SOCIETY, ECONOMICS, AND PHILOSOPHY

SOCIETY, ECONOMICS, AND PHILOSOPHY
Selected Papers

Michael Polanyi

edited by
R. T. Allen

Transaction Publishers
New Brunswick (U.S.A.) and London (U.K.)

First paperback publication 2016.
Copyright © 1997 by Transaction Publishers, New Brunswick, New Jersey.

Appendix I (Annotated Bibliography of Michael Polanyi's Publications on Society, Economics and Philosophy) Introduction and Appendix II (Summaries) © R.T. Allen
English translations of *To The Peace-makers* and *New Scepticism* © 1995 Endre J. Nagy.

This book is printed on acid-free paper that meets the American National Standard for Permanence of Paper for Printed Library Materials.

Library of Congress Catalog Number: 96-42469
ISBN 978-1-56000-278-9 (cloth); 978-1-4128-6403-9 (paper)
eBook: 978-1-4128-3462-9
Printed in the United States of America

Library of Congress Cataloging-in-Publication Data

Polanyi, Michael, 1891–
    Society, economics, and philosophy : selected papers / Michael Polanyi ; edited by R. T. Allen.
        p. cm.
    Includes bibliographical references and index.
    ISBN 1-56000-278-6 (cloth : alk. paper)
    1. Philosophy. 2. Political science—Philosophy. 3. Economics—Philosophy. I. Allen, R. T., 1941–   . II. Title.
B945.P583S63   1996
192—dc20
96-42469
                                                                            CIP

Contents

Part IV: Mind, Religion, Art

Acknowledgments

Firstly, I must thank Dr. David Lamb who first suggested this project in 1991, and then Prof. John Polanyi, FRS, who, as his father's literary executor, kindly gave it his endorsement. Next I wish to thank my colleagues on the committee of the former *Convivium* Group who provided financial assistance towards the collection of copies of Michael Polanyi's published papers.

In making that collection, and in compiling the Annotated Bibliography (reprinted here as Appendix I), I was assisted by the following persons and organisations: Prof. Klaus Allerbeck, J.-W. Goethe University, Frankfürt; Miss J. Crewdson, Oxford; Prof. Paul Nagy, The University of Indiana, Indianapolis; Mrs. P. Polanyi, Worthing; Prof. M. Rose, The University of Manchester; Mr. D. Taylor, Research Officer, The Local Studies Unit, The Central Library, Manchester; The staff of the British Library, at the Reading Room of the British Museum, the Newspaper Collection at Colindale, and at the Document Supply Centre, Boston Spa; The Library of the School of African and Oriental Studies, London.

I am especially grateful to Dr Francis Dunlop, of Norwich, for supplying notes for the summaries of the two articles in German, and to Dr Endre J. Nagy, of the Janus Pannonius University, Pécs, for responding to my request for English translations of Polanyi's first two non-scientific publications.

The following have kindly given permission for the reprinting of the respective articles:

The American Chemical Society for 'Creative imagination' and 'Life transcending physics and chemistry'; Blackwell Publishers for 'The struggle between truth and propaganda', 'The rights and duties of science', and 'Jewish problems'; Basil Blackwell Inc. for 'Do life processes transcend physics and chemistry?; Dr. W.R. Coulson for 'The Mind-Body Relation'; The Institute of European Defence and Strategic Studies for 'Towards a theory of conspicuous production'; Mr. M. Lasky for 'On Liberalism and liberty', 'The foolishness of history' and 'Polanyi's logic: answer'; Oxford University Press for 'Science and reality', 'The hypothesis of cybernetics' and 'What is a painting?' Routledge for 'A Postcript'; Springer Verlag for 'Why did we destroy Europe?'

I offer my due apologies to any owners of the copyrights for the remaining articles, whom I have made every effort to trace and contact.

Finally, I would like to express my gratitude to Transaction Publishers for accepting this project for publication.

R.T. Allen
Loughborough
Spring 1995

Introduction:
The Intention of this Collection

This collection contains published articles by Michael Polanyi on non-scientific subjects. It does not include any that were previously unpublished[1]. Furthermore it excludes all articles which were incorporated into *The Logic of Liberty* [60][2], *Personal Knowledge* [88] and *Knowing and Being* [134]. The intention is to make more readily available those from the remainder which include material not found in his books from *The Logic of Liberty* onwards, and thus to provide a supplement to those volumes. Inevitably it is a heterogenous selection, ranging from his first non-scientific publication in 1917 to his last but two in 1972, and makes no claim to balance. For example, there is a certain relative preponderance of articles on economic theory, for none of Polanyi's books since *The Logic of Liberty* (1951) has included anything on that subject even though Polanyi continued to write and publish articles upon economics.

When I took up Dr David Lamb's suggestion, made in the autumn of 1991, that there was scope for a collection such as this, my first task was to survey all of Polanyi's non-scientific articles. It soon became obvious that more than a few of his articles were versions of each other, and, in order to put on record exactly how they were related to each other, I compiled and published privately the Annotated Bibliography which is reprinted here as Appendix I[3].

My next task was the actual selection of those that I thought worthy of republication. Obviously those that are verbal duplicates of others immediately eliminated themselves. So also did those which added but little to what Polanyi had written elsewhere. In this category are some lengthy articles published just before or after *Knowing and Being,* and which restate his philosophy of tacit integration in more or less familiar terms and apply it to topics treated elsewhere. I also eliminated those, usually shorter items, which were more ephemeral in their contents, unless, like those first two articles and 'Jewish problems' (6, [18]), they are likely to have a particular value for those interested in Polanyi's life and work. In some cases, that still left me with similar treatments of the same theme, such as 'Clues to an understanding of mind and body' [108], 'The body-mind relation' (22 [132]) and 'On body and mind' [133], where it was a matter of picking, rather arbitrarily, one rather another. As a result of these negative principles of selection, I was left with the twenty-five articles which are included in this volume.

All of them, in my judgment, include matters of either intrinsic or personal interest which are not available elsewhere. Undoubtedly there is often an overlap with others of his publications, but I have assumed that it is not my place to alter them except in minor details: viz. to introduce a uniform style of spelling and of continuously numbered end-notes, and silently to correct some obvious mistakes without, I hope, introducing others. All editorial insertions are placed in square brackets and added notes are marked with asterisks or daggers.

In order to give to complete the intention of providing a supplement to Polanyi's books, I have given in Appendix II summaries of the principal contents of those articles which were not included either in them or in this collection. Where the articles restate, with only a few additions, familiar themes, such his analysis of the organisation of science or his philosophy of tacit integration, I have given only the briefest of summaries despite the length of some of the items in question. In this way I have tried to put on record something of the whole body of Polanyi's non-scientific publications, except for two of which I have not been able to trace any copies. Those who wish to pursue further their interest in Polanyi's writings may find Appendix II a helpful guide in deciding which other articles they would like to obtain.

The articles in this collection represent almost the whole range of Polanyi's interests outside his scientific research and teaching: economics, politics, society, philosophy, philosophy of science, religion and Positivist obstacles to it, and aesthetics. Only the more specialist subjects of the making of diagrammatic films, in which Polanyi was a pioneer, and of reform of the patent laws, are not represented in any way. The selected items range from lengthy articles to short notes such as 'Polanyi's logic—answer' (17 [119]), and provide, I hope, a valuable supplement to his books.

Despite overlaps among their contents or themes, I have arranged the twenty-five selected articles into four groups: Political Questions, Economics and Social Theory, The Theory and Practice of Science, and Mind, Religion and Art.

But what claim do these articles have upon the attention of the reader? To answer that question I shall now give, for those unfamiliar with Polanyi, a brief outline of his life and work, and of his place in the history of thought.

Polanyi's Life and Work

Michael Polanyi, FRS, was born Polányi Mihály (in the Hungarian style), in Budapest in 1891, into a liberal Jewish family. His father was a railway engineer and entrepreneur who built much of Hungary's railway system but then lost a lot of money. After his death, Michael's elder brother Karl (Károly) looked after him, and their mother, Cecilia, continued to run a salon right up to her death in 1939.

Michael studied medicine in Budapest but his interests were always turned to research in chemistry. After graduating he went to the Technische Hochschule in Karlsruhe but returned to serve as a medical officer on the Serbian front in the Austro-Hungarian army during the First World War. While recovering from diphtheria, he wrote his Ph.D. thesis on his theory of adsorption (see 'The potential theory of adsorption' [113]). But his interests were not confined to science. He had been active in the Galileo Circle, a students' group formed by his brother Karl, but unlike Karl, and many others in the circles in which they grew up, he was sceptical of Socialism. With the other members of the Galileo Circle he supported Oskár Jászi, 'the Father of Hungarian Liberalism', and his journal *Huzsadik Század* (*Twentieth Century*). Polanyi also supported the new government of an independent Hungarian republic established in October 1918 by Count Mihály Károlyi, in which Jászi became Minister for Nationalities, and served in the Ministry of Health. His first non-scientific publications were 'To the peace-makers' (1917) (1 [1]) and 'New scepticism' (1919) (2 [2]). Although he refused to join the Red Army, when Béla Kun introduced an Hungarian Soviet régime in March 1919, that did not help him when Kun was defeated by an invading Romanian army and a National Army raised by Admiral Horthy, who avoided conflict with the Romanians. Horthy headed the new régime and later was elected Regent of Hungary. Along with many other Hungarians, especially of Jewish descent, both supporters and opponents of the Kun régime, including his brother Karl, Oskár Jászi and Karl Mannheim, a friend of the Polanyi brothers, Michael Polanyi left Hungary and returned to Karlsruhe before joining the Institute of Fibre Chemistry in Berlin, and then, in 1926, the Institute for Physical Chemistry. He maintained contact with Hungary and acted as a consultant for Tangsram, an Hungarian company manufacturing electrical equipment. During his years in Germany he published only scientific papers and there is little in his unpublished papers to indicate that he still took an interest in other matters.

Having earlier refused an invitation to go to Manchester as Professor of Physical Chemistry, he accepted it in 1933, when Hitler began to remove Jews from public positions. Visits to the Soviet Union, and especially a meeting with Bukharin in 1935, led to the first of many further publications on economic, political and philosophical themes, four of which were collected as *The Contempt of Liberty*, 1940 [12]. He took up the challenge of Marxist proposals for the planning of science, and this led him to formulate his distinction between corporate (or centrally planned) order and spontaneous (or polycentric) order and to apply it both to the organisation of scientific research and to industrial economies. Further articles on those topics were republished as *The Logic of Liberty* (1951) [60]. Previously, in 1946, he had published *Science, Faith and Society* [42], in which he explored the fiduciary roots of science and of scientific and political freedom.

Although he published, often jointly, over 200 scientific papers and was elected a Fellow of the Royal Society in 1944, his extra-scientific interests were becoming more important to him and in 1948 he gave up scientific work for a personal chair in Social Studies, especially created for him at Manchester, so that he could formulate his philosophical ideas, to be presented as the Gifford Lectures in 1951–2, and published as *Personal Knowledge* [88]. In that work he set forth his philosophy of tacit integration in knowing and being, which he extended in his later publications, beginning with the first Lindsay Memorial Lectures at the University of Keele, given in 1958 and published as *The Study of Man* [93].

He helped to form the Society for Freedom in Science, of which he became chairman, and then the Congress for Cultural Freedom. He was also a member of the Mont Pelérin Society, and gave radio talks in Hungarian on RIAS.

He left Manchester in 1959 to become a Senior Research Fellow at Merton College, Oxford, but found more of an audience in America, where he paid several visits to give courses of lectures. Some of those were published as *The Tacit Dimension* [123] and a later series was edited by Prof. Harry Prosch, when Polanyi's memory began to fail, as *Meaning* [143]. Dr Marjorie Greene had previously collected and edited a selection of articles, first published between 1959 and 1968, as *Knowing and Being* (1969) [134]. Polanyi died in 1976.

Michael and Magda had two sons, George (1922–75) who became an economist, and John (b.1929) who is now Professor of Chemistry in the University of Toronto, and a joint winner of the Nobel Prize for Chemistry.

Polanyi's Place in the History of Thought

Michael Polanyi is probably best known for the statement, '*We know more than we can tell*' (*TD* p.4). Throughout the ages many philosophers have been aware of limits to what we can make explicit but they did not pursue the theme, perhaps because it was an embarrassment. For a powerful motive in modern philosophy has been the desire to be in complete control of oneself: intellectually and epistemologically, in order not to be led into error; and morally and politically, in order not to be subject to another's will or external law. But can we be assured of being in control only in respect of what we can make explicit to ourselves, of what we both know and know that we know. This ideal of total self-determination is radically challenged by Polanyi's demonstrations that our knowledge and action are always tacit integrations in which we attend *from* one set of things *to* another. Though we can often make explicit and put into articulate form some of the subsidiary clues from which we attend, we can never make all of them explicit nor the ways in which we integrate them. Moreover, to switch one's focus to the subsidiary details is sooner or later to destroy the sense, perception or meaning of the focal whole or action into which one previously had integrated them. I shall not elaborate Polanyi's account of tacit integration here, and those unfamiliar with it can find expositions of it in two articles included in this collection: 'The scientific revolution' and 'Creative imagination'.[4]

Only Merleau-Ponty, in his *Phenomenology of Perception,* approaches Polanyi in focusing upon and arguing from the tacit dimensions of our experience, yet even he does not formulate the structure of the tacit integration of the two modes of awareness, *from* the subsidiary and *to* the focal. It is that structure, both epistemological and ontological (for our integration of clues into wholes reconstitutes the hierarchical organisation of the comprehensive entities which we know), which is distinctive and unique to Polanyi's philosophy and defines his place in the history of thought.

Of the many consequences of the frank acceptance of these tacit dimensions, I shall briefly mention here only a few. The first is that the ideal of a complete, precise and fully articulate body of knowledge is both impossible and dangerous. All our knowledge, even in the most exact sciences, is never fully precise, as Polanyi first pointed out in 1935 ('The value of the inexact' [5]). It follows that inexactness and impression are not *per se* fatal flaws. The second is that the ideal of a detached and impersonal body of knowledge, knowledge without a knower to which the knower contributes nothing, is also false and dangerous. All knowledge is *personal* knowledge, shaped and upheld by a tacit and personal co-efficient, without which it would not be knowledge. Another is that the contrast between an precise, quantifiable and impersonal knowledge of fact, as supposedly to be found in natural science, especially physics, and an imprecise, qualitative and personal (or 'subjective') assessment of values, as in the humanities and everyday practical knowledge, is also false and dangerous. All knowledge is personally, tacitly and passionately endorsed as *true and valid* on the basis of standards to which the knower is committed. For those, 'Objectivists' and 'Positivists' of various persuasions, who do uphold these unattainable ideals, Polanyi's philosophy inevitably appears to be 'subjectivist' and to endorse 'subjectivism' and irresponsibility. (Yet, of course, to say that is itself to express commitment to ideals and standards of responsibility which, according to Objectivist and Positivist philosophies, are necessarily 'merely subjective'). What in fact Polanyi offers is something that transcends this vicious dichotomy of Objectivism or Subjectivism, a responsible, personal way of knowing and acting.

For the most part, the articles in this collection which employ Polanyi's philosophy of tacit integration deal with its further ramifications: such as his analysis of 'moral inversion'; his arguments for the distinctiveness of biology and the impossibility of reducing it to physics and chemistry; his account of the mind as the meaning of the body, a meaning which is lost if we explicitly attend to it; the methods actually, and mostly tacitly, followed in natural science; his arguments against the Weberian distinction in the humanities between noting others' acts of evaluations, which is necessary, and endorsing or criticising them, which is to be abjured; and the role of tacit integration in our apprehension of works of art.

Other articles lie outside the concerns of that philosophy, most notably his first two non-scientific publications and 'Jewish problems', which have been included for the light they throw upon Polanyi's development and his more personal interests. In between lie the other political essays in the first group and those upon economic and social theory. Some of them do employ aspects of the philosophy of tacit integration whereas others do not. As was briefly indicated in the first part of this Introduction, Polanyi's was spurred into philosophical reflection by the Marxist movement for the planning of science. That led him to see how Positivist accounts of science which deny its bearing upon reality and its claim to be true, and Utilitarian evaluations of it as technically and economically useful, denied it any value and significance in itself and thus any claim it might make freely to cultivate itself without subservience to outside interests. At this point, we meet a second and independent interest in economics, the origins of which are not indicated in the unpublished papers which I have read. Polanyi's study of Soviet economics, which I have not included because of its mass of detail which has no interest today, appears to have been undertaken as a separate by-product of his visits to the USSR. These two interests converged when Polanyi took the spontaneous and self-co-ordinating organisation of scientific research as a model for the similar structure of an economy.

As was mentioned above, none of Polanyi's books since *The Logic of Liberty* have included sections or previously published articles on economic theory. And interest in Polanyi's economic writings seems to have been noticeably less than that in his other non-scientific writings. Yet they have their own importance in the history of thought. For, as Prof. Paul Craig Roberts has pointed out[5], Polanyi provided an explanation of the impossibility of central planning more radical than those given by von Mises and Hayek. It is not just that central planners would need prices for the rational allocation of resources and thus a market somewhere to determine them (von Mises), or that the knowledge that operates an exchange economy is dispersed and fragmented (Hayek), but that the span of control that a given mind can employ is necessarily limited. It follows that what was called 'central planning' in the Soviet and satellite economies was no such thing, it being logically impossible. What went on there was dispersed and self-adjusting, 'polycentric', managerial decisions within each centre of production and distribution, as under private enterprise, plus a central allocation of capital funds, as with nationalised industries in largely privately owned economies.

It seems from the published evidence, and from much of the unpublished work, that Polanyi's economic thought continued to develop somewhat independently of his philosophy of tacit integration, except, of course, for their convergence in respect of political and economic freedom. Perhaps that is one reason for its comparative neglect. The republication of six articles on economic theory in this collection may do something to restore the balance.

Further comments upon each group of articles and each article will be found, respectively, in the Introductions to each part of this collection and to each individual article, where I shall indicate the place of each in Polanyi's life and work and what is distinctive and notable about its contents.

Notes

1. Polanyi's unpublished papers are held in the Special Collections Department of the Joseph Regenstein Library at the University of Chicago.
2. The numbers in square brackets are those of Polanyi's publications as listed in the Bibliography in Appendix I, and the others are those of the ones as reprinted in this selection.
   Polanyi's books will be referred to by means of the usual abbreviations:
   KB   = *Knowing and Being*
   LL   = *The Logic of Liberty*
   M   = *Meaning*
   PK   = *Personal Knowledge*
   SFS = *Science, Faith and Society*
   SOM = *The Study of Man*
   TD   = *The Tacit Dimension*
3. Two items not listed in other bibliographies are 'To the peacemakers' and 'New scepticism'. I had already been to the Polanyi Memorial Conference, held in Budapest in 1991 by the Michael Polanyi Liberal Philosophical Association of Hungary, at which I was shown copies of them.
4. Perhaps the best ways into Polanyi's thought are his shorter volumes, especially *The Study of Man* and *The Tacit Dimension*. Several introductions to Polanyi's work have been published: R.T. Allen: *Polanyi* (London, Claridge Press, 1990); R. Gelwick: *The Way of Discovery* (New York, OUP, 1977); H. Prosch: *Michael Polanyi: A Critical Exposition* (New York, State University of New York Press, 1986); Dru Scott: *Everyman Revived* (Lewes, The Book Guild, 1985).
5. *Alienation and the Soviet Economy* (2nd. ed. New York, Holmes and Meier, 1990). One aspect of Polanyi's economic and political thought which is not represented in this collection is his acceptance of Keynes' general theory and prescriptions

for dealing with failures in gross demand and consequent widespread unemployment. For, on the one hand, Polanyi merely mentioned Keynes in some of his shorter and more ephemeral pieces, and, on the other, gave an exposition of his own understanding of Keynes in *Full Employment and Free Trade* [30] which was much too long to be considered for this collection. On that book see Paul Craig Roberts, 'Idealism in public choice theory', *J. of Monetary Economics,* 4 (1978).

Part I

Political Questions

Introduction to Part I

The eight articles included in Part I range from Polanyi's earliest, apart from scientific publications, published in 1917, to one of his last, published in 1970. They are all responses to the momentous events in the twentieth century: the political and moral collapse of the First World War, the rise of totalitarianism and the passions that drove and supported it, and the position and tasks of Jews in the modern world.

The first two are included because of the light they throw upon the development of Polanyi's thinking about society and politics and because they have never before appeared outside Hungary and in English. The third, 'Jewish problems', appears because it expresses Polanyi's views upon matters that touched him personally.

With 'The struggle between truth and propaganda' (1936) and 'The rights and duties of science' (1939), we come to the events which led Polanyi once more to write and publish upon matters outside of his professional work in natural science: the Marxist demand for the planning of science along with everything else and the need, in the face of that threat, to defend the freedom of scientific research and with it freedom in society at large and in the market economy that supports it. 'The rights and duties of science' could also have be placed in Part III, but it has been included here because of the political context of its account of science and how it differs from applied science.

We then jump over several other essays on political matters, which have been reprinted in Polanyi's books or include nothing of wider interest that is not found elsewhere, to three articles which develop Polanyi's account of 'moral inversion' as first presented in 'The magic of Marxism' [74] (PK pp.226–48). The modern world is replete with explicit expressions of contempt for morality and its restraints and with explicit avowals of unscupulousness and ruthlessness, born of scepticism and accompanied by assertions of the 'honesty' of those attitudes in contrast to the 'hypocrisy' and 'dishonesty' of explicitly moral appeals. In 'The magic of Marxism' Polanyi explained how the explicit avowal of unscrupulousness and violence is accompanied by a tacit use of moral appeals. This conjunction, Polanyi explains, 'enables the modern mind, tortured by moral self-doubt, to indulge its moral passions in terms which also satisfy its passion for ruthless objectivity' (PK p.228), especially when, as in Marxism, the latter are identified with something taken to be simple fact, e.g., the Marxist laws of history and the inevitable arrival of the classless society. Though they overlap with that article, and with 'Beyond Nihilism' [95] and 'The message of the Hungarian revolution' [121], and with each other, they each add something to Polanyi's account of the great evils that have beset our era.

1

To the Peacemakers: Views on the
Prerequisites of War and Peace in Europe

*Huszadik Század was founded by Oskár Jászi, who, with Count
Mihály Károlyi, founder of the Hungarian Independence Party, at-
tended the Conference of the League of Lasting Peace held in Bern
in November 1917 at which he propounded his scheme for a feder-
ated Austro-Hungarian empire, later a Danubian federation. Apart
from the personal interest of this plea, this article is also notewor-
thy for its prophetic recognition of the error of concluding peace in
the spirit of war.*

When Will it Come to an End?

For many months now a great many outstanding men have been struggling all over the world to break a path to peace and to rescue us, the
peoples of Europe, from the devastation in which we have become more
and more deeply entangled each day. At the outset most of us believed
that the first self-determination of peoples and the first manifestation of
the idea of peace would put an end to the war at an irresistible speed.
However, in spite of this and being bitterly worried, we have to see the
obstacles become daily more powerful, and a successful outcome to the
work of the peace delegates looks more and more unlikely. And one breaks
out in angry words: Do our delegates consider their work in the right
way? Does the true spirit of peace live in these men? Has the vision of a
new age in the future been opened before their eyes?

[1]. Published as a pamphlet in Budapest 1917, 15 pp., and republished in *Huszadik
Század (Twentieth Century),* 1917, no. 2, pp. 165–176. Translated by Endre J. Nagy.

Each question entails new doubts. What, so far, have they mostly talked about? First the various peace conditions: Alsace, Trentino, indemnity to Belgium and Serbia; after that, arbitration and arms limitations.

Even the sequence indicates the unfortunate and sterile spirit of these talks!

The delegates of all peoples ought, first, to agree on the institutional bases of an unshakeable system of international law, and then the questions relating to the dignity and integrity of States would settle themselves; but, in spite of this, once plunged into conflicts in a war-like spirit, they will not be able to establish a firm basis for international peace, without which, as governments have already declared, a short cease-fire would be possible but no peace could ever be achieved that would mean tranquillity and prosperity for Europe.

For, who determines the peace conditions determines also the war conditions. Thus, the first result of the peace talks, on this interpretation, has been only the declaration of this: that the territorial affiliation of Trentino, the question of Alsace, some millions of indemnity, were sound and just reasons for bringing about the war. Yet the foundations of the future tranquillity of Europe cannot be laid in the spirit of such a declaration, and, as long as we are informed by this spirit, the war goes on. It would be a disastrous mistake, if the those preparing the peace, were, like typical diplomats, to see their mission as being to try to heal the injuries inflicted by European States on each other's sovereignty, since they would thereby only admit what they ought to struggle against. For, as long European States continue to possess their present unlimited sovereignty, this war will go on. And peace will come when and only when we, the peoples of Europe, have become aware of the idea of the internal co-operation and a close system of law and order among European States, and, accordingly, controversies about power, have disappeared from our agenda.

To develop this position will be my task in what follows.

The Causes of the War

Let us examine, first, what the sovereignty of a European State consists of today and what its effects are.

The territory of Europe is divided among six large States, each of which is prepared to raise an army of 6 to 10 million soldiers. The people of every State esteem the greatness and wealth of their own State much more than those of any other State, and if a foreign State seeks to impair this greatness and wealth all the people of each State are willing to send all their army for to fight the menacing neighbour. Thus, like competitors, each State must be permanently on stand-by both to defend its territory and, on occasion and by a swift invasion, to enlarge it. It is for this same reason that States must keep their power, plans and alliances secret from each other, and it also entails that this secret power be placed in the hands of 2–3 men, if possible.

The six secretive centres of incalculable devastation in Europe thus formed have certainly kept the peoples of Europe in mutual fear and uncertainty. An army endowed with motor transport can invade the larger part of a neighbouring country within a few days. Thus preparations must be prevented by quicker preparations and invasions by a quicker invasions; no power can avoid this. This is an outline of the origins of the war.

And why just now, not sooner or later, did the war start?

Because recent decades European States have become more dangerous to each other as a result of the technical development of railways, motor vehicles and artillery. This has finally brought European States to a position where, lest they be accused of negligence, they could not do other than invade the territory of a neighbouring country in order to prevent the enemy's attack.

Lest there be any mistake, I shall explain this statement in more detail. Thus, I do not claim that the existence of two sovereign States on the globe necessarily means eternal war between them! Even though it is certain that there will always be a legitimate distrust between two States, which fosters the germ of war, if both adversaries are hardly able to pose a sudden threat to each other, and if it takes weeks or months to launch their armies against each other, no serious word can then be voiced for the argument that it is the prevention of an enemy invasion that makes it a duty for the leaders of each State to overrun an adversary. However, if the war breaks out, the distrust will be but an insignificant cause among many others, and the real causes will be material or moral ambitions which they seek to realise by waging war.

In contrast, European States are at the opposite extreme by virtue of the unprecedented expansion of the danger of one to another. It was just under these circumstances that mutual and legitimate precautions must have exploded into declarations of war in the quickening succession of effects and counter-effects. In this situation the much mentioned causes of the war, i.e. moral and material war ambitions must be considered as of secondary importance as giving the last impetus the jolt that was to overthrow the balance of power.

Daily we feel more strongly that the world war is a fatal catastrophe of quite particular importance, that it is essentially different from any kind of war waged in the past. Accordingly, the significant trait of it is as follows: the world war essentially and first of all is not a complex of campaigns (as we thought it to be), but the only stable situation which corresponds to the principle of the sovereignty of European States in respect of their actual danger.

However much this assumption may perhaps seem to be a paradox, let us remember that the first event of the war was actually an invasion, with thousands of motorised vehicles, that was so powerful and light-ning-fast that even the Reichstag was informed about it only when and as the Chancellor made the statement: 'Our troops crossed the Belgian bor-der last night'. An irresistible drive on Paris must have been planned that would have decided the war within ten days. And it is also certain that this attack would have prevented a similar shock-action of the enemy, that is, the invasion by the Russians of East Prussia, which would have been really fatal to the Germans.

Nonetheless, the fact that the German attack was but the ultimate result of legitimate and preventive actions will become clear if we put aside our common mistrust for a moment and listen to the great powers' own arguments. Each of them says that it was not it who started the war, and plainly demonstrates that the other side had previously taken mea-sures which had put it into jeopardy. It does not follow from this that either one or the other, or both of them, is lying. The facts they put forward are all beyond doubt, so the correct conclusion is that both of them are right. It is true that Germany could not wait once Russia had mobilised, and Russia had mobilised because Austria had mobilised, and Austria could not wait for Serbia had offended her and her authority was at stake. All this is not, of course, to say that the 'sufficient cause' was (Gavrilo) Princip, but, on the contrary, I am saying that in whatever direction one follows the series of mutual alarms which exploded into war, the series of causes leads to smaller and smaller events which can-not be considered as being 'sufficient causes' of the subsequent actual events, and, therefore, the sufficient cause is the situation itself in which small events can trigger epidemics of distrust epidemics which increase like avalanches. This state of affairs consists, as I said above, in the power of European States that are able at any moment to cast all their devastating forces on their neighbours, and that power is but a logical consequence of the idea of unlimited sovereignty, i.e. that the greatness and welfare of one's own state is more important than those of the others.

Who is to Blame for the War?

The start of the peace talks is encumbered by the fact that the hostile parties want, first, to make clear 'who is to blame for the war'. They cannot agree on this question because both sides are caught in their policy started at the outset of the war, and therefore the one accuses the other. Yet, one state seems to have no more right to accuse the other than a brick under the ruins of a collapsed house which would blame the others for the collapse.

The peace delegates, I think, are right if they want to start with an investigation into the causes of the war. For the causes of the outbreak of the war do not cease to exist even now and because of them the war is still going on. So the politicians of the peace should not cling to the declarations made at the outset of the war. When the world gets to be out of joint and runs in an unknown new age, they should not search for formulae of political consistency. Only then will they get rid of the ridiculous obsession about which particular states caused the disaster. The cause of the catastrophe has been the old-fashioned setting of Europe: the existence of six great powers of unlimited sovereignty within a confined space. And we, the people of Europe, are to be blamed for the war, for we believe in these six great powers.

Who is Responsible for Furthering the War?

As long as the great European powers do not renounce the free exercise of their power, all their honest endeavours for peace will be fruitless. For any peace that could be concluded now would merely restore the circumstances as they were before the war, i.e. the situation of which the burdens and dangers propelled us into war. Since that time the burdens and dangers have got heavier: the great European powers have become more dangerous to each other, their production of arms, artillery and trained troops has been multiplied. They fear more from each other, and they have a hundred times more reason for it than before the war. On this basis peace cannot be concluded. The soldiers can withdraws from each other for a breathing-space at best and only in order to be able to attack each other anew and with more force. And please do not object against us that the powers have taken to heart the lesson from their actual costs and now will find it hard to go to war. Have we seen that the neutral states have learned anything from the damage that we have suffered? Have not they joined in the war one after another? There is no question about it: the state, the 'people's machine', cannot be instructed, since it can work only in the way that its structure requires.

Before the war the situation of the peoples in Europe was like that of a mountain climber who has come on the frozen shelf of a cliff. By any movement by which he may try to escape from his disastrous situation he would slip further and further down the slope. What should he do? Shall he succumb there on the frozen shelf? No, he tries to perform his last movement. And falls down…

Yet, suppose that the climber in danger should stay on the wall of the shelf because of a miracle and succeed in climbing back onto the edge, or, to put it otherwise, that Europe should succeed in concluding peace on the bases of the status quo. Has our man learned to sit peacefully on the frozen shelf? Will he behave more prudently? No, he will wriggle and then fall down again.

Why do you, politicians of peace, leaders of Europe, want us to climb back onto the ledge of the cliff onto which we have fallen, back onto the fatal edge? Take us to the place where a path leads out from the depths onto the rich lowlands.

The State—A Religious Idea

Among many critical points that can be brought against me, I shall deal only with one. I have to hark back to the point where the common-place causal argument diverges from mine. This point can be found where we feel we have come to a deadlock after having followed the argument of official declarations or else we finally across either the bullet of (Gavrilo) Princip or the passport of Major Tankosic*, or some other

---

* I have not been able to trace the incident to which Polanyi refers. Princip, of course, was the Serbian who assassinated the Archduke Ferdinand in Sarajevo.

event of infinite insignificance. At this point the public at large (which is always sceptical and contrary, and does not want to believe that governments are as stupid as it says they are) will continue to argue as follows: since it is impossible that they could push the world into catastrophe for such a nothing, the official statements must accordingly be lies, and the real causes are material and moral aspirations: Alsace, Berlin, Baghdad! The Yugoslav question! Irredentism. The Eastern question! Briefly, a hundred slogans which were shouted out loud at the outset of the war.

I do not want to deny that the public was right to point out these causes (slogans about which were, by the way, disseminated quite certainly by the governments themselves among the citizens). The public was wrong only in that they considered the war to have been an undertaking embarked upon for the realisation of these slogans. Or else, we are wrong if we understand the word 'undertaking' in terms of its ordinary meaning, i.e. as a deliberated activity aiming at human interests.

To make this point clear I have to develop my own position about these goals of the war. I described above the nature of State sovereignty as the jealous love of people for the greatness and wealth of their own State. I omitted the analysis of the term 'greatness and wealth of the State', the meaning of which does not present itself by itself. Well, these slogans—Alsace, Constantinople, Salonika, etc.—have actually the meaning that we understand by them. Up to this point I am on the same track as public opinion but henceforth we take leave from each other.

The commonplace opinion is that putting these slogans into effect serves the interests of the State's population or, at least, that of class within it. Nevertheless, about this opinion many outstanding minds, from Voltaire to Norman Angell[†], have convincingly demonstrated that it must be considered as being completely wrong with respect to the disasters of war and its blind chances. And those who have not yet been convinced by these authors that the war is a bad business must be convinced by now, in the fourth year of the war (when property to a value of 300 billion has been destroyed, 10 millions of our fellow human beings have been killed, and 5 millions have been handicapped) that these ways were hardly skilful methods to perform such tricks as 'Alsace', 'Baghdad', 'Constantinople', etc.

[†] Sir Norman Angell (1873–1967) had published in 1910 *The Great Illusion*, soon translated into many languages, in which he argued against the belief that war and conquest can bring economic advantages such as access to markets and raw materials.

Still, what sort of event would still shock us? What kind of event would makes us think deeply about it, and, at the same time, would be the one that bring us insight into the real connexions? When, recently, the socialists gathered in Stockholm, their first utterances were: 'Alsace!', 'indemnity', 'Trentino'!?

If I have succeeded in getting the reader actually to think about this fact, he or she will also accept the lesson to be driven home: we must transcend the materialist prejudice, still living obstinately in us, according to which the actions of the masses are primarily motivated by insight into their interests. For it is not interest that voices from the delegates in Stockholm but the idea of the power of States, the idea, as I explained above, whose vitality in the masses brought Europe to the plight of world war, and now makes this plight still uncertain. And what we must clearly perceive at this point is that the idea of the State does not take its power from the strength of the interest of the people who form the whole of the State or a part of it. The war is a bad business. But the State goes to war, not as an association of interests, but as an idea, and what is a bad business for an association of interests is vital food for the idea. Business requires rational investments, an idea demands bloody sacrifices. If the State acted in the interests of its citizens, it would join its neighbours in a permanent and stable co-operative effort, i.e. it would cease to exist in a sovereign way! But the State is an idea that lives for itself, for its own interests, the names of which are: Trentino, Alsace, indemnity, etc. These interests are those of no living man, but are those of the State, the idea of which is living in its people.

I know that this tenet of mine has nothing to do with ordinary materialis thought and will provoke objections. Discussion of them is out of place here; therefore I want to give the core of my defence in a few words. Despite the fact that our age has denied 'all prejudices', it has not freed itself from prejudices at all. For they are rooted in tacit presuppositions which determine our thoughts without our being aware of them. That is why they cannot be renounced. Only if we thoroughly clarify our concepts can we then take notice of them, and only this can free us from them—if they are false. It might be that our age has materialist prejudices which, someday in the future, will seem to be fancies as wild as do those of the past today. Thus, those who try to explain by people's material interests the phenomenon that the peoples of Europe are perishing away in the hell of war, instead of enjoying for some years—even, in a broader sense, for decades—the prosperity of a world at peace, should stop and think it over. They should stop and analyse more thoroughly their argument: in the adoption of concepts such as 'the interest of the ruling classes', 'army contractors', 'bureaucratic and military ambitions', 'economic expansion', is not an ignominious prejudice hidden? Are these arguments firm enough to ground so horrible an assumption as the one that they want to demonstrate?

This critical work it is not my task to perform here. I only want to make reference in passing to the theoretical bearing of the tenet in terms of which the world war is but a stabilisation, logically occurring, of the powerful idea still dominating the peoples of Europe today, i.e. that the peoples of all States must esteem the greatness and wealth of their own State more than those of any other. The war is a bad business but—sorry to say—it is more than that: the most devastating crusade for which the religious idea has ever sacrificed its believers. And this religion is tantamount to the cult of State sovereignty.

Why Have the Socialists not Prevented the War?

In peace time, Socialist literature always emphasised that war was nothing other than a disguised capitalist undertaking. However, when the war broke out, they unhesitatingly discarded the flag of the Internationale and promptly sided by the State. As we see it today with enlightened eyes, the truth is that Socialists of the world have never seriously thought through and felt the significance of the ideas of the Internationale to their final consequences. All that happened was, rather, an attempt, a first effort, to get away from the magnetic power of the idea of the State, but they have, thereby, never arrived at the point of transplanting their ideals into their own and their fellows' flesh and blood. What remained in their flesh and blood was the vital susceptibility to be pained by everything that would impair the greatness and wealth of their country. And when the alarm-bells were suddenly tolled throughout Europe, this pain became urgent while cosmopolitan speculations vanished. Their behaviour resembles the well-known atheists of the nineteenth century who grew up in a religious spirit, and, when they felt the approach of death, converted in the arms of the Church.

At that time, at that stage of Socialism, it was explained that the power of the State was in the interest even of the working class. We were optimists! In terms of the strange optimism of Materialism one sought to discover calculation in what was only a devastating movement of ideas ruling over humanity.

So far I have tried to explain that the situation of world war has to be considered as being a stable state of affairs which is appropriate to the idea of the sovereignty of the great powers in Europe and to the dangers which they actually pose. These dangers cause the epidemics of legitimate distrust and the mutual fear that can burst forth only in world war. I have argued that this tremendous danger could not be diminished without restricting sovereignty, and that it would cut deep into the idea of the State, that is, into the warm feelings which fostered towards the greatness and wealth of their own State. I do not see the effective power of the alleged causes of the war, like 'Alsace', 'competition', 'Salonika', etc., in some human interest being attached to them, but in the fact that they are attributes of the greatness and wealth of the State. I have represented the world war as a bloody sacrifice made by the peoples of Europe for the idea of the State.

Finally, I pointed out that the idea of the State is actually alive within the minds of the people as a whole, including the minds of Socialists, and it was this that made the Internationale fail at the outbreak of the war.

The European Idea

And at this point I address everyone who wants to bring peace to us, his suffering fellows: he should realise that he cannot create a new Internationale as he is now trying to do—and we need one which will not be a timid fumbling but will be our flesh and blood—unless he first creates its prerequisites in his own mind. If our feelings remain such as they were before the war, then we shall deserve the war as much as we have so far. We must not fear the armies of the enemy, we must not put on our lips the guilty slogans of States; let us realise that they are pitfalls which will whirl us back into the turmoil of devastation. Let us recognise that the Internationale and the establishment of a legal order in Europe will divest these words of their meaning and obliterate the danger of the biggest armies. We must love a united Europe, the re-creation of our truncated life. People leading the world should release themselves from mutual fear and from dams built against each other. They should seek to exploit the forces of nature and the riches of the earth, and, henceforth, a new age of riches and welfare, never seen before, will open up before us.

The peace delegates should retire within themselves and be fully aware of whether they want to create this new Internationale, or else, if they want a peace that would only cover over the still glowing embers of the war for some years. They should retire within themselves! If they really want us to escape from the evil storm, it is themselves that they first must make pure, and then they can be our guides towards the new life!

About the Revolution that Everybody is Talking About

Yet, if my arguments are insufficient, and if, because of that, the peace delegates, as good materialists, do not recognise the bitter logic of the devastation of Europe, and if they cannot imagine that European civilisation may fall prey, today or tomorrow, to a tremendous misconception, then I shall speak to them as politicians: take a look around, and recognise that the last hour has arrived. By what means do they hope to stop the danger more dreadful than the war itself that menaces Europe more openly day after day? One hears the name of this danger on the lips of all, on those of governments and of people as well; it is spoken in the rooms of legislative bodies and on the markets in concert, and the world as a whole proclaims it as heedlessly as the word for war used to be uttered, i.e. they are saying simply: 'This will lead to revolution...' Do you realise what this would mean if it were to take flesh? That the sufferings caused by the war would be dwarfed in our memory by the revolution if it should come about!

And should not we do something about it? Peace workers!, the only way to prevent the revolution is to create a system of law and order in Europe! For what does the revolution, that everyone has been talking about, consist of in its very essence? It is the move of the people's conscience that is seeking to be free from the idea of the State.

Accordingly, who could not perceive what is happening in the mind of the world as it bleeds? Let us remember how all this began: when, after the first frightening movement of armies, the words burst out with religious anger: 'This is the very reality, the fatherland is the truth!' The State idea got hold of people by a force which they never suspected. It seized millions of Socialists whom we expected to have shaken off its mental influence. And the fever of war continued to seize, day after day the intellectuals of Europe, those thousands of people who spoke alike the languages of Europe and whose minds were alike fostered by the culture of each of them; thus these hundreds and thousands of lonely minds, who sought independence, denied, one after another, the idea of the Internationale, of which each of them, with respect to his whole mental outlook, was a living document!

Thousand of crises used to happen and to result in the victory of the masses. Thousands of youngsters and men were hesitating throughout Europe in the conscience-splitting noise of the war at the outset while they searched for the truth, the one which should have sprung from their hearts so as to give them strength in their loneliness. We know that most of them did not find the answer and that they ran along with the crowd, and many of them silently, others loudly, but each hiding his doubting and worried heart in his bosom. It was at that time that the idea of the State lived in the strongest heyday of its realisation: the first casualties only fostered the magnetic, continuously spreading power of the war.

However, three years have passed since that time!... The peoples of Europe hardly remember what had preceded those years, for everything has changed so much during this time. Work, hope, death—life in its entirety is different, the colour of the sky and the taste of bread: everything has changed. All sounds have other echoes, all words have other meanings: millions of hearts full of bitterness are longing for relief. Revolting pain is throbbing in the veins of millions. Clamorous ideas of the war have long since quietened, and only the deeper constraints and laws of unconscious action still have mankind in their power. Muddled swearwords and slogans can be heard everywhere and people are stuck in their present ways only because they do not know what else to do. Despair is grappling with the inner moral force of the idea of the State in their minds. Despair is growing day by day, but it has not yet found the ultimate force by which the mind can depart from the old ground. They are still saying, 'What else can we do?', but the disastrous alternative has not yet been voiced: 'Rather anything!' But let us take notice of the first step that has already been already taken. The people of Russia tried to deny the existence of State power by bloody riots and condemned as guilty the holiest aspirations of the State. It also happened that their armies in battle refused to obey in the defence of their fatherland. In Russia there exists order again for the time being. For the time being. Yet the struggle in the minds of the people continues.

Peace workers and politicians, you must retain the initiative as long as you have it in your hands! The maintenance of our civilisation can be guaranteed only by the idea of a united Europe; we should not wait until the despair of the people will bring it about through the suffering brought by revolution. Do not be cautious and diffident, for that would be a disastrous caution. Only a quick, determined and far-reaching settlement can keep Europe, on the basis of the right of nations to self-determination, from convulsions that would be more disastrous than those we have so far experienced.

The Peace

Our fear that organic development cannot turn the present organisation of Europe for war into an organisation for peace, and that a revolution is necessary to bring it about, becomes only stronger if we try to determine the guarantees of the peace. For those considerations lead to the conclusion that only the elimination of the sovereignty of States in Europe the and establishment of a joint army (police) can render the peace certain, and that all intermediate states of affairs which we could arrange by arbitration, arms limitations, etc. could hardly restrain the possibility of war! Since, as long as States can, however little, feel threatened by each other, no agreement will hinder them from taking preventative measures, and war will then break out within the shortest time from the increase of preventative measures. Once the slightest reason for mistrust exists between them, so it will create, by itself and from itself a hundred other powerful reasons. Thus, as long as the State itself remains the supreme executive within the State, no agreement can prevent the State from developing itself to its furthest extent.

The idea of power is alive in the minds of people. Since people think that the existence of that from which power emanates is the source of them all, a mortal fright seizes them if they feel it threatened. Thus, as long as the State is the supreme power, the idea of State power will endure and all agreements running counter to this fundamental idea will break down.

It is no use if States sign contracts which are contrary to their nature. There is only one solution: to place the supreme power above the nations, to set up a permanent European army which would guarantee, along with the United States, the rule of our civilisation on the earth.

By taking intermediate measures we perform a Sysiphean task. However far the shoulders of Sysiphus shove the rocks upwards on the slope, they roll tumbling downwards to the bottom if he leaves them. Until he finally rolls them over the summit, he cannot rest from his ever-lasting labours.

Peoples of Europe, our infinite pains will not be relieved until our true alliance is fully achieved.

2

New Scepticism

Szabadgondolat *was the journal of the Galileo Circle and was edited by the president, Karl (Károly) Polanyi, Michael's elder brother. This article, published during the government of Count Károlyi, demonstrates Polanyi's scepticism with regard to the materialistic reduction of politics to competing interests and to grandiose political scheme. It goes further to express a scepticism regarding all politics at least for a while.*

Before the war the position of artists and scientists was like that of a poor nobleman who had married into a rich tradesman's family. Politicians regarded artists and scientists as being very prestigious burdens, while the latter looked down on involvement in politics, although they liked to be on good terms with politicians.

However, when the war broke out, the belittling smile froze on the despising lips, for politics suddenly and unexpectedly became decisive and powerful. It was tragic that artists and scientists became so frightened that they lost their sense of being distinguished and they fell on their knees before the facts of politics.

Now there is revolution; later on peace will arrive.

Artists and we who are devoted to research feel obliged to make it finally clear how we stand with politics. Therefore, artists and scientists are organising themselves throughout Europe to defend their interests and to strengthen their impact upon society. I believe that is not the right way. Our real task in one sentence is as follows:

On account of the devastations brought by wars and revolutions we need to awaken to the fact that popular belief in politics disintegrates our

---

[2]. Published in *Szabadgondolat (Free Thought)*, 1, Feb. 1919, pp. 53–56. Translated by Endre J. Nagy.

societies and sweeps everything away. Thus we must enlighten people about this fact and refute their belief in politics.

Politics is not what we have thought it to be and what the public still thinks it to be, that is, a result of people's competing interests. Society is so complicated that even science cannot calculate the future effects either of any institution or of any measure, and people involved in politics, with their rough minds and passionate fancies, are a thousand times less able to foresee whether the institutions they demand will meet their interests in the last analysis. People see only misty outlines of society. Accordingly, merely by the fact that they project their purposes on society, although they cannot be well up in it, they disobey the rules of sober consideration by which they reckon their interests on other occasions.

Thus man in politics does not advance towards goals but aims at illusions which seize his imagination.

These political illusions are brought about by the torturing insecurity in which one is kept by society with respect to one's prosperity. As the savage groping about in the jungle feels surrounded by ghosts, so our contemporary struggling in the trackless forest of our civilisation weaves around the constituents of society with illusions. When our fate is swayed by the events of society with an inscrutable speed, we shake off the rule of reason, and imbued with hope and fear, snatching about and turning to any direction, we embellish the dim multitude of our fellow men around us with encouraging or threatening illusions.

Politics is a blind eruption of fear and hope. Accordingly, the social materialism, according to which people follow their interests in public affairs and also the democracy justified by this theory, are themselves mere illusions.

Unlike the teachings of schools that flatter democracy, political struggles, as blind battles of fear and hope, do not ensure progress but are aimless devastations caused by irrational passions.

People of reason and of imagination must not get involved in politics, that is to say, they must not add to the fatal disorder with their illusions. We must preserve our interests but that is tantamount to preserving culture: to destroy political authority and to refute belief in it.

What will be left for men after that? Don't worry about it. Illusions do not die, for their death, like that of kings, crowns their successors because hope and fear continue to live as sources of illusion. Let us adopt the ancient traditions of the Sceptics, and, while looking at people of our age who are lost among misconceptions, let us enlighten their minds. Let us leave it to people to find less dangerous misconceptions in the place of those of our time.

It may happen that, after having stoned us—as it has happened so many times in the course of centuries—people will cry: 'Brutus must become Caesar', and will enter into the Church of our Scepticism in order to pray. But our aim is not that. Ruling means behaving in such a way that others are obedient—to which we are not prone. It is not the task of the author to implant with flattery his teaching into the imaginations of the masses. The Word would have been frozen on the lips of Christ if he could have seen his future Church. Nietzsche would have put his pen aside if he could have imagined his Nietzscheans, and also Marx would have done the same if he could have seen his followers in our time.

Our job is exploring the truth; dissecting the confused images of politics and analysing the belief in political concepts; finding the originating conditions of political illusions and what animates the imagination to fix illusions to certain objects. We need to construct a picture of contemporary society by aggregating the inclinations of a hundred million people towards such illusions.

For such a job a sociology is needed that acknowledges only those concepts which it can lead back without remainder to actually experienced mental states of human beings, a sociology in which, accordingly, generalisations like 'development', 'class interests', 'ideologies', could only be problems to be analysed and not solutions. In order to perform this task we have to solve the paradox of how the spontaneously aggressive and independent action of all comes about in this society in which almost everyone can be drawn to do anything if the others, who can also be drawn to do anything, want them to do so. We have to discover here an operation like that of integration in higher mathematics that supplies the whole path of a line if the positions of all its points to the neighbouring ones are known.

We have to present such a picture of society on the bases of which reformers, publicists, politicians and the lower clergy of the Spirit*, will construct henceforth a community less dangerous to itself than today's, one without politics and democracy, that is to say, one in which people

---

* This refers to Hegel's notion of Spirit and thus more to people such as artists, scientists and scholars, rather than to ministers of religion as such.

leave their activity focusing on society, not to mass, avaricious passions and to illusions triggered by them, but demonstrating as much self-control and consideration in their public affairs as they usually do in their private ones.

—This will be their task.

Until then the exploring mind can confront politics only as with his enemy whom he is always about to contend ,as much within his own soul as beyond it.

3

Jewish Problems

The Polanyi family, originally 'Pollacsek', came from Ungvár, now Uzhgorod, in Ukraine, south of the Carpathians. Michael Polanyi's father, Mihály Pollacsek, Magyarised the name to 'Polanyi' and married Cecilia Wohl, whose father was a rabbi from Vilnius in Lithuania. Michael Polanyi was their fourth child and married Magda Kémeny, his student at Karlsruhe, the first woman to enrol to read engineering in Budapest, and a Roman Catholic. He was therefore an example of that assimiliation about which he writes, although it has been suggested that one reason why he read medicine at the University of Budapest, despite the fact that his interests were in scientific research, was that, as a Jew, it was easier for him to enter that faculty. Sir Lewis Namier, of Polish Jewish descent and with an Anglicised name, was Professor of History at Manchester, and there is, in the Polanyi collection in the library of the University of Chicago, a letter from Polanyi to him, from the same period of this article, expressing Polanyi's opposition to Zionism.

To live as a Jew is a peculiar and sometimes perplexing task. There is no accepted doctrine as to what obligations one Jew owes to another; how far they belong together within one country or across the frontiers. Zionists regard Jews as a nation of Hebrews. Their opponents, pursuing assimilation, insist that Jews must remain a mere religious denomination; that they are just Englishmen, Scotsmen, Frenchmen, Americans, Russians, etc.—as it may be—who happen to be of the Judaic faith.

---

[18]. An address delivered to the Manchester Branch of the Trades Advisory Council of the Board of Deputies of British Jews, 24th. September 1942. Reprinted, with permission from Blackwell Publishers, from *Political Quarterly*, XIV, Jan.–Mar. 1943, pp.33–45.

Both views are obviously forced—expressing somewhat crudely a particular programme, rather than facing the facts. Actually, some Jews best known as such to the world were men like Heine, Marx, Disraeli, Einstein, who neither spoke Hebrew nor professed the Jewish faith; and there are a great many people of this kind, commonly called Jews, who do not belong to any visible kind of Jewish community but whose lives, nevertheless, are profoundly affected by the fact of their Jewish descent—just as on the other hand the existence of these Jews is of decisive importance to the whole Jewish community, down even to its most orthodox roots.

The fact that official spokesmen of a community should give two conflicting definitions of its membership—both of them bluntly excluding a great number of the men who are best known to the world as the representatives of that group, does indeed reveal an extraordinary and perplexing situation. Jews cannot expect to play a reasonable part in the world unless they first clarify their views concerning themselves as a group. This is not impossible if only one is prepared to face the facts. I believe that a glance at Jewish history will show that the present internal conflicts and ambiguities between Jews merely reflect the unavoidable difficulties of their historical situation and I am confident that once these difficulties are squarely met they need not confuse us much longer nor weaken our standing and future action.

II

The position of Jews to-day is determined in the first instance by the fact that their forefathers 2500 years ago made the momentous innovation of adopting a single God of righteousness as their tribal deity. The fervour of the Bible was the fervour of the Israelites, and much of it continues to live in their descendants to-day. Religious fervour brought the Palestinian history of the Jews to an end when, by colliding head on with the claims of the Roman Empire, it involved the country in complete destruction and caused the Jews to be dispersed through the whole world. Soon after came a second collision when Rome became Christian, and the great rival religion, an offspring itself of Judaic fervour, became dominant over the western world. The new religion, now in power, reduced the adherents of the old one to the position of a hardly tolerated, contemptuously treated sect. But, fortunately for the Jews, the Roman Empire did not outlast this event very long and it was not until the time of the Norman Conquest that Christianity once more succeeded in consolidating its power over Europe. Up to that time the Jews, often in contact with the Arabs, continued to develop their intellectual heritage and remained well at the head of the cultural élite of the West.

The decisive blows against Jewry which were to fix our position until the opening of the 19th century, began to fall thick and fast soon after the forces of the new Christian civilisation deployed their might. Christendom in its medieval glory could tolerate no heretics. The Jews were overpowered, exiled, hunted, and finally their remnants imprisoned within the walls of the Ghetto.

The process went on in different ways in the various parts of Europe, but was practically completed everywhere by the close of the Middle Ages. For the then following 500 years, that is all through the formative period of the Modern Age, the Jews lived in isolation. It was a case of purely religious persecution. The situation was maintained by the pressure of one religion from one side and the unyielding tenacity of another religion from the other side. The Jews accepted at this time in the Shulchan Aruch a newly defined ritual code of unsurpassed strictness, regulating every detail of orthodox life. Every action and every thought was ruled by a meticulous discipline and any sign of laxity was watched and checked as a portent of defection. In fact while the physical gates of the Ghetto were guarded from outside, its spiritual and intellectual gates were locked from within. During the 500 years of isolation in the Ghetto, Jewry produced nothing of general human value. Rabbinic scholarship, maintained with unfailing devotion, was largely wasted in elaborating fruitless talmudist speculations. In the world around us men were embarking on great oceans of new inspirations and were discovering continent after continent of new truth; but we remained sitting in the dark, visited in our seclusion only by occasional waves of crude, fanatical visions of a national Messiah. The brute force of the Christian authorities, helped by the vigilance of the Jews, succeeded in reducing the heritage of Jewry to stagnation and decay.

III

Then came the time when modern civilisation began to spread from England and France to the less advanced countries of the world.

Modernisation was a military and economic necessity and it engaged the political and intellectual eagerness of progressive forces everywhere. Enlightened rulers from Peter the Great to Kemal Ata Turk started it with a strong hand from above, while national leaders from Kossuth to Sun Yat Sen spread it through the masses below. It created nation-states; merging the population inside their frontier into one mass of equal citizenship under one common law; educating the population to speak the national language and to feel themselves different from people elsewhere; exacting national loyalty unconditionally and to the exclusion of any other allegiance.

Had the Jews at this time been living together on one patch of land, the process of their modernisation would have occurred similarly and a Jewish nation would have been born. Some Peter would have risen to cut off forelocks and beards and some Ata Turk to scrap skull caps and kaftans. Perhaps the Yiddish vernacular would have been standardised or Hebrew been revived as our common language. In any case, after overcoming the usual resistance of antiquated opinions and claims, the reformers would have established a more or less westernised Jewish national State.

But the Jews were dispersed, living in small settlements surrounded by vast majority of other kinds of people. Their westernisation could not be achieved by a national renaissance. If they were to become citizens of a modern State at all, this could happen only by disrupting their own internal cohesion: by cutting their internal bonds, all along the frontiers of the new national territories, and allowing each separate section to become absorbed by the country to, which it would thus become apportioned.

To this new situation a certain number of Jews did respond. The modern rationalist ideas had penetrated into the Ghetto and weakened the hold of religious customs. The new latitudinarianism showed the way to relax ritual while retaining religion in a more spiritualised form. The outlook of equal citizenship within the national state offered tempting facilities for a broader and more useful life. Many of our ancestors, recognising themselves disgracefully backward, were overwhelmed by the contact with a superior culture. They rebelled against the ties of orthodoxy and entered on the path of assimilation.

Such a process could possibly take place in two ways: either in groups, that is by reform of general Jewish customs on modern lines, or else individually by the action of single persons deciding to give up their Jewish characteristics and to mix with the surrounding national community. The dispersion of the Jews, placing small separate colonies in widely different conditions, hindered a movement of reform in large coherent masses. It increased, on the other hand, the opportunities for contacts which could lead to individual assimilation. Hence the latter process became altogether prevalent and it is mainly the progress of individual assimilation which has determined the position of the Jews to-day.

IV

All through the period of Jewish seclusion there was a trickle of individual Jewish assimilation going on and in the 17th century one of the outcasts from Jewry, a grinder of lenses in Amsterdam, Baruch Spinoza, gave a world-wide demonstration of the fruitfulness of the process, by establishing a new great system of rational philosophy. But when about the time of Napoleon Jewish assimilation started in numbers, there occurred a veritable invasion of intellectual life by Jewish newcomers. The list of their great names has often been compiled and is mentioned with pride by many a Jewish writer.

Yet in a sense the event does by no means represent a straightforward Jewish success. The names of Heine, of Mendelssohn-Bartholdy, of Ricardo, Marx, Disraeli, do prove the presence of genius among Jews. But since all these were baptised Jews, their achievements may also indicate that Jewish talent is most effectively released by baptism. Or at least that Jewish triumphs are bound up with the neglect of distinctive Jewish traditions.

In fact, the process of assimilation has, I believe, demonstrated this beyond a doubt. For over a century there kept pouring forth from the Jewish community a stream of individual Jews possessing more or less talent or genius, undergoing baptism or retaining their religion only in an abstract and often quite superficial form while actually severing their ties to Jewish tradition and Jewish circles. Why did these men abandon their tradition and the community of their kinsfolk? They were the same stock which had so often braved the stake for its religion. Some of them, like Marx gave examples of great courage in facing exile and poverty for the sake of an idea. These men were not tempted by the easy fruits of apostasy. The reason for their desertion lay not in the lack of moral scruples, but sprang, on the contrary, from a profound urge to embrace the greater causes of mankind. They rebelled against the Jewish tradition which they found narrow and uninspiring; and they were found justified when, by stepping into the current or modern civilisation, they succeeded in making a major contribution to it.

Usually a people is best represented by its most eminent sons. Frederick II and Goethe—are Germany; Peter the Great and Tolstoi—are Russia; Louis XIV, Descartes, Pascal, Voltaire, Rousseau—they are France; and they represent these nations at their peak. But the more eminent a modern Jew is, the less is he usually concerned with Jewry, the less is he attached to Judaism. Our great men do not demonstrate the greatness of our distinctive tradition, but rather reveal, by the success of those who abandoned that tradition, its state of sheer exhaustion.

The broad masses of Jewry were not reached by the movement towards modernisation until well after the process of individual assimilation had got on its way. General, reform, like individual assimilation, involved a hard struggle against orthodoxy, and around the middle of last century this struggle led to the splitting of Jewry into two parts: an orthodox community retaining its old elaborate distinctive ritual and a new body of Judaism following a more spiritualised form of the faith. Reform brought parts of the Jewish masses nearer to the position of the assimilated vanguard, but the separation continued essentially as before. It remained true that in general the higher a Jew rose in the world, the more he became removed from Jewry.

V

The various degrees of assimilation, achieved by the various groups of Jews, have led to a second dispersal of Jewry. Jews are now not only spread out over all countries, but also spread out over a wide range of Jewishness in each country. There is a mass of orthodox Jewry, speaking Yiddish, their men with forelocks, their married women with wigs over their shaven skulls. They recall the original mass of medieval degradation and mental narrowness to which most of our ancestors belonged about 150 years back. And there exist various Jewish communities and circles representing all stages between the original Ghetto and the final dilution of the Jewish blood through intermarriage to a point where it loses all recollection of its own sources.

Those at the head of these straggling columns progressing towards complete assimilation are not the leaders of those behind them, but often seem rather to be running away from them. They are not supported, but only hampered by those who follow them. Their tendency is to cut themselves loose from the less assimilated Jews, because that facilitates the more intensified contacts which they are establishing with the non-Jewish world. The advance guard of assimilation may therefore be inclined to lose their feeling of solidarity with the less assimilated Jews, who are to them a constant source of embarrassment in the task of assimilation.

Naturally, the Jews left behind sometimes resent their treatment by the more prosperous and distinguished Jews whom they see drawing away from them to gain firmer ground in non-Jewish circles. They feel deserted by the more successful Jews who leave them, the poorer people possessing no exceptional gifts for advancement, to carry the burden of a more rigorous Judaic tradition.

Moreover, the reactions of the outside world to assimilation tend to increase the disruption of the Jewish community. Assimilation was sponsored by the modern idea of equal national citizenship. It flourished during the forward march of the new democratic nationalism in the latter half of the 19th century. But as opposition to democracy gathered force, there arose—first in Germany during the economic crisis of the seventies—a new political form of Jew-baiting which became known by the scholarly name of Anti-Semitism. Those Jews who, by assimilation, had ceased to be subject to religious persecution, were henceforth met by an attack based on racial discrimination. Each different stage of assimilation was faced with its special kind of opposition and each Jew had to fight his separate battle according to his grade on the scale of assimilation. These new diversified troubles increased the estrangement and distrust between the various grades of Jews.

VI

In the last years of the 19th century, there arose among the Jews themselves a vigorous reaction against assimilation. Jewish nationalism, buried for almost a century, rose again with the appearance in 1896 of Theodor Herzl, a Jewish lawyer from Budapest. Another, even more important beginning was started during the last war by a chemist, the Polish Jew, Chaim Weismann, then living in Manchester.

This movement, which became known as Zionism, attempted to collect once more all Jews dispersed by the process of assimilation. It caused some Jews, well distinguished in the non-Jewish world, to reaffirm more closely their community with the poorest and most backward of their fellow-Jews. They proposed to do for these what so many other leaders had done for their people during the period of Modernisation. To weld them into a modern political state and to fill them with a new national consciousness by reviving the long disused language of their ancestors. The task involved in this case the return to the ancient home country: thus raising special problems of great political and moral difficulty with regard to the now indigenous population of that country.

With these special problems I need not deal here. Even had they not arisen, the impression of Zionism on most of the Jews advancing towards assimilation would yet have remained slight, so long as the path of assimilation was generally kept open. But a great change occurred with the advent of Hitler to power in 1933. When Hitler condemned all Jews in Germany—the orthodox, the reformed, the baptised and even those with only a fraction of Jewish blood alike—to the same common destruction, Zionism suddenly appeared in a new prophetic light. The fall of German Jewry was taken to demonstrate the failure of assimilation in the very land of its greatest success and to justify by contrast the national conception of Jewry. When all Jews once more become outcasts, Jewish unity is automatically restored and at the same time the Holy Land may appear as the only true refuge from persecution.

VII

The time, however, has now passed when Hitler's rise was accepted as the verdict of history; when his successes over European progress, his destruction of the Law, of Religion, of free Science, were accepted as the proofs of decay—if not of ultimate failure—of these great causes of our civilisation. The time is now to fight him. And when victory comes, Hitler's fall must be made a token for all times of the invincible force of progress towards civilised life.

What then—in the light of this true verdict of history—can justify a return to Messianic traditions, from which the best of our forefathers 100 and 150 years ago turned away with such energy and contempt? How can this faith which seemed outworn and even degrading to men who were brought up in it, now inspire their descendants, educated, and often highly distinguished, in the arts of Western culture?

My answer is—in all reverence to the earnest endeavour of the Zionists—that in reality very little of such inspiration exists. I can see the
practical and humane undertaking of settling some Jews in Palestine.
There is here an enterprise in colonisation which offers a refuge to some
oppressed people and an adventure to some enterprising ones. The colo-
nists are Jews, a race inclined to reflection, the soil on which they settle
is that of the Holy Land, unparalleled on this planet for its associations.
That soil is bound to move them, as it moved so many mere travellers:
'the clime, and the land, and the name of the land, with all its mighty
import'. It is bound to move them the more if they speak Hebrew and
cultivate other Jewish reminiscences.

So far I will go, with willing admiration for settlers and organisers alike.
I can see good reason for supporting their scheme so long as it does not
conflict with more important interests. But I cannot accept that this scheme
represents a genuine revival of Jewish national feeling among Jews in general. And it seems to me that even in a good number of Zionists, including
some of their leaders, no genuine revival of this kind has occurred.

Zionist ideas have been recently reformulated by Professor L B. Namier
in a collection of remarkable essays[1]. He reveals most penetratingly the
moral ordeal of assimilation and through page after page that will long
remain classic, he lays bare the painful anomalies of our position. 'The
obvious conclusion of it all'—he writes—'is that a situation which produces such results should not be continued indefinitely' (p.132.) And a
little later (p.156) he declares: 'we have adhered to our own religion for
thousands of years, whatever price we had to pay for it; our religion is
essentially national in character; and the core of both our religion and
our nationalism has always been the return to the land which the Lord
has given to us and to our fathers from old and even evermore'.

These declarations, however, seem to me to reflect a sentiment rather
than to define an actual course of action. Most Zionists in England and
America show no practical intention of going to Palestine. For all their
feelings against assimilation, they take no steps to discontinue the process. In spite of their high emphasis on the Jewish religion with its Messianic traditions, they may be often found not to believe in that religion at
all. In fact some of the most eminent Zionists are—as Professor Namier
describes for his own case (p.172)—almost ignorant of Judaism, while
the flower of Jewish settlers in Palestine itself, the Chaluzim, are practically without any religion at all. Similarly, while Zionists express the

desire that we should all speak Hebrew (p.167)—they continue to speak and write in excellent English.

Zionism declares that it is not so much concerned with the fate of individual Jews as with their collective existence: 'For the sense of grandeur men derive only from the collectivity—the nation' (p.133). Yet by their practical programme they clearly show that this is not to be taken literally. Jewish organisations have ceased to complain about the fate of the largest single body of Jews, living in the Soviet Union, although there Zionism is prohibited, the use of the Hebrew language suppressed and Judasm, like other religions, is distinctly discouraged. Leading Zionists express acquiescence and even satisfaction with these conditions; apparently because they consider it more important that the Soviets have abolished Anti-Semitism[2]. The practical concern of Zionists is clearly with the victims of Anti-Semitism whom they desire to rescue from their plight and, not with the Jewish collectivity or the Jewish sense of grandeur. And that is as it should be.[3]

For the enormous majority of Jews who propose to go on living in the various countries of Europe and America, and who are bringing up a family with that future in mind, the declarations of their eternal faith in a return to Palestine can express no real conviction. And the same must be said of all Zionists who do not actually go to live in Palestine as soon as that is physically possible at whatever cost and sacrifice. A faith is not real unless we are prepared to live by its precepts. And we must live by it ourselves; not make others live by it on our behalf.

VIII

No, the Jews are not a nation, nor are they just Englishmen, Scotsmen, Frenchmen, etc., who happen to be of the Judaic religion. They are the descendants of a religious tribe which having given the Bible to the world, ran into a heavy conflict with the later developments of its own ideas, and was ever since left more or less outside the main flow of humanity. They are still recovering from the last 500 years of utter isolation, which was brought to an end only, in the course of the past few generations.

The recovery is being achieved by assimilation. We must realise more clearly the great difficulties of this task and face them with determination. This by itself will dissolve most of their confusing and weakening effects. I name only a few points which have to be recognised. Jews are still backward in various ways, and have yet more to learn from the great nations who built up our modern civilisation. We are newcomers; and hence, while we must never allow the legal recognition of our equal citizenship to suffer the slightest limitation, we must realise that it cannot yet be put into full and general operation. The degree to which any Jew can speak for the nation to which he belongs—and will be recognised by his non-Jewish compatriots to have the right to do so—will vary in the most complex fashion with the person of the Jew and the nature of the occasion. Consequently the proper relationships between the Jews themselves are also difficult to define in general terms. Assimilation necessarily means getting away from one another; but it must not mean the casting off of mutual obligations which decency requires between people of one kinship especially when faced with common troubles.

On all these problems there is a great deal of hard work to be done. For this work a higher mood of candour is need than has yet been general in Jewish literature. We must get rid of the self-praise and self-pity with which some minor Jewish publicists have been disgracing their fellows. It would also be better to leave to others the trouncing of Anti-Semitism, especially within the English-speaking world. We may trust a people who inspired these lines:

> *We could establish those of kindlier build,*
> *In fair compassion skilled,*
> *Men of deep art in life-development;*
> *Watchers and warders of thy varied lands,*
> *Men surfeited of laying heavy hands*
> *Upon the innocent...*

Let us rather guard our own steps, and restrain such gestures, of truculence, as when a Zionist leader quotes himself saying that he considers himself to be 'first a Jew and only in the second place a human being'. Such defiance only frightens our friends while causing delight to our enemies. In fact what I needed most, I think, is a thorough course of Jewish self-criticism, scourging all their weaknesses in the style of the ancient prophets. That would establish the right kind of solidarity among ourselves and provide the right tonic to our self-esteem.

IX

Men born to a lesser status must have the candour and humility to face their condition calmly and with the determination to shoulder the task. The acceptance of our inevitable limitations sets our souls free and establishes our human equality. We may then be able to discover any special opportunities that are implied in the disabilities imposed on us. In the case of Jewry such opportunities will be found to arise from the fact of their cosmopolitan outlook. The world is now heading towards a new Western Commonwealth, comprising Europe and North America, in which men of a cosmopolitan kind will be needed. Twice already the Jews, by their dispersion, have been the carriers of universal thought through Europe. During the first three centuries of our era Christianity spread from one Jewish settlement to another. Then, only a generation ago, the Jews helped to spread Socialism from country to country. The Soviet Government found good use for the Jews because in view of their antecedents their loyalty could always be relied upon. The Western Commonwealth of the future—which for generations to come will be in danger of particularist dissensions—should be able to rely in a similar fashion on Jews throughout Europe and America.

It is as well—from this point of view—that the Jews should have as yet become only half assimilated. The other half of the process will be achieved during the consolidation of the Western Commonwealth of the future. In order to form that Commonwealth all people of the West will have to undergo some assimilation towards a more uniform type of man. The cosmopolitan character of the Jews will give them a start in this direction. It will provide in their midst a natural affinity to the spirit of the new commonwealth and quality them to become its most devoted servants.

In certain, ways the future Western world will resemble the Roman Empire about the time of Constantine. Its basis will be the rule of law, equal citizenship and a religion rather similar to early Christianity with its admixture of Greek philosophy. The dispersed settlements of the Jews today are the most genuine residue of the old Roman Empire and they will fit quite easily into its modern equivalent. The world is changing in a way which will make it into a better home for the Jews. So it will in any case appear to us, once we discover how we can serve it best in our own particular way.

Notes

1. L.B. Namier, *Conflicts*, Macmillan & Co., 1942.

2. Compare, e.g. Norman Bentwich, *New Statesman*, 25th July 1942, and *Conflicts*, pp. 152, 159.
3. In *Conflicts*, on p. 115 it is said that after the war a 'certain number of Jews from countries where the Jewish problem is not patently acute' will desire to settle in Palestine. These countries contain 10–11 million Jews (p. 150). All evidence indicates that Zionists expect 99 per cent of these to stay where they are.

4

The Struggle Between Truth and Propaganda

The Webbs, famous Socialists and authors of the constitution of the Labour Party with its commitment, in Clause 4, to complete nationalisation, were among many duped by, or duping themselves about, the nature of the Soviet régime even in its most repressive years under Stalin. From his own first-hand knowledge and with evidence from within the book itself, Polanyi exposes the Webbs' suppression of their critical powers.

While under the Holy Alliance stillness reigned over Europe, modern dictatorships resound with the voice of enthusiastic crowds. While absolute monarchy claimed all public matters for itself bidding the citizens to keep quiet and to mind their private affairs, party dictatorship demands active participation of all men and women in public life; the machine of democracy is kept in full swing, not indeed to give opportunity for expression of opposition views, but to let the people show their enthusiasm for the reigning party and to let them discuss how they could even more zealously fulfil its policy. Freedom today is drowned in popular emotion.

The democratic machinery can be safely used in this fashion as a drilling ground for professions of loyalty if only every public body is watched by a sufficient number of determined party members who, in their turn, can rely on swift and merciless action of the police. Experience shows that a few per cent. of party members backed by police can bully the rest of any public meeting composed of indifferent or unorganised opponents of the government into loyalty, making the gathering appear

[4]. A review of *Soviet Communism: A New Civilisation?* by S. and B. Webb. Reprinted, with permission from Blackwells Publishers, from *The Manchester School of Economic and Social Studies,* Vol. VII, 1936, pp. 96–116.

or even to be full of enthusiasm. However, even a considerable proportion of party members has proved to be in effective if, as in the case of the Protestant Church in Germany, they are not supported ruthlessly by the police. The use of the democratic machinery for the subjection of the people is thus seen to depend ultimately on police terror. Every citizen has to know that he is under surveillance of an armed force wielding arbitrary powers to imprison or execute him on the suspicion of opposing the government's policy. Dictatorship wishing to control the totality of human life in its territory will try to extend the democratic machinery as far as possible; it will draw the whole adult and juvenile population into participation while at the same time widening the scope of public life to include activities formerly private, such as, for example, sports, love or cooking. The democratic machinery is tested periodically by its rulers through the taking of votes. On these occasions the party uses its powers of persuasion, surveillance and intimidation to the utmost. An efficient dictatorship will obtain practically unanimous votes even though admitting widest franchise and secret voting, while polling will reach percentages ranging up to figures unheard of in democratic countries.

The more cruel a dictatorship the more democratic can—and will, in general—be its institutions. Hitler has often defied the very much milder Austrian government to follow his example in taking a popular vote on its policy; and there is little doubt that if he once should rule in Vienna he would bring general franchise and the secret ballot to the people of Austria, who will by these channels approve his policy as emphatically as did, for example, the inmates of the concentration camp of Dachau in 1934.

The dictatorial use of the democratic machinery was first developed in the war. Propaganda ministries wielded emergency powers to impart orthodox information, ideas and feelings and to stamp out other views. Modern dictatorships are well aware of the use of war methods in their home policy. They constantly refer to their activities in military terms, and they justify their arbitrary powers by keeping up a state of warlike emergency, real or imaginary.

This mechanism of modern dictatorship seems obvious to any observer who is out of sympathy with the reigning party. If he cares little for either Communism or Fascism, the similarity of the various Party dictatorships will seem equally obvious to him. The non-Communist reader will, therefore, be deeply struck by Mr. and Mrs. Webb's account[1] of the political system of the U.S.S.R., which conveys a very different impression. On close examination of the book he will find the following explanation of the discrepancy.

The authors trace the main outlines of the political system by presenting its legal structure and its most patent facts. Accordingly, they draw a monumental picture of its public life which embraces the young and the adult at work and at leisure, operating through millions of meetings and discussions, based on a wide franchise and on pollings ranging up to almost one hundred per cent. We are made to admire the functioning of the democratic machinery-which under dictatorship rattles the louder the more effective the secret terror is which controls it from below-and we are made to delight in the freedom enjoyed by the citizen. No single detail of this account is literally incorrect; it is mainly by the space given to the description of the structure and operation of the democratic machinery and by the enthusiastic comments accompanying it that the picture of a free and powerful democracy is impressed on the reader.

Nor are the actually operating powers of the dictatorship such as Stalin, the Party, the OGPU left undiscussed. But the references to these are not allowed to destroy the picture of a great democracy; they become assimilated to the main argument or else, where some circumstances are admitted to be at variance with it, their weight is reduced to that of merely passing or at the most, unfortunately unavoidable minor circumstances.

The result is a presentation which, at first sight and probably to most of the readers, conveys nothing else but a monumental apologia of Soviet institutions and of the freedom enjoyed under them, while, on closer examination it proves to be so full of nicely adjusted reservations and containing so many details incompatible with the main argument that the careful student finds it impossible to form any picture whatever of the political system of the country.

The greater part of the book bears directly or indirectly on the political system; the other parts dealing with economic matters, social service and scientific work are built up by a method similar to that used for the presentation of the political system. The authors base their main argument on the information given to them or to other writers by the Soviet government. This material, underlined here and there by the authors' enthusiastic comments and accompanied by their interesting reflexions, makes easy reading to the general public. The material, however, having been originally issued with a view to propaganda, is unsystematic and, therefore, most unhelpful to a student seeking serious information on any particular subject. On careful reading one finds, indeed, that the gaps, inconsistencies and vague points are so numerous that it is not possible to draw any definite conclusions of a general kind from this material.

I will now quote some specific evidence in support of this general criticism, drawing it mainly from the authors' discussion of the political system which dominates their account of the U.S.S.R.

The first volume (528 pp.) deals with the Constitution of the U.S.S.R. as the authors see it. They claim that this is composed of—

(1) The legally instituted political bodies described in the section 'Man as a Citizen'.

(2) The Trades Unions in conjunction with the parallel bodies of the non-wage earning population forming together the organisation of 'Man as a Producer'.

(3) The co-operative shops, comprising 'Man as a Consumer', and

(4) The Communist Party, which is described in a chapter entitled 'The Vocation of Leadership'.

In the introductory chapter on 'The Constitution as a Whole', it is pointed out that these four organisations are the most important of half a dozen 'pyramidal structures' each 'based, according to a common pattern, upon a vast number of relatively small meetings of associated citizens for almost continuous discussion, and for the periodical direct election or primary representative councils. Each of these structures rises tier after tier, through successive stages of councils, governing ever-widening areas and constituted by indirect election, up to a group which is supreme for each particular mass. These half a dozen culminating groups, in different combinations, and by more or less formal joint consultations, constitute the source of all governmental authority, whether legislative or executive' (p.4). The principle of self-government incorporated in these pyramids is further emphasised on the page entitled 'The Power Cable': 'The power needed for administration may be generated in the innumerable meetings of electors, producers, consumers and members of the Communist Party, which everywhere form the base of the constitutional structure. It is transmitted through the tiers of councils as by a mighty conducting cable, working, as it passes, the machinery of government in village and city, district and province and republic. It is this conception of an upward stream of continuously generated power, through multiform mass organisation, to be transformed at the apex into a downward stream of authoritative laws and decrees and directives', that is indicated by its inventors by the term 'democratic centralism' (p. 7).

The next 150 pages deal with 'Man as a Citizen'. In the sub-section 'The Base of the Pyramid', the electoral franchise is carefully compared with western systems and its extraordinary wideness emphasised. Directing our attention more particularly to the political rights of the rural population we find that in the meetings of the village electors 'the discussions range over the whole field of public interests'. 'The village meeting may pass resolutions in the nature of suggestions or instructions on any subject whatsoever....' (p. 25). As to the village Soviets elected by these meetings 'the newest decree insists that it should consider and discuss also affairs of rayon*, oblast, republic and even U.S.S.R. importance' (p. 29), and further we read that according to Soviet jurists 'within the village the selo- (village-) soviet is "sovereign"; meaning that nothing which it does requires the sanction of any higher authority before it is put in operation' (p. 30), a statement to which the authors add the exclamation 'This does not look as if the Soviet Government was afraid of the peasant, or distrustful of popular democracy!' (p. 30).

The rural part of the population of U.S.S.R. was up to 1928 more than eighty per cent. and is even now not less than seventy-five per cent. of the total. We are told that this numerical preponderance always outweighed the less favourable rate of representation of the rural population so that 'the delegates deriving their mandates ultimately from the village soviets at all times constituted the majority of the All-Union Congress of Soviets' (p. 445), which is the supreme body in the Soviet Hierarchy. This body elects a Central Executive Committee called 'TSIK' to which, we are told, is entrusted 'all legislative and executive power' in the interval between the biennial meeting of the Congress which lasts only a week or so (see pp. 83 and 87).

We are thus led to understand that the political system of the U.S.S.R. is that of popular self-government which, owing to the overwhelming numerical excess of the agricultural population, naturally leads to a preponderance of the rural representatives. Nor should we doubt that the people make effective use of the wide liberties granted to them, since

---

* 'Rayon' is the original and clearly refers to an administrative unit or district, not the fabric.

according to the authors 'nowhere in the world outside the U.S.S.R. is there such a continuous volume of pitiless criticism of every branch of government' (p. 773), and at the close of their book they re-emphasise it that 'there is, as the student will have concluded, no country in the world in which there is actually so much widespread public criticism of the government and such incessant revelation of its shortcomings, as in the U.S.S.R.' (pp.1026–1027).

Nor should any apprehension that the Communist Party might exercise undemocratic pressure on the decision of the people be sustained, since 'neither the organisation nor the activities of the Communist Party are so much as mentioned in the "Fundamental Law" or in any statutory amendments of it. Nor has the Party any legal authority over the inhabitants of the U.S.S.R., not even over its own members!' (p.340), and accordingly, 'If the Party influences or directs the policy of individuals or public authorities, it does so only by persuasion. If it exercises power, it does so by "keeping the conscience" of its own members, and getting them elected to office by the popular vote' (p.340).

These statements should establish it beyond doubt that the U.S.S.R. is the freest peasant democracy of the world. The reader is, therefore, deeply puzzled how to reconcile them with the action described in the section pp. 237–272, by which the Government of the U.S.S.R. transformed the majority of the peasant holdings into collective farms, overcoming—as the authors tell us—the fierce opposition of the whole agricultural population.

The authors do not refer to the discrepancy of this action with the statements made in the course of their principal argument quoted above; instead, they introduce the subject as follows: After the civil war in which the peasants supported the Red Armies 'the peasants, poor, middle or kulak, now imagining themselves proprietors of the land they tilled, demurred to parting with their produce to feed the cities, even at free market prices, so long as these prices did not enable them to obtain the manufactured commodities they desired at something like the old customary rates. The peasants, moreover, even the very considerable proportion of them to whom the revolution had given land for nothing, resented, like peasant proprietors all over the world, the levying on them of any direct taxes. Nor did the marked development, in the village, of the characteristic peasant vices of greed and cunning, varied by outbursts of drunkenness and recurrent periods of sloth, produce anything like general prosperity, nor even any common improvement in agricultural methods. What became apparent was that the peasant, formerly servile, was becoming rebellious' (pp. 238–239).

For an appreciation of this passage we have to recollect two facts not directly pointed out in the book:

(1) The peasants in Russia were at all times much poorer than the urban population.[2]

(2) The direct tax claimed by the Soviet Government and actually obtained after collectivisation amounts to about 40 per cent. of the net income of the farmer.[3] This is illustrated unintentionally in the book by the account given of a successful collective farm by which '227 tons of grain was sold [in 1932] to the Government out of a total grain crop of 619 tons' (p. 280). 'Selling' to the Government means grain delivery at a nominal price, the amount delivered in this case is—deducing 10 per cent, for re-sowing—40 per cent. of the net crop.[4]

Carrying these facts in mind one might well be struck by the tone of ironic deprecation in which we are told that the peasants 'resented, like peasant proprietors all over the world, the levying on them *of any direct taxes*', even though *'the revolution had given the land for nothing'*. How mean of the peasants—we are asked to feel—not to pay gladly to 'the revolution' some 40 per cent. of their income in return for its gift! And we actually hear the masses of the poor defamed as greedy and cunning drunkards because they are unwilling to be taxed at the rate of 40 per cent. by a Government supported only by a small relatively prosperous minority.

In other places and at other times it used to be rather the Governments acting in such manner which were reproached of greed and cunning by the advocates of justice and freedom, but the authors do not consider this alternative; feeling that the Soviet Government has no other purpose than 'to obtain for all the conditions of the good life' (p. 1018), they freely speak of '120 millions of peasantry steeped in ignorance, suspicion and obstinacy' (p. 245), without giving any consideration to the wishes and rights of these millions, not noticing that their attitude justifies Hitler and Mussolini, Colonial Imperialism and the Holy Inquisition as well as a number of less illustrious tyrannies who all are or were seeking the conditions of good life for those oppressed by them—as sincerely as do the Soviets. To them it seems, 'where systems differ is in who wields the bludgeon and with what purpose' (p. 1032); so long as they approve of the bludgeoner and his purpose they call it democracy.

The authors' reluctance to adopt this doctrine consciously and openly seems responsible for the various paradoxes in which they get involved. Of these the following is a further example close at hand.

We are told that the fight over collectivisation was at its height in the year 1931. 'Beginning with the calamitous slaughter of livestock in many areas in 1929–1930, the recalcitrant peasants defeated, during the years 1931 and 1932, all the efforts of the Soviet Government to get the land adequately cultivated' (p. 265); yet have we not learned on an earlier page that during the same period the Communist Party was enormously popular among the peasants? We have been told that 'it is significant of the character and popularity of the Party that out of 59,797 village soviets at the 1931 election, 35,155 chose a Parry member as elected president, who is always a member of the local presidium, whilst 3,242 others elected a Comsomol' (pp. 31–32). We are thus asked to believe that at a time when the peasants were killing their cows in a desperate struggle against the communist policy, the popularity of the Party among them was so great that it caused them to elect a member of the Party as soviet chairman practically whenever or wherever they could find one. One is left to wonder whether perhaps the word 'character' associated with the word 'popularity' in the above passage might not indicate a reservation which resolves the paradox: 'character' might perhaps stand for 'terroristic character'.

The short chapter entitled 'In Whose Interest Does the Government Act?' (p. 449) suggests, however, that the village soviet chairmen of 1931 are only a special case of a more comprehensive paradox. It seems that in Russia it is quite customary for the agricultural population to elect representatives who are opposed to their own interests. Only this can explain the fact stated in this chapter that up to 1927 the Government acted only in the interests of 'the urban or industrial manual-working wage-earners', that is, of about 15 per cent. of the population. Later on, it is true, at least one class of the peasants seems to have become more mindful of their interests or more enlightened in the choice of their representatives, for 'since 1928 the Government may be deemed to have in view also the interests of the kolkhosniki, the owner-producers in agriculture who have joined together in collective farms'. The reader, bearing in mind the events of 1929–1932 to which I referred before, will ponder on the carefully chosen words 'may be deemed to have in view' in this curious passage, and he might wonder whether the 'interests of the kolkhosniki' are meant to be distinguished from their wishes, and if not, what would have become of the Government if the wishes of the kolkhosniki of 1929–1932 had been fulfilled.

But whatever may be the reader's reflexions on these points, one thing appears clearly to him both from the history of Collectivisation, as told by the authors, and from the last quoted passage, namely, that the Government has at all times, strongly opposed the interests of the individual peasants, whom they subjected to detrimental taxation (p.116) and other discriminating measures. Yet on page 725 he finds: 'Adhesion to the collective farm is entirely voluntary'. So he again feels much puzzled.

The reader comes across more paradoxes if he examines the authors' favourite argument in proof of free speech in the U.S.S.R.: 'It may surprise those who assume the existence of a dictatorship, and deny that of free speech, to learn that, for nearly three years (1925–1928) the issue [of agricultural policy] was the subject of heated public controversy in articles, pamphlets and books, widely circulating in large editions, as well as prolonged committee debate in the Central Executive Council and within the Communist Party' (pp. 242–243). The argument is repeated in various forms on pages 348, 367, 448 and 1099.

But can, the reader will wonder, the struggle between Stalin and Trotsky, ending at the close of 1927 with the victory of the former, be adduced as an illustration of common usage in present-day Russia? The fact reported on page 619 that immediately after the close of the debate Trotsky and hundreds of his followers were exiled to remote parts of the land and that, as we know from other parts of the book, later on most of the others who stood on the losing side of that debate lost their life or their liberty at the hands of the secret police, must certainly discourage the present-day Russian to look upon that debate as a precedent on which to base his claim to free speech; the more so, since it seems that the Soviet Government does not at all wish it to be considered in such a light. An official publication of 1933, quoted by the authors, refers to the debate in the following terms: 'The Five-Year Plan was born in the midst of a fierce class struggle around the question of the main road [or] means of socialist construction. Notwithstanding the counter-revolutionary resistance of the Rights and the Trotskyists, the Communist Party and the Soviet Government adopted the Five-Year Plan…' (p.621). What the authors ask us to consider as a typical example of a free debate, the Soviet publication quoted by the authors calls 'class war' and 'counter-revolution'.

But even the authors themselves seem unable to make up their minds on this matter. While a footnote on page 1100 explains that it was only the persistence of Trotsky in his factious conduct after the Party decision of December 1927 which led to his persecution, the 'Index of Persons' attached to the book states that Trotsky 'after Lenin's illness became persistently in opposition to the Party policy and was transferred from Commissariat of War to that of Transport; expelled from Party 1927, and exiled to Alma Ata' (p. 1159). Since 'opposition to Party policy' is equivalent to 'counter-revolutionary resistance' this passage condemns as strongly as the Soviet source quoted before the use which Trotsky made of the alleged right of tree speech and it contradicts flatly all the previous arguments of the authors on this matter.

The puzzled reader wonders that the authors should quote this so doubtful example of the exercise of free speech no less than five times, giving not a single other case of a public discussion on important political matters. Supposing that it is the only example they know, how can they venture to use it at all?

Another little example of the method by which the authors assimilate a piece of evidence to their main argument that the U.S.S.R. is not a dictatorship but enjoys freedom of thought and expression is found on page 435. We read: 'It is not easy to get hold of copies of the pamphlets surreptitiously circulated in opposition to the present Government of the U.S.S.R.' Then follows a list of objections made by one of these pamphlets, and the following conclusion is drawn: 'It will be seen that these criticisms of the U.S.S.R. Government are exactly parallel in substance and in form with those that are made by a Parliamentary opposition to the policy of a Prime Minister in a Parliamentary democracy. They do not reveal anything peculiar to a dictatorship as such'.

It is not the fact that criticism, which would be freely admitted in a democracy, can be circulated only surreptitiously in Russia that appears significant to the authors; the conclusion which they draw is that there is no dictatorship because it is not mentioned in the pamphlet. The writer of the pamphlet, they imply, had no objection to be threatened by imprisonment or execution, since he makes no statement to the contrary. I will conclude my demonstration of the authors' inconsistencies (which could be continued indefinitely) by showing how the main outlines of the actual political system of the U.S.S.R., so unlike the picture which the authors try to impress upon us, can be made perfectly clear by collecting some of their own statements. We read: 'There can be no doubt that Stalin correctly described the situation when he referred to "the supreme expression of the guiding function of our Party. In the Soviet Union, in the land where the dictatorship of the proletariat is in force, no important political or organisational problem is ever decided by our soviets and other mass organisations, without directives from our Party. In this sense, we may say that the dictatorship of the proletariat is, substantially, the dictatorship of the Party as the force which effectively guides the proletariat"' (p. 370). The method by which the Party, which, we are told, includes 3 per cent. of the voters, exercises its rule is also described: 'The highest governing bodies in all these hierarchies are found to be almost wholly composed of Party members' (p. 353). 'The Party members who are office-bearers, and who are all pledged to complete obedience to the dictates of the Party authorities, have assumed as their main vocation the supreme direction of policy and the most important parts of its execution, in every branch of public administration in the U.S.S.R., where public administration covers a much larger part of the common life than it does in any other country' (p. 354). Even out of office we hear that a Party member 'on announcing his Party membership, will usually be able to secure obedience, or, if not, he can command any militiaman (police constable) or local official to take action' (p. 355).

In the last resort the Party dictatorship relies on the ruthless use of the armed forces, including the secret police: 'It can be inferred that it was actually expected that to carry to completion the new agrarian revolution would involve the summary ejection from their relatively successful holdings, of something like a million families. Strong must have been the faith and resolute the will of the men who, in the interest of what seemed to them the public good, could take so momentous a decision' (p. 563). These men certainly showed supreme faith in the police. We might, therefore, agree that 'without the G.P.U there would be no Communist Party in Russia today, no Union of Socialist Soviet Republics'.[5]

The Party exercises the legislative powers through two alternative channels. Firstly, as already stated, they secure for themselves the majority of the seats in the higher representative bodies. For example: 'At Moscow in 1931 it was they who saw to it that two-thirds of all the candidates who survived to the final votes belonged to the all-powerful communist organisation' (p.460. Secondly, since 1928 legislation is more frequently enacted simply by orders of the Central Committee of the Party, which 'does not limit its intervention in the government of the U.S.S.R. to what may be considered legislation, even in its widest sense'; but also 'is perpetually directing the executive work of the far-flung Party membership' (p. 370).

The real power resides with a small Committee called Politbureau (p. 366). In the Politbureau the influence of Stalin is dominant. On account of the 'Adulation of the Leader', referred to on page 439, 'he may be thought to have become irremovable from his position of supreme leadership of the Party, and therefore of the government' (p.438).

The rules of the Party require that 'once any issue is authoritatively decided by the Party, in the All-Union Party Congress or its Central Committee, all argument and all public criticism, as well as all opposition, must cease' (p. 348). Since changes of policy cannot be discussed without criticising the accepted policy, it follows that no important political discussion whatever is permitted.

Thus the simple and well-known truth emerges that the U.S.S.R. is ruled by the Communist Party, under the orders of the Politbureau which is dominated by the unassailable power of Stalin. Had the authors started off from these facts instead of trying to submerge them in a flood of argument on freedom and democracy, they would have, no doubt, arrived at a more consistent and intelligible account of the political system of the U.S.S.R.

Next to the political system of the U.S.S.R. to which the greatest part of the book relates, the system of socialist economy is its most important subject. It is, however, impossible to understand from their book how this system works, since the authors do not tell us how outputs and prices are fixed. We are told that 'Gosplan has to compare the aggregate expected demand for each commodity or service.... with the amounts that the productive enterprises are severally proposing to turn out...' (p. 629). We might expect these two quantities to be different in general; but we hear nothing of the principles by which the decision is taken between the two possible alternates by which their disparity can be bridged: to change the output or to adjust the price. Since the authors give no consideration to this question, and, especially, do not mention pricing at all, their account leaves the reader completely in the dark as to the economic mechanism of the U.S.S.R.

On the factual side the book is equally deficient. It is written—as are, for example, pages 650–657 on the results of planning—in the form of an enthusiastic catalogue of disconnected items without even an attempt at a statistical analysis of the crude data. Students wishing to find out facts on any particular subject, let it be taxes, wages prices, housing, morbidity or education will find that the material presented is so full of gaps, so crude and so vague in its foundations as to be of little help to them for any serious study on the subject. In the chapter on 'The Good Life' we are told that the enterprise of the Soviets is like the undertaking of a great engineering work of uncertain success. 'Whilst the work is in progress any public expression of doubt, or even of fear that the plan will not be successful, is an act of disloyalty, and even of treachery, because of its possible effect on the wills and on the efforts of the rest of the staff' (p. 1038). I cannot remember any engineering project from the Suez Canal to the flight of the Graf Zeppelin or the draining of the Zuider Zee during which the public expression of doubt was made a capital offence, or was not, indeed, quite customary. The great feats of civilisation have not been accomplished by dictatorial efficiency nor have they needed for their protection that atmosphere of enthusiasm combined with panic which is supposed to be required for the creation of the conditions of 'The Good Life'.

It is deeply regrettable that the authors make it their task to discover new arguments for the protection of governments stampeding their peoples into 'The Good Life' against the interference from those who seek the truth. Such sacrifice of the intellect benefits all dictators equally, and on balance amounts to an injection of more venom into the issues of Europe's civil strife.

If such philosophy prevails there is little hope that the admirable advice given to both the economists of the U.S.S.R. and those of the western world 'that the reciprocal ignoring of each other's studies and the reciprocal contempt for each other's arguments is, on both sides, unworthy of what should be a matter of serious common investigation' (p.675), will gain acceptance. Still less can we hope for that reconciliation of rival social doctrines which alone can save Europe from dissolution. Such an aim can only be attained by tolerance, that is, restraint imposed by those who seek the truth on governments bludgeoning their peoples into Goodness.

Many thinkers today do not believe in truth; of those who do, few consider it right to tell the truth regardless of political consequences; thinkers have thus forfeited their right to restrain governments in the name of truth. Unless intellectuals make a new departure, inspired by unflinching veracity, truth will remain powerless against propaganda.

Notes

1. *Soviet Communism: A New Civilisation?* by Sidney and Beatrice Webb, 2 vols. (Longmans Green. pp. 1174).
2. *Summary of the Fulfillment of the First Five-Year Plan,* Moscow 1933, states on p.197 'peasants and collective farmers drawn into industry have raised their living standards 2.5 to 3 times'.
3. See M. Polanyi, *U.S.S.R. Economics,* Manchester University Press, 1936; p. 7; and Knickerbocker, *Rote Wirtschaft und Weisser Wohlstand,* Rowohlt, Berlin 1935, pp. 49–50 where the Government prices paid for wheat are compared with the price of bread sold by the Government.
4. The lack of any direct statement on the rate of the grain levy is one of the most serious gaps in the book. The report on Taxation, pp.116–7, mentions a single agricultural tax 'on all agricultural enterprises' (which is said to be much in favour of the collective farms as compared with the individual peasant), but no rates are quoted—although the figures for the 'progressive income tax' are given in detail. The grain levy is at the bottom of all the main political, social and economic events of the past nineteen years in the U.S.S.R. The reader who is left uninformed about the actual size of this levy cannot possibly understand any of these events.
5. From a statement quoted on p.586 as coming from 'a foreign resident of candour and experience'.

5

Rights and Duties of Science

This is the first statement of Polanyi's case against the planning of science, against which he actively campaigned from when it was first mooted by the British Association for the Advancement in Science in August 1938 (see SFS, 2nd ed., p. 7) and for the next seven or eight years. Though that campaign was won, in more recent years radical sociologists have revived the notion that science is 'ideological', and many people still fail to grasp the difference between natural science and its technological and thence economic applications. This article, therefore, continues to have more than a merely historical interest.

In the years since the World Crisis of 1929/33 a movement has grown up in England and to some extent also in the United States and France, putting forward a claim for the reconsideration of the position of science in the light of Marxist philosophy. More recently, it seems to me, this movement while further gathering in breadth, is adopting a less orthodox attitude. It is trying to win the support also of non-Socialists, mainly by emphasising that no restriction of the freedom of science is intended. The able and powerful treatise of Professor Bernal[1] represents this attitude. While he emphatically advocates Socialism, he does not suggest that scientists should join the Party but only that they support the Popular Front (p.404). His ruling passion is a profound resentment of delays in the achievement of plenitude, health and enlightenment to which, he believes, science even now holds the door open. To attain these, he demands a reorganisation of science on the basis of Marxist philosophy.

---

[10]. A review of J.D. Bernal's *The Social Function of Science*. Reprinted, with permission from Blackwells Publishers, from *The Manchester School of Economic and Social Studies*, Vol VII, 1936, pp. 96–116.

Throughout he is guided by the doctrine: 'The mode of production of the material means of life determines, in general, the social, political and intellectual processes of life. It is not the consciousness of human beings that determines their existence, but, on the contrary, it is their social existence that determines their consciousness'[2]. He wants science to be re-organised so that it may consciously, and hence, in his view, more efficiently, fulfil its social functions as outlined by Marx in this quotation. This, he asserts, should not interfere with the freedom of science. In fact, he professes that the very essence of science is the spirit of free enquiry (p.410); that science must be able and willing to defend its theses against all comers, not excluding but encouraging critics of all kinds (p.278); that we should guard against the possible risk of restricting the freedom of science or limiting its imaginative possibilities (p.261).

My purpose of this article is to examine briefly the Marxist claims, and those of Professor Bernal in particular, for a radical reconsideration and re-adjustment of the duties of science and the assurances accompanying these claims, that they will not impair the vital rights of science.

Science: Pure and Applied

The main points at issue are comprised in the relationship of pure and applied science; I will, therefore, deal with this relationship in some detail.

In Marxism a distinction between *pure science*, which seeks to find truth for its own sake, and the *application of science* to practical purposes is not admitted because all intellectual processes are assumed to be equally determined by the mode of production of the material means of life. The orthodox Marxist doctrine is correctly expressed by Dr. Ruhemann, in Appendix VII of Professor Bernal's book, 'The view prevailing in the Soviet Union as to the social function of science is roughly as follows: In the U.S.S.R. as in all other countries, science is the product of economical conditions of society, and its social function is to benefit the ruling classes of society'. (These classes in U.S.S.R. are said to comprise the vast majority of the people). He continues: 'In spite of this conscious interdependence of science and industry, plenty of work is being done in the Soviet laboratories which would in Western Europe be termed "pure science". But this term is not required in the U.S.S.R. as it is unnecessary to justify curiosity regarding the laws of nature with the help of idealistic doctrines'.

The Marxist position was made especially clear to me by a talk with Bucharin in 1935. He explained that the distinction between pure and applied science made in capitalist countries was due only to the inner conflict of a type of society which deprived scientists of the consciousness of their social functions, thus creating in them the illusion of pure science. Accordingly, Bucharin said, the distinction between pure and applied science was inapplicable in U.S.S.R. In his view this implied no limitation on the freedom of research; scientists could follow their interests freely in U.S.S.R., but owing to the complete internal harmony of Socialist society they would, in actual fact, inevitably be led to lines of research which would benefit the current Five Years' Plan. And accordingly, comprehensive planning of all research was to be regarded merely as a conscious confirmation of the pre-existing harmony of scientific and social aims.

Before discussing the position of Professor Bernal, which, although perhaps less intransigent in form than these orthodox Marxist statements, does not differ from them in effect, I will try to restate in some detail the liberal view—widely held, I believe—concerning the distinction between pure and applied science, and concerning the relation of science and society. To the Liberal, science represents in the first place a body of valid ideas. The origin of their validity can be observed most clearly in the major branches of science, such as mathematics, physics, chemistry, biology. Each new addition to these branches is the product of a continued application of certain methods of thought and observation which are characteristic of the branch in question. The results obtained are incorporated into accepted knowledge only after they have passed the standard tests of recognised experts. Thus the methods by which a branch of science makes its new acquisitions ensure its own standards of validity. The methods of science also ensure that every new addition to knowledge should enlarge the organism of ideas to which it accedes. New findings even though valid, are not considered interesting to science, unless they are related to some of the fundamental ideas which govern its various branches, and can be shown to confirm, expand or modify to some extent, these guiding principles. It is, in fact, precisely in this sense that the Liberal regards science as a body of valid ideas. Science consists of autonomous branches, ruled by their several systems of ideas; each of these are continuously producing new minor propositions suitable for scientific verification; and by these verifications they are being steadily strengthened and revised, in order to approximate more and more closely to truth.

Nothing has proved as permanent as these systems of science. Waves of civilisation have come and gone over Mesopotamia, Egypt and Europe, and while their creeds and laws, and often even their crafts, may have been forgotten, their contributions to systematic science have been preserved. It seems that an ordered framework of ideas in which each single part is borne out by the cohesion of the whole is of supreme attraction to the human mind. Struggling for a foothold in a shifting world, the mind clings persistently to these rare structures of sound and consistent ideas. It is in these structures, accordingly, that all scientific interest resides. No unconnected single fact, however momentous it might be, possesses any scientific interest. His own birth, his future death, the existence of the Universe, are supreme facts in a man's life; since they cannot be related scientifically to other data, they do not interest man as a scientist. This is not to say that the intrinsic interest of events is lost on the scientific mind. The more important an event is in itself, the more interesting is it to deal with it scientifically. This is equally true whether the interest in the subject matter is mainly contemplative or mainly practical. In fact, these two types will be often found blended to a general *human* interest, reflecting the essential connection of man's interest in the contemplation of his own nature and of his position in the Universe, with his urge to dominate and draw profit from his surroundings.

But it is essential for the Liberal distinction between pure and applied science to keep steadily in mind that the direct appeal of a subject, however strong, does never in itself signify scientific interest. Although every moment of man's life depends on his handling of practical knowledge, yet none of this is science. A new-born child sucking his first meal makes use of practical knowledge of vital significance, and so does the constructor of a skyscraper or the surgeon opening a skull; yet none of this is science. No amount of ingenuity, be it conscious or instinctive, employed in the process of handling knowledge in these ways, can make it into science. In fact, so long as knowledge is merely viewed in its practical context, it can have no scientific interest; and it acquires such interest only if and when its relations to one of the great schemes of ideas governing some branch of science can be clearly demonstrated. The scientific interest of such a demonstration consists entirely in the disclosure of the theoretical significance of the knowledge in question; but the practical value of the subject need not be forgotten in the process; its recollection will, on the contrary, quite justifiably enhance the interest in its scientific investigation.

Some kinds of practical knowledge are almost entirely empirical while other kinds are more rational. The ancient crafts, such as beer brewing and pottery, depended purely on experiment, whilst cases of reasoned industrial procedure are found rather among modern manufacturers in industries such as electrical and mechanical engineering, and in the production of chemicals. Medical healing is even to-day almost entirely empirical, while surgery is mostly rational. The difference between these two kinds of practice (which jointly partake in varying proportions in all technical processes) clearly consists in their relation to extraneous experience. he empirical solution of a practical problem is mere guesswork, and its finding, therefore, constitutes a new discovery. The rational solution, on the other hand, makes use of previous experience to devise a new contrivance: its finding marks an invention in the modern sense of the word.

The experience on which the rational solutions of practical problems are based is, of course, mostly drawn from every-day life, or else from scientific knowledge which is so ancient as to have become almost generally known. But some inventions draw also on experience gained by scientific investigations dating from modern times—say of the last few centuries—which is not yet taught in all schools. This type of work is done by scientifically trained inventors who in the past fifty years have become responsible for an increasing part (the extent of which is customarily exaggerated) of the innovations in industrial practice. This is called the *application of science* to industry; and hence comes the term 'applied science' in contrast to which *science* is then styled 'pure science'.

The existence of far reaching mutual interactions between science and practical knowledge, and, in particular, between science and 'applied science' should now be clear. The discoveries made by the empirical crafts often prove later to be interesting objects of scientific investigation ('stimulation of science by industry'); and, on the other hand, knowledge gained and stored up by science is widely used by the modern inventor to contrive new processes and new apparatus ('application of science to industry'). But it should also be clear from our description of science as an organism of ideas, that scientific research, which is the growth of the organism, cannot be deflected from its internal necessities by the prospects of useful application—any more than the empirical search for a practical advantage can turn aside to consider what interest science might take in the result.

It is curious that the existence of common data, forming part of science as well as of industrial practice, should constantly lead to the suggestion that the progress of science and industry should be organised jointly—although the absurdity of harnessing together other pairs of occupations on such grounds, would appear obvious. For example, the boring of mines and the excavation of railway tunnels both involve similar operations. Can they be combined? While tracing a tunnel can we be guided by the possibilities of using it as a mine? Or can we, while boring for minerals give preference to places in which perhaps tunnels might be built later? Obviously not, because generally speaking, while we are guided by the immediate considerations arising from one pattern of thought, we cannot give attention to the part which our object may perhaps play in a second entirely different pattern.

Reluctance to accept this fact, leading to attempts to direct research towards results of possible practical applicability, cannot lead to a growth of science which is of much value. A consistent policy conducted on these tines would actually stop the development of science altogether, turning, in effect, the efforts now devoted to scientific research into attempts to discover empirical solutions for practical problems. If a line of compromise were chosen, leaving science 'half free', the result is likely to be the stimulation of comparatively meagre investigations similar to those that are called forth nowadays by the large endowments given to special fields—as in the case of cancer research. I doubt whether these endowments have promoted to any considerable extent the scientific understanding or even the treatment of cancer, since the main progress concerning both, has been achieved in principle by workers outside the domain of cancer endowments. This could not be otherwise because 'cancer research' does not form a branch of science based on a specific system of ideas. For all its practical interest, knowledge of cancer can only advance if and when the progress of physiology, biochemistry, cytology, and other branches of science, does throw from tie to time new light on one or other of its aspects—a process which cannot be appreciably hastened by the endowment of research on cancer. Moreover, all such progress is wholly derived from the freedom of the systematic branches of science to pursue their own specific scientific aims.If a policy of endowing research for practical aims were universally adopted, such benefit as any particular practical task now derives from the general progress of science would be altogether eliminated. Science would immediately come to a standstill and its practical applications would gradually become exhausted.

Hence the position assigned by liberalism to science in society is this. Society cultivates science as an organism of ideas which powerfully attracts the minds of intelligent people. Science as a whole, as well as the various branches of science, are valued for two combined reasons—the intrinsic appeal of the subject matter and the power of the theoretical interpretation. Society cultivates science also in order to increase the store of knowledge available for practical application. Whichever of these motives prevails, the resulting endowment should always be given freely, for science to pursue its own aim; namely, the further development of its several branches.

To the Liberal this position of science in society is a significant example of the principles of liberty. Science, munificently showering gifts on all men, when allowed freely to pursue its own spiritual aims but collapsing into barren torpor if required to serve the needs of society, makes a powerful argument for liberty. An argument which can be readily extended to other systems of ideas, which possess independent existence of their own, forming systems of consistent ideas, which can grow only in accordance with their own fundamental principle—I mean, the whole spiritual realm of truth, justice, humaneness, beauty and their organisations in the forms of laws, politics, moral customs, arts, religion. The same reasons which cause science to be paralysed by any imposition of secular authority, makes all the wealth of this realm turn to dust the moment it is made subject to the demands of the State.

The Marxist doctrine of social determinism and the kindred teachings of Fascism, claiming that thought is the product of society and ought, therefore, to serve the State, removes all ground on which to consolidate an authority, to which man could justifiably appeal against the commands of the State. If on the other hand it is admitted that the realm of thought possesses its own life, then freedom is not only made possible but its institution becomes a social necessity. Freedom is made *possible* by this doctrine because it implies that truth, justice, humaneness will stand above society, and hence the institutions which exist to cultivate these ideals, such as the Press, the law, the religions, will be safely established and available to receive complaints of all men against the State and, if need be, to oppose it. Freedom also becomes *necessary* because the State cannot maintain and augment the sphere of thought which can only live in pursuit of its own internal necessities, unless it refrains from all attempts to dominate it, and further undertakes to protect all men and women who would devote themselves to the service of thought, from interference by their fellow citizens, private or official—whether prompted by prejudice or guided by enlightened plans.

The position of science in society is thus seen to be merely a special feature of the position of thought in society. Its consideration is so important because it strikingly points to the general fact that society must cultivate thought and not attempt to dominate it—for fear of seeing it drowned in the morass of some eternally stagnant orthodoxy—and also because it shows how society, in order to perform this spiritual duty, must grant to its citizens freedom to devote themselves to the sphere of ideas, and must secure them the right to appeal from its own commands to the superior judgment of this realm. Such principles concerning the relation of science and society are, of course, familiar to Professor Bernal. In his chapter on 'The Ideal of Pure Science' he presents them in a superb quotation from Thomas Henry Huxley, the greater part of which I reproduce here:

'In fact, the history of physical science teaches (and we cannot too carefully take the lesson to heart) that the practical advantages, attainable through its agency, never have been, and never will be, sufficiently attractive to men inspired by the inborn genius of the interpreter of Nature, to give them courage to undergo the toils and make the sacrifices which that calling required from its votaries. That which stirs their pulses is the love of knowledge and the joy of discovery of the causes of things sung by the old poet—the supreme delight of extending the realm of law and order ever farther towards the unattainable goals of the infinitely great and the infinitely small, between which our little race of life is run. In the course of this work, the physical philosopher, sometimes intentionally, much more often unintentionally, lights upon something which proves to be of practical value. Great is the rejoicing of those who are benefited thereby; and, for the moment, science is the Diana of all the craftsmen. But, even while the cries of jubilation resound and this flotsam and jetsam of the tide of investigation is being turned into the wages of workmen and the wealth of capitalists, the crest of the wave of scientific investigation is far away on its course over the illimitable oceans of the unknown'.

'Thus, without for a moment pretending to despise the practical results of the improvement of natural knowledge, and its beneficial influence on material civilisation, it might, I think, be admitted that the great ideas, some of which I have indicated, and the ethical spirit which I have endeavoured to sketch, in the few moments which remained at my disposal, constitute the real and permanent significance of natural knowledge'.

To which Professor Bernal adds the comment:

> 'In another sense the ideal of pure science was a form of snobbery, a sign of the scientist aping the don and the gentleman. An applied scientist must needs appear somewhat of a tradesman; he risked losing his amateur status. By insisting on science for its own sake the pure scientist repudiated the sordid material foundation on which his work is based'.

And discussing the ideal of pure science further he finds that it makes science into a mere pastime like cross-word puzzles (p.97), a game, which can give no full satisfaction for a life work. For such satisfaction 'men require that what they do has social importance as well'. The more so since 'whatever the scientists themselves may think there is no economic system which is willing to pay scientists just to amuse themselves'.

Professor Bernal does not, of course, deny that in actual fact pure science exists as distinct from applied science. His book is full of most illuminating information and discussion on this subject. Even in his own plans outlined in the chapter on 'The Re-organisation of Research' he recognises that 'the old sciences.... like astronomy and chemistry have accumulated centuries of autonomous tradition; they have whole sections which are separate both from technical theory and from technical practice and develop to a considerable extent according to their own internal necessities' (p.280). But the recognition is only *de facto* not *de jure*: on the same page, when outlining scientific organisations, we read that their first stage 'will be occupied mainly with what has been called pure, but should more accurately be called sophisticated science'.

Scornfully the Marxist rejects here any claim of science to be pursued merely for the sake of discovering truth. Although it is recognised that the desire to discover and to understand the external world is at present a motive to scientific endeavour and though such motive is even approved as part of the disposition of the socially minded scientist of the future (p.97 and p.273) it is thought absurd that any economic system would pay a scientist just to search for truth.

One is tempted to return the charge of snobbism: We scientists who know so well the delight of study, the excitement at the dawn of understanding, the profound satisfaction in mastering thought; we whose daily work is stirred by such emotions; we citizens of a scientific world solely concerned with work of this character; should we deny that other people than ourselves are also capable to enjoy the study and understanding of truth, the spectacle of its progress through discovery? That they can feel sufficiently moved by their desire for enlightenment, by their admiration of science, to pay a fractional part of their incomes, amounting on the average to a farthing in the £, in order to secure the continuation of research? Surely scientists cannot assume that they form a race apart governed throughout by motives which are quite absent in other human beings!

And yet this is precisely what the scornful rejection of the ideal of pure science by Marxists amounts to.

Curiously enough Professor Bernal does not fail to point out that the great scientific controversies of the nineteenth century such as that of evolution were fought out in the field of ideas (p.29). Nor would he deny, I am sure, the earlier great struggles between Church and Science in the sixteenth, seventeenth and eighteenth centuries; and that all through the centuries from the Renaissance onwards, a wide general public was passionately concerned with these struggles (pp. 89 and 323). He also admits that in modern Britain there is a considerable popular interest in science (p.87), and indicates that this interest is strongly directed towards contemplating the marvelous working of the universe, trying to extend the mind, as T.H. Huxley says, 'towards the infinitely large and infinitely small'—but he treats such manifestations of popular scientific interest with contempt (pp.87,89, 229, 306). Instead of 'meditating on the mysteries of the universe' people should read books in which 'science is related to common human needs and aspirations', and for this he recommends repeatedly and emphatically (pp. 260, 360) the books of L. Hogben in particular his *Science for the Citizen*.

This recommendation provides an opportunity to acknowledge the weightier nature of Professor Bernal's book compared with the writings of Professor Hogben, which belong to the same movement of thought. But in this particular connection Hogben's outlook would suit Bernal's contention. The idea repeatedly implied in *Science for the Citizen* that certain discoveries were made 'to measure' to satisfy certain social needs, is certainly the most radical attempt to extinguish all interest in the *object* of scientific discovery—which is the existence of certain laws of nature. Who could, indeed, stay to ponder on the Universe when he is told that the position of the Earth as the centre of the Universe was only abandoned when clockmakers found that they had to shorten their pendulums if exporting clocks to the tropics?[3] May we not even abandon again, now that we all carry watches, the sophisticated idea of the Earth going round the Sun—as a useless meditation on the Universe?

Science Organized to Promote Welfare

But what is the purpose of all this trend of thought? The ironical belittling of the motive of science, the implied denial of a popular interest in knowledge for its own sake, the annoyance at the sight of its manifestations, the attempts to divert it into purely utilitarian channels—are all these professed only to fulfil the doctrine—'the modes of production determine the intellectual processes of life?' Not altogether. The major force behind this attitude is the passionate desire to put science into the consciously organised service of human welfare. It is the demand for this adjustment of science to its social function which dominates the book and which precludes the acceptance of science for its own sake. To illustrate this we may quote this emphatic passage which refers to the reciprocal stimulation of science and industry.

'This double process has indeed been taking place throughout the whole of the history of science. What has happened now is that we are just beginning to be aware of it and could replace the clumsy and casual adaption of the structure of science to this double flow by a more consciously thought out scheme of what may be called a vertical organisation of science. To a certain extent this has already been done in the Soviet Union. Indeed the idea derives directly from Marxist thought and is so obvious and true that the difficulty is not to justify it but to explain why people never saw it' (p.279).

The institutions to which Professor Bernal wishes to entrust this new direction of science are similar to those in existence today, but they would assume new tasks. The academies would plan the fields of science in which research is to be conducted, seeking, in consultation with industrialists, to adjust science to its social functions. Though it is repeatedly stated that this scheme can only become fully effective under Socialism, it is implied that a start could be made before this state is achieved.

However, all the brilliant and instructive pages of the book have no answer to the question: how should the progress of science be directed in order that it may benefit human welfare? The process remains mysterious up to the end. On p.415 we read the emphatic statement 'Science will come to be recognised as the chief factor in fundamental social change...Science should provide a continuous series of unpredictable radical changes in the techniques [of the economic and social system]'. But a moment later 'Whether these changes fit in or fail to fit in with human and social needs is the measure of how far science has been adjusted to its social functions'. It is difficult enough to see how society can do anything to adjust what is admittedly unpredictable, to the service of welfare. But still, it might do its best, as Professor Bernal suggests, by favouring certain directions of research which are thought likely to produce the unpredictable. But the major question is still there. How can science, if it has to submit to adjustment to its social function at the hands of society, maintain its essence, the spirit of free enquiry?

Let us put the case concretely. It is generally accepted that in the last 40 years physics have advanced on a scale which is unsurpassed in any previous period of similar length. This advance has, no doubt, enlarged the outlook of industrial physicists and has in many unspecifiable ways assisted them in their inventive tasks. But it seems to me that the only invention which may be said to have arisen directly from this era of discoveries is the modern discharge lamp which is now coming into use for the illumination of roads. Now the theory which has been utilised for this invention was built up between 1900 and 1912 in a series of giant strokes by Planck, Einstein, Rutherford and Bohr. Suppose then that 'the socialised, integrated, scientific world organisation', the coming of which is prophesied by Professor Bernal (p.409), would have existed in 1900, with its 'unified and co-ordinated, and above all, conscious control of the whole of social life'. How would this organisation have 'adjusted' the inclination of Planck, Einstein Rutherford and Bohr to discover the atomic theory to the increased need for street lighting which was to arise 20 years later in connection with the popular use of motor cars, undreamed of in 1900? Would scientific world control have foreseen, not merely this future need but also the fact that it might be satisfied by a discharge lamp based on the discoveries which were about to be made? And, then the crucial question. Supposing the likely case that the scientific world controllers would not have performed this miracle of foresight, would they then have had to reduce their support of the investigations which were leading to the discovery of atomic structure?

I think Professor Bernal will agree, with pleasure, that there is no scientist who would answer this last question in the affirmative. But then, it would be admitted that Scientific World Control could do nothing better than public authorities do today—lending support to scientists of recognised ability, to extend in any way that they think fit, ever further, T. H. Huxley's 'realm of law and order'. And this would amount to the complete abandoning of the planning of science for social purposes, and of the Marxist philosophy of science.

Truth or Propaganda?

The fact that the main point which Professor Bernal raises is not once critically faced by him, is characteristic of a propagandist attitude to which Marxist thinkers of the highest intellectual and moral qualifications succumb, through their disbelief in the power of truth and their rejection of our duty to serve it for its own sake, which are taught by their philosophy. I will now show how this attitude, believing itself justified by a passion for human welfare, to override the most elementary intellectual scruples, leads, in spite of all the accompanying protestations of loyalty to freedom of thought, inexorably to the result which its philosophy implies, namely the approval of merciless oppression of intellectual liberty, if only it is perpetrated in pursuit of approved political aims.

Throughout the book capitalist institutions are relentlessly criticised. Fascism is violently exposed. Soviet Russia is constantly held up as an example to be followed. Any school-boy knows that such comparisons are useless unless they include a discussion as to what extent any particular evil of Capitalism or of Fascism is also present in U.S.S.R. Another elementary rule of reasoning is to examine what possible disadvantages may have arisen in U.S.S.R. in connection with the elimination of the evil under consideration. The complete omission of these simplest critical precautions is a characteristic of propaganda.

We are told at length how under Capitalism scientists are induced to conformity with the general views prevailing in the State (p.388) and that they might feel unable to refuse assistance in war work for fear of losing their jobs (p.387). That in psychology and the social sciences studies are greatly hindered by the fact that they 'may be banned as tendentious, if they seem to imply that the world may be run in a different way' (p.342); that teaching often shows a definite bias in favour of certain orthodox views, sometimes taking up the subtle form of pretence of a strictly scientific attitude (p.259). All these things happen under Capitalism.

It is then vigorously emphasised that conditions under Fascism are infinitely worse. Here scientists who think for themselves outside their own fields are exposed to 'sanctions' (p.403). Social sciences are so grossly distorted as to be removed from scientific study altogether (p.259), and psychology is in a similar position (R. A. Brady, quoted on p.233). It is also particularly noted that 'Italian scientists have been largely cut off from their fellow scientists abroad, partly on account of political unreliability and partly from lack of means to travel' (p.211).

In the U.S.S.R., on the other hand, to which constant reference is made, as to the only example of the application of Marxism in practice, Professor Bernal finds nothing to criticise. Actually scientific thought is, I believe, nowhere oppressed so comprehensively as in U.S.S.R. and this is due precisely to the fact that the thrust of violence is guided here by Marxism, which is a more intelligent and more complete philosophy of oppression than is either Italian or German Fascism. I will briefly outline the position.

The U.S.S.R. is the only country in the world which is dominated by an elaborate orthodoxy. The writings of Marx, Engels, Lenin and Stalin are all above criticism. Not only can none of their views be called into question, but any criticism of any detail of the enormous volume of publications by these authors, covering almost all conceivable subjects, would be considered as a counter revolutionary act, punishable by death. The imposition of Marxism includes the compulsory acceptance of all writers approved by Marx or Engels; on these grounds authors as widely varied as Epicurus, Darwin and Balzac are above criticism. The first because he was favourably discussed in Marx's doctoral dissertation, the latter [sic] because Marx praised him in his private correspondence. This reference of Marx to Balzac has actually become the foundation of the literary doctrine of 'Socialist Realism' now enforced in the U.S.S.R. 'Socialist Realism', 'Soviet classicism' are examples of modern Marxist doctrines, which are proclaimed from time to time by the party authorities. They are compulsory.

Up till 1932 the Communist way of discussing any theoretical problem of science, engineering, art or society was to seek for a text in the then authoritative writings and Party lines which would apply to the case. In important questions the Party might intervene giving a final decision absolutely binding to everyone.

The most important new scientific periodical of the U.S.S.R. which was started early in 1932 (*Zeitschrift für Physik der Sovjetunion*) contains an editorial preface mentioning the application of Dialectical Materialism to physics as one of the purposes of the new journal. Not one in a hundred physicists believed in this nonsense, but no one could dare to contradict the statement publicly. A few months later the Party decided against the continued application in detail of Dialectical Materialism in the exact sciences. A number of essays were then exposed to ridicule by the Party organs. I quote a few of their titles from an account of Sydney and Beatrice Webb,[4] Marxism and Surgery, The Dialectics of Graded Steel, The Dialectics of an Internal Combustion Motor. *A Journal for Marxist-Leninist Natural Science* was published regularly cultivating such branches of knowledge. Not before this lunacy was eventually abolished by the Party in the fifteenth year of the revolution, could any scientist of the U.S.S.R. raise his voice against it.[5]

Dialectical Materialism remains, of course, beyond criticism in [the] U.S.S.R. This philosophy, which most scientists do not believe to have much sense in its general form, than in its just quoted special applications current until 1932, is still being thrust down the throats of Soviet scientists, who must not contradict [it]. A report on a discussion couched in scholastic terms referring to the Soviet orthodoxy, which was conducted at the end of 1936 in the Lenin Academy of Natural Sciences on a problem of genetics appeared in Nature (1937), 140, p.296.

By a decree of the Communist Party dated July 4, 1936 the application of Binet-Simon intelligence tests to children was declared as a counter-revolutionary science. I quote after Lady Simon from Moscow News, September 23, 1936, a few words illustrating the inquisitorial atmosphere of a meeting in which the educationists concerned (called 'pedologists') received this decree: 'Most significant was the speech of Professor G. P.Blonsky. "I personally feel the full weight of responsibility for the offences of pedology", he said, "I knew all along that bourgeois pedology does not accept the Marxist basis but I continued using tests and measurements, which are a means of bolstering up the exploiting classes"'.[6] Psycho-analysis is also banned in U.S.S.R., in none of its institutions is its teaching or its practice permitted.

Soviet scientists feel, I suppose, just as any other educated people would feel under this regime of intellectual dragooning. They are well paid, but, nevertheless, the Government does not let them go abroad, believing that many of them would prefer not to return. When permission to travel is granted to a scientist his wife is retained in Russia to ensure his return. But it appears that for more than two years now not a single

Soviet scientist has been allowed to cross the border. The precaution is not unreasonable. A few years ago V. N. Ipatieff, the best organic chemist of Russia, fled the country. He was followed to the United States by G. Gamow, the most successful Russian theoretical physicist. In respect to experimental physics the Soviets have been more fortunate. In September, 1934, they succeeded in capturing an eminent representative of this branch, Peter Kapitza, while he was staying in [the] U.S.S.R. on a holiday from Cambridge, where he held a professorship and had resided for many years. Many well-known young scientists have been imprisoned in the course of the last year, no one knows why or for how long. Their names can be mentioned only in a whisper. Reference to papers by such political outcasts are banned.[7]

All this is quite well known, and should have been discussed by Professor Bernal, as showing the results of the only hitherto known large scale attempt to adjust science to its social functions. It would have thrown light on the otherwise mysterious aspect of freedom in Socialism, as outlined for example in the emphatic statement on p.381. 'The freedom of the nineteenth century was a seeming thing.... In an integrated and conscious society this conception of freedom is bound to be replaced by another—freedom as the understanding of necessity. Each man will be free in so far as he realises that he is taking a conscious and determinate part in a common enterprise. This kind of freedom is most difficult for us to understand and appreciate; indeed, it can only be appreciated to the full by living it'.

Dragooned into the lip service of a preposterous orthodoxy, harried by the crazy suspicions of omnipotent officials, arbitrarily imprisoned, or in constant danger of such imprisonment, the scientist in Soviet Russia is told, from England, that the liberty which he enjoys can only be appreciated by living it. Since the terms of this liberty prevent him from answering to his British colleague, I have taken it upon me to point out the anomaly of the situation.

Unless we fully re-establish man's right to pursue truth regardless of social interests, and unless we again dedicate ourselves to the duty of this pursuit, such anomalies cannot be eliminated, but must go on growing into a suffocating tangle of fallacies; and presently this generation which was itself—in the phrase of Lionel Robbins—'betrayed beyond belief by those who should have been its intellectual leaders'—will find, too late, that it has opened wide the pass to the barbarians.

Notes

1. *The Social Function of Science.* By J.D. Bernal. Routledge. Pp. xvi+482.
2. Karl Marx, *A Contribution to the Critique of Political Economy* (Preface).
3. 'From the landsman's point of view the earth remained at rest till it was discovered that pendulum clocks lose time if taken to places near the equator. After the invention of Huyghens the earth's axial motion was a socially necessary foundation for the colonial export of pendulum clocks'. *Science for the Citizen*, p.232.
4. S. and B. Webb, *Soviet Communism: A New Civilisation?* p.1000.
5. A lone exception was made in favour of the famous Ivan P. Pavlov who was free at least to talk as he pleased. Pavlov died in 1936 at the age of 86. During the era of Stalin, beginning about 1927, his activities were naturally very limited by his age.
6. Lady E. D. Simon, *Moscow in the Making*, 1937, p.130.
7. See *Modern Quarterly*, 1938. Vol. 1. p.371 footnote.

6

History and Hope: An Analysis of Our Age

This article develops Polanyi's account of 'moral inversion' and his analysis of the dangers inherent in the modern union of scepticism and zeal for reform, the logical consequences of which are totalitarian attempts to recreate society at will and to be inhumane in the interests of humanity. Polanyi expounded that analysis in several articles. Of those that were not reprinted in Personal Knowledge *and* Knowing and Being, *this is the most extensive and links moral inversion to the materialist reductionism which claims to base itself on natural science and the scientific outlook.*

My title may sound strange: 'History and Hope'. Yet these words refer to plain facts. The history of mankind falls into two sharply divided periods, into two periods of vastly different lengths. The first extends from the beginnings of human society and all through recorded history up to the American and French revolutions. All during these ages men had accepted existing custom and law as the foundation of society. There had been changes and some great reforms, but never had the deliberate contriving of unlimited social improvement been elevated to a dominant principle. The first government to adopt this principle was that established by the French Revolution. Thus, the end of the eighteenth century marks the dividing line between the immense expanse of essentially static societies and the brief period during which public life has become increasingly dominated by fervent expectations of a better future. Such is the history—the short history—of hope as a political and social force; such the justification of entitling an analysis of our age 'History and Hope'.

[105]. Reprinted with permission from *The Virginia Quarterly Review*, XXXVIII 2, Spring 1962, pp. 177–95.

In the Western countries where they had their origin, the pursuit of these hopes achieved in the course of the nineteenth and twentieth centuries the most humane and freest societies the world had ever seen. It engendered an intellectual life of unprecedented range and led to a new flowering of the arts, which rivalled the splendours of Greece and the Renaissance. It created immense wealth, more equally distributed than before and nearly abolished poverty.

But another stream of the same flow led to different results. It established the Soviet empire which has spread its power and influence during the last forty-four years over a major part of the globe. Thus, hardly had the march of humanity towards its new hopes got under way than it divided mankind into two rival camps, mortally opposed to each other by their different visions of progress.

Last June the leaders of these two camps met in Vienna and one of these, President Kennedy, reported on his return that the Soviets and we have wholly different views of right and wrong and above all have wholly different concepts of where the world stands and where it is going.

The situation is terrifying; but here I am only concerned with understanding it. We must ask how the pursuit of progress has engendered and established over vast areas a system of ideas which mortally conflicts with the original hopes of human progress.

We might be tempted to think that the dominance of Soviet ideologies was imposed by sheer force of arms, but this would leave unexplained how the power of Communist governments originally came into existence at the centres from which it subsequently spread to other parts. We must face the fact that these centres of power were originally established by groups of deeply convinced adherents, who gained influence over broad masses. And we must face also the fact that these ideas, so different from our own, are still echoing round the globe and gaining followers, particularly among the more educated people. We must acknowledge that these converts embrace these ideas with fervent hopes for humanity, and that they are dedicated to fight and suppress any opposition to them.

The main difficulty in understanding this rise of modern totalitarian ideas lies in the habit of thinking of it in terms of a conflict between progress and reaction. That is false; the revolutions of the twentieth century are not of this kind. They do not aim at restoring either the dogmas or the authorities shattered by the French Revolution. They are dogmatic and oppressive in an entirely new way which, by a curious process, harnesses to its purpose the great intellectual and moral passions by which free thought and popular government were first achieved in Europe and America.

This strange transmutation was first achieved by Karl Marx. In his biography of Marx, Isaiah Berlin describes him at work: 'The manuscripts of the numerous manifestos, professions of faith and programmes of action to which he appended his name still bear the strokes of the pen and the fierce marginal comments with which he sought to obliterate all references to eternal justice, the equality of man, the right of individuals or nations, the liberty of conscience, the fight for civilisation, and other such phrases which were the stock in trade...of the democratic movements of his time; he looked upon these as so much worthless cant, indicating confusion of thought and ineffectiveness in action'.

Marx obliterated all references to moral ideals from his manifestos, for he believed he had far better, more honest, and more intelligent grounds on which to achieve these very ideals. He wrote: 'It is not the consciousness of human beings that determines their existence, but conversely their social existence that determines their consciousness'. To Marx, therefore, a revolution which would transform the existence of society became the only possible embodiment of social ideals. Otherwise, these were just empty words. Even his own resolve to fight for that revolution was cast in the form of a scientific sociology which predicted that the revolution was both inevitable and imminent, owing to the material fact that it would release an immensely increased productive capacity.

Marxism transmuted the ideals of human progress into a doctrine of violence. It proclaimed a new vision of reality in politics and history, reducing all morality to underlying economic necessities. Moral forces then become illusory and economic forces alone are accepted as real. This is the famous transformation of utopia into a science. In the name of science Marxism destroys the moral image of man and affirms that human ideals are mere derivatives of power and profit.

But it would be a mistake to accept at its face value this description that Marxism gives of itself. The image of a mechanical process of history leading to the establishment of socialism could never inspire revolutionary passion. But Marxism does inspire powerful passions. The secret of this contradiction lies in the fact that the Marxist conception of history does not eliminate—as it pretends to do—the moral ideals of progress, but absorbs them into its vision of this process. The mechanical machinery of history is in fact seen and deeply felt as the embodiment of all the moral aspirations of man, which, being thus embodied, are assured of inevitable victory by the mechanical laws of history.

The Soviet régime is an exact replica of the machinery of history as conceived by Marx. It claims to be intellectually superior to all other governments, both past and present, by conducting itself on strictly scientific lines. Hence the fierce struggle between rival Communist factions over the correct interpretation of the historical situation of the day, and over the correct application of Marxist theory to this situation. Arguments on deciding the Party line are conducted in the sociological terms of Marxism. Yet all the time this allegedly cold, calculating machinery is fuelled by the fierce passions of utopian aspirations; the régime relies for its driving force on the very motives which its scientific theory claims to have exposed as ineffectual.

But this unfortunately does not mean that a government thus constituted is guided by moral considerations. It will no doubt occasionally respond to them, but it will do so only by departing from its theoretical principles. The main behaviour of the régime will conform to its theory, relegating the moral passions of socialism to the role of a fuel which blindly drives the machinery of revolutionary power. But when used as a fuel, the moral force of socialism is torn from its original context. It becomes inaccessible to moral, or indeed to any reasonable argument. This is fanaticism; a fanaticism of a kind the world has never seen before. For it is a fanaticism induced by scepticism, which turns to science for denying the reality of moral motives and for reducing them to mere reflections of economic necessities. Communist fanaticism is clearly a product of the scientific age.

But we must recognise also that moral scepticism would never have produced modern fanaticism but for the great new tide of political and social hopes engendered by the revolutions of the eighteenth century. I have spoken of the progress achieved by these forces during the nineteenth and twentieth centuries in all Western countries. Progress has been slower in areas more distant from its original centres. But the demand for progress has been all the more insistent in these lands among the individuals who fully realised the backwardness of their country. Today, demands for progress and social justice have reached a range and force altogether without precedent in the history of mankind. Thus the catastrophic eruption of Communist fanaticism has been due to the confluence of the two main ideas of the French Revolution. Both scientific scepticism, which originally liberated free thought, and the new tide of humane sentiments, which inspired subsequent reforms, were combined in it. Modern sceptical fanaticism unites these progressive forces in a deadlock which turns scepticism into dogmatism and morality into contempt for morality. This is what I meant by saying that modern totalitarian tyranny does not go back on the French Revolution, but is an outcome of it: that it is another branch of the same pursuit of progress which has brought forth the comprehensive humanisation of Western society since the French Revolution.

Some people have described Soviet morality as an extreme form of hypocrisy. It is true that Soviet representatives sometimes sound unbearably sanctimonious, but the true strength of the Bolsheviks lies in being frankly hard-boiled. We have seen Marx engaged in furiously eliminating all moral professions from his manifestos. An American analysis of the chief propagandistic writings of Lenin and Stalin shows that ninety-four to ninety-nine per cent of the references to the Communist Party and its activities describe it as seizing, manipulating, and consolidating power. This is not hypocrisy. It is the inverse of hypocrisy—a sceptical fanaticism, contemptuous of moral motives which it yet uses as raw fuel to feed the cylinders of its political machinery. For some years past, I have used the term 'moral inversion' as a label for this peculiar mental structure. The term is useful and I shall introduce it here again as a guide to those states of mind, both inside and outside Communism, that can be best understood as variants of moral inversion.

But I have not yet sufficiently consolidated this concept of moral inversion as applied to the Soviet régime itself. It might be objected that it is simpler to say—as it is commonly said—that the Soviet régime is crassly materialistic and hence blind to all moral considerations. But I deny this; I deny that the Soviet régime is materialistic. Materialism is an indulgence of appetites and a love of comfort. A materialistic economic life is one that concentrates excessively on material comforts. The Russian economic system is the opposite of this. It neglects the most desperate popular needs—e.g., for better housing—in favour of ornate skyscrapers and underground marble halls. It deflects untold treasures from the use of consumers in order to plant a pennant on the face of the moon. It revels in production and shies away from consumption. Comfort is sacrificed to the passionate endeavour to conduct production in a particular way that is deemed socialistic, and thus to erect a monumental symbol of the march of Communism to world supremacy. Indeed, we in the West should watch keenly and hopefully for any sign of a true materialism in Soviet Russia. For if the régime once turned to the pursuit of material advantages, it would have lost its fanaticism. Love of comfort may be ignoble, but one may trust it to be reasonable.

The Soviet economic system is in fact another instance of inversion. Just as moral inversion transforms morality into the service of power, so the satisfaction of men's needs is transformed into the service of public splendour. The machinery of industry, invented to provide material comforts, is transformed into an altar for material sacrifice. Western scholars will never understand the Soviet economic system, until they realise the full extent of this transformation.

Inversion applies also, and with disastrous consequences, to the domain of artistic life in the Soviet empire. Just as the ideals of freedom and democracy are unmasked as bourgeois pretences, while a party dictatorship is endowed instead with the quality of being intrinsically free and democratic, so also bourgeois art and literature are unmasked, and the glorification of socialism is proclaimed instead as true art and literature. Mental inversion goes indeed beyond this. It inevitably engulfs the very conception of truth; the truth of ordinary matters of fact. It is difficult to say how far the personal obsessions of Stalin have contributed to the creation of that universe of fictitious allegations, on the grounds of which millions of harmless Soviet citizens were sent to the frozen wastes of Siberia. However that may be, Stalin was certainly supported in the vagaries of his imagination by the principle that objective truth was a bourgeois pretence which must be cast out by affirming the partisan character of all truth. He could always rely on the doctrine that party truth was sacred and was to be protected by terror against objections based on mere facts. A belief in factual reality is indeed a subversive principle under totalitarianism.

Admittedly, the pervasive mendacity of the Soviet régime, relying on the principle of party truth, eventually overreached itself and evoked the first major revulsion against the Soviet régime. But this event belongs to a later period.

This may remind us that my analysis has so far given no direct answer to the question why the ideas of modern Communism have exercised such fascination far beyond the domains of the Soviet Union, and indeed for some time gained the allegiance of many men of highest intellectual distinction throughout the West. But it is clear already from what I have said hat Marxism could satisfy simultaneously the two most active demands of the modern mind. It appealed both to scientific objectivity and to the ideals of social justice. It satisfied the scientific outlook by interpreting man and history in terms of power and profit, and assured at the same time the highest social expectations by identifying social progress with the irresistible course of history.

But one may still ask: Did those responding to Marxism not see the ruthless oppression of their most cherished ideals in the Soviet Union? They did, but they disregarded it. For they had accepted the doctrine of moral inversion according to which the victory of the Revolution was the embodiment of all moral values and was, therefore, not subject to judgment by moral standards. The Soviets' declared resolve to act unscrupulously was taken to certify their intrinsic supremacy over any moral considerations. As Hannah Arendt rightly observed, 'Bolshevik assurances inside and outside Russia that they do not recognise ordinary moral standards, have become a mainstay of Communist propaganda'.

Soviet Communism has been the most important revolutionary movement of the twentieth century, and the only one effectively articulated in an elaborate theory of itself. The revolutions of Mussolini and Hitler were by comparison amorphous affairs, relying on the incitement of hysterical masses by a turgid rhetoric. Yet the way in which Fascist dictators transmuted the patriotic sentiments of the masses into a cult of naked power had the structure of a moral inversion. Hitler's frenzy was primarily evil, but its appeal to the German youth was moral. Their response was determined by convictions similar to those which Marx held about the nature of moral motives in public life; they believed that all decency was hypocritical and that brutality alone was honest. Hence their disgust of moralising and their moral passion for unscrupulous violence.

Since popular nationalism was as much an outcome of the French Revolution as were the hopes of unlimited social progress, we may say that all forms of modern totalitarianism have a similar structure. Unscrupulous tyranny is justified throughout by a moral scepticism which converts a flow of generous motives into the blind fuel of naked power. Thus in every case the two main forces of the French Revolution, its scepticism and its generous hopes, destroyed each other in modern totalitarianism and revealed thereby a catastrophic contradiction between the major ideas of that great revolution.

But do ideas actually make history? Could the internal contradiction in the ideas which first generated modern liberty, have actually caused in our days a widespread collapse of liberty? Ideas certainly provide the shape, or at least the possible shapes, of historic transformations. It is a moot point how far the French Revolution was caused by the ideas of the philosophic Enlightenment which preceded it; but there is no doubt that the ideas which the French Revolution proclaimed and spread through-out the world were those of the Enlightenment. And just as this philo-sophic movement has determined the character and the teachings of the French Revolution, so, I believe, the internal contradictions of these teach-ings have eventually determined in their turn the character and teachings of modern totalitarianism.

This is borne out by the profound influence which the self-destructive tendencies, inherent in the ideals of the Enlightenment, have exercised on modern minds apart from its bearing on politics. Just look how in France itself, where the dawn of unlimited hopes first arose in the eighteenth century, the continuous pursuit of these great hopes has led the present generation of writers to a philosophy and a literature of despair. How, actually using 'The Age of Reason' as his title, Sartre demonstrates that the ultimate outcome of the age of Reason is a recognition of the total absurdity of man and the universe, and finds that this reduces man's freedom to a total arbitrariness. Look how this sense of total absurdity is combined with a violent moral protest. Roquentin, the hero of Sartre's novel *La Nausée*, expands his metaphysical nihilism into an attack on the complacency of the fat bourgeois dignitaries, whose portraits he views in the municipal picture gallery. This is a combination of logically in-compatible affirmations; for if moral values do not exist, no one can be said to be morally defective and still less can such an accusation be made with an outburst of moral indignation. These logical incompatibles are fused together here in the same way in which Marx transmuted an abso-lute moral scepticism into a moral indignation at bourgeois hypocrisy. Such is the structure of all modern nihilism, in the sense I shall use the term here. It is a fierce moral scepticism fired by moral indignation. Its structure is exactly the same as that of the moral inversion underlying modern totalitarianism. Herein lies, in great part, the susceptibility of the modern Western intellectual to the ideas of totalitarianism.

Of course, in ordinary parlance, 'nihilism' often means moral depravity or moral indifference. But I regard this kind of nihilism as unimportant both for the history of ideas and the origin of revolutions. Depraved individuals have often joined company with true nihilists and have become instruments of revolutions. There was a vicious madness in Hitler and Stalin, and they attracted criminal types to their service. But by itself such mentality can produce only a crime wave—not inspire great literature or make a revolution. This mentality is poles apart from that of the personage first identified a hundred years ago as a nihilist by Turgenev in his hero, Bazarov. This character, which has made history, represents the rebellious Russian intelligentsia of the 1860's, who repudiated all existing bonds of society in the name of a scientific materialism, by which they hoped to liberate men and make them all brothers. The romantic variant of nihilism that Nietzsche introduced in Germany was likewise a moral protest against existing morality. 'This shop', wrote Nietzsche, 'where they manufacture ideals seems to me to stink of lies'. It is in disgust with these lies that he proclaims magnificent brutality as something supremely authentic, honest, and admirable.

In France the beginnings of a nihilism motivated by moral protest go back two hundred years. Diderot speaks of it already in 1763 in *The Nephew of Rameau*, whose immoralism justifies itself by the hypocrisy of society. Soon after, Rousseau in his *Confessions* proudly acknowledged his own vices in the name of nature's naked truth. And later in the century the Marquis de Sade gave an extensive account of his cruelties and lust, deriving a sense of intellectual and moral superiority from a conception of man as a mere machine, and from the theory that law is but the will of the stronger.

In nineteenth-century France, the first major figure of modern nihilism was that of Baudelaire. After him, the distinguished representatives of this mentality became too numerous to be named here, while around them a whole new social stratum emerged in the modern bohémiens, popularising the rebellious amoralism of their masters. A similar mentality spread at that time through the Russian intelligentsia and penetrated by the beginning of this century into Germany, particularly in the form of the Youth Movement, and to Italy, in the form of Futurism. It has been that European Revolutions are made by the armed bohémians. It is certainly true that the rebellious intellectuals of the European continent were receptive to the ideas of totalitarianism, and I believe indeed that their contribution to the rise of totalitarianism was decisive.

But we must stop here and face the fact that these subversive intellectuals of the nineteenth and twentieth centuries have brought forth achievements of supreme distinction in the arts and letters, and we must acknowledge also that their great works were not unconnected with that very mentality which had such ill consequences in politics. Nihilism has served for a century as an inspiration to literature and philosophy, both by itself and by provoking a reaction to itself. A loathing for burgeois society, a rebellious immoralism, and a mood of despair have been prevailing themes of great fiction, poetry, and philosophy on the Continent of Europe since the middle of the nineteenth century. Modern painting and music have risen rebelliously within this milieu, by a deliberate rejection of socially accepted standards. We may actually commemorate the centenary of this great outburst today for it was just one hundred years ago that Eduard Manet painted his immortal 'Le déjeuner sur l'herbe'. Rejected by the official exhibition of paintings, Manet and his rapidly multiplying followers soon founded their own exhibition under the title *Salon des réfusés*, the Salon of the rejected. The advent of modern music was accompanied by similar public clashes. Throughout the subsequent decades modern art went on battling with academicism. We have got so accustomed to this spectacle that it is generally overlooked that nothing like it had ever happened before. Great artists had sometimes gone unrecognised during their lifetime, but never had a whole artistic culture gone flowering through successive generations in systematic opposition to the prevailing standards of the age. Let us face the fact that the heroism of the modern intellectuals, to which we owe the victory in this long battle, arose from the same subversive temper which often made the influence of these intellectuals politically disastrous.

And there is more to this. Modern art has arisen from a persistently continued destruction of existing artistic realities for the sake of penetrating to strata of harder, more genuine forms of reality. So the 'poetic' has vanished from our poetry, the 'picturesque' from our painting, the 'harmonious' from our music; gone are heroes and heroines from our novels and plays. All these were rejected in the pursuit of a harsher artistic truth. But can this process go on indefinitely? Must it not presently lead to a complete destruction of meaning? *Dr. Faustus* by Thomas Mann is an inquiry into this question. 'In a work [of art]', Mann writes in one place, 'there is much seeming and sham...The question is whether at the present stage of our consciousness, our knowledge, our sense of truth, this little game is still permissible, still intellectually possible [whether it] still stands in any legitimate relation to the complete insecurity, problematic conditions, and lack of harmony of our social situation; whether all seeming, even the most beautiful, even precisely the beautiful, has not today become a lie'.

So in the end beauty itself and all standards of art are unmasked as lies. Tortured by fear of banality, modern art takes refuge in a complex formalism bereft of subject matter, or else in a naked subject matter so harsh as to exclude any suspicion of humane ideals. Bawdiness has never been lacking in literature and art, but this has been always a form of levity; it was left to our age to discover a sombre and fantastic obscenity, as an ultimate token of intellectual honesty. It seems obvious that the rebellion which evoked modern art and moved it on for a century cannot fail to exhaust itself, once its product will have ceased to affirm anything and hence leave nothing more to rebel against.

But is not science itself—true science, which was the main source of philosophic enlightenment and from which grew the great movement of modern rebellious scepticism—is it not a safe haven against all the harms of excessive doubt that I have described in politics, in personal morality, in artistic endeavour? Alas, it is not. Scientific rationalism has indeed been the main guide to intellectual, moral, and social progress since the idea of progress first gained popular acceptance about a hundred and fifty years ago. But unfortunately, the basic ideals of science are nonsensical. For science does not recognise the existence of any ultimate irreducible entities above the level of elementary particles or their wavefunctions. Thus all life, all human beings, and all works of man—including Shakespeare's sonnets and Kant's *Critique of Pure Reason*—are ultimately to be represented in terms of these ultimate particles.

The ideal of science remains in fact what it had been in the time of Laplace; namely, to replace all human knowledge by a complete knowledge of atoms in motion. Laplace said that if we knew at one moment of time the exact positions and velocities of every particle of matter in the universe, as well as the forces acting between the particles, we could compute the positions and velocities of the same particles at any other date, whether past or future. To a mind thus equipped, he wrote, all things to come and all things gone by would be equally revealed. This is precisely what science still accepts today as its ideal of perfect knowledge; and this ideal is nonsensical, for such universal knowledge would tell us absolutely nothing that we are interested in. Take any question to which you want to know the answer. For example, having planted some primroses today you would like to know whether they will bear blossoms next spring. This question is obviously not answered by a list of atomic positions and velocities at some moment on May 1, 1962; it must be answered in terms of primrose blossoms. The universal mind is utterly useless for this purpose, unless it can go beyond predicting atomic data and tell us what they imply for the future blossoming of primroses.

Never mind whether we could actually infer something about primroses, or about anything else that we may be interested in, from a topography of atomic positions and velocities. It is enough to make clear that, as it stands, Laplace's representation of the universe ignores all our normal experience and can answer no questions about it—that the Laplacian ideal of universal knowledge is actually a state of complete ignorance.

Science has achieved magnificent results in the pursuit of this absurd ideal, but at some point it must always lead science to an impasse and reveal its absurdity.

Take, for example, modern neurology. Its discoveries are unrivalled in beauty and usefulness. But neurology reflects the ideal of science by assuming that man is a mechanical automaton, and hence it cannot account for human consciousness and must in fact deny its existence. Three authoritative contributors to the international Symposium on Brain Mechanism and Consciousness, held in Paris in 1954, said this clearly. The first said: 'The existence of something called consciousness is a venerable hypothesis; not a datum, not directly observable....' The second: 'Although we cannot get along without the concept of consciousness, actually there is no such thing'. The third: 'The knower as an entity is an unnecessary postulate'. These statements express, of course, only the theoretical opinion of the three distinguished scientists. Actually, they know like everybody else that consciousness, as for example pain, exists, and that other states of consciousness also clearly differ from unconsciousness. But as scientists they feel compelled to make statements to the contrary.

We meet the same situation in the study of society. Anthropologists must endeavour to describe social groups in strictly scientific terms. And most anthropologists will insist, therefore, on carrying out their analysis

of society without reference to good or evil. Two distinguished anthropologists of Harvard have represented the unspeakably cruel murder of
supposed witches as a cultural achievement. 'Some social systems', they
write, 'are much more efficient than others in directing aggression into
oblique or non-disruptive channels. There is no doubt that witchcraft is
Navaho culture's principal answer to the problem that every society faces:
how to satisfy hate and still keep the core of society solid'*. Another
anthropologist has described head-hunting as fulfilling an essential function in the societies in which it is practised. 'The religion of Edistone
Islanders', we read, 'provided a motive for living and kept an economic
system functioning'†. Head-hunting proved wrong in this view only because it kept down numbers and so made technical progress superfluous,
eventually leaving the islanders a prey to British conquerors.

For this kind of scientific anthropology, social stability is the only
accepted value and becomes therefore the supreme value. Yet all the time
we know, and the anthropologist knows it like everybody else, that the
stability of evil is the worst of evils. He ignores this only in order to
maintain a purely descriptive attitude towards his subject, in accordance
with the ideals of the natural sciences. Admittedly, such anthropology
avoids the mistakes of earlier explorers who made no efforts to understand the internal structure of primitive cultures and condemned their
practices out of hand. Yet on the other hand, the modern anthropologist
will tend to draw from his observations such fantastic and morally scandalous conclusions as I have just quoted and, what is more, his method
will blind him to the forces of moral progress in the societies that he
investigates.

This attitude of scientific detachment pervades our minds today. When
we hear that the Soviets and we have totally different views of right and
wrong, our immediate reaction is to look for the economic and social
structure, to which the peculiar ideas of the Soviets of what is right and
wrong may seem appropriate. When Khrushchev denounced Stalin's
monstrous régime at the Twentieth Party Congress, a leading English
newspaper could not help remarking that the historic necessities to which
Stalin's actions responded must not be overlooked.

---

* C. Kluckholn and D. Leighton: *The Navaho* (Harvard, 1946), p.177. Quoted in 'On
  the introduction of science into moral subjects' [67], p.196.
† G. Childe: *What Happened in History* (Pelican ed.) p.15. Quoted in the same place.

Scholars, bent on interpreting the economic and social policies of the Soviet regime as rational responses to historic necessities, have woven a texture of speculations no less fanciful than those I have quoted from the works of some anthropologists. And again, these rationalisations—just like those of the anthropological analysis of primitive societies—have obscured the moral and intellectual forces rebelling against the evils of Soviet society. Yet this rebellion has, I believe, been the most powerful trend of thought during the past ten years all over the globe. The belief that the rule of the Communist party embodies all the hopes of humanity, and that its very existence is a full compensation for the fact that it does not fulfil these hopes, that its successes should be ascribed to its peculiar excellence, while its failures should always be regarded as incidental; this peculiar bias of the twentieth century, which protects its own blazing credulity by a steel armour of scepticism; this condition, capable of combining highest intelligence and morality in a teaching which reduces both of these to mere derivatives of power and profit: this has ceased to be as stable and seductive as it used to be.

Nor was this merely a weakening of fervour due to lassitude. No, it was a passionate movement of minds long starved of spiritual substance. We have seen this in the insurrections in Poland and above all in Hungary. These were not rebellions against the Communists but a change of mind of leading Communists. The Hungarian rising went a long way towards victory as a revulsion of Communist intellectuals, without aid from other quarters. They demanded freedom to write the truth; to write about real people, real sentiments and problems; to report truthfully on current events and on matters of history. In demanding this they reverted to beliefs they had previously abhorred and even violently suppressed. I quote this from a speech by a formerly leading Stalinist, a young man called Gimes, who has since been hanged by Kadar in Hungary. He spoke of the doctrine of party truth which 'affected not only those who invented the faked political trials, but often infested even the victims; this outlook, which poisoned our whole public life, penetrated the remotest corners of our thinking, obscured our vision, paralysed our critical faculties, and which finally rendered many of us incapable of simply sensing or apprehending any truth'.

This is where the régime overreached itself. The last forty years have shown that while it is possible to impose unlimited material sacrifices in the name of a revolutionary doctrine; while its immoralism may actually strengthen its hold by appealing to the hardboiled moral scepticism of our age; the mendacity of such a régime finally becomes unbearable. Fanatical Communists, who had at first resolutely accepted its dishonest paintings and novels, and even its theory of party truth, eventually got sick of these. They had to vomit. The word 'vomiting' has actually become a technical term in Poland and Hungary for this reversal of inverted man; the act by which he violently turns himself right-way-up.

I have said before that the totalitarianism of the twentieth century did not go back of the French Revolution, but went forward from it to a consummation of its internal contradictions. The rebellion of the Polish and Hungarian Communists and the revisionist movement throughout the Soviet empire and beyond it attempt to reverse this consummation. These movements express the demand to go back to the original Enlightenment, before the movements of scientism and romanticism had clashed with the new tide of social hopes and fused with it into mutual destruction.

But can we revert to that time today? No, I believe that the lessons of the Hungarian Revolution and of the world-wide tendencies pointing in the same direction must go beyond this aim. They challenge us to revise rationalist enlightenment and to purge it of its fateful deficiencies. It is for us today to realise the difficulties of the modern mind to the full, and for us to accept these difficulties as our problem.

The passionate awakening of minds in the Soviet empire may momentarily sweep aside these logical difficulties. But they will presently reassert themselves and paralyse or pervert once more the revival of freedom.

No, at our present level of consciousness we cannot build safely on the metaphysical presuppositions of a free society, while holding fast to principles of free thought and free individualism which refuse any commitment to such presuppositions. The modern mind must continue to work its own destruction, and to work it most vigorously when it is at its most incisive and most generous, so long as it fails to reach a vision of itself—and of the universe around itself—within which the unlimited demands of the modern mind can be seen to require their own framework of intrinsic limitations. Towards such a vision and framework many are striving today on different paths. This paper is an attempt to enlist sympathy for these efforts.

7

A Postscript

This article, although overlapping with the previous one, has been included because it develops even further Polanyi's account of moral inversion and of alternatives to it in response to a discussion of his 'Beyond nihilism' [95] published as History and Hope.

On returning from his meeting with Krushchev, held over the first week-end of June 1961, President Kennedy reported:

> 'The facts of the matter are that the Soviets and ourselves give wholly different meanings to the same words: war, peace, democracy and popular will. We have wholly different views of right and wrong and what is an internal affair and what is aggression. And above all, we have wholly different concepts of where the world is and where it is going'.

How did we get here and where do we go from here? This was, in effect, the question I put to the meeting in Berlin, a year earlier, by asking them to discuss my paper 'Beyond Nihilism'.

Confronted with this question, people think first of the impact of industrialisation. But sitting as we did in the Congress Hall of Berlin, a few hundred yards from the Brandenburg Gate—which marks the frontier between the two halves of the world dominated by the two different systems of ideas—it was obvious that their disparity would not be explained by differences in industrial development. There is no great difference in this respect on either side of the Brandenburg Gate, and what is more, there is no difference in the degree or history of industrialisation of the 'Federal Republic of Germany' under Adenauer and the 'German Democratic Republic' under Ulbricht. Industrialisation may offer an

[111]. Reprinted, with permission from Routledge, from *History and Hope*, ed. K.A. Jelenski (New York, F. A. Praeger, 1963), pp. 185–96.

opportunity for the spreading of new ideas, but it neither produces them nor lends them power to convince men.

The immediate reason for the dominance of distinctive ideas all over the eastern zone of Germany is obviously the presence of some twenty divisions of Russian troops ready to uphold the Communist government against the opposition which would otherwise have swept it away along with the whole system of distinctive ideas which it imposed on its people.

But this cannot either be the root of the matter. It leaves unexplained how the power of Communist governments originally came into existence at the centres from which it subsequently spread to other parts of the world. And it leaves unexplained also how a system of ideas, in many ways similar to that of Communism, had established, less than twenty years earlier, the equally oppressive rule of National Socialism all over Germany.

We must face the fact that these disasters of the twentieth century were primarily brought about by groups of fanatics who gained influence over broad masses. We must recognise indeed that these ideas so different from our own, which President Kennedy met with in Vienna, are still echoing throughout the planet and still gain adherents, particularly among the more educated people. We must acknowledge that these people embrace these ideas with fervent hopes for humanity, dedicated to fight for them and to suppress any opposition to them.

The main difficulty in understanding the power of modern totalitarian ideas is the habit of thinking of them in terms of the conflict between progress and reaction. They are not part of the struggle that has dominated men's minds since the Enlightenment shattered Christian dogmas and the French Revolution shattered feudalism in Europe. The revolutions of the twentieth century are not in line with this conflict. They do not aim at restoring either the dogmas or authorities against which the Enlightenment and the French Revolution fought. They are dogmatic and oppressive in an entirely new way which—by a strange logical process—assimilates for its purposes the great passions of scepticism and social reform which first achieved free thought and popular government in Europe and America.

The biography of Karl Marx by Isaiah Berlin has a passage which reveals this transmutation. It reads:

'The manuscripts of the numerous manifestos, professions of faith and programmes of action to which he [Marx] appended his name, still bear the strokes of the pen and the fierce comments with which he sought to obliterate all references to eternal justice, the equality of man, the rights of individuals or nations, the liberty of conscience, the fight for civilisation and other such phrases which were the stock in trade...of the democratic movements of his time; he looked upon these as so much worthless cant indicating confusion of thought and ineffectiveness in action'.

Why did Marx so fiercely obliterate all references to justice, equality and freedom from his manifestos? Because he believed he had far better, more honest and intelligent grounds on which to achieve these aims. He had written:

'It is not the consciousness of human beings that determines their existence but conversely it is their social existence that determines their consciousness'.

To him, therefore, the revolution which would transform the existence of society became the primary aim and a true embodiment of his demand for righteousness. Even his own resolve to fight for this revolution was disguised in the form of a scientific sociology which predicted its inevitable approach, by virtue of its immensely increased productive capacity.

Such an ideology simultaneously satisfies both the demands for scientific objectivity and the ideals of social justice, by interpreting man and history in terms of power and profit, while injecting into this materialistic reality the messianic passion for a free and righteous society.

The potency of this combination has its counterpart in the weakness of the position confronting it: the position that we ourselves are trying to uphold. Our scientific outlook conflicts with our moral convictions, as it denies their objective justification. Our most fervent beliefs falter on our lips as their authenticity is questioned by our critical powers. Words like those of Woodrow Wilson invoking the conscience of world opinion, which once aroused Europe, sound hollow today. Our intellectual conscience has driven our moral convictions underground. But these antinomies which make the liberal mind stagger and fumble, are the joy and strength of Marxism: for the more far-flung are our moral aspirations and the more severely objectivistic is our outlook, the more powerful is a combination in which these contradictory principles mutually reinforce each other. We must face the fact that our own ideals, though true and right, are cramped by an internal conflict and tortured by a self-doubt which our opponents have eliminated, by embodying their moral aspirations in a scientism which defines their own power as the ultimate goal and moral purpose of mankind.

Some contributors to the discussion of my paper have called this hypocrisy. It is actually the inverse of it. Hypocrisy conceals lust for power behind a screen of moral professions; but Bolsheviks silence their moral aspirations and identify them with an unconditional support of Bolshevik power. They may sometimes sound sanctimonious, but their strength lies in being frankly hard-boiled. An analysis of the chief propagandistic writings of Lenin and Stalin shows that ninety-four to ninety-nine per cent of the references to the Communist Party and its activities describe it as seizing, manipulating and consolidating power.[1]

This, surely, is the inverse of hypocrisy. Its spearhead is indeed to accuse our own society as hypocritical, for professing ideals of truth, liberty and justice against which it often offends—and cannot help offending. I have described therefore the structure of Marxism as a form of 'moral inversion' and under this label I have classed it with other mentalities which have a similar structure and are, moreover, rooted in the same historical antecedents.[2] This kinship has been criticised in the discussion, as if it identified the political types linked by kinship. But elephants and whales are both mammals and yet quite different animals. Marxism and Nazism are also very different, even though they have a similar structure and spring from common origins. Their kindred structures have different contents; Marxism is a revolutionary utilitarianism, Nazism a revolutionary romanticism. But their seductivity is of a similar kind; it lies in offering paths of intense political action to men estranged by a moral rebellion armed with moral scepticism, a combination which I have equated—not without historical reasons—with nihilism.

I must digress here to impress on the reader that I have not invented the problem which I am trying to solve here. Many authors have seen it. It was brilliantly introduced by Roger Callois.[3] Marx and Engels, he says, built up their formidable theory for the purpose of concealing from themselves and others that they were following the voice of their generous conscience, instilled by a education which their theory unmasked as fundamentally hypocritical. They transmuted their moral demands by uttering them in the form of scientific predictions. J. Plamenatz[4] struggled with the same paradox and concluded '"Scientific socialism" is a logical absurdity, a myth, a revolutionary slogan, the happy inspiration of two moralists who wanted to be unlike all moralists before them'. H. B. Acton[5] examines this logical absurdity and hints at the origins of its convincing power: 'The Marxist can derive moral precepts from his social science...to the extent that they already form, because of the vocabulary used, a concealed and unacknowledged part of it'. Carew Hunt[6] reveals this practice in the following quotation from Lenin: 'Morality is what serves to destroy the old exploiting society'. The struggle for power is set up here as the ultimate criterion of morality in words justifying this struggle by a moral condemnation of capitalism. The period of pre-Marxist Russian nihilism in which moral passions were first embodied in the revolutionary struggle for power is described by E. H. Carr[7] in his biography of Bakunin. It was Nechayev, around 1870, who took the final step of abandoning the romantic aspirations of the previous generation and raising revolution to the status of an absolute good, overriding any moral obligations. The ensuing internal contradiction is analysed for Russian Marxism by Bochenski.[8] Moral laws, he says, are appealed to and then it is denied that any such laws exist. In describing the militant mentality of the Soviets, Richard Lowenthal reveals its contradictions in paradoxical terms. He speaks of an 'unconscious and indeed fanatical hypocrisy—[a] ruthless immoralism justified by the subjectively sincere belief in the millennial rule of saints'. But how can hypocrisy, which is a pretence, be fanatical? And how can it be also an immoralism—that is, an open denial of the ideas invoked by hypocrisy? Lowenthal joins issue with me for rejecting the current description of the Soviet mentality as a 'secular religion'. I regard this term as misleading for it might equally apply to any fervent patriotic or social movement forming part of the liberal tradition which is the primary opponent of Communism.[9] The problem I want to face was clearly formulated by Hannah Arendt[10]: 'Bolshevik assurance inside and outside Russia that they do not recognize ordinary moral standards have become a mainstay of Communist propaganda…' An attempt to explain why this concealment of more purpose behind professions of immoralism is so stable and seductive has recently been made by E. E. Hirscmann[11]: 'We must realise that this disregard [of humanitarian idealism] has been a source of strength not of weakness. For because men in their moral professions have for so long not meant what they said, because the moral will has not seemed a reality which men could trust, therefore, by seeming to depend less on moral profession and moral will, they seemed the more to mean what they said and the more to rely upon realities'. Mr. Hirschinann sees a kindred tendency underlying 'the greatest self-conscious assault on humanitarian ideals yet seen in history, that of the Rome-Berlin-Tokyo axis'. Nearly forty years earlier

Meinecke[12] had interpreted the tragic failure of imperial German mentality as due to the idea that the only true morality of a nation was immanent in its will to power. I think one could use the term 'immanent morality' instead of 'inverted morality' and I have occasionally done so. But 'immanence' lacks the terrifying overtones of 'inversion', as a state in which moral passions are transmuted into the hidden fuel of absolute violence.

The morally inverted mentality can be individualistic, unpolitical—this I call nihilism. In my paper, 'nihilism' means neither moral depravity nor moral indifference. Depraved individuals have often joined company with modern nihilists and become instruments of the revolutions of the twentieth century. But by themselves they could have only produced a crime-wave—not made revolutions. Their mentality is poles apart from that of the personage first identified as a nihilist by Turgenev in his hero Bazarov. This character, which has made history, represents the rebellious Russian intelligentsia of the 1860's who repudiated all existing bonds of society in the name of an absolute utilitarianism, of which they hoped that it would liberate men and make them all brothers.

The romantic nihilism first propounded by Nietzsche in Germany, was likewise a moral protest against existing morality. 'This shop', writes Nietzsche, 'where they manufacture ideals seems to me to stink of lies'. In place of this hypocrisy he sets the noble ideal of 'something perfect, wholly achieved, happy, magnificently triumphant, something still capable of inspiring fear'. He finds it represented in Napoleon, 'that synthesis of the brutish with the more than human'.

The beginnings of a nihilism associated with moral protest go back further. Diderot speaks of it already in 1763 in *Le Neveu de Rameau* whose immoralism justifies itself by the hypocrisy of society. Soon after, Rousseau made a monumental declaration of moral independence in his *Confessions*, exhibiting his vices as nature's naked truth. And later in the century the Marquis de Sade gave an account of his cruelty and lust, deriving intellectual and moral superiority for his acts from a scientism which reduces man to a machine and a political theory which denounces laws as the will of the stronger.

Owing to its moral and intellectual appeal, nihilism has served as a cultural leaven throughout the past two centuries. A rebellious immoralism has bred the modern *bohémien* in France and the disaffected intellectual throughout the continent of Europe, and these alienated groups have contributed decisively to the renewal of art and thought since the second half of the nineteenth century. In this cultural process the two kinds of nihilism, the 'utilitarian' and the 'romantic', were interwoven. But I shall pick out one thread of the latter kind which leads us back to the social and political scene and to the romantic branch of modern totalitarianism. The movement which in France produced the *bohéme* and in Russia the revolutionary intelligentsia, found an even wider outlet in the German Youth Movement. From small beginnings at the end of the nineteenth century, it came to comprise millions of boys and girls by the end of the First World War. At a famous congress on the Hohe Meissner Mountain in 1913, it dedicated itself to a fervent 'inner truthfulness', condemning existing morality as a bondage imposed by a corrupt society and affirming instead the romantic values idealised by Nietzsche, Wagner and—more recently—Stefan George. I remember no instance in which this youth movement protested against the rise of National Socialism, while there is evidence that it amply contributed to the ranks of Hitler's supporters. The same romantic nihilism spoke as follows on the rise of Hitler to power in 1934 through Oswald Spengler: 'Man is a beast of prey... would be moralists...are only beasts of prey with their teeth broken ...remember the larger beasts of prey are noble creatures...without the hypocrisy of human morals due to weakness'.[13]

Nazi fanaticism was rooted in the same conviction of the irrelevance of moral motives in public life, which Marxism had expressed in terms of historic materialism, and which caused Marx to eliminate furiously any appeals to moral ideals from his manifestos. Fascists believed with Marx that such moral appeals were but rationalisations of power. Hence their contempt of moralising and their moral justifications of violence as the only honest mode of political action.

Such is the kinship between the ideas which gained fanatical support among revolutionaries and broad influence on the masses of our age. Such the convincing power of an inversion by which scepticism and moral passions reinforce each other in acting on minds whose moral convictions are hamstrung by scepticism. Revolutionary régimes admittedly continue to rule by oppressive violence; but their immense efforts of propaganda show that they rely on violence only in combination with the power of their ideas.

Whether we are to fight or to submit—to live or to die—first duty must be to recognize the awful fact that these are highly stable and seductive. And we must face also the fact that their force and seduction is not due—at least not primarily due—to an evocation of evil instincts, but is gained by satisfying in its own manner the same ideals which we ourselves hold and which we are defending against their attack.

So much in answer of the first part of our question. It explains how the world came to be where it is—divided as it is.

Now the second part of the question: Where does the world go from here? I must not respond to this without first making clear some obvious limitations of any answer I may give to it. The process of inversion which I have described has not taken place everywhere—this is precisely why the world is divided today. Even many revolutionary régimes of the twentieth century are untouched by inversion. Most of the new Asiatic and Africa countries have achieved independence upholding the traditional ideals of liberalism; I cannot take into account here the wide variety of conditions in these countries. Nor can I deal in detail with the great differences between the Communist countries, ranging from fanatical fury in China to the mere ritual observance of Marxism in Yugoslavia. I can only suggest that these differences be analysed in terms of the trends which I am trying to identify. Finally, though I may tell which way the world is going, I cannot prophesy where it will arrive.

I believe that the predominant trend of human thought in the last ten years has been a retreat from the most extreme forms of inversion. The belief that the rule of the Communist Party embodies all the hopes of humanity, and that its very existence is a full compensation for the fact that it does not fulfil them; that its successes should be ascribed to its peculiar excellence, while its failure be always regarded as incidental—this bias which thrives on its own absurdity, by rendering itself totally unapproachable to argument; this peculiar milieu of the twentieth century which protects its own blazing credulity by a steel armour of scepticism; this condition which is capable of combining highest intelligence and morality in a teaching which reduces them both to epiphenomena of power and profit [—] it is no longer as stable and seductive as it used to be.

This has been no mere weakening due to lassitude. It was a reaffirmation of truth and of morality and the arts, as intrinsic powers of the mind that caused the leading Hungarian Communist intellectuals to rebel against a régime which had showered them with benefits. This reaffirmation was momentous, not only because those who uttered it were abandoning a place in the sun for the shadow of death, but because it was the outcome of a bitter internal struggle in minds divided between two irreconcilable conceptions of conscience. This liberation and re-establishment of thought from its reduction to the functions of ideology has been the mainspring of all revisionism within the Soviet empire, and of the many defections from 'the god that failed' throughout the world.

This movement took on many forms, because any conviction that acknowledged the power of thought in its own right could equally express it. The beliefs to which the modern mind turns beyond nihilism, comprise all the main ideas which prevailed before the descent into nihilism. In my paper I gave a list of three, each defined by its historic past: nationalism, religion and sceptical enlightenment. Today I would add two more, namely romantic enlightenment and its descendant, modern existentialism. But the list is inexhaustible. A man who has broken out of prison might be found in any place to which he had access before he was imprisoned.

Some of those criticising nationalism or religion seem to have thought that they were opposing my apology of them. But I had merely said that minds recoiling from nihilism sometimes have done so by renewing their national or religious dedication, and I have spoken in the same breath also of sceptical enlightenment. I said that:

'...the sceptical mood of the enlightenment itself has been given a new lease of life. The more sober pragmatist attitude towards public affairs which has spread since 1950 through England and America, Germany and Austria reproduces in its repudiation of ideological strife the attitude of Voltaire and the Encyclopedists towards religious bigotry'.

This was indeed the only path in which I saw a hope for the future. 'Perhaps', I said, 'the present recoil may be stabilised by the upsurge of a more clear-sighted political conscience'. And I quoted as an example the way religious conflict had eventually been overcome in England and America.

'Civility prevailed over religious strife and a society was founded which was dynamic and yet united. May not Europe repeat this feat? May we not learn from the disasters of the past forty years to establish a civic partnership, united in its resolve on continuous reforms—our dynamism restrained by the knowledge that radicalism will throw us back into disaster the moment we try to act out its principles literally?'

I have repeated these words here in reply to Sidney Hook's essay 'Enlightenment and Radicalism' in which he too recommends a return to Enlightenment as a cure to our age, and—curiously—conveys this by a strong attack on my supposed denigration of the ideals of Enlightenment. This is due to the fact that he identifies these ideals with the American and British systems of continuous reform through self-government, while on the other hand be thinks that 'the chief causes of the Bolshevik and Nazi revolutions have very little to do with doctrinal beliefs. They are to be found in the First World War and its consequences'. So when I say that the catastrophes of the twentieth century were a manifestation 'of a sceptical rationalism combined with a secularised fervour of Christianity' he believes that I am attacking rationalism just as other authors have thought that I am attacking Christianity; while I have done neither.

In any case, whatever the proximate causes of our recent revolutions may have been, I think Sidney Hook would agree that their ideas, and the ideas represented by the Soviet government in particular, are still powerful and menacing. My analysis recognises that they possess this force and seductiveness only because they are deeply rooted in ideas which we share—and because we have also the same ancestry, which first laid the twin burdens of scepticism and social morality on mankind. If this is true, the impasse of completely different languages of which President Kennedy spoke, may not be unbridgeable. If the ideas so hostile to us derive their power from their kinship to our own, we might recognise in them our own problems. We shall then make contact with the internal difficulties of the Soviet mind which are leading it to revisionism. And we shall no longer see this process then merely as a weakening of our opponents, but recognize it as a struggle of minds like our own against a predicament similar to our own. The revisionist who breaks up the Marxist inversion of moral passions and recoils from its political immoralism, returns to our situation in which objectivism conflicts with the claims of moral judgment. He comes up then against our own problems.

A revisionist may expose the logical contradiction in Marxism in terms very similar to those of the academic critics I have quoted. Kolakowski says to the orthodox Communist:

'You do not let me measure your moves with a measuring rod of absolute values because in your opinion such values do not exist at all or are purely imagined. But on the other hand, you yourself talk about all human values which must be absolute; thus silently you introduce into your doctrine axiomatic absolutism in a vague and equivocal way in order to destroy it immediately with "historical relativism"'.[14]

And in him—a Communist who has survived Stalinism—this insight is far more vivid than it is in us. Problems which to us are speculative, are reopened by him as wounds, seemingly healed, that have started festering. This can teach those who take the foundations of liberalism to be self-evident, that they are in fact driven by a contradiction which only a faith more experienced than ours can validly transcend.

The problem of modern man is then everywhere the same. He must restore the balance between his critical powers and his moral demands—both of which are more relentless than ever. This may be the starting-point for a movement of intellectual solidarity between the civilisations arising beyond nihilism and the lands which have been spared the political consummation of nihilism. The common ground of this movement would overcome the division of the two mutually exclusive languages and might eventually guide our statesmen to find a way to co-existence and joint progress.

Notes

1. See G. A. Almond: *The Appeals of Communism*, Princeton, 1954, p. 22.
2. 'Moral inversion' can be understood as a counterpart to Freudian 'sublimation'. 'Sublimation' designates the (alleged) transmutation of sexual libido into nobler manifestations of the mind, while moral inversion refers to the opposite transformation of noble ideals into a quest for power and profit. Accordingly, I regard Freud's theory of sublimation as an expression of the same reductionist urge pervading our modern mentality, which, consistently applied, led to moral inversion.
3. Roger Callois: *Description du Marxisme* (Gallimard, 1950).
4. John Plamenatz: *German Marxism and Russian Communism* (1954), p. 50.
5. H. B. Acton: *The Illusion of an Epoch* (1959), p. 190.
6. R. N. Carew Hunt: *The Theory and Practice of Communism* (1950), p. 80.
7. E. H. Carr: *Michael Bakunin* (1937), p. 376.
8. Bochenski: *Der Sowietrussiche Dialektische Materialismus* (1950), p. 156.
9. The 'famous speech at Amsterdam on September 8, 1872' to which Lowenthal refers as contradicting my statement that for Marx violence was the proper aim of a scientific socialism is famous only because it is at variance with the most emphatic statements of Marx to the contrary:

   'The Communists disdain to conceal their views and aims. They openly declare that their ends can be attained only by the forcible overthrow of all existing social conditions. Let the ruling classes tremble at a Communistic revolution'.

   This peroration of the Communist Manifesto was a million times more effective as Marx's teaching than his speech in Amsterdam saying that in certain cases socialism could be achieved constitutionally.

   Lowenthal says that Marx has drawn up fairly precise outlines for his own Utopia. The only text I can think of consists of a few vague pages in the 'Critique of the Gotha Programme' written as a letter to Bracke—of which Engels found a copy among his papers in 1891, nine years after the death of Marx. On the eve of the Russian Revolution Lenin could find no other Marxian basis than this document left unpublished for sixteen years—first by Marx and then by Engels—for shaping the programme of the future society in *The State and Revolution* (1917).

10. Hannah Arendt: *The Burden of our Time* (1951), p. 301.
11. E. E Hirschmann: *On Human Unity* (1961), p. 124.
12. Meinecke: *Die Idee der Staatsraison* (1929), *passim*. Immanence is also called here 'Monismus' and related to Hegel's 'Identitätslehre'.
13. Oswald Spengler, *The Hour of Decision* (1934) quoted by Leslie Paul, *The Annihilation of Man* (London, 1944), p. 128.
14. L. Kolalowski, 'Responsibility and History', *Nowa Kultura*, September 1, 1957, Warsaw. Quoted by *East Europe*, December 1957, p. 12.

8

Why Did We Destroy Europe?

Again overlapping with the previous two articles, this one gives Polanyi's final analysis of the evils that have beset Europe in the twentieth century, along with a poignant contrast with the world of his youth.

My remembrance of these September days 60 years ago, when I entered the University of Budapest, shows me an almost forgotten past of peace, of bold intellectual and artistic enterprise and of continuous progress towards liberal ideals. And then, after a mere six years of this life full of confidence in the future, I see years of destruction and fear, extending up to this day through the major parts of Europe, of the Europe ranging in my time from the Atlantic to the Urals.

And I would suggest to you that we are not likely to understand our present predicament unless we can clear up what caused the disasters which have ravaged Europe in the twentieth century. For these causes are still with us today.

J. C. Eccles* has spoken of the danger arising through the modern scientific outlook which has destroyed the philosophies in which man's spiritual existence was grounded. I agree with this view, but we cannot expect to convince a public brought up to put all its hopes on the present scientific outlook, unless we can prove that the disasters of this century were caused by the errors of this scientific outlook. And we can hardly hope to discover and spread widely a truer world view, unless we can

[140]. Reprinted, with permission from Springer-Verlag, from *Studium Generale*, XXIII No 20, October 1970, pp.909–16.

* This refers to an article, 'Some Implications of the Scientiae for the Future of Mankind', also published in *Studium Generale* 23 and *Knowledge in Search of Understanding*.

effectively demonstrate that this truer world view will restore the kind of sanity which will stop the progress of disintegration in our times.

But the very first steps of such an enquiry lead up to a baffling result. It faces us with the fact that the great period of progress which preceded our disasters was inspired in its many achievements by the very outlook of science which we suspect to have caused our eventual destruction.

The nineteenth century was inspired in countless creative directions by the hope of unlimited progress, based on the scientific outlook. This hope was the inheritance of eighteenth-century Enlightenment, proclaimed by Condorcet at the close of that great century. And this hope was fulfilled. By battling against established authority, scientific scepticism did clear the way for political freedom and humanitarian reforms. Throughout the nineteenth century, scientifc rationalism inspired social and moral changes that have improved almost every human relationship—both private and public—throughout Western civilisation. Indeed, ever since the French Revolution and even up to our own days, scientific rationalism has been a major influence towards intellectual, moral and social progress. The damage done by the scientific outlook to religious beliefs fostered the humanitarian idealism of the age, for it transformed the hopes of salvation into an unprecedented fervour for social reforms.

This seems to query the view that the predicament of modern man is due to the destructive message of the scientific outlook. We seem forced to assume that about 50 years ago the scientific outlook changed altogether and took on pathological forms, new forms which virtually destroyed all the benefits that its ideas had previously brought to us—and at points caused us to descend to levels of evil hardly readied before in the history of mankind.

The supposition sounds strange, yet I think it is precisely this kind of pathological transformation of the scientific outlook which has brought about the destruction of Europe and which continues to menace us today with further extensions of this disaster.

But there are alternative explanations to be considered first. The destruction brought about by the first World War undoubtedly played a part in the degeneration of Europe in the twentieth century. About ten million Europeans were killed in battle between 1914 and 1918. But I do not think that this directly brought about the cultural destruction that was to follow. Losses in battle were twice as much in the second World War and yet its effects were on the whole rather favourable to the recovery of Europe, particularly in Germany and Italy. The peculiar effect of first World War consisted rather in shaking our confidence in the inevitable progress of humanity, as guided by modern enlightened reason. This loss of confidence released the destructive potentialities of the scientific outlook which had already been developing for some time in Europe.

But before analysing these mental antecedents, which I believe to have been decisive, there are yet other explanations of the European disasters to consider. The chain of our revolutions started in Russia in 1917 and in the popular mind this event is regarded as the overthrow of Czarism with its notorious tyranny. But the Czar was overthrown well before Lenin returned to Russia. And another six months passed before the Communists took power, and then they did so by violently suppressing all the parties which for many years had fought the Czarist system and had in fact overthrown it. Moreover, when the cruel tyranny of the Czars evoked indignation throughout Europe, including Russia itself, this was fully justified by the standards of the nineteenth century. But some of the pictures showing social revolutionaries as prisoners in Siberia, published in England to arouse indignation against the Czar, look by twentieth century standards like documents of unbelievable lenience and freedom under the Czars. A number of famous women revolutionaries, most of whom had the assassination of a high government official to her [*sic*] credit, can be seen having themselves photographed in prison as sitting in white blouses under two streamers displaying revolutionary slogans.[1] Whatever the justification of the Russian Revolution, it cannot be granted it for the abolition of a cruel tyranny.

The ridiculous idea that this was the best way of industrialising Russia, deserves but a passing mention, along with Mr. Geoffrey Gorer's hypothesis explaining the typical behaviour of Russians under Stalin 'in the main' by the habit of wrapping babies tightly.

Again, we are often told in England and America that the destruction of liberal standards in central Europe did not involve a deep change, since there had been no democratic tradition in those parts. We are told that the Germans had an 'Authoritarian Personality' and a 'Fear of Freedom'. I don't know what exactly these words mean, but I am sue that they cannot apply to Friedrich Nietzsche whose influence on Germans since the end of the nineteenth century has been paramount. Indeed, right through the nineteenth century, German individualism sharply contrasted with British and American conformism. And we shall see in a moment that it was precisely this individualism, embodied in the 'armed bohemian' which provided recruits for totalitarian revolutions on the Continent of Europe.

I shall spare you the refutation of further absurd explanations of the European disaster. The marching orders of my argument are set by my acceptance of the thesis that the modern scientific outlook—after having been the inspiration of humane progress in the nineteenth century, has become a danger to the spiritual conception of man and that this transformation has brought about the destruction of liberal societies over wide ranges of Europe. If we can demonstrate this sequence of events, any explanations referring only to parts of it will fall away automatically.

Let me define more closely what I mean by the *destruction of Europe*. The First World War claimed over ten million killed in battle, which figure includes a million killed in the Russian civil war. The Second World War killed twenty million men in battle, including four million civilians killed during the war in Germany, Poland and Russia. In addition, Germany has murdered about five million Jews and the deaths caused by the Soviets by the 1923 famine, by the collectivisation of peasants in 1932 and by other deportations and executions are estimated at 10 to 15 million. Thus the total of violent deaths during the years since 1914 may be assessed at forty-five to fifty millions, which leaves out the killings in the Spanish Civil War and other items I will not enumerate. We can speak of roundly 50 million killed.[2]

The death toll is high, but does not approach (in proportion) that of the Thirty Years' War, or of the Black Death in the fourteenth century; it impoverished Europe, but did not devastate it. It was the madness and the evil of the killing which was the destruction of Europe. The depth of this evil was reached in the intellectually decided and technically organised murder of five million Jews and in Stalin's insane purges. The destruction of Europe consisted in the corruption of the minds which made them do this evil. It lay in the enslavement which enforced this corruption by whole systems of madness, stupidity and lies. This is what I mean by the destruction of Europe.

The destruction of Europe is marked by the difference persisting to this day between what the centres of European thought and art were in 1914 and what the same places are today. Compare the Munich of 1914 with that town today, or today's Berlin, or its Gottingen, or its Leipzig, or its Prague, or its Vienna, or its Moscow, or its Budapest are, compared with what they were in 1914. Think of the fact that the genius of Russia which during the half century before the revolution produced a literature that included the greatest writers of Europe, has produced in the half century after this hardly any major literary work. This is where our Europe has been reduced to a mere fraction of its previous mental existence. Add to this the present division of Europe which before 1914 was one single freely responding area of art and thought and add the brutality and intellectual bigotry of its still enslaved parts, and add also the enfeeblement of the comparatively undamaged countries, such as France and England, owing to the destruction of Central and Eastern Europe, and you have before you the destruction of Europe, as I see it.

I have said that the destructive potentialities of the scientific outlook have been maturing in Europe well before their outburst was evoked by the First World War which shattered our belief in liberal progress. This disappointment did not happen over night. I can relive how the possibility first dawned upon us that the great hopes intrinsic to our every thought might fail us: that we may actually be witnessing the destruction of Europe. I remember how this hitherto inconceivable thought gradually took possession of our minds, and finally faced us as a fact. This was the moment when the eclipse of the liberal ideas of the nineteenth century began.

Yet there had been prophets who attacked these ideas. Three great names come to mind; the names of Dostojevski, of Nietzsche and of Marx. They aimed in three different directions, but they all started from the same point. Dostojevski warned that science must destroy the conception of moral responsibility. If there is no God, everything is permitted. And man, reduced to the level of a machine, will rather go mad than accept this condition. If there is no God, says Kiriloff in *The Devils*, then man is compelled to demonstrate his independent will, and Kiriloff demonstrates this sovereign will, by committing suicide. Nietzsche, twenty-two years younger than Dostojevski, came across one of Dostojevski's writings only after he had completed most of his own work, but he immediately recognised Dostojevski as his forerunner. Indeed, like Dostojevski, Nietzsche had declared that the critical powers of man, sharpened by science, unmask all morality as mere conventions. Man in his fullness must contemptuously brush aside any such restrictions of his sovereign choices. Let the ignoble masses bow to standards imposed upon them; superior man set free from such servitude must make his own laws, create his own person. Thus Nietzsche's argument is a variant of Dostojevski's. They both say that modern scepticism destroys the grounds of all accepted values and obliges man to assume total self-determination. Dostojevski sees the outcome of this in madness and suicide, while Nietzsche sees emerging from it a superior man, who, respecting no laws, is ready for violence beyond good and evil. Nietzsche spoke in paradoxes and parables, leaving always open the possibility that his words may be merely metaphorical. But the teachings he had left open vaguely, the twentieth century acted out clearly in their most cruel meaning. But before following up these Nietzschean doctrines, I must turn to the third of the prophets who undermined in his own way the partnership between scientific scepticism and liberal progress, the combination which had guided the nineteenth century to its achievements. Marx saw history as determined by the necessity of class wars which bring consecutive improvements in modes of production. The technical necessity of replacing capitalism, which had become unworkable, by the productive forces of socialism, would inevitably lead to the overthrow of Capitalism and the establishment of Socialism in its place. Since the moral principles of each period were determined by the interests of the ruling class there was no point in appealing for reforms to the feelings of justice and brotherhood, or the ideals of freedom. Nor was there any sense in respecting moral principles in carrying out the revolution that was historically necessary.

Engels was to describe this doctrine as transforming Socialism from a utopia to a science. But what it actually did, was to dress up a utopia as a science and thus render it unquestionable by an age to which science was the ultimate truth. But Marx did more than that. By endowing a machinery of history with the power to bring social salvation, he imbued its mechanism with all the passions of utopia. Hatred of capitalism, of its icy cash-nexus and of the wicked exploitation of the workers, and, correspondingly, the hopes of socialist brotherhood, were injected with all their fervour into the Marxist mechanism and made these passions serve this mechanism as its fuel. Marxism provided our scientific age with an ideology which made its boundless moral demands on society covertly and thus protected these moral demands from the knife of modern scepticism. Marxist man thus formed a combination of scepticism and fanaticism which no age had known before.

I have characterised already some years ago the condition when moral perfectionism is protected against scepticism by being embodied in a mechanical process, and I have given this structure the name of 'moral inversion'. In away moral inversion goes back to eighteenth-century utilitarianism. Bentham derided the social ideals of the French Revolution and claimed instead the greatest happiness of the greatest number as the only scientifically acceptable conception of social value. But since this principle was used by Bentham and his followers only to counteract unreasonable rigidity obstructing desirable reforms, he never came to realise that his teachings could justify the evils of a totalitarian regime. The alliance between scientific scepticism and liberal progress still held, because scepticism had not gained the degree of its modern incisiveness.

But turning once more to the twentieth century, we see moral inversion developed into totalitarianism. Totalitarian principles were proclaimed from the start by the Russian Revolution in 1917 and 1918. Lenin unhesitatingly outlawed in January 1918 the Social Revolutionaries forming the majority of the Constitutional Assembly which he had himself convened. By 1923 the canvassing of personal views was suppressed even within the Party. And soon the government wove through all domains a web of absurd falsehoods, often based on confessions extorted by torture. This was sanctioned as 'party-truth' the extension of which to all manner of arts subjected these too to the party line.

Totalitarianism was introduced into history by Marxism and its Fascist variety arose in 1921 at the hand of Mussolini following his victory over an Italian communist insurgence. In the fifteen years to follow, eleven other European countries fell under similar right wing dictatorships. Germany was one of the late comers; National Socialism came to power in 1933 as the sixth fascist regime established in the example of Italy. By 1939 the countries enjoying civic liberties in Europe had fallen to 14, equal to the number of dictatorships. Totalitarianism had become endemic in Europe.

By the time the Second World War broke out, the liberal heritage of the nineteenth century seemed doomed to extinction.

The right wing dictatorships justified their rule largely by an anti-communism echoing Soviet practices; only Mussolini and Hitler were more articulate. Much of their vocabulary was borrowed from Nietzsche's talk of the superman. But the doctrine that violence was the true principle of government had deeper roots. Sorel's *De La Violence* played its part. Germans had declared already in the first World War that Realpolitik alone was the true guide of international policies. They expressed contempt for the moral principles invoked by the Allied powers and denounced their moral claims as hypocritical. Writing in the years immediately following the First World War, Meinecke showed that the German identification of Right with Might in the actions of nations was the ultimate outcome of the Hegelian teaching of immanent reason. The strength of such immanent morality, would be testified by the violence of manifest immorality.

Immanent reason as well as the immanent morality claimed by Hegel for World Historical Personalities correspond closely to the conception of moral inversion that I derived from the Marxian theory of revolution. Marxism transposed Hegel's immanentism into a historic creed which claims the authority of science.

I have said that it was our modern perverted individualism, embodied in the 'armed bohemians' which provided many of the recruits for totalitarian revolutions. Let me describe these bohemians before they took arms in politics. Just as the First World War released the destructive powers of Marxian scientism, so it also released the Nietzschean ideal of absolute self determination, liberated from all moral standards of society. Take as an example the surrealist mentality in the years following the war. Its leader André Breton said: 'We were possessed by a will to total subversion'. Robert S. Short has recently wrote [*sic*] of Breton's followers, 'They extolled all forms of anti-social behaviour, crime, drug-addiction, suicide, insanity, as so many expressions of human freedom and revolt. They preferred the criminal to the political militant, since crime seemed to be a self-sufficient act...They called for crime on an inter-national scale: a second reign of terror or a wave of barbarian invasion from the East'.[3] Today, 40 years later, you find moral protest expressed by young people in similar demonstrations of nihilism. And, conversely, you could trace such principles of total subversion back to the Russian nihilists of a century ago. They based themselves on popular scientific writers describing man as a machine: on the same popular scientific writers, to whom Dostojevski refers in his *Notes from Underground* (1864) where he stated for the first time his aim to rescue man from the destruction of human responsibility by the mechanical outlook of science.

The surrealist mentality I have described before characterises the period of 1920 to 1925. It gives you a good example of a privately practised moral inversion, in other words, a fierce moral protest made in terms of a fantastic immorality. Soon after that the followers of Breton joined the Communist party. The bohemian took arms and converted his immanent moral passion into the fuel of a ruthless political machinery of subversion. You can see this happening today, as it has happened for a hundred years before, in the oscillation of youth between personal immoralism and its transposition into politics of violence.

I think this story resolves the paradox arising from John Eccles' account of the destructive ideas disseminated by science today. It shows that during the whole period before the great wars, while science led on to moral and social progress throughout Europe, the contradiction between science and human responsibility remained latent, though powerfully expressed by our prophets. And that this contradiction became effective after the world wars had caused a profound disappointment in liberal progress, so that the teachings of Marx and Nietzsche, based on this contradiction, became predominant. A moral perfectionism cast into private immoralism or totalitarian tyranny swept over Europe.

I think this is the situation we are facing today, a situation that is likely to get worse unless we can radically change and re-establish the grounds of human knowledge and thus make sense once more of man's life and of the kind of universe which is our home.

Notes

1. The photograph is to be found in Jaakoff Prelooker: *Heroes and Heroines of Russia*, pp.304–305, London: Simpkin, Marshall, Hamilton, Kent, 1908.—There is a title to it as follows: 'Girl Revolutionists in the Akatui Prison, Siberia. Below the photograph there is the following explanatory caption: 'From left to right: K. Fialka, A, Izmailovitch, M. Spiridonova, A. Bitzenko, A. Ezersky, M. Shkolnik. Inscription on Banner in the back-ground: "Glory to the martyred, Freedom to the living". From a photo taken in the prison'. There is a list of the acts for which these revolutionaries were sent to prison in Siberia, and this lists shows that five out of these had each killed one high government official.
2. The figures for men killed in the two world wars and the data on the spreading of Fascism following the rise of Mussolini are based on Martin Gilbert's *Recent History Atlas*, London: Weidenfeld and Nicholson, 1967.
3. For my quotation of Robert S. Short on surrealism, I must rely on imperfect notes telling only that this text was published about 1968 by *Survey* in London.

Part II

Economic and Social Theory

Introduction to Part II

The articles grouped together in Part II are of a more theoretical nature and deal principally with economic themes. With the exception of the last, they appear in chronological order which coincides with the logical development through them of Polanyi's arguments for the logical impossibility of the central planning of an economy, the respects in which he agreed and disagreed with both the opponents and proponents of planning, his account of what the Soviet economy actually was and how it in fact operated, and his demonstration of what is required for any rational activity in society. They span the years 1940 to 1960, for, although published in 1969, 'The determinants of social action' was written in 1950. They should be read in conjunction with Chaps. 8–10 of *The Logic of Liberty*.

To them I have appended 'On Liberalism and liberty', which, because it is primarily concerned with a political theme, could well have been placed in Part I. But because it looks back to debates about the possibility of central planning and its connection with totalitarianism and incompatibility with political freedom, before giving more of a positive account of political freedom, I have used it to close both Part I and Part II.

9

Collectivist Planning

This, the text of a talk given in April 1940, is Polanyi's first published statement of the impossibility of central planning and his explanation of what in fact passes under that name. Although the bankruptcy of collectivism is acknowledged today, after the collapse of the Soviet Union and its empire, there is still much misunderstanding and resentment of the invisible hand that feeds us. Polanyi's analyses of planning and supervision were elaborated, as 'corporate' and 'spontaneous' order respectively, in 'The growth of thought in society' [16], an article which, because of its central place in the development of Polanyi's political and economic ideas and because its contents were dispersed when reprinted in other articles and then again in The Logic of Liberty, *I almost included in this collection.*

In this article Polanyi also draws the analogy with the organisation of scientific research and argues for freedom for the great affairs of life—the cultivation of moral ideals, justice, knowledge, art, religion—because they are public and of public value, and hence require public protection. This is in direct contrast to the usual run of Liberal thinking which, with J.S. Mill, wants freedom for purely private concerns: see further, LL Chap. 10.

> *The whole of society will have become a single office and a single factory with equality of work and equality of pay.*
>
> *...we have a right to say with the fullest confidence that the expropriation of the capitalists will inevitably result in an enormous development of the productive forces of human society.*
>
> —Lenin, *State and Revolution* (1917).

[12]. Reprinted from *The Contempt of Freedom*, London, Watts, 1940, pp.27–60.

When I say we are stopping the economic retreat I do not
want to suggest that I have for a moment forgotten the
hellishly difficult conditions in which we find ourselves.

—Lenin, *Report of the Central Committee*, (March 1922).

The great collectivist powers have established themselves by revolutionary forces, which, thrusting aside the claims of individualist liberties as ignoble and unintelligent rudiments of the past, heralded in an era of ruthless efficiency. In Russia the spearhead of the thrust was the demand for social justice, in Italy and Germany it was the demand for national power; but the difference was only one of emphasis, the result being a nationalist Socialism on the one hand, and a socialist Nationalism on the other. In either case a State was established which, in principle, assumes the complete responsibility for the culture and welfare of its citizens. This is totalitarianism; a régime absorbing the whole life of the people, who live by it and live for it entirely.

Many reject such predominance of the State yet admire the efficiency of collectivist methods. The idea of planning the whole cultural and economic life of a country from one centre has a profound appeal for the contemporary mind; it fascinates above all the intelligent, the energetic, the forward looking minds, and makes them contemptuous of traditional individualist liberty.

Planning as opposed to aimless drifting is the natural inclination of a purposeful scientifically trained mind. Modern engineering is an inspiration to grandiose planning. The cutting of the great artificial waterways, the construction of modern dams and power stations, the erection of skyscrapers, the building of huge liners—these are the examples which fashion the engineers' approach to society. Here are great works achieved by forethought; a clear aim, a social good being recognised, a plan is conceived to attain it and an authority invested with the powers to carry it out. Why not deal in this way with society as a whole? The organisation of production in modern factories also affords stirring examples of planned action. Hundreds of working phases must fit together with clockwork precision to result in a modern locomotive. The whole process is planned in every detail by hundreds of separate workshop drawings. No wonder that the energetic man of the factory manager type will think of social reform on similar lines.

Comprehensive, provident action appeals also to moral feelings. Both the unselfish servant of a great enterprise and the leader resolutely imposing his authority for the sake of the public good are dedicated to noble forms of action. A unified purpose, which lifts the whole State to a higher plane, gives comfort to the individual who puts his trust in it, and diffuses widely a sense of public duty. These moral values are prominent in war-time, in particular in modern war, with its complete regimentation of whole peoples, and accordingly war and war preparation have been a constant source of inspiration for collectivism.

The military spirit is prevalent in the Fascist forms of collectivist planning; the Socialist form represented by Soviet planning has a more civilian outlook, being mainly influenced by American ideas of extreme mechanisation and of large scale construction and management. But technical enthusiasm, as represented by Futurism, also plays a part in Fascism; and on the other hand Lenin regarded the measures of rationing, commandeering, and industrial conscription taken in the World War of 1914–18 as pointers to Communism[1]. The Five Years' Plans have at all times been guided by military exigencies, to no less an extent than Germany's and Italy's economic régime.

The more explicit and more extreme forms of planning are professed by Socialism, as represented by the Soviet Union. Their Five Years' Plans, in which every single branch of production is given its task by the central directing authority, have created a profound impression on our age, and are largely responsible for the popularity of planning in the Western countries. Less well known perhaps are the efforts made in Soviet Russia to plan cultural life and in particular the progress of Science. But these also are highly significant, as representing the fundamental claim of the Collectivist State to dominate all mental efforts for its own purposes. These claims have been widely reaffirmed and expounded in the West by scientists of eminent standing.

In this essay I will first try to lay bare the exact meaning of planning, as demonstrated by such obvious cases, as, for example, the planning of a military action. This analysis should show that planning is not the only method of ordering human affairs, and that the alternative method is *Supervision*, which is almost the opposite of planning, in that it ultimately relies on a multitude of individual initiatives which planning would subordinate to a central will. We will then observe the course of some attempts at collectivist cultural and economic planning, and will see how the authorities, after having failed in this direction, turn to the establishment of general oppressive supervision of people's lives—from which only a liberal revolution can get them free.

Military Examples of Planning

The largest organisation directed to a single purpose, and firmly controlling all its members, has at all times been the army. When at war the State fights for its existence, and for this purpose it mobilises the full power of its population. But the distribution of arms alone bestows but little military power on a people. An unorganised swarm of men advances blindly wherever it finds no resistance, or else where it succeeds in overcoming it; such an army is an easy prey to a skillfully operating opponent, who, by creating diversions, disperses its masses and destroys its disjointed parts, one after the other. The power of an army, arising from its organisation, lies in its capacity for planned manoeuvres. These are operations, executed at the orders of one man, the Commander-in-Chief, in which the various parts of the army are purposefully co-ordinated. The first precondition of manoeuvring an army is, therefore, a division into parts, each under a separate subordinate commander, each of which can move independently of the others, at the directions of the C.-in-C. A manoeuvre is the conjunction of such movements. In principle, then, the larger the number of sections into which the army is divided, the greater the complexity of the manoeuvres of which it is capable But actually this advantage cannot be increased indefinitely, because a complexity, which is too great to be comprehended by one man cannot be utilised by its Commander; and an organisation which tends towards such complexity will only cause confusion. The number of subdivisions which is found to reach the limit of the span controllable by one man is about five[2]; in what follows we will use this number for the sake of illustration.

An army, then, of say half a million men, divided into five army corps, marches on the enemy. Each corps is given its programme by the supreme commander; it fulfil a certain function in a movement conceived as a whole. Operations will, in general, try to fix enemy at an awkward point, then to engage him fully where he is least prepared for it, and finally to throw in all reserves as a last hammer blow against a vital position. All these movements are consistently planned and replanned—that is, directed and co-ordinated at every stage by the C.-in-C. The five corps form a joint instrument at his command, like the five fingers of a hand; joint movements, precisely timed and placed, must fit together according to his intentions; these movements, quite meaningless in themselves, may gain in this conjunction the supreme power which military genius can impart to an army.

We see here the essence of comprehensive planning. A situation in which hundreds of thousands of men participate is reflected in the mind of one man, the leader, in a few bold outlines. If he is the right man the picture thus drawn will fully comprise the essence of the available military data, their complete joint significance. Based on this general aspect of the situation the leader conceives his plan, again in general outline only; and from stage to stage, as the campaign develops, he redraws his plans in similar terms, always preserving a general perspective.

It is the same in all kinds of planning; whether it is the planning of a house, of a machine, of a town or even of a work of art; the simple terms of one idea which can be conceived and handled by one man dominate a mass of details; the general idea is the plan, the details follow from it as its execution.

In the case which we are considering these details are filled in by the five corps commanders, in execution of the several programmes assigned to them by the chief. Each of these undertakes to solve, in accordance with prevailing circumstances, the definite task committed to him. The solution is issued by them in the form of sub-tasks to the divisions contained in the army corps; there will be four or five divisions to a corps. The division commanders reformulate the sub-tasks assigned to them, in terms of tasks of the third order which they give to subordinate brigades. And thus the tasks go on branching out further, right down to the platoon and the private in the line. No stage adds anything to the original plans conceived by the one man at the top; every further and further detail fits in to it, and has significance only as its execution; the plan does not change by being put into effect.

The chief directs his five army corps as wholes, not interfering with the way in which their commanders execute the tasks assigned to them in his plan; such interference would be beyond his capacities, since his full span of mental control is engaged already by the co-ordination of the five units as wholes. And as the plan branches out vertically in the course of its execution each commander in his turn sees below him only his four or five immediate subordinates, and their sections as wholes, the internal arrangements of each sub-section being left to the subordinate commander. Hence also reports, to be relevant to the superiors, must relegate internal affairs of the reporting unit to the background, emphasising only its position as a whole. As reports are handed on upwards a summary is made at each stage, sieving out that is irrelevant in this sense, so that finally the supreme chief receives only five brief reports from which he forms his comprehensive view of the military situation.

No authority can co-ordinate the movements of its subordinates, unless they obey its orders; discipline, therefore, is essential to planning. Some mutual contacts between equals under direction of the same command are, of course, necessary for an intelligent execution of orders; but such contacts must modify the plan which they are helping to execute. In an organisation acting according to plan there can be therefore, only one channel for essential communications: the vertical line of authority, through which orders travel downwards and information is given upwards. To the extent to which lateral communications in the horizontal plane are permitted to affect the movement of those receiving them, planning is being relaxed; if lateral impulses become essential, planning will have ceased to take effect and the authority above, hitherto executing a plan, will change into an authority responsible for supervisory functions, as described in the next section of this essay.

We can illustrate the change-over of a central power to a supervisory function in the case of military operations when, instead of freely manoeuvring troops, as described before, we consider trench warfare, with two lines of soldiers pressing against each other all along the border between warring territories. In such a battle of lines a breach made at any point in the opposing line is followed up by putting all reserves into action, first those locally available, then, as and when further successes are achieved, adding the reserves available farther and farther back, until the whole of the available forces may be absorbed by the action. Capt. Liddell Hart, describing this method of the 'expanding torrent', remarks that its semi-automatic mechanism leaves the initiative to the lower commands, and these again leave it to their subordinates, so that the effect is an 'anonymous battle'. Marshal Foch many years before this (when holding only the rank of a colonel) already noted with apprehension the possibility of future 'wars of the line' in which the supreme command would be ineffective—since, as he says, the battles would be won by the private soldiers individually[3].

Supervisory Authority

We have shown that the essence of planning is the absorption of the actions held under control by a single comprehensive scheme imposed from above. It is a co-ordination of those actions by means of vertical lines of authority which impose a specific task on each subordinate unit. As the lines of authority branch out at each successive stage of their downward course the scope of these tasks is narrowed down to a insignificant detail of the total operation. The plan is not communicated to the subordinate unit, which must not consider the general purpose in which it participates, but attend exclusively to the execution of the specific orders received. The subordinate, who is thus entirely cut off from the fundamental ideas which he is serving, Is also separated from other subordinates in equal positions. Vital lines of vertical authority admit no direct horizontal contacts; two units of the same plane are connected only through the circuit of a slender thread where high up in the scale of the hierarchy there is a commander common to both.

These characteristics sharply distinguish the functions of a planning authority from those of a regulative or supervisory authority, the task of which is, in fact, of an almost opposite nature. Supervision presupposes human activities which are initiated from a great multitude of centres, and it aims at regulating these manifold impulses in conformity with their inherent purpose. It achieves this by making generally available social machinery and other regulated opportunities for independent action, and by letting all the individual agents interact through a medium of freely circulating ideas and information.

It is evident that such functions of public authority can be exercised only in a Liberal society to which the cultivation of widely dispersed sources of initiative is essential and in which mental communications are open throughout the community. Public supervisory powers are in fact the vital safeguards of independent forces of individual initiative in society, the integrity of which they am to protect against private corruption as well, as against oppression by collectivist tendencies of the State. This is why collectivist, thinkers ignore or deny the principles of supervisory authority[4]. They can see in supervision only a veiled method of domination which the collectivist State would achieve more honestly and efficiently by the method of straight-forward planning. The true scope of supervision is therefore of crucial importance for the issue of social planning.

Supervision is in the first place the method by which the cultivation of things of the mind is regulated. We may see it at work—while avoiding for the moment any major issues—by observing the harmless case of the cultivation of chess. Chess organisations arrange contests, subsidise players, elucidate a codify the rules of the game, record advances in chess problems and chess moves, and generally encourage the discussion and dissemination of the theory of chess. In short, they do all in their power to provide the best opportunities for the practice and perfecting of chess-playing, but they would never think of directing the individual games of chess, which, indeed, would be a useless, if not altogether meaningless, thing to do, and would certainly not contribute to the cultivation of the game.

In a Liberal society there is a wide domain of activities: in which ideas are cultivated under the supervision of organisations or public authorities. Artistic pursuits, religious worship, the administration of justice, scientific research are the main manifestations of the permanent principles to the cultivation of which such a society is pledged. Supervising authorities guard the occasions and regulate the channels for these manifestations, and they keep communication tree for public discussion and :instruction concerning them, but must not interfere with their substance.

When, for example, legal justice is administered, the State provides the machinery of the police, of the courts and prisons, and all sanctions legal procedure and lays down the law to be applied, but it rigorously guards the decisions of the court from public influence. The courts are sole masters of their conscience and interpretations under the law which they are required to apply and as they make their decisions, these are instantly added as amplifications, valid throughout the land, to the law from which they have just been derived.

Thus, wherever permanent principles of society are cultivated under public supervision, the authorities set up machinery and lay down rules as channels for their manifestation, leaving it to individuals, who are called upon by virtue of their special gifts, or else just as ordinary citizens, to make use of these opportunities; to write, to preach, to address meetings, to give evidence in court, or to undertake any other of the numerous tasks which offer expression to general guiding principles. It is by the devotion of men and women to these tasks that the fundamental ideas cultivated by society are continuously elucidated and advanced. Under supervision the individual action springs forth from direct communion with the social heritage, and its outcome returns directly to the same common fund. This is in complete contrast to the way in which a subordinate unit obediently follows the lead of a single vertical line of authority, which keeps it ignorant of the general plans of those in command and at the same time isolates it entirely from its fellows placed under the same authority.

A further function of supervision lies in economic field. It represents here the method for ordering the satisfaction of individual needs in accordance with personal wishes. In so far as a State consents to grant such satisfaction—and none can entirely refuse it—it recognises yet another field in which it submits to a diversity of decisions by a multitude of individuals. This field, therefore, cannot be managed by the imposition of a governmental plan, but must, on the contrary, be cultivated by a supervisory authority which assures the individuals of suitably regulated opportunities for giving effect to their desires. Supervision in the case of individual economic desires is embodied in the machinery of commerce, operating through the market which keeps commercial ideas and information in universal circulation. This machinery will be discussed later in more detail.

Meanwhile we may sum up the position now reached. There are two alternative methods of ordering human affairs: Planning and Supervision. In an ordered society every activity which affects the community is either subordinated to an authoritative scheme or is, on the contrary, stimulated to individual manifestations under the protection of public supervision. As long as certain guiding principles—of truth, of justice, of religious faith, of decency and equity—are being cultivated, and as long as commerce is protected, the sphere of supervision will predominate and planning will be limited to isolated patches and streaks. Conversely, if comprehensive planning were to prevail, this would imply the abolition of both the cultivation of guiding principles and the pursuit of commerce, with all the liberties inherent in these forms of life. Hence collectivist revolution must aim at the destruction of liberty, and in particular must suppress the privileges under which Universities, Law Courts, Churches, and the Press are upholding their ideals, and attack the rights of individual enterprise under which trade is conducted.

This outline may be borne in mind while we pass on to describe some entanglements to which collectivist planning has led in practice. In the course of these we shall see the authorities recoiling at various points from the destruction of wealth and culture caused by their attempts at total planning, yet rallying to a general campaign of hostile supervision for the dragooning of the lives which they are unable to dominate but dare not set free.

Planning of Science

It is usually thought that a poem or a painting, or else a scientific discovery, springs from a unique mental situation which is entirely personal, and humanity used to respect such solitary inspiration.

But collectivists do not recognise the inherent autonomy of the creative act. For example, in science they would not be content that the state should provide opportunities for research, leaving the scientist to choose his own task, but would wish to subordinate scientific research to a general plan devised by a central authority. The isolation of various discoveries, they say, is only apparent; their results are found to fit together and to produce important joint consequences. Much better, therefore, that research should be consciously co-ordinated, even while discovery is in progress.

In order to consider this collectivist suggestion I will survey the main acts of scientific life as it is conducted to-day.

The mental situation which produces scientific discovery is built up laboriously by the scientist through a number of years. From a general scientific education he tends at an early stage to turn towards a side which appeals to the play of his first tentative efforts. Roamings in this direction over various fields finally confirm an even more definite interest. Thus attracted, the young scientist comes in contact with the living masters of the selected branch, and may join the team of a research school. There follow years of study under a master's guidance, and of devotion of body and soul, day and night, to patient research work. As this goes on, the young scientist may begin to feel his way to independence. He has been settling down more and more to the type of work suitable to his special gifts, and intimations of the problems around him are now taking shape in his mind. These first intimations will probably be the humus from which his whole life's work will grow. As he follows one or the other of them the fascination becomes more intense, the preoccupation more passionate, and his mental position becomes more and more unique. He now sees daily such things as no one saw before him. He has established a new line of research, which is his own personal, his own vital contact with nature. On the inherent fruitfulness of this contact, as on his own skill and unfailing vigilance, will depend the discoveries which he will henceforth make.

Discoveries, as well as minor observations, are published as soon as they are sufficiently assured to be of use to other scientists. It is the scientist's ambition to secure credit by anticipating his rivals, but he is restrained from publishing preliminary speculations or results which as yet lack confirmation, because these would cause more confusion than their useful stimulus might justify. The personal intuitive feelings, which are the most valuable, element of the creative situation, cannot be appreciated by anyone but the most intimate associates, and are therefore not to be discussed in public.

Since thus from the moment of its birth all new knowledge becomes common property, the ground from which all lines of research take their origin is the same all over the planet. It is usual, there-fore, to find lines which run parallel, as mental efforts, however intensely personal, are bound to do, when starting from identical premises. It happens every day that two men fall in love with the same woman from the very depth of their hearts; the course of creative imagination is determined by the objective situation in which it arises.

The mutual consistence between discoveries simultaneously or in close succession to one another requires no explanation to those who recognise the existence of Truth. A statement which is part of Truth will always be consistent with another part of Truth; and both parts together will reveal a further, more comprehensive aspect of Truth. This is just as necessary as that two pieces which fit into neighbouring gaps of an unfinished jigsaw puzzle must also fit to one another.

We recognise here that a large number of independent activities can form a system of close co-operation. In fact we see that this type of co-operation must necessarily prevail if, as in the case of science, the workers all intercommunicate by rapidly publishing the results achieved in cultivating different arts of the same major task. This is the co-operation of independent minds devoted to the pursuit of an aim which, though it is beyond the perception of any, yet is jointly guiding their several thoughts. It is the co-operation which arises by the pursuit of truth and other parts of human culture. In the Liberal State the cultivation of science is public concern, in the performance of which the community is guided by scientific public opinion. Recognised scientific ability forms a claim to official support, and new branches of knowledge are similarly taken up officially, once they are recognised by science. Thus science governs itself under the goodwill of Society. The State fulfil its supervisory duties by protecting and subsidising science as a whole, while letting the administration of scientific affairs operate under the control of scientific opinion.

We can now take up in contrast with this the collectivist demand for a central planning of scientific research. In its logical form its meaning is quite clear; it says that, just as the head of a research department directs half a dozen collaborators who form his team, thus the whole of science ought to receive directions for its daily tasks from a central authority. Collectivists point out that the usefulness of team-work being proved by the case of the research school, there is no reason not to expand this method to the, whole of science under a central authority.

To this must be objected that a small team of collaborators is merely an extension of the physical possibilities of the director of research; they help him in his experiments and carry out measurements set up under his supervision. A leader of research who extends the number of collaborators to a point where he cannot actually see their experiments being performed, but has essentially to rely on their reports is in danger of losing the solid ground of his work; Once he gives up wrestling at close quarters with the data of observation he relaxes his hold on reality, like a judge who has no time to examine witnesses and relies on hearsay evidence. Few scientists can do good work with more than a dozen personal collaborators, and there is in consequence no large scientific institution in the world the scientific work of which is directed by one scientist.

But what if, in spite of all such experience, the State, guided by collectivist passion, should nevertheless erect a central authority for the planning of science? What would be its function? Clearly the authority would first have to form a view of the position of science as a whole, then to conceive a plan for the progress of science as a whole; and to give orders to the different parts of science to advance according to this plan.

The information available to the central authority for establishing the position of science as a whole is the aggregate of available text-books and publications. This is accessible to everyone, but no one has yet been able to obtain from it a comprehensive conception of the position of science, nor any idea as to the direction in which it should advance as a whole. In fact these phrases are meaningless to a scientist, because it is of the essence of science, in contrast to scholastic speculation, that it advances piecemeal, by extending knowledge wherever discoveries can be made and not with reference to a central problem. Science has emerged from medieval scholasticism precisely by abandoning such comprehensive tasks as the search for the Philosopher's Stone and for the Elixir of

Life, and by applying itself instead to specialised pieces of research, knowing that the parts of truth thus discovered must form a joint pattern in the end. A comprehensive view of science is a superficial and an ignorant view of all parts of science; it is a view which contains no working knowledge of science, and from which no suggestions for research can be made which would not be recognised by scientists at a glance as either impracticable or childishly mediocre.

Unless the central authority is prepared to go to the extreme of pressing suggestions of this kind on scientists, and thereby putting an end to all real research and replacing it by futile performances, it will have to give up the planning of science. But it may then try to save its face by calling on individual scientists to send in their own plans, which it would send back endorsed with its approval. This useless procedure has actually emerged in Soviet Russia, where the initial attempt at centralised planning having failed, a system called 'decentralised planning' was introduced on the above lines. The term 'decentralised planning' is, however, contradictory. The essence of planning is unity achieved by control from a centre. The decision about what is to be done cannot be made both centrally and locally, and hence, if the essential decisions are local, the central decisions can be of no importance. The central authority can then retain only functions of a supervisory nature. How far the supervision entailed in this pretence of planning becomes oppressive depends on the temper of the political situation and of the persons partaking in this procedure. To assess this, we must remember that behind the pretence of planning there lurks the determined denial by collectivism of that independence of thought of which modern science is the child and the representative. In every politically difficult period, therefore, there is likely to come a sharpening of the conflict. Thus successive waves of suspicion rose up against the intelligentsia in the U.S.S.R. in the years 1918–20, 1927–30, and 1935–37, leading to persecution of every kind. Some of its members were imprisoned, others shot, the rest were forced to demonstrate their loyalty by fervent declarations in support of the official philosophy of the State. But naturally the more extravagant such declarations become, the less their sincerity is trusted by the authorities. Nothing can appease the collectivist, who knows that his victim cannot be sincere so long as he is oppressed, but who dare not set him free, well knowing that there can be no peace between collectivism and free thought[5].

Economic Planning

The classical aim of collectivism is the placing of all production and distribution under control of the State. The resources of the community should be exploited not for commercial gain but according to a central plan which aims directly at the satisfaction of the needs of the population as ascertained by the authorities. To examine this programme I will first briefly summarise the principal features of economic life based on individual enterprise and individual choice.

Humanity living in society earns its livelihood by divided labour; hardly any human being could survive in Europe if each adult had to provide himself with his own shelter, clothing, and tools. In any case the population would be decimated and its residue levelled down to a brutish existence, if deprived, of the device of divided labour. Such, division implies the exchange of products between the producers, and as the division of labour becomes increasingly differentiated the exchange of products becomes more complex. To-day few of us consume anything that we produce ourselves; we live entirely by making things for others, or giving services to others, in order to receive from them in exchange the means of our livelihood. The process is performed by use of the market. On the market we sell our produce, or else it is sold on our behalf by the manager of the firm or head of the institution in which we participate. We spend the proceeds in the same market to cover our needs. Thus the total exchange takes place. Looking at it in greater detail, we should see the goods in the production of which we took part distributed among thousands of customers of our firm Sometimes, being used as raw: materials, they are handed on from the first customer, after being used in a process of manufacture, to a second set of customers, and often this process is repeated before the product is finally used up. And the connections established by our daily purchases are equally complex. In the course of a year we buy thousands of different types of merchandise and services which require for their production hundreds of different raw materials. Tracing these to their ultimate producers we should see that the most modest of us draws supplies from millions of his fellows on this planet. These supplies, we know, are received in exchange for what was distributed by ourselves, or on our behalf, as the product of our labour. Since our customers, to which this distribution went, are not the same people from whom we make our purchases, it follows that our outline of the circle of exchange is yet incomplete; that we have to add to it a series of exchanges between those to whom we sell and those from whom we buy. The entire multitude of all these exchanges, running into millions, are required to implement the existing division of labour, when any of us makes his living to-day. Selling and buying is by agreement. The sum of both is commerce, comprising all agreed exchanges which arise from the division of labour. The State supervises commerce by controlling the standard forms of contracts through which it operates and by supporting the organisation of markets which offer scope for public competition.

Apart from this production for individual use, there are, of course, provisions made by the authorities for communal use. Things which can be used only in common, like roads, town halls, and armaments, are obvious cases in point. But the modern State goes far beyond this in making common provisions: it considers, in particular, that the care for children, for the sick, the old, and the unemployed is a public concern, and it provides services for these from public funds. Wherever a comprehensive interest of society can be demonstrated, which is distinct from the sum of satisfactions given by the exchanges made through the market, there is a recognised obligation for the public authorities to safeguard it; this, in general, will involve public expenditure and thus imply a certain amount of central economic functions. The great majority of human satisfactions are, however, of distinctly individual character, and are parcelled out through the market to individual consumers on commercial basis.

Let us now turn to the idea of collectivist planned economy. This would base a system of divided labour with subsequent exchange of products not on the mutual agreement of those exchanging them, but on a plan based on a comprehensive view of economic life as a whole. Economic life, however, consists of the satisfaction gained by millions of individuals in thousands of different ways which have no comprehensive meaning, such as can be given to millions of bricks shaped to a house or to millions of soldiers operating as an army. The compilation of statistics on objects consumed, comprising the number of handkerchiefs, spectacles, prayer books, and countless other kinds of merchandise, are as meaningless from this point of view as would be the valuation of the National Gallery by square yards of canvas or pounds of paint. Production statistics may be related to satisfaction so long as the market functions well enough to attribute comparative values to each item, but they mean next to nothing unless that condition is fulfilled. Those who try to interpret the statistics of the Soviet Union, where the market has not recovered from its periodic suppressions by the State, know how profoundly the significance of production-statistics has been impaired thereby. The prices given in rubles have become almost meaningless, and a laborious and uncertain process of reassessment of every available item by reference to British or American prices is necessary in order to obtain even a rough estimate of the value of production. In his *Critique of Russian Statistics* Mr. Colin Clark finds, in the course of an analysis of this kind, anomalies of Russian valuation which even within one group of articles of consumption amount to more than tenfold distortions of relative values. Assuming that no vestige of market valuation would be remembered nor be available in another country, it would be impossible to gather anything but the vaguest idea of the satisfaction which a certain list of goods gives or may give to a population. As in, the case of science, the comprehensive view is not an essential view but a superficial view and an ignorant view. From it not a single business proposition could be made which would not be rejected out of hand by any business man of special experience as grossly unprofitable, and which hence—in nine cases out of ten—would not also be grossly wasteful from the point of view of society as a whole.

Far from being able to summarise the essence of an economic situation independently of the autonomous exchanges which go on in the course of marketing, and to replace their operations by a comprehensive scheme of its own, the Government finds that all it can see of economic life is based on the valuations arising from these exchanges. While it might feel able to correct these valuations here and there, where the participants are taking a too narrow point of view, the Government must recognise that it has no comprehensive set of alternative valuations to replace them. It is unable, therefore, to remove the course of economic life from the essential control of individual agreements, and to subordinate it instead to a co-ordination according to a central plan of its own.

In view of this position, there are, as in the some what analogous case of the attempted planning of science, two courses open to the Government. The one is to give up actual planning and to content itself with a more or less oppressive supervision of the autonomous operations of commerce, while adding to this sphere of individual use, which will supply the main livelihood of the people, as many public works and services for communal use as possible. Or it may take the ruthless course of imposing its determination to plan, at least to the extent that it puts an end to all exchange by mutual agreement—by destroying the functions of the market. It may take over plants, and, refusing to sell their products, ration them out to consumers; it may make trading illegal and debase currency to the point of making the use of money impossible.

But, since the Government can possess no point of view of its own by which it could direct the millions of exchanges entailed in the maintenance of divided labour, its efforts to do this will be grossly ineffective. Therefore, if the suppression of the market is inexorably put into effect, the consequence is an almost complete stoppage in the exchange of goods, followed by a total breakdown of production and widespread famine, as occurred in 1921 in consequence of the measures by which the Soviet Government had paralysed trade.

Soviet Communism

The attempt made in Russia twenty years ago to abolish the market broke down in disaster. 'We have suffered', said Lenin in 1921, 'a defeat on the economic front more severe than any previous military reverse'. With this he gave the signal for that new economic policy which he called the great retreat from Communism. Its purpose was to readmit so much commercial life as was necessary to restore a minimum of prosperity, while at the same time systematically learning to use 'capitalist methods' in the conduct of State enterprise.

The lesson which was then learned at the sacrifice of millions of lives that the market, far from being a domain of anarchy, is the vital principle by which alone ordered co-operation can be maintained in a system of divided labour, ought to be a permanent acquisition of the human mind. It means that economic life by divided labour is a business to be settled mainly between the multitude of individuals dividing the labour between them, and that planning which would prevent this spells disaster.

Unfortunately this lesson was demonstrated under dictatorship the political strength of which is nourished by a fanatical hatred of the market and a prophecy of salvation through its final destruction. Thus the surge of prosperity gained by re-admission of trading was a political peril to the Communist Government.

In order to reassert its waning power, the Soviet Government therefore again went on the offensive in 1927. Private shops and enterprises
were again destroyed and a vast programme of state enterprises was
launched. Three years after this a new economic disaster forced Stalin
once more to a retreat. Again the market was reintroduced, but this time
State ownership in industry and commerce was fully retained. Thus the
experience of the Soviets has now proved that, even though the State is
owner of all enterprises, it yet cannot decide on its own accord what to
produce, but has to rely on the profitability of sales to indicate the usefulness of every particular activity. Commercial management is now revealed as far more fundamental than the system of ownership, which can
vary widely while the market persists.

Clearly, for political reasons, the Soviet Government must do everything in its power to prevent the honest recognition of this state of affairs[6]. Hence the confusion, the obscure war permeating its whole life.
Production based on the individual efforts of the many State enterprises
and the millions of peasant organisations could go on well enough and
gradually restore a measure of prosperity. But the Government, intent on
imposing its initiative on economic life, must ever again renew its spec-
tacular efforts, at huge investments. It must be constantly 'showing off'.
Where the consequent dislocation causes confusion it suspects sabotage;
to suppress it, it spreads terror, causing more confusion and creating
further suspicion of sabotage, and so on. If, to prevent complete catastrophe, the Government then once more relaxes its hold, the wave of
consequent recovery restores the position of a more or less business life
with an inherent tendency to escape from the control of the Government
and to accumulate political power in opposition to it. Thus the struggle
must be renewed; collectivist fanaticism fighting for its life against the
necessity of the market and the independence which commerce restores
in the people[7].

The Return of Liberalism

Is it, then, time for Liberalism to return to charge with the fervour of
its early intransigence, which it professed up to about seventy years ago,
before beginning to give way to the growing claims of collectivist ideas?
I believe this to be justified to certain extent.

Extreme Liberalism in all its crudity is a source of material and moral
blessings when it serves to release society from medieval fetters or from

paralysis by State-imposed restrictions of trade. The phenomenal success gained at the beginning of the nineteenth century by the opening of the channels of trade could be once more achieved to-day merely by wiping out the collectivist structure of industry and commerce in Russia, Germany, and the countries around them—along with a few hundred tariffs and exchange regulations all over the planet. Such a New Economic Policy, to call it by the name of the first retreat from collectivism in Russia, would bring an immeasurable increase of wealth and liberty to Europe. In this sense the revival of crude Liberalism would be as justified and desirable to-day as it was 150 years ago; but in this sense only. For a Liberalism which believes in preserving every evil consequence of trading, and objects on principle to every sort of State enterprise, is contrary to very principles of civilisation.

The fact that certain individual actions are under public protection does not characterise them as *private affairs*. On the contrary; while it is true that private matters deserve protection, they require it only in exceptional cases, when they attract unjustifiable public interest and this interference or intolerance has to be averted. Public protection should, as a rule, be given to such individual actions in which there is a real public interest to preserve; and naturally not in disregard of the action's social consequences, but precisely because of them. Disregard of social consequences is equivalent to anarchy, which may amount to barbarism. The protection given to barbarous anarchy in the illusion of vindicating freedom, as demanded by the doctrine of *laissez faire*, has been most effective in bringing contempt on the name of freedom; it sought to deprive it of all public conscience, and thereby supported the claim of Collectivism to be the sole guardian of social interests.

Liberalism was misled to extremism mainly by failure to understand unemployment. It believed that this evil could be avoided by the prevalence of free trade. This view arose as a vague generalisation of the theory of maximum benefit which is provided by an economic equilibrium, freely established. It was thus held that all measures reducing the income of the rich and increasing that of the poor must produce unemployment; and most of the other proverbially dismal and inhuman conclusions of economic science arose from this central error. Among them the most important, because most recent, was the attitude of Liberal economists to the last World Crisis, in which they maintained that it was the duty of the State not to interfere, if it did not wish to aggravate the depression. I believe that the adoption by Brüning in 1932 of a policy of retrenchment and deflation, conforming to this error of extreme Liberalism, was one of the most potent immediate reasons of the Nazi revolution, which might have been avoided by a policy of financial expansion, as inaugurated by Roosevelt a few months later.

There is an element of superstitious fear in the idea of orthodox Liberals that the market takes revenge on society for any interference with its mechanism, by inflicting on it the curse of unemployment, and this mystical element seems akin in its origin to the obsessions of collectivists about the evil powers of the market. The orthodox Liberals maintain that, if the market is limited by the fixation of some of its elements, then it must cease to function, the implication being that there exists a logical system of complete *laissez faire*, the only rational alternative to which is collectivism. That is precisely the position which collectivists want us to take up when asserting that none of the evils of the market can be alleviated except by destroying the whole institution root and branch.

Instead of accepting this point view of orthodox Liberals and collectivists, I consider that the alternative to the planning of cultural and economic life is not some inconceivable system of absolute *laissez faire* in which the State is supposed to wither away, but that the alternative is freedom under law and custom as laid down, and amended when necessary by the State and public opinion. It is law, custom and public opinion which ought to govern society in such a way that by the guidance of their principles the energies of individual exertions are sustained and limited. The benefits of culture in the form of science, of religion, of the arts, and of the manners of intercourse are developed by individuals protected by law and encouraged by the response of society. The division of labour and the many commercial devices for the exchange of products are all subject to law and custom; money is a legal invention, and so are all the forms of contract, of company laws, all the statutory forms of business life. Supervision is a positive, ancient, and fundamental responsibility of Society which it must accept with respect to every individual action affecting wider circles. In fact, civilisation consists mainly in the system of behaviour by the observance of which men and women will benefit rather than injure their fellows while pursuing their own personal interests in life.

General planning is wholesale destruction of freedom; cultural planning would be the end of all inspired enquiry, of every creative effort, and planned economy would make life into something between a universal monastery and a forced labour camp. Our aim must be not to destroy the mechanism of liberty but to amend it by renewing the rules and principles on which individuals are called upon to act. Common sense will not admit that the only alternative to unemployment, to unjust gains, and to undeserved poverty is to bind ourselves hand and foot, to gag our mouths and blindfold our eyes. But common sense will not be heard until we rid ourselves of magic beliefs. We must realise that planing, as applied to social affairs, does not in general mean order and intelligent foresight; and at the same time we have to reduce the market in our minds to its proper position of an element of social machinery, subordinate to our will, so long as it is used in conformity with its inherent mechanism.

A more sober approach may not in itself eliminate conflict, but it will replace conflicting obsessions for which there is no solution, by conflicting interests which admit of compromise and by rival valuations to be adjusted by mutual toleration.

Notes

1. 'We have received the means and weapons from the capitalist State at war—the grain monopoly, the bread cards, and the universal labour service'.—Lenin, *Can the Bolsheviks Retain State Power?* October, 1917 (*Selected Works*, Vol., 6, p.269).
2. For 'Span of Control' in administration see Graicunas in *Papers on the Science of Administration*, edited by Luther Gulick and L. Urwick (Columbia University, 1937).
3. 'Anonymous battle' and 'expanding torrent' are described by Liddell Hart in *The Defence of Britain* (1939). For 'battle of the line' see Foch, *The Science of War*. Other parts of this section are based on Foch's 'unity of time and place' as the essence of manoeuvre.
4. The cultivation of liberty under the law has been greatly clarified by Walter Lippmann in his *Good Society*. The collectivist denial of such a possibility was forcibly expressed by Lenin in *State and Revolution* (1917), approving of Engels, who 'mercilessly ridiculed the absurdity of combining the words Freedom and State', and continuing: 'While the State exists there is no freedom. When freedom exists there will be no state'.
5. By a decree of November, 1926, the Communist Academy was constituted as the highest of All-Union learned institutions, charged with the strict advocacy of the stand-point of dialectical materialism both in the social and the natural sciences, Membership was confined to the party. The central planning of science having proved impracticable, 'decentralisation' was decreed in 1932, under which planning is delegated to individual scientific institutions (S. and B. Webb, *Soviet Communism*, pp. 959, 967, 969). This system is described by J. G. Crowther (*Manchester Guardian Commercial*, 2nd June, 1934) in connection with the Physico-Technical Institute of Kharkow: 'Each department draws up a plan for work from January 1 to December 31 of each year. The plan is given in detail for

each quarter, and there must even be a suggestion of what will be done on each day. At the end of each month, the research worker assesses what percentage he has accomplished of his plan. This is usually about 80 per cent. to 90 per cent., and the assessments are notably honest. The workers in each department are organised as a team or brigade, and each holds frequent meetings to discuss its own work and the policy of the institute'.

This disgusting comedy was, of course, only a pretence kept up for the satisfaction of official requirements; on my various visits to scientific institutions in the U.S.S.R. I never heard it mentioned except in contemptuous jokes; yet the procedure is reaffirmed in J. D. Bernal's *Social Functions of Science*, by Ruhemann in the Appendix (p. 447). The political atmosphere of this attempt to subject science to the orders of the authorities is characterised for the year 1930 by S. and B. Webb (l.c., p.553) as follows: 'This much-discussed prosecution of Professor Ramzin and his colleagues inaugurated a veritable reign of terror against the intelligentsia. Nobody regarded himself as beyond suspicion. Men and women lived in daily dread of arrest. Thousands were sent on administrative exile to distant parts of the country. Evidence was not necessary. The title of engineer served as sufficient condemnation. The jails were filled....', Meanwhile 'the strengthening of the dictatorship in philosophy' by the imposition of dialectical materialism (J. G. Crowther, *Manchester Guardian*, 18th March, 1935) proceeded apace. Recent evidence of the type of ideological lip service by which eminent scientists were forced to propitiate the authorities was published by Professor A. V. Hill (*New Statesman*, 17th February, 1940) from the *Astronomical Journal* of the Soviet Union, December 1938:–

'(1) Modern bourgeois cosmogony is in a state of deep ideological confusion resulting from its refusal to accept the only true dialectic-materialistic concept, namely, the infinity of the universe with respect to space as well as time.

'(2) The hostile work of the agents of Fascism, who at one time managed to penetrate to leading positions in certain astronomical and other institutions as well as in the press, has led to revolting propaganda of counter-revolutionary bourgeois ideology in the literature'...and so on.

At the outbreak of the present war a considerable number of scientists were kept imprisoned in the U.S.S.R. Though no mention of this is made in Marxist literature, it is involuntarily revealed in a footnote on p. 371 of the *Modern Quarterly* (1938), which blandly mentions that the publication of a bibliography of a scientific bibliography was cancelled on account of the number of names included of scientists under political persecution. 'In a bibliography of genetical literate which has been prepared, the publishing office pointed out that a number of names were included of scientific workers who had either been convicted of Trotskyism or who had long been resident in capitals such as Paris or Berlin. While it was not seriously contended that the work of such men must be so deeply vitiated by their political ideas or their residence abroad as to justify their original papers being omitted from the bibliography, the office could yet not bring itself to take the responsibility of publishing the full list, and the bibliography has not so far appeared'.

6. In a recent publication (*Two Systems: Socialist Economy and Capitalist Economy*, 1939, by Eugene Varga) the following official explanation is given by the Soviets. The transfer of products from one enterprise to another and to the final con-

sumer is by sale and purchase (p.97). But it is not competition which determines the price and it is not the prospect of profits which determines which goods are to be produced (p.96). We are also told that planning is guided by the trend of purchase (p.120) but no explanation is given as to how this is done, while disregarding profits. Actually nothing is mentioned about the way in which planning is accomplished except in a footnote which says that it is too complicated to be explained briefly (p.225).

7. The contention that the market should be used and combined with economic planning in the Socialist State has become fairly common among the younger Socialist economists. The presentation of this doctrine in its recent and perhaps most able formulation by H.D.Dickinson (*Economics of Socialism*, 1940) vividly recalls the course of events in the Russian Revolution. At the beginning (pp.14–15) there is an emphatic declaration of economic planning. A Supreme Economic Council will decide what is to be produced and to whom it is to be allocated, on the basis of a comprehensive survey of the economic system as a whole. 'In the ultimate analysis the responsibility for economic decisions must be single and undivided...and...must create a deliberate conscious control of economic life'. But as the torrent widens toward the ocean, we come (on page 222) to the following summary of the Socialist system in its final form. 'In one or two matters, perhaps, considerations of social policy would be planned on their merits. (But even here the tendency would be to make specific grants to particular undertakings or to lay specific burdens upon particular branches of production, and then to leave them to the quasi-automatic working of market forces.) In all other matters, and in all questions of detail even within the special schemes, the normal indices of prices and cost would be decisive. The great majority of lines of production would be carried on automatically within the given framework of costs and prices so as to supply goods to consumers according to their preferences as indicated by the market'.

The upraised fist of Moscow dissolves into the invisible hand of old days. Unfortunately, in real life, once revolutionary powers are called forth to dominate every particle of the people's life, they do not renounce their position when realising the necessity of free commerce. Their resistance keeps the State in perpetual struggle, within and without.

10

Profits and Private Enterprise

Polanyi read this paper in a discussion arranged by the Central Joint Advisory Committee on Tutorial Classes, and replied to one by Dickinson. (For more details of Dickinson's arguments, in this and other writings, see the previous article, n.7, and Paul Craig Roberts, Alienation and the Soviet Economy.*) It goes beyond von Mises' argument that central planning is impossible because, to be rational, it needs prices that can be derived only from a market, by demonstrating that even in the most simplified form, that of distribution alone where production is taken for granted (as Socialists usually do take it, regarding it as a purely technical problem of manufacture—see the note on 'Economics on the screen' [13] in Appendix II), the problems of economics are essentially 'polycentric' and cannot ever be formulated, let alone solved, in terms of central planning. The same is then shown to apply to production and to the allocation of capital. Furthermore, there has to be a visible, foreseeable and equitable way of persuading those engaged in production and the allocation of capital to carry out their responsibilities, i.e. a system of rewards, whether they operate in a privately or publicly owned enterprise.*

I will try to put before you one or two points of view which perhaps one gets more easily as a scientist than otherwise.

Mr. Dickinson has played a part in a very important discussion to which my subject is somewhat related, and I would like to use the opportunity of having him here to give a brief outline of the history of that discussion.

[49]. Reprinted from *Economic Problems in a Free Society*, London, Central Joint Advisory Committee on Tutorial Classes, 1948.

The problem of social control over production was introduced in history for the first time in an effective fashion by the Socialist movement, and its starting point, I understand, was the Russian Revolution of 1917. The Socialist assumption is that, if a properly constituted Government takes over the direction of economic activities, both on the productive and distributive side, then, in view of the fact that the Government represents the public, it both can and will carry out this task of organising economic life in the best possible way in the interests of its citizens. It will achieve efficiency and justice, and will also fulfil any other requirements that can be reasonably expected. It will at the same time (and this also played a part in the motives of the Revolution of 1917) be able to run the economic system most scientifically because it will be able to gather *all* the available information abut the economic situation and base its decisions upon it. Thus it will substitute a central decision based upon *all* the available information for a number of inclusive decisions based upon imperfect information made by separate economic agents acting in ignorance of one another's actions. Each single decision will thus reflect the economic position as a whole instead of a number of imperfect and partial appreciations of it. This latter aspect is usually called 'The possibility of Central Planning'. It involves the elimination of the market as a method of taking economic decisions. Now, this purpose was put into effect during the stormy period of the Russian Revolution, about which I would not like to speak in detail, and it was during this stormy period of 1917–1921 that the first studies of this general purpose of Socialism in a critical sense were started by Ludwig Von Mises in 1920 and then in 1922. He published theses in which he averred that it was impossible to achieve the purpose of nationalisation, because it was impossible to run the economic system centrally. It was impossible for two reasons: first, because in the absence of a market there could exist no rational principle of valuation for the goods to be produced and the resources to be used; secondly, because, in the absence of a market, there was no rational basis for the allocation of capital as between different uses. Hence, Mises concluded, the only possible way of running an economic system was that based upon individual decisions, and he private property, the price system, and profits.

This challenge of Mises was not taken up for a considerable time by Socialist theorists. It was eventually taken up by Mr Dickinson in 1933. He met Mises's objection to the central running of economic life under nationalisation by asserting that nationalisation need not involve central running or central direction of the economic life in the sense assumed by Mises, but might very well be combined with a market economy, with decisions taken by individual enterprises, acting on behalf of the public treasury, but guided by the same method essentially as guides individual enterprises in a system of private enterprise. This point of view was elaborated by Mr. Dickinson in 1938 in his *Economics of Socialism*. While, as I understand him, he still maintains that it would be possible to take all these decisions in a rational way without recourse to the market mechanism, he had clearly placed the greatest emphasis in his thesis on the fact that this was not necessary—that the nationalised economy could be run, as he had already suggested in 1933, on principles of market economy.

Mr. Dickinson, in following this line, met with the criticism of other Socialist writers who thought that this was not a solution of Socialism, but away from the original Socialist gospel. Mr Maurice Dobb in 1937 rejects this whole system by saying, 'Either planning means overriding the autonomy of separate decisions, or it apparently means nothing at all'. Again: 'that in a Socialist economy it should be thought necessary for the managers of various plants, having ascertained the necessary data about productivities, to use these data to play an elaborate game of bidding for capital on a market, instead of transmitting the information direct to some planning authority, is a "Heath Robinson" kind of suggestion which it is hard to take seriously'.

You find here the original point of view which has been modified by Mr. Dickinson and his fellows. I will leave out some other stages of the argument and come to its final stage, which I believe Mr Dickinson accepts as satisfactory in every way: that which Mr Lerner has laid down in the *Economics of Control* (1944).

Mr Lerner rejects entirely in distinction from Mr Dickinson the possibility of directing economic activities from a centre, and he maintains that this could lead only to utter paralysis and confusion; so that now the only solution for a nationalised economy is that, according to Lerner, of running it through the market. But Mr Lerner suggests emphatically (and here he develops something which Mr Dickinson has already suggested before) that a great improvement is possible through nationalisation, because individual enterprises would not be compelled to maximise profits in the same way in which they would in a private economy. They would, it is true, try to reduce costs as much as possible and increase revenue, but not by every means at their disposal. They would have to renounce the means which monopolists use, and that they would do by following what Mr Lerner calls 'the rule', namely the rule that they have to expand production up to the point where the price is equal to the marginal cost of production.

My own thesis, which I would like to outline to you today, is that this statement of new possibilities which Lerner gives is groundless—that it is impossible to apply to the nationalised economy a new rule for the processes of the market, except to the extent to which this is possible under private enterprise. In order to show you my reasons for saying this, I have now to cover briefly the theoretical ground, having already given you an outline of the historical. Now, the theoretical ground, I think, can be conveyed most conveniently if we first of all imagine an economy in which things grow on trees. Or, to put it differently; the total of products is given to us without expenditure of labour, and the economy is concerned only with the distribution of these products—rational distribution among millions of consumers having different wants, different tastes, different situations in life, different viewpoints, and so on.

Now, the first difficulty, which usually comes to the mind if one considers the possibility of distributing a flow of goods from a central position of authority, is: that the central authority, however properly constituted it may be as a government, is in fact ignorant of the desires of its constituents as far as their day-to-day wants are concerned. Let us suppose a group of housewives living in one street saying, 'We will elect in our street someone to do our shopping for us'. However careful and democratic the election might be, the thing would still be very unsatisfactory. Now, this argument against the central allocation of resources is based on the subjectivity, on the delicacy, and on the complexity of individual desires. This argument has been the subject of much discussion. It has been maintained that the attempt to satisfy desires by allocating goods according to the decisions of a central authority (e.g. rationing) would lead to hardship, loss of freedom, waste and so on. This contention is sound enough up to a point, but I want to point out that it is not very important. First of all, no government would fall into that mistake, and secondly, it is not a great difficulty, even in the field of distribution, that we do not know the desires of people.

That is the point which I want to bring out now. Supposing we wanted to know the desires of the people, we could do it, according to economic theory, by presenting the government with the 'substitution curves', as they are called, according to age, wealth and parentage of all the population with respect to all the goods available. Well, that is one way of doing it, but it is too difficult to go into it here before you, to elaborate what the result would be, although it would perhaps be possible to say that the government could not do anything at all with the substitution curves.

I think one could get the position more clearly as follows: let us assume that subjectivity is eliminated. Let us replace individual human beings with all their feelings and desires by robots; by machines which simply score satisfaction. We feel holidays and railway journeys, and all kinds of things which are enjoyable. They score satisfaction automatically. They have substitution curves: they can score the same degree of satisfaction by an indefinite number of combination of goods. They behave like individuals in modern economic communities, with all the choices before them, on which depends their satisfaction. I submit to you that if the engineering problem were now presented to the government, to achieve a maximum total score on the indicators o these robots, it would be an entirely insoluble problem.

The way one would attempt to solve it would be this: first of all we would define a rational solution. We could say that a rational solution would be one in which it would not be possible to take away from Robot A something and give it to Robot B, in exchange for which B would give something to A. That is, it would not be possible to have any redistribution to the advantage of anyone. In other words, it would not be possible to keep any of the scores constant while increasing the score of the residual robots. If you had N individuals, you could not keep the scores of N-1 constant and increase that of the Nth individual. That is essentially the rational condition for maximum satisfaction; that it is impossible for anyone to gain without any body else losing. Now, this is not sufficient condition—it is a rational condition but not a sufficient condition. We come one step further by establishing the fact that in addition to this rational condition we assume the existence of rates of exchange. That is, that every kind of good can be exchanged for every other at a certain rate which is constant at any given time throughout the system of robots having these goods; or—to put it theoretically—the rates of substitution are the same for all; the marginal rates are the same for all robots.

Now, I maintain then that the only way to go one step further would be this. One would have to establish some kind of income distribution between the robots. One would have to say, 'How should their shares be related to one another'. You might say that each should have the same share, or you might establish any other pattern of income-distribution. But it would not be possible to solve the engineering problem of the maximum scoring, under this particular condition or any other similar condition, except by distributing money among the robots and allocating some money to each, which would then be spent on behalf of that robot at prices which we could guess to be the right prices for equating supply and demand. If we can guess that successfully, and if we spend these sums on behalf of each robot at the public stores, then we have solved the problem. It is another way of saying that one of the conditions of the solution of the problem is that no robot can exchange with another at a gain to himself.

This whole argument brings out the following conclusion namely, that the very fact of a number of centres being involved in a problem of distribution makes it impossible to solve that problem centrally. Here it is, I think, that scientific experience comes in useful, because nothing is more common than this experience, as soon as you have a large number of centres interacting and mutually adjusting themselves according to certain laws. For example, you have to plan a rigid structure, where struts are pinned together at certain points, and these points are subject to certain conditions of pull, due to certain weights. If you have to calculate the deformation which you expect to occur in such a structure, the only way to do it is to use a system of successive approximations in which you first of all consider one single pin-point, one centre in general, and the interactions of that one centre with all the others. Meanwhile you keep yourself in ignorance of the interaction of all the others with one another. You then solve this problem for one centre and proceed to the next centre, and again go on as you did for the first time and solve it for that centre. So you proceed from one centre to the other adjusting it according to the condition of the problem to all the rest, and as you go all over your centres you finally solve the problem of the whole rigid framework under the weights. This is the type of method of successive approximation by proceeding from one centre to the next which is quite universally used in all polycentric problems, and in our particular case of an attempt being made to run the economic system from one administrative centre it yields the following conclusion: that this is impossible and has to be replaced by a method in which we take one centre at a time, one robot at a time, and instead of using al the information at our disposal we use only that information at that time which is relevant to the condition of the single one which we are concerned with: so that the central authority, if it wants to solve the problem at all, has to abandon its advantageous position of universal knowledge and reduce itself to the position of an individual ignorant of anything else but this one particular problem; or else it has to abandon its powers altogether—relinquish them and allow the individual to operate according to those conditions which allow him to operate by the knowledge which he has of his own problem alone. This mode of operating, of course, is that of a market economy. That is, the problem of distributing all those resources by the government would then be solved by distributing a certain amount of money among the citizens and pricing the goods which it is producing—and allowing the citizens to buy those goods according to prices which are adjusted until they are such that supply is equal to demand.

Now let us take the next step of this theoretical outline. It consists of admitting that goods are not supplied in this gratuitous way by nature, but have to be produced, and they have to be produced in industrial enterprises conducted by managers, who are responsible for buying resources and consuming them for the purpose of production.

Now, again we are faced with problems of a similar kind. These managers must know what is needed of them. In order to know it they must get from the people who have to be supplied an expression of desire in the form of some objective measure, some criterion, such as the readiness to buy the goods by spending money on them. Secondly, having taken notice in this way of desire which they could not otherwise assess, they must again solve a problem similar to that which we solved in the case of distribution of goods between the robots to achieve a maximum score of satisfaction between them. We must distribute this money, or else (let us go one stage back) they must utilise resources in such a way as to maximise the product which they are going to sell, and thus acquire a maximum amount of the money which expresses that desire. In order to do that (this finishes the circle) they offer money in order to induce others to offer their labour for the purpose of applying it to the making of the products under their management. The managers offer this money to the labourers and the labourers are induced in this way to do the particular kind of things which are conducive to the satisfaction of the wants of the community.

This, then, really duplicates the same problem which we have met in the distribution of goods. There is the indication of desire through the use of money, and the maximisation of a satisfaction through the allocation of resources in the way which will produce a maximum of profitability. The whole thing amounts also to a system of control. I will come to that a little more fully in a moment. The managers are controlled in the matter of whether they are doing their job well by the fact that they have to earn the maximum amount of money; unless they do they are reduced to bankruptcy. There is a control of the labourers employed by the manager. (I leave out land as we are not primarily interested in that. Let us take labour as the only factor of production.) There is a control on them too, because they have to comply with the need of earning this money which is offered to them in return for satisfying the desire of the community under the direction of the managers. So that there is, as it were, a control exercised by man as consumer over man as producer, via the managers who are themselves controlled in the process, and the control functions through the circulation of money which is paid out by the managers to man as producer, and is received by the managers from man as consumer.

That is how the whole system becomes totally decentralised, and there is only one element to be added to it: we must know where the money comes from, and how it gets into the hands of the managers. Now, this is the question of finance, and here it is necessary that somebody who produces the money (say, the government) should have agents at its disposal who will allocate these goods to the various alternative uses of investment. Again we have a polycentric problem; this is actually the third we have. First, the distribution among consumers; then the distribution among the factors of production or the man [as] producer; and now we have a polycentric problem among the various persons who would be in charge of this distribution of money for the purpose of investment: that is, placing that money in the hands of the managers, who would then be in a position to use it for production by paying labourers. Now, here we must consider the fact that anybody who would do this function of placing money at the disposal of managers would again have to be controlled, and in this case there is again a question of control by the need of doing the thing well. What he has to do well in particular is to assess the risk which he is incurring in giving the money to a particular manager rather than to another, and therefore he must be rewarded according to whether he has taken that risk well or not, so that he will probably be paid in accordance with the gains or losses which have resulted from his operations. He may be a tenant of the government, or a trustee of the government in charge of a certain sum of money, or it may be that it [*sic*] would be just an official in a government department. There apparently would be a difference in that respect between private and public ownership. In the case of private ownership he would have inherited his position, or have got the position in some other way; but otherwise he would operate on similar principles.

This brings me to my final point which I think is the one where there is, possibly, some real difference of opinion between myself and Mr Dickinson. All this, I think, would be accepted by most theoreticians of Socialism today, but they would argue that it is not necessary for the system to operate in this way, by trying to maximise profits. Instead of imposing upon each manager the condition that he must earn as much profit as possible, the theoreticians propose that each manager should be subject to the condition, which may lead to losses in some cases, that all units must expand production up to the point where the marginal yield (that is, the price) is equal to the marginal value of the factors used; that is, roughly speaking, marginal return is equal to marginal cost.

There has been a great deal of discussion recently in economic journals about the question of whether this criterion is a practical one or not, and what kind of result it would yield. It is one of the most important subjects of discussion at this moment in economic literature. I will not enter into that question, because I think it is irrelevant to the problem. It is irrelevant to the problem of further nationalisation. Does it make any difference or not to the possibilities of running economic life rationally? Because there are obviously two alternatives: either this criterion is applicable or it is not applicable, and I think that in both cases nationalisation makes no difference. Now we have seen that the running of an economic system involves *three* polycentric problems: (i) the problem of distributing goods among consumers; (ii) the problem of using different resources (including labour) to produce goods; (iii) the problem of allocating command over money (capital) to the managers of the productive enterprises. In each case the acceptance of the fact that a polycentric problem exists, involves a surrender of direction by the government: it has to pass on the initiative, which it originally had the power to exercise, to a number of separate individuals. But there is a fundamental difference between (i) the problem of the consumers on the one hand, and on the other hand problems (ii) and (iii), the problems of production out of investment. Something is involved in the two latter cases that is not present in the case of the consumer. While the consumers are using their discretionary powers to satisfy their own needs, the managers (and the workers under their control) and the directors of investment are not satisfying their own needs but are doing something which is not primarily in their own interests at all. They are not interested in producing those goods or in doing the work towards producing goods, except for the fact that in the second instance at a remoter stage they will be rewarded for it; but that reward is not a primary result—must be provided for; that is, there is a problem of government involved here.

You solve the polycentric problems in this case by laying down the rule which directs people to do something which they would not otherwise do, but which you want them to do: which will reward them if they do what you direct them to do, and punish them if they do otherwise: which will give them a claim to reward if they do what you want them to do, and which will give them a claim to a fair reward. That will place them in the position of people governed, which means they have the right to be governed fairly and with justice. Now, the question is, can we say that we possess a rule which is fair and just? Let us examine it in the following way: if the rule is to be operated fairly it must be certain. Everyone must know, first, what is expected of him; next, how he is to show results for the purpose of achieving reward; and that no other person is going to falsify the criterion of success and get away with rewards which are denied to him.

That is the criterion, I think, of fair government. I submit then that either this new rule is fair and reliable too, so that everybody knows how success is to be achieved under this rule; in that case I think there is no difficulty in applying it whether you have nationalised the system or not: or else it is not of this character. If it is uncertain; if it leaves open opportunities for wangling, for pretending success when you have not really achieved it, or for differences of opinion which cannot be solved by any foreseeable rational principle: then I submit it cannot be used either as a rule which has to be followed by the manager or the Socialist industry and nor [sic] can it be used as a rule to be applied to private industry. Let me make this more precise: supposing we introduce this new rule, people having enterprise will be rewarded; the manager will be rewarded not in proportion to the profit which he has achieved but according to profits and some other criterion. Now then, let us operate this in a private enterprise. The managers will then, if they make a loss but they achieve success in the light of that other criterion, have the possibility of claiming a reward. They will have the possibility of claiming the reward for themselves and obviously for the capital invested in the enterprise. Otherwise the capital cannot rationally invested in one enterprise rather than another. The private capitalist will, therefore, have every reason to invest the capital in the enterprise which earns these new rewards, these new rewards allocated according to these new principles. In other words, if these new rewards do in fact represent the social benefits earned by the enterprise, and they represent it in a foreseeable way which can be rationally achieved, then there is no difficulty whatever in offering to private capitalists the possibility of henceforth investing their capital in various enterprises according to their capacity of earning reward in respect of the social benefits which they achieve. If they do not do that; if the social benefit cannot be properly estimated by some other new criterion which operates with certainty and is foreseeable; then I submit it will corrupt all the administration of socialised industry as well, because the agents of the government which would be in charge of the allocation of capital could not foresee what the possibilities are of achieving success, promotion, security of tenure, and other advantages which they rationally claim. They would be placed in the position of people who are obliged to enter into a competition of wire-pulling and persuading the government—the superior authorities—that they have done something when there is no definite criterion by which they can actually show that they have done or achieved something.

That is the problem I want to put before you and with one more concluding word I will sit down. Let me go back to the original proposition which has played an enormous role in the history of our time, and the history of the world: that a properly constituted government represents the public good, and if we entrust to them the conduct of the economic process, then it will apply its powers to the best possible effect through this process; that it will secure economic efficiency and social justice and will be in a position to apply a scientific, comprehensive view: that it will, in fact, be able to achieve any reasonable success. Anything that can be conceived as right could be expected to be done by an authority which represents the public good, and is unaffected by any private vested interest. I submit that we have found profound qualifications to this generous vision. First because of the polycentric nature of the problem, which makes the scientific treatment not one which takes the problem as a whole, but—on the contrary—one which proceeds by successive approximations, and at every stage requires only that part of the problem, which can be seen from one centre. Secondly, that we have seen another set of limitations arising from the fact that these individual centres have to be governed. They have to be given the rules by which they can be expected to live, and to act in expectation of being rewarded fairly for their labours. We have seen that these conditions seriously impair the general proposition that the public good can be achieved through properly constituted government in the sphere of economic life, and we are warned that the way to argue was fundamentally wrong, so that I think that in future the argument has to be changed.

In future, I think, if we find imperfections in economic life; if we find, and we certainly can, a long list of irrationalities, of injustices, of all kinds of objectionable features in economic life, then we cannot in general say, 'Let the government take power over this whole system and achieve the public good'. That argument is, I think, not right. We have in every such case to consider whether there is any possibility of improvement involved in nationalisation at all—and the likelihood is that there is not. We have to accept the possibility that most of these imperfections do not constitute an argument for nationalisation at all, but simply an argument for stating that some—and perhaps most—economic problems are unmanageable: that which we call an economic system is just one single instance out of a million in which there is a relative unmanageability of economic affairs.

If I had time I would perhaps try to amuse you by imagining economic systems galore which are entirely unmanageable. For example, the possibility of all costs being social costs, and all benefits being social benefits. Take just the case of—well, I do not want to go into that. There are any number of such cases.

I do not want to end on the note of socialisation, but rather to end on this general note: that the alternative to our miseries is not one which is available to us in the positive sense, but in general may—on closer examination—be simply the establishment of the fact that we have either to give up this kind of production—or that particular kind of mode of production—or accept it as an unmanageable, or relatively unmanageable, form of activity.

Well, I do hope that I will have an opportunity of elucidating some of these points further in my discussion.

11

The Foolishness of History:
November 1917–November 1957

I have placed this article after the previous two because it gives chapter and verse for the real nature of Communist ambitions and their erroneous interpretation by their opponents as well as by Communists themselves.

It is often said that our scientific approach to history debars us from discriminating between good and evil; but the real trouble is not that this method blinds us to crime (which we still continue to recognise in spite of our sophistication) but that it renders us incapable of envisaging folly. And yet it is folly that has made *our* history; follies so vast that they appear almost inexplicable the moment they are recognised as such. Many of these follies are still so widespread, so nobly popular, and so ingrained in our own habits of mind, that their recognition remains difficult, wavering, incomplete. Remember how twenty years ago practically everyone in Britain believed firmly the slogan of 'poverty in the midst of plenty'? It was regarded as axiomatic that opulence was at hand for the mere asking. And not only in Britain, but everywhere—in Italy and Greece, in Turkey and Ceylon, in Borneo and the Gran Chaco. Just like that. The Children's Crusades delivering boat loads of boys and girls into the hands of oriental slave-dealers were perhaps less reckless than the enterprises undertaken by modern political movements on the grounds of our latter-day delusions; for now the fate of the entire human race is at stake.

Volume upon volume of excellent scholarship is rapidly accumulating on the history of the Russian Revolution, but as I read these books I find

---

[81]. Reprinted, with the permission of Mr. M. Lasky, from *Encounter*, IX, November 1957, pp. 33–37.

my own recollection of this event dissolving bit by bit. In these carefully researched accounts, we see people being driven by conflicting conceptions of reality; but each of these conceptions appears quite reasonable in its own way. So when two sides clash, we merely see the stronger eliminating the weaker; and nothing is left behind. The Revolution is about to be quietly enshrined under a pyramid of monographs.

Yet I know that it was something quite different. Not only when it actually happened; but all along, up to this day—for it still lives in our own blood. It was boundless; it was infinitely potent; it was an act of madness. A great number of men—led by one man possessing genius set themselves limitless aims that had no bearing at all on reality. They detested everything in existence and were convinced therefore that the total destruction of existing society and the establishment of their own absolute power on its ruins would bring total happiness to humanity. That was—unbelievable as it may seem—literally the whole substance of their projects for a new economic, political, and social system of mankind.

Today, if you are resolved to flout the obvious requirements of common sense and decide to plunge the world into obscurantism, you naturally invoke the justification of science. This is what the famous transformation of socialism from an Utopia to a Science amounted to. Scientific socialism banned as 'unscientific' any enquiry into, or even speculation about, the nature of socialism. Its success was complete, the darkness remained unbroken. During all the decades preceding the Russian Revolution, decades in which Marxist socialism became an intellectual world movement, only a few obscure scraps were published on the nature and functioning of socialism.

This is how it happened that two small pages of Marx became the fundamental text for Lenin's economic principles. Lenin discovered them in a paper now known as the *Critique of the Gotha Programme*, which Marx wrote in 1875 for the information of five leaders of the German Socialist Party. A copy of this was found fifteen years later among Marx's papers and was published by Engels in the *Neue Zeit*. Lenin read this article at the beginning of 1917 and wrote down in his notes:

'Thus here two phases of communist society are dearly, precisely, and exactly distinguished. The *lower* (the 'first')—distribution of articles of labour "proportionately" to the quantity of labour contributed by each to society. The "*higher*"—from each according to his ability, to each according to needs'.

Six months later Lenin triumphantly quoted from these pages in *The State and Revolution*, to refute writers who doubted that Socialism could succeed in abolishing inequality. This objection, Lenin replied, flourishing his new-found text, 'only proves the extreme ignorance of Messieurs the bourgeois ideologists'.

Nor is the level of his argument substantially raised as he proceeds to formulate the immediate aims thus set to Communism. Let me repeat a few lines of his statement, even though the place is well known. This is how, according to Lenin, the economic system will work:

'The means of production belong to the whole of society. Every member of society, performing a certain part of socially necessary labour, receives a certificate from society to the effect that he has done such and such an amount of work. And with this certificate, he draws from the social stock of means of consumption, a corresponding quantity of product'.

Not a word about the method of distributing labour, of supplying raw materials, of securing even the most elementary economic rationality. We are left to guess the answers to such problems from the sentence

'The whole of society will become a single office and a single factory with equality of labour and equality of pay'.

The quality of thought behind this announcement can be gauged from two further paragraphs which form the emphatic conclusion of the chapter.

'For when *all* have learned to administer, and actually do administer social production independently, independently keep account and exercise control over the idlers, the gentlefolk, the swindlers, and similar "guardians of capitalist traditions", the escape from this national accounting and control will inevitably become so incredibly difficult, such a rare exception, and will probably be accompanied by such swift and severe punishment (for the armed workers are practical men and not sentimental intellectuals, and they will scarcely allow anyone to trifle with them), that very soon the *necessity* of observing the simple, fundamental rules of human intercourse will become a *habit.*

'And then the door will be wide open for the transition from the first phase of communist society to its higher phase, and with it to the complete withering away of the state'.

These words were written exactly forty years ago. The movement which followed their lead has since caused (directly or indirectly) the death through famine, persecution, or war, of ten, twenty, thirty, or forty million people, depending on how you count them. Do we at last see plainly today that they mean precisely nothing? I wonder.

There was one writer who clearly realised that these rhetorical pronouncements were utterly nonsensical and saw what they must amount to in practice. This writer was Ludwig von Mises. In a paper published in 1920 he observed that economic management is impossible unless you can ascribe a rational price to every unit of resources and labour on the one hand, and to every parcel of products on the other hand. Mises concluded from this fact that you cannot run an economic system as a single enterprise. The only way to conduct industrial life was to parcel out resources between a large number of firms, each of which will make the most profitable use of its lot for the purpose of supplying a single common market.

This may, of course, sound strange. If you have all the pieces of a whole within your power, why not consider them jointly and combine them to that grand whole? Why divide them instead into thousands of separate lots and place the operation of each one in charge of a manager who knows nothing of all the others; or, at least, knows no more of these than is remotely noticeable by the repercussions which their operations may have on the market?

Why, indeed? I suppose the only people who know indisputably from their own experience why you cannot direct all the resources of an industrial system from one centre, are those who have tried it. The only full-scale attempt to do this was the one undertaken in Soviet Russia during the last six or eight months of 1920; and the results were disastrous. By December 1920 even Trotsky, who had been a most rigorous central planner, began to feel uneasy about the assumptions underlying this policy. He replied to a delegation complaining of the mounting economic hardships:

'All this is easily said, but even in a small farm of 500 *desjatines*, in which there are various agricultural branches represented, it is necessary to preserve certain proportions; to regulate our vast, far-flung disorganised economic life so that the various boards should maintain the necessary cross-connections and feed each other, so to speak—for example when it is necessary to build workers' houses, one board should give so many nails as the other gives planks and the third building materials—to achieve such proportionality, such internal correspondence, that is a difficult task which the Soviet power has yet to achieve'.

And ten years later Trotsky, in exile, had been sobered to the point of declaring that only a Universal Mind as conceived by Laplace could successfully conduct a centrally directed economy. Ludwig von Mises had been proved right.

Yes, I believe the rulers of the Soviet Union know, better than anyone else, the impossibility of genuine central planning; they know it in their bones, but their lips are sealed. The project of a centrally directed industrial system died in March 1921, and the system of commercial state capitalism was promptly invented to replace it. But the dead ideology of socialism was not buried. Far from it. When the great Soliman was killed during the siege of Szigetvár, the Turks concealed his death and paraded a dummy in the dead Sultan's garments until victory was secured; and the Communists acted similarly when their first, truly socialist, system collapsed. The Five Year Plans with all their sound and fury are but the parading of a dummy dressed up in the likeness of the original purpose of socialism.

To be sure, the sound and fury have not been altogether empty. A government posturing as the planner of every economic transaction in the country will do as much as any government can, and often quite a bit more, to impress its performances on its own people and on the world at large. By setting up large plants, which have their own inherent operational logic and the technology of which has been developed in a market economy abroad, it will establish areas of reasonable economic relations and thus cover the country widely with patches of technically fixed economic rationality. The easiest choice, unfortunately, will be to embark on a huge armaments programme, simply because modern armament manufacture was originally developed under governmental management and has remained therefore technically suitable to be conducted by a government. The senseless concentration on heavy industry is also due to the fact that such production lends itself more easily to centralisation: one can set 'targets' and mobilise the nation's energies and resources to reach them—whether or not these 'targets' have any organic connection with the rest of the economy. Much was done in this way that was useful, and the prestige and power of a revolutionary government were always available to curb any resistance to its policies. The devastations accompanying such achievements only added to their potency as a ritual celebrating the splendours of long-dead socialist aspirations.

The system often broke down exactly in the way Trotsky described it in the speech I quoted; even the Soviet textbook mentions such examples: 'If the production of a certain number of motor cars is planned but the production of the requisite quantity of steel sheets is not planned, this may cause the plan for the production of motor cars to remain unfulfilled'. But under cover of the noise made by the Five Year Plans the Government went on quietly fitting into place one piece of commercial (i.e., 'capitalist') economic machinery after another. Bit by bit every economic operation was fully commercialised. Adam Smith would have marvelled at this strange return of the 'invisible hand', doubly invisible as the carefully camouflaged secret of 'socialist' successes. Nothing could indeed be funnier than the way this kind of economics is taught in the Soviet Union. The official textbook is in two parts, nicknamed by Soviet students the Old and New Testament. The 'Old Testament' tells you all about the evils of commercialism, of production for profit, of the fetishism of commodities, of social relations being degraded to relations between goods, of the alienation of man within an acquisitive economy producing for the market. In the 'New Testament' each of these commercial features is re-introduced, with each time renewed apologies, explaining that under socialism they are really and essentially different from what they were before, and that besides they are only temporary, etc., etc.

When you read these justifications carefully, you see that they coincide exactly with the thesis of Ludwig von Mises: it is impossible to organise a nation's production centrally; one has to rely instead on the commercial operations of numerous independent enterprises. Whether these are privately owned or state owned turns out to make not as much difference as one might think. The managers and executives run the enterprise in pretty much the same way and always for the same purpose: a profit on their books.

But unfortunately, Professor von Mises had claimed too much. He had not foreseen that a system of nationalised enterprises could be run on commercial lines. He denied this. So he and his followers now changed their grounds. In 1947 Mises denounced the Soviet Government for wickedly doing precisely that which in 1920 he had proved to be impossible. He wrote:

'Men must choose between the market economy and socialism. The state can preserve the market economy...or it can itself control the conduct of all production activities. If it is not the consumers by means of demand and supply on the market, it must be the government by compulsion'.

This became the line of the post-war anti-socialist movement. It was the argument of *The Road to Serfdom* published by Hayek in 1944.

Of all the intellectual triumphs of the Communist régime—and they are vast—it seems to me the greatest is to have made these eminent and influential writers so completely lose their heads. Could anything please that régime better than to hear itself proclaimed by its leading opponents as an omnipotent, omniscient, omnipresent socialist planner? That is precisely the picture of itself which the régime was so desperately struggling to keep up. Such accusations supply the Soviet government with an incontestable 'testimony' of having achieved the impossible aspirations of socialism, when in fact it has simply set up a system of state capitalism—a goal which leaves the régime next door to where it started.

We have forgotten what the Russian Revolution was about: that it set out to establish a money-less industrial system, free from the chaotic and sordid automatism of the market and directed instead scientifically by one single comprehensive plan. This was to be the lower stage of 'Communism', on which the higher stage would follow. These have remained up to this day the supreme ideological purposes of the Communist régime, and the source of its emotional power. Hence its perpetual state of turmoil. The fantastic demands of its ideology must struggle unceasingly against the limitations of reality. The administrative apparatus must be constantly stretched to the breaking point in the attempt to achieve a task which exceeds many millionfold the span of control of any administrative machinery. And the mountainous hierarchy created for this absurd purpose lives by this 'function' it has assigned itself and holds on to power grimly in its name.

To-day, when our only hope for the future lies in conquering the minds of our opponents, we must concentrate on this crucial truth. We are faced with the force of moral passions, armed with weapons of mass destruction, but this fearful combination hinges simply on a false conception of administrative possibilities; and this very point may therefore be susceptible to persuasion by argument.

So foolish is history.

12

Toward a Theory of Conspicuous Production

This article develops further the arguments of the preceding ones against the possibility of central planning, and, with reference to objections to Polanyi's arguments and to descriptions from within of the workings of a supposedly planned economy, it shows in more detail how such an economy did in fact work and what motivated it. The allocation of resources to individual centres of production in the Soviet Union, and likewise in its satellites, was a matter neither of central planning, as was claimed, nor of commercial contracts within a market, but of bureaucratic allotment based on directives to increase the production achieved in the last period by a stated percentage. The whole system is one of 'conspicuous production', in which the physical objects produced—so many thousands or millions of tons of steel and wheat, of loaves, shoes, houses and machine tools—are fallaciously equated with the satisfaction of consumers' desires. That fallacy was exposed to full view when the Soviet empire, and Comecon with it, collapsed in 1989–90, although even then some in Western European governments and inter-governmental institutions refused to see it and insultingly proposed that Western Europe should use its money to subsidise exports from the former satellites to Russia, which would have perpetuated the chronic dissatisfaction of Russian consumers and the international uncompetitiveness of the industries of the former satellites.

During the decades before 1917 in which Marxist socialism had grown into a world movement, any discussion of the way the future socialist system would function was banned as unscientific utopianism. As a re-

[98]. Reprinted, with permission from the Institute of European Defence and Strategic Studies, from *Soviet Survey*, XXXIV, Oct–Dec 1960, pp. 90–99.

sult, when the Bolsheviks achieved supreme power, the original aspirations of pre-Marxian socialism emerged in their pristine crudity as the principles of their new economic system. Lenin had declared a few months before: 'The whole of society will become a single office and a single factory...', and the Soviet Government put this programme into effect by deciding to direct all economic activities centrally in the form of a single comprehensive economic plan.

This decision both satisfied the deepest hopes of the revolution and appeared obviously rational. Once the state had legal control of all enterprises, it would decide the allocation of resources and determine production to the public advantage. Government by the people would govern economic life for the people, and being fully informed at every moment of all the particulars of the economic situation, it would take into account all these particulars in every single economic decision. Thus it would establish a brotherly and scientific co-operation among men in place of self-seeking, impersonal, chaotic commodity production. How could it be otherwise?

Yet this idea, so plausible and exhilarating, is quite absurd. Its internal contradiction has caused the convulsive course of internal Soviet history, leading up to the present method of conducting economic life which can be understood only as an outcome of this contradiction. The first battle between socialism and reality was joined in 1920. Central direction made its full impact during the second half of that year and extreme measures of centralisation continued during the last two months of 1920 and up to March 1921. The attempt at suppressing all commercial relations and the very use of money, in favour of a central allocation of resources and distribution of products, was bitterly sustained until economic disaster ensued. When production fell nearly to zero, the troops mutinied, workers struck and Lenin was forced to restore commerce throughout the economic system. Then production recovered, and rose to [its] pre-war level.

At first, Lenin had frankly declared that his New Economic Policy was a retreat from a rash effort at establishing socialism, but soon the myth of the party's infallibility was restored by describing the drive towards central direction as an emergency measure due to the war. It has since been known as 'war communism'—in spite of the fact that its principal measures were issued at a time when fighting had ceased, and that the consequent collapse was manifestly cured by reversing these measures.

For the Soviets this falsification of history was a matter of routine and they did not in fact deceive themselves. They never repeated the experiment of totally suppressing the market in favour of a central direction of industry. But curiously enough, the covering up by the Soviets of the decisive defeat suffered by the original socialist programme has been accepted throughout Western literature. Distinguished scholars of Soviet affairs up to this day use the term 'war communism' and describe its policies (extending up to March 1921) as desperate expedients to which the Soviets were compelled to resort in their struggle for survival—without even mentioning any possible doubt of this interpretation[1].

Two reasons seem to induce the Western mind to submit to such deception. First, the adoption of a scientific attitude towards history makes us reluctant to ascribe any great public events to mere error; they must be historically justified. And second, we still lack a clear understanding of the utter folly of attempting the central direction of a modern industrial system. These remain indeed the main obstacles to a complete understanding of the present system of economic management in the Soviet empire.

We can see this from the history of the movement which Ludwig von Mises started in 1920 by attempting to prove that central economic direction is impossible. He argued that without a market, productive sources cannot be allocated economically and hence you cannot run a modern economic system as a single enterprise. What Mises said was true but he failed to prove it so. This became apparent when the Soviet government put an end to the NEP and got its Five-Year Plans going, as a system of state owned industries. By 1936 the argument of Mises came under fire by F. H. Knight, himself a passionate supporter of the system of private enterprise. He said that Mises was wrong in using market theory to deny the possibility of central direction. The government could satisfy all the requirements of economic theory directly. Governmental direction could indeed surpass the market by including the processes of taxation, taking account of social costs, as well as correcting other imperfections of the market. The objection to this system was—Knight declared—not economic but political: it involved the total suppression of liberty. This argument was given powerful expression by Hayek's *Road to Serfdom* (1944). Mises himself then denounced (1947) the Soviet government for wickedly doing that which in 1920 he himself had affirmed to be impossible.

Churchill spoke on similar lines against socialism in his election addresses of 1945, and this argument has indeed become the predominant interpretation of the Soviet system by Western opinion. It forms our warning to newly developing countries. We tell them that they could get rich by the Soviet method only at the cost of sacrificing their liberty. This theory may actually favour communism, for it may appeal to local élites who might expect to become the planners producing wealth by enslaving their fellow citizens; while many of the latter, borne down by abject poverty, may think opulence cheap at the price of liberty. We should be the last to spread this view—the less so since there is little truth in it.

Mises' original thesis, though true, cannot be upheld on its own grounds, for it does not explain why resources can be allocated economically within one enterprise without establishing a commercial network between individual users, and why this cannot be done between a number of industrial plants. This can be explained only by assessing the limits of administrative feasibility. F. H. Knight was right in denying that economic theory could prove the necessity of the market, but he went widely astray by suggesting that the market could be replaced by administrative action guided by the marginal theory of productivity. This feat would immeasurably exceed the capacity of any administrative machinery.

For my part, I have argued (1948)* that the possibility of replacing market operations by central direction must be categorically denied in view of the intrinsic limits of administrative control. Wherever a number of units are formed to achieve a joint purpose by mutually adjusting themselves to each other, this mutual adjustment cannot be replaced by the directives of a superior authority.

This principle has, in its most general form, nothing to do with the claims of individual freedom, or indeed with human affairs. It applies to a sack of potatoes. Consider how ingeniously the knobs of each potato fit into the hollows of a neighbour. Weeks of careful planning by a team of engineers equipped with a complete set of cross-sections for each potato would not reduce the total volume filled by the potatoes in the sack so effectively as a good shaking and a few kicks will do. Passing on to human affairs, take a soccer team of eleven mutually adjusting at every moment their play to each other, and pit it against a team each member of which has to wait before making a move for the orders of a captain controlling the players by radio. Central direction would spell paralysis.

---

* *The Logic of Liberty.*

This is not to place mutual adjustment generally above central direction. These two principal ways of ordering human affairs have each their proper functions. A hierarchic order controlled from one centre is proper to a task which can be subdivided by stages into consecutive details. Consecutive stages are then assigned to descending tiers of authority, down to the individuals actually handling the task of the organisation at the base of the pyramid. This is how a million soldiers are directed to carry out a single strategic or tactical manoeuvre decided upon by their supreme commander. And in spite of modern attempts at mitigating its hierarchic structure, this is how the distribution of resources and tasks within an industrial enterprise must be organised. Any attempt to replace lines of authority, fanning out by successive stages from one centre, by allowing individuals to adjust themselves mutually for going into battle or for working a mine, would result in total chaos. Anarchists in Spain trying to dispense with the lines of command in armies and to run railways without time-tables have proved (if proof were needed) the madness of such ideas.

The impossibility of replacing the market by central direction is but a particular instance of the fact that no process of mutual adjustment can be so replaced. The Soviet experiment of 1920 was a sustained attempt to replace the market by central direction, and it did spell complete paralysis. The Soviets have never forgotten this lesson and never repeated the experiment. Their present system, which does function, cannot, therefore, be centrally directed—as it pretends to be—and our problem is to find out how it does function in reality.

Three qualifications must be borne in mind applying these principles. The first two will be made in order to block irrelevant side-issues, the third, on the contrary, to broaden the scope of my thesis.

1. I submit that we can distinguish in practice between the decisions which *determine* a man's task and the circumstances which *condition* his performance of it. While a centrally directed hierarchy determines the tasks of each subordinate, it allows and may even require the execution of these tasks to be conditioned by mutual adjustments between subordinates, for example between neighbouring units in the line of battle. But it still remains true that any hierarchic order is instantly destroyed the moment its subordinates determine their tasks by mutual adjustment, and that the converse holds equally.

2. When I say that mutual adjustment through a market cannot be replaced by central direction I have in mind *the useful functions* of the

market. Economic science has during the past decades developed complex theories of the intrinsic limitations to which a market is subject. I accept these limitations, of which I could give a list here—and accept also any other limitations I may not know of. My argument assumes only that the market does perform vital functions in a commercial economic system, and affirms that these functions cannot be replaced by central direction.

I emphasise this, for the discussion on central economic direction has been obscured by the battle between the partisans of laissez faire and the critics of the market. There was a tendency on both sides to assume that this issue involved a decision between capitalism and socialism, or, more precisely, between market relations and central direction. This is not the case. Shortcomings of the market do offer a prima facie case for intervention by the public authorities, whether by legislation or administrative action, while it is also true that public authorities can often do little about such defects, with which we then have to put up. In any case, these functions of the public authorities are a necessary corollary of the market, as they serve to regulate, guide, correct and supplement the market, without ever trying to suppress and replace it. I shall describe these public functions as 'overall planning', and whenever I speak of a market *I will mean a market within a framework of overall planning.*

3. Public agencies charged with distributing scarce commodities arbitrate between rival claims by some system of licensing according to rules determining priorities. Since such a process mediates the mutual adjustments of individual initiatives, it forms part of overall planning. The allocation of public expenditure between numerous rival government departments (absorbing between themselves a considerable part of the national income), is commonly determined by this kind of mutual adjustment.

Central agencies can be used for the mutual adjustment only of [a] few centres, the relations of which change but slowly. Yet even where all enterprises are nationalised, distribution of investments by the interplay of rival pressure groups—each supported by its own mixture of economic and political arguments—can thus replace the capital market[2]. Mises failed to foresee this (admittedly cumbersome) possibility of mutual adjustment between rival capital allocations and declared therefore that public ownership would render economic life in a modern industrial system altogether impossible. By 1948 it was, of course, easy to see this mistake. I argued also that the mutual adjustments required *for the running of enterprises* were many million times more complex, more rapidly changing and far more dependent on subjective valuations than the mutual adjustments *for allocating investments to them*, and I concluded that publicly owned enterprises must therefore operate through a market even though this may be heavily overlaid by a pretence of central direction.

The following features of Soviet economics seemed to confirm that such was actually the case in the Soviet Union:

1. First, there was the fact that accounting in terms of money was introduced and has been enforced since the early thirties. The standard textbook of economics published in 1951 abounds in arguments to justify the use of money within a system of central direction. These excuses show clearly that money was introduced in opposition to a strong ideological reluctance, and we may conclude therefore that it does play a role that is indispensable to the conduct of economic life. And we may conclude further that, since money can be effective only by offering the opportunity for alternative choices to its users, managers of enterprises using money must be making choices which essentially control the course of economic life. I shall amplify this point later.

2. Next, the wholesale adoption of Western technological processes may be seen to introduce a set of concealed market relations within the system of central planning in Russia. For the rationality of such manufacturing processes was originally based on the comparative costs of resources and prices of products in a market economy. Insofar then as a technical process was transplanted unchanged, this act engrafted the network of commercial relations which originally justified the technical process, even though failing to take into account the difference in the relevant value relations.

3. Another feature which, from the start (1935), made me suspect that central planning could not be a coherent act of central direction, was the official applause given to 'overfulfillment'. This attitude is inconsistent with any effective co-ordination of productive efforts. If a bridge is planned, the over fulfillment of one pillar is not taken to compensate for the underfulfillment of another.

4. There was also a growing volume of evidence that illegal transactions between enterprises were playing a major part in Soviet economic life and served as the covert basis of an ostensible superstructure of central planning.

5. Lastly, there were reports that the plans are worked out by first issuing directives to enterprises in a preliminary form and requesting them to suggest modifications to them, a continuous flow of exchanges being maintained between the top and the base of the hierarchy. In such a system the initiative could pass over more or less to the enterprises, and to this extent the directives eventually issued from the centre would be merely an aggregate of the individual plans made by enterprises operating a network of mutual adjustments at the base.

I still think that these symptoms do suggest that the economic system of the Soviets is not operated by central direction, and I shall come back to them later in this connection. But first I must give full weight to some indications which speak to the contrary, and have indeed quite rightly been raised as objections to my view that the Soviet economy is based on camouflaged market operations. There are two such objections[3].

1. Reliable descriptions of the conduct of Soviet enterprises, of which Janos Kornai's *Overcentralisation in Economic Administration* (1959), gives perhaps the most detailed and recent account, leave no doubt that enterprises do receive detailed instructions which closely determine their programme of production. Managers strive strenuously to fulfil these targets so as to earn the substantial premia awarded for such achievements. These are an essential source of their income, while the profitability of their enterprises is of secondary importance to them. This situation does not seem to allow effective scope for the operation of market relations.

2. If it be true that the Soviet system is a distorted market economy, its productivity should be found to be defective to a degree corresponding to this distortion. For one thing, the cost of the top-heavy bureaucracy ruling the system should markedly depress its yield. Yet all indications seem to suggest that its productivity is rather higher than that of a Western market economy.

I shall take up the second point first, by asking the question: Could it not be that the distortions of the market actually favour production? This may sound absurd, until we recall a paradox that has often puzzled Western observers. Berliner voiced it in his study *Factory and Manager in the USSR* (Harvard, 1957, p. 326).

> The elements of inefficiency are so striking that they may create the impression that Soviet industry is grossly ineffectual and scarcely to be taken seriously. Such an impression would fly in the face of all we know about Soviet industrial performance.

Ely Devons says it even more forcefully in his review (*Manchester Guardian*, 22 October 1959) of Kornai's book.

> It adds up to a damning indictment of detailed central planning. Indeed, as one reads of one inefficiency after another, one begins to wonder how the system produced anything at all. And yet according to figures given by Kornai production in Hungarian light industry doubled between 1949 and 1955[4].

Most curious of all perhaps is the fact that the great many shortcomings of which Kornai complains are invariably identified and condemned by comparison with a capitalistic market. He takes these commercial standards unquestioningly for granted.

A first hint toward the solution of these conundrums is thrown out by Kornai when criticising Stalin's praise of the Soviets' sellers' market. Stalin says that: 'with us in the Soviet Union the consumption of the masses is constantly growing, outstripping the growth of production and thus stimulating production'. Kornai replies that this may stimulate the planners but it does not induce enterprises to do better work; rather it induces laziness, negligence, disregard of the buyers' requirements.

But why should the superior authorities responsible for directing enterprises on the lines of a minutely detailed plan be highly satisfied when production is generally disorganised? The answer may be found by evoking the picture of a sellers' market operating through a system of fairly rigid prices, as we had in England during the years immediately following the last war. Let us bear in mind in this connection that chronic suppressed inflation has been observed throughout the Soviet empire ever since the inception of the Five-Year Plans in 1928, and also that the Soviet government can keep prices rigidly fixed and may, in any case, disregard any inflation of profits in the allocation of investments, thus avoiding an inflationary spiral, even while it puts the economy under a powerful draft. The consequences will be as follows:

1. Full employment, to the very limit.

2. Defective co-ordination between resources supplied to factories and consequent waste of resources.

3. Defective timing in the supply of resources, resulting in stoppages and waste of capacity.

4. Reduction of consumers' satisfaction by their being forced to buy what happens to be available. More particularly, the satisfaction given by any given parcel of commodities is lowered by reduction of assort-

ment, slowing down of innovation, and erratic distribution under pressure of demand[5].

5. These factors tend to reduce costs of production and distribution. The favourable production statistics of countries with suppressed inflation suggest that its stimulus to productivity measured in physical terms (along with the high level of employment) tends to offset the impairment of physical productivity caused by the defective co-ordination and timing of productive supplies. So planners aiming at high production statistics may well be satisfied when production is disorganised by an excessive pressure of aggregate demand!

But their statistics are misleading; economic productivity must be judged by the creation of economic value. Products are not goods by virtue of their bodily existence; as such they are merely potential goods. Their value as goods depends on their aptness to the recipients' needs. To value a list of goods at our own market prices is to assume that they are delivered to recipients as aptly as goods are normally delivered in our particular state of the market. I shall call this their *normal market value*. In a sellers' market the same products have a *lower value*, which we may call their *actual value in this market*, or simply their *actual value*.

It is difficult to measure the actual value produced in a sellers' market. But we may roughly estimate the possible reduction in actual value by comparing prices paid for a less discriminating allocation, such as a meal from a single fixed menu, with that of a meal from a rich *à la carte* choice; prices of clothes ordered in advance for delivery at specified intervals, compared with the same clothes purchased at the users' convenience; prices of uniforms compared with a normal assortment of suits, etc. *From such examples we may estimate that the value produced by satisfying less discriminating users may be less than one half the value of the same physical goods satisfying a normal market demand.*

Once this reduction is taken into account, the real value of the total yield of a sellers' market is likely no longer to appear higher, but substantially lower than that of a normal market. The planners' satisfaction with the increased output of a sellers' market then appears to be based on a statistical delusion.

This delusion is intensified by the myth of a centrally directed economic system. Central direction aims at replacing commercially justified production programmes by production targets. It would thus extend 'target production' from the field of public services, to which it necessarily applies, to the much larger assembly of more mobile enterprises serving individual needs. The result is then as follows:

1. The process of mutual adjustment by central authorities, which is barely manageable in respect of a set of comparatively few and fairly steady public interests, becomes altogether unmanageable when extended to a much more numerous set of productive centres supplying more flexible needs.

2. Such an extension would be all-embracing and eliminate the commercial milieu within which the costs of a limited number of rival public interests can be weighed up against each other (as could still be done fairly well for the production of diverse armaments in wartime).

3. Public authorities can be kept informed by public opinion of the strength of rival public interests, but they have no similar guidance concerning the preferences of individual consumers; the latter can be established only by making competitive offers to serve the consumers and accepting their choices as guides to production. To set production targets centrally is to forgo this guidance and miss the predominant purpose of production.

Factors 1. and 2. render it doubtful, if not impossible, to ensure that targets are mutually compatible, and certainly make it impossible for them to be chosen with due regard to relative costs. Factor 3. tends to reduce greatly the value of targets as satisfiers of consumer needs. The situation resembles in outline that of suppressed inflation, with which it is usually combined. The stoppages due to the setting of incompatible targets and to manifestly uneconomic choices of targets are counteracted by a concomitant reduction of costs due to the disregard of consumers' choices. Once more, therefore, as in a sellers' market, *total production measured in physical units may increase, even while its total actual value is reduced below that yielded by a system of normal market relations.*

The ideology of central direction blinds the public to this negative overall result of target production by acknowledging physical units as goods, irrespective of the satisfaction they give to their recipients. Hence statistical results which in a normal market would be signs of much increased material satisfaction are accepted as such in circumstances where they actually give no increased satisfaction. The illusion of increased productivity is also reinforced by the basic socialist urge to exalt collective achievements at the expense of individual interests. This urge suffuses the process of production by a satisfaction of collective pride which compensates people as citizens for the corresponding loss of their satisfaction as individuals. We may call this a system of conspicuous production.

The wastefulness of conspicuous production is reduced to the point of allowing an accompanying increase in physical productivity, by the effect of two factors. The first of these is the presence of the crude commercial standards that I have already mentioned. These standards are imposed in the first place by a technology borrowed from a market economy, and are sustained further by the existing system of prices. Though prices are relatively inflexible and sometimes appear arbitrary, they certainly give (as I have said before) an indispensable measure of guidance to economic decisions. Actually, the total value of products, assessed at ruling prices, is extensively used to define production targets, and this would hardly be done if prices did not give some guidance for assessing the approximate equivalence of alternative products. It is also clear that commercial considerations are strong enough to enable a prevailing excessive aggregate demand to produce the characteristic symptoms of a sellers' market[6]. We should remember, also, the widespread illegal transactions which often prevent the incoherence in a system of targets from causing stoppages or other blatant wastages. Taken together, these commercial factors (technology, prices, and black marketing) may be said to form a *para-economic framework which effectively reduces the arbitrariness and incoherence of target production*.

The second circumstance that additionally reduces the inherent wastefulness of target production consists in the fact that the aims of target setting are far more restricted in practice than they appear in the theoretical image of central direction. The vision of a scientifically conducted economic life in which all particulars are simultaneously balanced against each other by a single directing centre and so made to serve the best interests of society as a whole—this original aim of socialist planning— has been abandoned in practice, ever since the first attempt at its realisation collapsed in 1921. The process now called central direction has accepted everywhere as its starting point a previously established commercial network, and directives issued after that time have also been always based on an actually existing network of supply and demand flowing between enterprises.

What is more, as Kornai makes emphatically clear, no binding directives are issued for more than three months ahead. And even so the range of these quarterly plans is in effect usually much less, since they are decided with a view to the results of the previous quarter, reports of which become available only after the final rush for the fulfillment of quarterly targets is over. Plans for such short periods can prescribe only small changes. Nor do these prescribed perceptual changes vary discriminatingly for each enterprise. All enterprises are kept under pressure to expand production, and this pressure is subject to variations only in accordance with overall planning. 'Planning' consists therefore—apart from the founding of new enterprises—principally in ordering a small percentage of expansion (or improvement) of production of existing enterprise for the next two or three months.

To this must be added a final and decisive restriction on the setting of targets. At the end of each quarter some enterprises will be found to have exceeded and others to have fallen short of their targets. Their immediate superior authority will reward the former and penalise the latter, but will itself be said to have fulfilled its own target even if its subordinate enterprises have only fulfilled their targets on the average, with under-fulfillments balanced by over-fulfillments. Consider also that the superior authority's knowledge of the present productive capacity of its enterprises rests principally on their last reported achievements. It therefore need do little else—nor can it in practice do little more—than fix the next task of each enterprise in proportion to its last achievement. Kornai tells of managers worried at having their targets raised, if they are found doing too well, and mentions also that the authority above will tend to reduce the next target of an enterprise if its performance has lagged behind in the previous period.

Here we see emerging the essential formula of so-called total economic planning. The target of the next two or three months is fixed by adding to the results of the last period a small percentage of expansion. Thus the planning authorities merely impose the continuous general expansion of an existing network of mutual adjustment, as established within a prevailing para-economic framework. This ubiquitous pressure is graded by the 'overall planning' of economic progress, much as it is under capitalism for the purpose of the industrialisation of new areas. But all detailed directives—which are the characteristic feature of Soviet planning—are determined by the local successes and failures of individual enterprises in fulfilling demands made on them in proportion to their last successes or failures, which themselves had been achieved in response to previous demands fixed in the same way in proportion to still earlier outputs, and so on indefinitely.

This is not central direction but a ubiquitous central pressure, which forces enterprises to operate constantly to the limits of their capacity and to widen this capacity from quarter to quarter by a process of trial and error.

But there still remains the question how can enterprises rely on each other to supply them with raw materials, semi-finished products, machines and spare parts, and all other requirements of production? We must accept the fact that enterprises are prevented from attracting these supplies by offering to buy them at competitive prices. For even supposing that they might circumvent the prohibition against such procedure, they would not find prospective suppliers readily responsive to buying offers, since the primary interest of these lies in fulfilling their targets (and earning the attached premia) rather than in increasing their income by profitable sales. A black market can function therefore only marginally, and the main contractual lines must be established non-commercially by superior authorities responsible for the continued operation of the whole group of enterprises which mutually rely on supplies from each other.

We may ask then: does not the establishment of such supply-links by a superior authority contradict my thesis that the network of economic adjustments between enterprises must be left to their peripheral mutual interaction? Does it not entail indeed, the kind of central planning which I have declared to be impossible and non-existent?

The second question is the more important and also the easier one to answer. Whatever the procedure may be which induces enterprises to supply each other, it does not centrally direct their production. The production of each enterprise is determined primarily by its response to a ubiquitous expansionist pressure from above, as described in the previous sections. The ability of superior authorities to secure delivery of resources by one plant to the other will doubtless affect this response, but cannot be said to determine it, let alone to do so in the light of a consideration of all possible alternative allocations of resources in conjunction with all possible alternative programmes of production. The function of the superior authority can be only to mediate between enterprises striving to fulfil their pre-given targets, by satisfying the increased supply claims of each expanding enterprise from the increased production of all other, also expanding, enterprises. Though the authorities, who thus continually expand the network of supplies between plants frequently have to trade the priorities of rival claims, it still remains true that both the supplies becoming available and the demands made for them, have their origin locally within the several enterprises responding to a universal production drive. To this extent, then, the superior agencies whose function it is to expand from quarter to quarter—as best they can—the network of supplies, are acting as the agents for the supply claims of enterprises and are exercising their authority on behalf of these by binding other enterprises contractually to service them.

This is not central planning, but neither is it a system guided by a market, for targets are not set in response to a commercial demand made at competitive prices. Output is demanded as part of a desire to produce more, and the availability of resources is then taken into account as a limit to the expansion of productive capacity. The mutual compatibility of targets is secured up to a point by the para-economic standards inherent in technology and a system of not altogether uneconomic prices, and, in any case, targets only represent fairly monotonous increases on the last actually achieved figures. The task of effecting a corresponding expansion in the network of supplies is therefore also very monotonous as compared with the speed and complexity of re-adjustments in a modern market.

Even so, the adjustment of supplies is the field of notorious failures. It is largely because of the wasteful failures of this system of supplies that Western observers have been so puzzled by seeing the vast flow of goods produced by Soviet enterprises. These wastages (stoppages and misuse of resources) will, of course, tend to reduce production, but the damage will be counteracted, as we have seen, by a stimulus to physical output due to the fact that production is carried on unhampered by close attention to the demands of ultimate consumers. The fallacy of identifying certain physical objects as such with economic goods, and of equating their real value with their normal value, is the gold mine of conspicuous production, which pays for this double extravagance.

I have tried to show that the absurdities of conspicuous production form a system which the Soviets hit on in their fierce endeavour to act out as far as possible the original vision of a universally planned, strictly non-commercial economy. An integral part of this system is its way of testing and rewarding the fulfillment of targets. In the absence of an effective profit motive, productive achievements must be assessed either in terms of physical quantities or of values at controlled prices. But with all its shortcomings, commercial profitability does offer a more rational measure of economic efficiency than any set of such quantities can do. Whatever indices of this kind are tried, they give results that are scandalous in the light of obvious economic standards. Kornai's book presents a systematic study of these anomalies of target-production

They are of two kinds. First, enterprises will use the margin of freedom granted by any given set of efficiency tests to meet the tests by short-cuts, the possibility of which the superior authorities had overlooked. Thus they will earn important premia by manifestly wasteful methods. If such practices are then blocked by making tests more specific, the operation of enterprises will be so narrowed down that at the next turn of some unforeseen situation, they will be unable to take the obviously requisite line of action.

Consequently, tests are continuously readjusted in an attempt to make them sufficiently stringent and yet not excessively restrictive; as a result of which we see wastages caused by efforts to circumvent tests alternating with wastages due to the paralysis of obviously necessary operations. Kornai regards this situation as an internal contradiction of the system; I would consider it rather as a marginal outcrop of the great conflict between the vision of a centrally directed economy and the necessity of deciding true economic actions by the direct mutual adjustment of the participant units; a necessity to which the system covertly submits, but only up to the point required for producing physical objects, which are falsely identified as goods of normal value, in view of their conspicuous appearance.

If I cannot curb the current urge to understand the follies of men 'from their own point of view', I may try at least to anticipate some of its manifestations.

It will be said that Soviet Russia is too poor to serve its consumers more delicately. Certainly, poor populations everywhere are supplied with less varied choices, for this is cheaper. But this is no justification for putting very effort into producing a great bulk of goods with little regard for people's wants. There is no need to incur the wastages of target production in order to manufacture cheap goods. Ideological passion alone can justify such a system.

It may be objected that capitalism starves the collective interests of society and that the Soviet system restores this balance. Perhaps it does, though its authoritarian structure renders its assessment of collective satisfaction dubious; but even so, the major purpose of economic life remains the satisfaction of individual needs, and the aggregate of these individual needs is not and must not be administered as if it were a collective satisfaction. This error, once more, is purely ideological.

Finally, we may ask: If central direction is impossible and its alleged practice mythical, is there any difference left between the Soviet system and capitalism? The difference is that the profit motive is largely replaced by a scramble for target premia: to this extent the conduct of enterprises is integrated towards the achievement of public recognition, and made less responsive to consumers' preferences: and again to this extent, *targets* are produced in place of *commodities* and the consumer is despoiled for the sake of serving the rulers' prestige.

This system is not directed centrally, but is ordered, like commercial production, by the mutual adjustment of individual peripheral efforts. Yet the manner of mutual adjustment differs from that of a market and justifies calling it a system of conspicuous production. Its propagandistic advantages for sustaining the claim of having achieved socialism are prodigious. The Soviet government could hardly survive the reduction of the system to straight-forward marketing. Yet once we recognise what is actually going on here in the name of socialism, the whole exercise appears trivial: a pitiful simulacrum of the Messianic vision which had inspired a century of revolutionary aspirations.

Notes

1. Cf e.g. Merle Fainsod, *Smolensk Under Soviet Rule* (Harvard, 1958), p.7.
2. Bela A. Balassa, *The Hungarian Experience in Economic Planning* (Yale, 1959), p. 79–83, gives a vivid description of the bargaining and pressuring between rival government departments seeking investment allocation in Soviet Hungary.
3. See Peter Wiles in *The Soviet Economy* (London, 1956).
4. The problem is raised likewise by Andrew Shonfield (*Observer*, 14 June 1959). He speaks of the 'hideous and cumbersome paraphernalia of central planning' and writes: 'Yet...Soviet industry continues to pour out more and more goods'.
5. The quality of products also deteriorates, but it may be assumed that this is taken into account in identifying a given parcel of commodities.
6. Balassa, loc. cit, p. 95, describes price-guided choices in investment, production, exports and the labour market.

13

The Determinants of Social Action

This article elaborates Polanyi's account of polycentricity by showing how the five determinants of social action which he identifies are necessary to both privately owned and nationalised concerns. In Kantian terms, it offers a 'transcendental deduction' of five institutional arrangements required for rational action in society: the definition of current powers; the definition of an order of succession; the guidance of men's labours; control over what they have achieved; and provision of adequate rewards for their efforts. Polanyi also shows that these are necessary both for nationalised and privately owned concerns and must take broadly the same forms in each. An important collorary is a theme that runs throughout Polanyi's writings on society: because nationalisation (in this instance and revolutionary total restructuring in others) can introduce no other motivations or radical alternatives, then we have to accept the fact that there will always be imperfections in human affairs.

The essay I am offering here for the celebration of my honoured friend Fritz Hayek is on a subject close to his major interest. It bears on the foundations of individualism in economic life and argues that these must be equally respected whether ownership is public or private.

I think I have proved in earlier writings that the production and distribution of modern technological products can be conducted only polycentrically, that is, by essentially independent productive centres distributing their products through a market. From this I concluded that the claim of the Soviets of having a centrally directed production and distri-

[135]. Reprinted from *Roads to Freedom: Festschrift for F.A. von Hayek* (ed. E. Stressler, London, Routledge, 1969), pp.165–79.

bution was essentially fictitious.[1] This opinion conflicted sharply with the views prevailing at the time both among supporters and opponents of the Soviet regime. While the supporters applauded the practice of central direction, the opponents deplored it because it was deemed damaging to liberty.

It seemed pointless at the time to publish a study which elaborated my thesis that central direction was impossible. I set aside therefore the present paper, which I had first presented in the University of Chicago in 1950. Though Arthur Lewis accepted it for the Manchester School, I felt that publication would be useless at that moment. But since the time of Liberman's critique of the economic practices of the Soviet Union, the situation has changed. The existence of central direction in Russia came to be doubted. Besides, during the past ten years or so expectations attached to nationalisation in some Western countries have been much reduced. It may be of interest now to develop further the principles of polycentricity, which have proved broadly correct in contradicting the opinions predominantly accepted at the time and during years to follow.

I shall take for granted here the following assumptions which I believe to have established in previously published work.

There are two and only two ways in which the full-time activities of men can be co-ordinated in the achievement of a joint task. One is incorporation in a hierarchy of command, on the lines on which for example an army is organised when it goes into action. The other method is that of self co-ordination. In this case the initiative lies with the individuals (or individual centres) taking part in the joint co-ordinated activity. Each has to adjust himself to the situation created by the others and by doing so he contributes to the adjustment of all to their common task.

It is postulated further that these two distinctive methods of co-ordinating the full-time activities of men are applicable to the performance of different kinds of joint tasks. The performance of an army or a fleet in action must rely for its co-ordination on a hierarchical chain of command. And the same is true of the internal co-ordination of a factory or any business enterprise. But there exist other tasks which involve the mutual adjustment of a much larger number of relations and which cannot be performed by subordinating its participants to a pyramid of corporate order but can be carried out—if at all—only by a suitable process of self co-ordination. It is submitted, in particular, that the allocation of a multitude of resources to a large number of productive centres for the purpose of producing and distributing a great variety of commodities can be carried out in an orderly manner only by a system of mutual adjustments. This is to say that the task of *modern technology is of a polycentric character and that polycentric tasks can be solved only by mutual adjustment.*

I wish to enlarge on these postulates here by showing that either method of co-ordination—the authoritarian as well as the self-adjusting or individualistic method—must be implemented by institutions fulfilling a certain set of criteria which I shall call the determinants of social action. I shall argue further that these institutional requirements sharply restrict the scope of social reform and shall illustrate this by the example of a universal nationalisation of industry. I shall try to show that the State cannot make the managers of nationalised enterprises act in any very different manner from that in which they would act as managers of privately owned companies.

Let me embark now on this programme by defining what are the general conditions for *responsible action* in society—for actions which are *rationally determinate*, as opposed to inconsistent, meaningless actions.

A man can of course act rationally—just as other animals can—in solitary situations, unaffected by social relations. A man living by himself on an island solves all his practical problems for himself. He makes the best use of his resources according to his skill and prudence, without any institutional framework to guide his actions rationally.

The same is still largely true of a self-subsistent farmer cultivating his land within a community of other such farmers. The only institutional element that is indispensable in such a situation is that each member of the group should know what area he is entitled to cultivate. Each must be assigned definite powers over a particular area. These powers must be secure and continuous, so that he who has sown shall also reap. But there must also be established some determinate process by which the powers of landholding are transferred from one person to another, particularly on the death of the landholder. In other words, there must be institutional arrangements in force both (1) for defining current powers and (2) for defining an order of succession by which these powers are re-assigned.

This conclusion can be seen to apply over a wide field. Since man almost invariably uses some tools for his work, his rational behaviour in society will always require that he be assigned some definite powers, and that there should exist an order of succession by which these powers are reassigned.

If we now look at more complex societal situations, we shall readily discover *another three* institutional requirements of rational action in society. Whenever some people are to rely regularly on the services of others, the labours of the latter must be societally determined in three respects. Persons working for other people must rely on these people (1) for *guiding* their labours, (2) *controlling* what they have achieved and (3) providing adequate *rewards* for their efforts. The first two of these determinants will have to be present even when an action is unremunerated and in such cases we can observe them in isolation. Let us take a student in a university pursuing for example a course in medicine. He must both know what he is expected to learn and what kind of examination he is expected to pass. He should not primarily learn in order to pass examinations, for that would replace education by cramming. But while he must apply himself in the first place to the task of his medical studies, he must also learn how to place his knowledge on record by replying to certain questions set to him by examiners. For if the knowledge of candidates for the medical profession could not be tested by examinations, no objective recognition could be granted to medical qualifications; society could not rely on professionally acknowledged medical practitioners and no organised medical service could be sustained.

We have here an illustration for the twin principles of guidance and control, which must operate in every case when individuals are to render regular services to others. The first determines the *task* of a person, the second fixes the *tests* by which the performance of the task will be judged.

Lastly, we have *rewards*. Persons who do not produce anything that primarily satisfies their own needs must produce goods or services for which they will be rewarded by others. In order to act rationally, they should know what reward to expect for their services.

This completes our list of the five determinants of societal action, which, for the sake of further discussion, I should prefer to write in the sequence: Powers, Tasks, Tests, Rewards, Accession. For a general theory of rational action in society these determinants would have to be reformulated so as to include all spheres of intellectual activities, in which case we should have to allow for the fact that intellectually creative people are to some extent judges in their own cause. They have a voice in shaping the standards by which they will be judged, and their creative acts may be important precisely in opening the way for the establishment of new standards. But to begin with, I shall simplify my task by disregarding the special problems of creative intellectual activities and shall be satisfied in formulating the five determinants, as I have just done in the more straightforward manner in which they apply to other than intellectually creative activities and particularly to a modern system of economic life. Even so, we shall have our hands full in tracing the five determinants through the strikingly different forms which they assume for different classes of people who operate in economic life and in evaluating on this basis the scope of state control over industry.

The five determinants are easy to identify within an hierarchical organisation, such as a business corporation. Take the familiar chart showing the branching out of authority downward from tier to tier and let us direct our attention on any member of the corporation except its chief; that is on any single subordinate member of the hierarchy.

(1) It is immediately apparent that every such member, must have definite powers. He must know which are his own subordinates whose performances he is supposed to direct, or—if he is at the bottom of the hierarchy—he must know what are the tools which he may handle, what offices are at his disposal, etc. Any uncertainty in this respect will lead to people receiving contradictory orders from several persons, whom they] believe to be their superiors, and will result similarly in daily conflicts over the use of machinery and offices. A corporation, in which there is general uncertainty as to the powers of each member, will be subjected to chronic unrest. Writers on business administration have often pointed out that such ill-organised corporations will inevitably be 'shot through with politics'. To avoid this, a clear definition of responsibilities, or powers, is indispensable.

(2) Next it is indispensable that each subordinate should know what he is expected to do. Unless his task is laid down clearly he cannot act purposefully. Unless he knows what are his obligations he cannot act responsibly. The task of a subordinate will be assigned to him by his superior and renewed or shaped in its particulars from time to time by the day-to-day directives given to him by his superior.

(3) In this sense the subordinate must do what he is told, but this does not fully determine his actions. In the performance of his task he must exercise his own judgment. He must take into account for example the particular circumstances in which his job is to be carried out. He must

also apply to it his personal skill. In a sense, of course, his is a definite job to start with, but it yet depends on him what job he makes of it. And on this result he will have to report to his superior. The subordinate's report is a summary of what he has achieved, or thinks to have achieved, and also a claim to the recognition of this achievement. If a workman is on piece-work, he will present his score to the foreman and ask for its inclusion in his weekly total. But even when the report made to the superior is not as simple as that, it will always represent a summary of some kind in terms of certain significant features of what has been achieved. In other words, it will be stated in terms of certain data which the superior may be expected to accept as tests of the degree to which the task entrusted to the subordinate has been accomplished.

The problem of providing proper tests for the satisfactory performance of tasks which one person undertakes for another is of great importance for the question which I propose to examine in this essay. We should note in particular that tests must be fair. They must represent a true measure of the achievement of which they form the test, and be definite and objective. For if the tests by which a subordinate can claim to have acquired merit are hazy and based on objectively not controllable data, this offers excessive temptation for specious window dressing, while it penalises the honest scorer. Nothing is more demoralising to the conscientious worker than to find his performances classed below those of a colleague who makes up for his lack of true merit by effective talking points which impress his superiors. This must be avoided.

(4) The question of tests is of course closely linked to that of rewards. Rewards are not indispensable as incentives to every human effort. When people write poetry or save a child from drowning, their actions carry much of their rewards in themselves. But this is not so for the production of shoe-laces, toothbrushes, radiators, etc., which is also a satisfying occupation but not in itself. It satisfies you only if you know that you have provided something that was wanted by others. Therefore the proper measure for your own satisfaction in this case will be whatever your work will fetch from those who buy its products. It follows that a business corporation must pay for the services of its employees and try to pay them fairly, in proportion to their usefulness to the company. In saying this I do not wish to minimise the importance of praise or dispraise; I only affirm that in a business enterprise moral incentives are not enough. Employees must be paid and paid according

to their performance. If there had been any doubt about this, the disastrous experience of Russia in trying to dispense with graded material incentives should dispose of these doubts definitively. The proper grading of incentives is indispensable both in order to satisfy a sense of justice within the corporation and thus avoid demoralisation, as well as in order to stimulate efforts in the direction in which such exertions are most useful to the company.

(5) Naturally, there must be also an order of succession must get their powers assigned to them when they undertake tasks within the corporation, accepting certain tests that are to be and the prospect of certain rewards thus to be gained. New powers will have to be assigned and existing powers modified or revoked. This procedure is included among the incentives to the extent as it is covered by promotion or demotion. To this we must add, however, the process of new enrollments. Speaking of corporate bodies in general, new enrollments can be by initiation, as in a monastery, by conscription as in the army, while in the case of business corporations they will be by contract.

Within a corporate body all five determinants are operated by the authority at its head. In the case of business enterprises, they all emanate from proprietary and contractual powers vested in the head of the enterprise. These powers, however, form part of a framework of institutions that lie outside the corporation. Our next task will be to define the nature of this framework from which the corporation as a whole derives its powers and within which its actions are rationally determined.

Business corporations operate in the solving of the polycentric task of producing and distributing material goods by modern technical processes. Our task is now to identify in this system of polycentric adjustments the institutions which provide the persons making decisions with the five factors of responsible societal action. In other words, we ask what institutions are required in order to determine the powers, the tasks, the tests, the rewards, and the order of succession, for each individual engaged in adjusting himself to the position of other individuals within a polycentric system, of production and consumption?

I shall define firstly the nature of the powers which these individuals must possess. In the economic system there are three kinds of people who have to allocate resources: the W (Workers) allocate their labour, the L (Landowners) dispose of certain plots of land, the I (Investors) assign certain sums of capital.

$$W \searrow$$
$$L \leftrightarrow M \leftrightarrow C$$
$$I \nearrow$$

To be more precise, the W's allocate themselves to jobs offered by M (Managers) while M's give jobs to W's. Similarly the L's assign sites to one of the plants controlled by an M, while an M decides to put his plant on a site placed at his disposal by an L. The I's allocate capital between different M's, while the M's allocate their ideas to one of the I's. On the right of the M's we see them distributing their products between the C's (Consumers) while the C's choose between different M's in allocating their custom. These two way processes are expressed by the double-headed arrows connecting the symbols in the outline of the economic system.

We have seen that the polycentric nature of the overall task in the solution of which this system is engaged demands it that each W, L, I, M and C, should act on his own initiative. Each must therefore possess personal powers to dispose of the things which it is his function to allocate. In order to define these powers more closely, we have to consider the peculiar two-sidedness of each allocation. It is inherent in the nature of the adjustments occurring within this system that in each adjustment the allocations of two independently acting individuals must exactly coincide. Such coincidence can only be due to agreement between the two individuals in question. In other words, all allocations must be made on a contractual basis. We must have labour-contracts, leases of land, subscription of capital, and on the other side sales to consumers. We may sum up this by saying that from the polycentric nature of the economic system we have derived the necessity that individuals should have powers to make contracts for the allocation of resources and the purchase of products. And we may add that these contracts must be enforceable by a legal order of private law.

Professor Samuel Dobrin of the University of Manchester has shown that even in the Soviet Union the desirability of a reliably operating system of contractual relations has been recognised, and that they have enacted therefore a Civil Code similar to that of capitalist countries, which the Soviet government has tried to enforce by urging its enterprises to go into court against each other for the vindication of their contractual rights.

There is another institution which is a corollary to contractual allocations in a polycentric system, and which is also common both to private capitalism and to a system of universal state ownership. This is the institution of prices expressed in money. In order that a large number of individual allocations may be mutually adjusted there must be a public indicator of available alternatives and such indicators must make generally known the rates at which alternatives are currently substituted for one another. Such an indicator is a ruling price. Mutual adjustments take place through the fact that all individuals act on the basis of the same price (signifying availability of alternatives) and that the prices are readjusted in response to underbidding sellers or outbidding buyers.

It is also clear that prices must be expressed in *numbers* assigned to each piece that is to be allocated. For this has the decisive advantage that, by adding up such numbers, any combination of things can be recognised as an available alternative of any other combination the numbers of which add up to the same figure. That makes a rapid choice of alternatives possible. Once you have prices fixed in numbers you can use money, provided that the W's, L's, and I's whom the M's would pay in money can become C's and buy from the M's for their money the finished articles that these have produced by aid of the resources purchased from the W's, L's and I's. The M's of course must also be paid in money. They retain some of the money in payment of their own services as the flow passes through their hands from 'west' to 'east'. Each joins then the rank of the C's and makes his purchase from other M's, just as the rest of the C's do.

To complete the picture of the self-co-ordinating economic system we have yet to recall that each of the symbols, W, L…C stands for a multitude of individuals, whose every self-adjustment competes with that of all the others. It is these myriads of competitive outbiddings that establish jointly a relative economic optimum within the economic system. Soon, however, we shall at last arrive at a point where there is some difference between a privately and a publicly owned industrial system. This will become apparent by setting out explicitly the determinants of societal action apply to individuals within a competitive system of production and distribution. I have already said something about *powers*. Polycentricity requires that at every centre there should be independent powers for disposing commercially over the things that participate in the economic system at that centre. These powers to sell or hire out for business purposes one's own labour, or certain areas of land, or certain sums of money, we shall call proprietary powers. Such proprietary powers must be present in any polycentric economic system, whether its industries are privately or publicly owned.

Next we come to *tasks*. It follows from the principle of polycentric adjustment that proprietary powers must be used by their holders at their own initiative and (own) discretion. They must set themselves their own tasks: each must allocate, or transform by manufacture, to the best advantage the resources which he controls or the money which he has to spend. Perhaps we may say that self-co-ordination assigns to the individual a general problem within which he has to decide on his own particular task.

Next we come to *tests* and *rewards* which, for the sake of brevity, we shall discuss jointly. For this we must remember that in a polycentric economic system the choice of a task is always bilateral. It is laid down in a contractual agreement of two partners. In fulfilling his contract either partner's position in respect of the other is similar to that of a subordinate carrying out the directions of his superior. His performance must fulfil certain specifiable criteria. By fulfilling the tests of the contract, either partner can claim from the other the compensation agreed upon in the contract. And again, tests must be fair and objectively ascertainable. The old proverb says so: *clara pacta, boni amici.* Obscurity in a contract leads inevitably to conflicting interpretations by both sides and results in quarrels. If tests are inadequate and do not properly define the task to be performed, a partner may be able to claim the agreed payment without performing or fully performing the agreed task. Bad laws and bad contracts will frequently permit this to happen; and it is the principal purpose of good laws and carefully drawn up contracts to prevent such abuses. We have here a contractual framework of tests and rewards within a polycentric economic system; and there is so far no difference apparent between private and public ownership of industry.

There is one contractual relationship within the economic system in respect to which this identity between capitalism and socialism should be particularly pointed out. Within both systems there are certain people, the I's, whose function it is to allocate money between competing projects represented by their acting or prospective managers, the M's. Under capitalism the I's are private citizens while under socialism they are government officials. (The same holds for the L's who allocate sites for different productive uses; but for the sake of brevity we shall not mention the L's always separately, but concentrate our attention on the I's and speak of them as if they comprised also the L's.) Whether industry is financed by the State or by private capitalists, the subscription of capital must be by contract between the I's and the M's in which the M's agree to use the money remuneratively, and in both cases the test of this will in general consist in making a profit in money. For, other things being equal, profits are the greater the more economically the process of production is conducted and the more closely the distribution of the products conforms to the needs of the consumers.

And here at last our analytical quests are rewarded by a glimpse of our problem in a new setting. Our problem now boils down to this: Are the I's in their contracts with the M's in a better position to include adequate tests for the performance of the M's, in the case that they, the I's, are government officials as compared with the case that they are private individuals? But before trying to answer this question let us complete our survey of the determinants by passing on to the order of accession.

The power of the W's to allocate their labour is extinguished on their death or retirement and the new generation of W's grows up with power over their own labour. Similarly, the power of the C's to allocate their custom dies with them and arises naturally in new generations of C's as they reach maturity—these are trivial points which we need not elaborate here any further. The M's will invariably be appointed by those who allocate to them the wealth for the administration of which they are responsible. In other words the M's receive their powers from the I's, whether the latter are private citizens or government officials. The difference between capitalism and socialism lies in the order of accession of the I's. Under socialism these are appointed by the public authorities, while under capitalism they acquire their powers over investable sums of money either by saving up part of their incomes or, perhaps more usually, by inheriting the investments of deceased relatives. The powers of private capitalists are largely hereditary, but the power to invest smaller sums is possessed by every adult citizen under capitalism.

Here is laid bare the only great difference between capitalism and socialism. In the Soviet Union a private citizen may make a lot of money and he may save it. He may buy government bonds on which he will receive good returns, which at times were as high as 7 per cent. But he cannot subscribe any industrial shares. All allocation of capital is in the hands of public officials. All risks of enterprise are pooled in the public treasury. The State bears all the losses and takes all the profits—apart from a relatively small percentage of them which benefits the so-called 'Directors' Fund' of the enterprises in which a profit was made.

The doctrine of Keynes that saving and investment are two entirely separate activities is strikingly illustrated by the constitution of the Soviet Union, where all saving is private while all investment is public. The officials acting as investors are, accordingly, devoid of certain powers which their opposite numbers under capitalism possess. They can only choose between different channels of investment and they can presumably also wait and leave some funds uninvested for the time being, but they have no power to spend the funds at their disposal for their own pleasure. They have no right to sell out the factories which they have financed and consume the proceeds. In other words, they have no powers to 'dis-save'.

I shall add the last touches to my distinction between the systems of private and public enterprise, by taking up once more a point hinted at before about the defectiveness of competition between the I's, the investors, if they are not private citizens but employees of the government. If all the financing of industry is done exclusively by public authorities, there cannot be such a large number of independent initiatives among the I's as if anyone can become an investor who has saved or inherited some money. In the competitive order I↔M, we still have the managers boosting their projects in competition with each other and trying to attract capital in the direction of greatest profitability; but the I's being all officials of the same government cannot possibly pursue as many different and conflicting opinions as private individuals could. It is true that the government is not one person. There are different departments, different branches of the state bank and a multitude of local authorities which will more or less independently seek openings for useful investments. There are also the thousands of individual enterprises reinvesting their own profits sometimes on quite new lines. All these modes of investment can be observed for example in the Soviet Union. There is a great multitude of I's, but yet not as many and as varied and independent of each other's policies as in a system of private enterprise. Nor is there an organised capital market available which would allow for rapid mutual adjustments between the actions of the I's. Herein lies a serious imperfection of a system of public enterprise. Its mode of capital allocation is comparatively clumsy, as compared with that of a system of private enterprise. Government investors are not likely to probe as quickly and completely as private investors into all avenues of advantageous investment and to react as sensitively to changing circumstances by an appropriate re-shifting of investments all over the field of enterprises.

This is—rather surprisingly—all the difference there is between a system of private and public enterprise; at any rate so far as public enterprise is conducted in accordance with the polycentric nature of the modern economic task and with due regard to the necessity for providing a complete set of determinants—Powers, Tasks, Tests, Rewards, Accession—for each person participating in the system, so that he may be in a position to act in a definite and responsible manner. Of course, if a socialist government continues to pursue the pretence that it is centrally directing its economic system it will deflect the system from its rational course and cause much confusion, conflict and even violence. Such a government may, moreover, adopt a conception of man and history which leads logically to totalitarianism and it may actually use its power in a totalitarian manner.

In this paper I have tried to purify the concept of state ownership from the illusions of central direction usually attached to it, as well as from the totalitarian political theories which have in fact always been linked in past history to a programme of universal nationalisation. I can now proceed to answer explicitly the question which I have set myself here, namely, how far the system of state ownership can modify the economic optimum which a system of competitive enterprises is tending to achieve. Or anticipating my answer to this question—how is it to be explained that even though the public authorities appoint all the managers, as well as the investors, they cannot exercise more—or much more—control over them than if investment were private and managers were appointed by directors elected by shareholders?

In trying to answer this question—or rather to substantiate the assertion implied in it—I must refer briefly to the various imperfections of existing systems of private enterprise. When a manufacturer considers the costs of a project he adds up his accounts in terms of the resources which he would use up. He ignores the wider repercussions which the operation of his proposed factory may spread in various directions. The noise and smoke, the pollution of rivers, the defacing of the landscape and all this kind of nuisance, should be counted among the costs of manufacture, but the manufacturer is not directly affected by them and may leave them entirely out of account. Such costs are social costs and it falls to the public authorities to assess them and to act accordingly, either by making restrictive regulations to which manufacturers have to conform or, in some cases, by imposing special taxes on the production of certain articles which will bring home the social costs to the manufacturer. Similarly, there are enterprises which spread benefits, or supposed benefits, far beyond the range of the primary customers who pay for the products. Universities are sometimes classed in this category; it is assumed that the fees students are prepared to pay do not represent the full value of the universities' services to the community. For a student does not consume the education which he receives as he would consume a slab of ice cream, but embodies some of it in his personality and spreads it around himself throughout his lifetime. Consequently, the public authorities, or public benefactors consider it proper to make up the difference between the proceeds from students' fees and the costs incurred by universities. And there are many other instances in which the public benefits originating in an enterprise will justly the granting of subsidies to such enterprises. It is in general the proper function of a government to assess all diffuse social costs and social benefits, and to impose restrictive regulations and special taxes in respect to the former and grant subsidies to compensate for the latter.

Compare now the position of the public authorities in carving out this function in the two systems, that of private and that of public enterprise. In neither case can it deal with every individual enterprise. That in general will exceed its span of control. It must formulate general rules and apply certain definite tests in applying these rules. Every manager must be able to assess in advance how these rules will affect him. The tests should be fair, that is of a definite character, and such as are quickly ascertainable by objective methods. Otherwise the regulations, taxes and subsidies will inevitably result in capricious decisions and corrupt practices.

In this respect there is no difference between a system of private and public enterprise. Regulations, taxes, and subsidies, which can be rationally applied to a few hundred thousand private enterprises can be equally applied to a similar number of public enterprises, and regulations which would operate capriciously if applied to private enterprises, could not be applied to public enterprises either. The administrative problem of the government in a nationalised is obviously compounded from its two functions, first as the universal provider of capital and second, as the guardian of the social interest in respect to diffuse costs and diffuse benefits. The first of these functions is vested in the investment departments. As investors, they can rationally control the managers in charge of investments only by the same tests which private investors would use. They must see to it that the enterprises which they finance make profits and the more the better. This conclusion is clearly borne out by the granting of profit premiums to the 'Directors' Funds' in the Soviet Union. On the other hand, those government departments which are concerned with social costs and social benefits not accounted for in profits, must impose conditions on profit-seeking which will safeguard the general welfare. It appears obvious now that the administrative task facing these welfare departments in trying to control the managers of state-owned enterprises, is exactly the same as if enterprises were owned by individual shareholders.

I need go no further: this conclusion can be readily generalised to cover all other suggested improvements of a marketing system that have been recently advocated, such as the replacement of the profit motive by the equalisation of marginal costs and marginal incomes. If these proposals can be formulated in terms of regulations that can be applied to a panel of a few hundred thousand state appointed managers, so that their performances can be fairly assessed and rewarded in the light of the new criteria, then the same rules will operate with equal success in respect to a similar number of privately owned enterprises. For the administrative problem is once more the same in both cases. Public ownership of industry creates no new powers to eliminate the various imperfections of private capitalism.

Note

1. See Michael Polanyi, *The Logic of Liberty*, London and Chicago, 1951.
    The semblance of central planning was analysed in *Towards a Theory of Conspicuous Production** (*Survey*, London No. 34, Oct.–Dec. 1960, pp.90–99) and in *Theory of Conspicuous Production* (Colloque de Rheinfelden, Calman Levy, Paris, 1960); more concisely stated in *Quest* (Bombay No. 41 April–June 1964); as broadcast by RIAS Berlin, December 1962. For a further development see P. C. Roberts, 'The Polycentric Soviet Economy', *The Journal of Law and Economics*, XII (April 1969).

---

* See No. 12 in this collection.

14

On Liberalism and Liberty

Although the topical references are no longer relevant, this article does elaborate some of Polanyi's arguments concerning the bases of a free society and threats to it. I have appended it to the previous articles because its begins with a distinction between totalitarianism and central planning and goes on to give more of a positive account of what a free society is. In the Preface to The Logic of Liberty *Polanyi had explicitly repudiated Popper's 'Open Society': 'Private individualism is no important pillar of public liberty. A free society is not an Open Society, but one fully dedicated to a distinctive set of beliefs'. This article specifies tradition and traditional restraints, tacitly understood and tacitly transmitted, and a sense of civic conviviality, as parts of what a free society needs to be dedicated to.*

For many years, the discussion of public affairs throughout the free world has been dominated by a controversy over economic planning. Anti-planners have warned that planning would inevitably suppress liberty as it had in Russia, while the planners have answered that these political consequences could and should be avoided. Both sides seemed to agree that, in Russia at any rate, totalitarianism arose as a by-product of economic planning.

Yet this assumption has little root in historical fact: Lenin published his intention to establish a new type of state, which was to supersede parliamentary democracy, upon his arrival in Russia on April 17th, 1917. In the course of the following weeks, he identified this new state with the 'dictatorship of the proletariat', which was to be 'an authority not based

---

[69]. Reprinted with the permission of Mr. M. Lasky from *Encounter,* IV, Mar. 1955, pp. 29–34.

on law, not on elections, but directly on the armed force of some portion of the population'. Nor was this an improvisation: in 1906 Lenin had already demanded 'unrestricted power, beyond law, resting on force in the strictest sense of the word'. Thus the suppression by the Bolsheviks of the Russian Constituent Assembly, the proscription of all opposition, the lawless rule of the secret police, and the universal imposition of a Marxist ideology, were all long premeditated as purely political principles. They were in fact put into execution in the first years immediately following the revolution, before any extensive measures of economic planning had been undertaken.

The true relationship between totalitarianism and economic planning s obscured by the ambiguity of the term 'planning'. Economic planning, in the sense of replacing the functions of the market by the central direction of all industrial production, is a clear conception, and it was this kind of planning that the Bolsheviks originally intended to institute. A resolute attempt to put it into operation was undertaken by the Soviet Government in 1920, but the attempt broke down so quickly that the Government could successfully conceal ever having made it. It blanketed the event under the name of 'War Communism' dismissing it thereby as a purely accidental phenomenon. Though this effort was never repeated, the claim of conducting economic life according to plan was nevertheless vigorously upheld.

Yet Russian economic planning consists now merely in the Government's undertaking a number of heavy investments and ostentatious building schemes, combined with a general hue and cry for more production everywhere. Firms may exceed their planned production to any extent and are celebrated for it, without any questions being asked about how the plan should be readjusted accordingly. Overproduction in one field is actually taken to compensate for a short fall below the planned target in another—imagine a bridge builder who would acclaim the 'overfulfillment' of one pillar as compensation for the 'underfulfillment' of another! What is called 'planning' here is a loose collection of enterprises, initiated centrally, which the managers on the spot are left to adjust to each other by competitively scrambling for materials and men through a system of more or less regulated, and more or less legal, markets. Such co-ordination as this economic system shows is due to the commercial character of the day-to-day decisions taken by the managers in the pursuit of the well-being of their particular enterprises. While the planners continue to dramatise the system as 'central planning', by dressing it up in an elaborate socialist nomenclature and accompanying its operations by much tub-thumping and posturing, it is a market-economy, rigged to a considerable extent by government intervention It is not appreciably nearer to the original Communist idea of an economic system not dependent on the market than are the systems prevailing in Britain, France, or the United States.

It is true, of course, that in capturing power and suppressing liberty Lenin aimed at the abolition of capitalism. But the establishment of a totalitarian dictatorship came first, and this dictatorship was continued, not for the purpose of carrying out an economic revolution, but—on the contrary—to take its place emotionally. Far from being a mere incident in the establishment of a new economic system, monolithic discipline itself became the dynamic principle of the Russian Revolution It feeds the fire of its illusions, among which the pretence of having created a new economic system is still vital to the régime.

It is well to remember that Hitler established a totalitarian system in Germany without any pronounced hostility towards private enterprise or any intention of comprehensive economic planing. The totalitarian revolutions of our time have been actual primarily by political, not by economic motives. What were these motives? I should like to suggest that they were supplied by the liberal movement itself, wherever, unrestrained by respect for proper authority, it degenerated into nihilism.

Freedom and Civility

Political and cultural freedom, in the absolute sense, is incompatible with the existence of fixed social relations. Freedom can operate in society only within such limits as are set to it by the established political authority and the established moral consensus, both of which define and preserve the existing social framework. Liberalism differs from other systems of social relations in the nature of the authority to which it submits. However, any attempt by liberalism to define this authority ends by revealing a crucial ambiguity in the liberal position.

Free institutions themselves, like parliaments, independent law courts, a free press, are of course legally established in free countries, and are supported there by the authority and power of the government But such institutions inevitably also legalise ample opportunities for their own paralysis and possible destruction. Hitler was legally appointed Chancellor on January 30th, 1933 by President Hindenburg, just as Béla Kun had been legally appointed Prime Minister of Hungary on March 21st, 1919 by President Karolyi. Senator McCarthy has shown that Congressional Committees could legally exercise powers which would destroy democratic government in the United States. Weakest perhaps against legal subversion are the free institutions of Britain, which could all be abolished by a simple majority in Parliament.

Moreover, there is a difference in the nature of the authority exercised by free institutions, as compared with the authority of despotism, which makes despotism more stable than freedom. Free institutions can function only in a society spontaneously united in giving support to them, and no power can enforce such spontaneous collaboration. You cannot suppress a determined rebellion without sharply curtailing freedom. Even such a comparatively harmless conspiratorial activity as that of the Irish Republican Army in England during 1939 could only be met by a virtual suspension of the habeas corpus. The physical suppression of a more widespread terrorist movement, like that of the Arabs in Morocco, may give rise to terroristic countermeasures, such as the clubbing by French soldiers of sixty thousand suspects, of whom twenty died, in Port Lyautey in August 1954. However that may be, any resolute conspiracy determined to subvert by force a free government necessarily reduces the area of freedom; the government can neither stand fast against it, nor retreat from it, without some sacrifice of freedom.

Admittedly, no government, however tyrannical, can remain in power entirely by force; it must have at least a Praetorian guard of devoted followers on whose loyalty it can rely. The *apparat* organised by Stalin could reduce this requirement to a minimum, but only because it was built into a milieu that, though resenting Stalin's personal rule, was loyal to Communism, which would have been endangered by the overthrow of Stalin. Moreover, a police state can gradually enforce sufficient voluntary concord by a monopoly of publicity and education. It is not inconceivable that in the course of time, a modern despotic government may thus make itself ideologically so secure that it could continue to rule without using more force than free governments do.

Just as the practice of freedom cannot be secured by any set of formal rules, so also the essential meaning of freedom will always escape any attempt at a formal definition. It must be defined in terms of specific examples, if it is to be distinguished from servitude. Only within a free society can free institutions preserve freedom, as the Soviet constitution and Soviet elections remind us; and the very words 'freedom' and 'servitude' can carry their true connotations only when uttered within a free country.

The authority to which political and cultural freedom is correlated is, therefore, the authority which prevails in fact in what we regard as free countries; not in the explicit content of their constitutional rules, but in the tacit practice of interpreting these rules. It is on this unspecifiable art of conducting free activities that the preservation of freedom must rely; and similarly, all formulations of liberal principles must derive their meaning from a prior knowledge, diffused inarticulately among the citizens of free countries, of what freedom is. Thus, both the meaning and stability of freedom appears rooted in the liberal tradition, the presence of which we accredit in certain countries acknowledged to be free. The political and moral authority correlated to freedom is the authority of this tradition, as established in these countries.

This authority dwells within the peoples of free countries and is only occasionally reaffirmed symbolically by national rituals, solemn or joyful. But all forms of freedom, such as self-government, the rule of law, and tolerance of religious and irreligious convictions, are sustained by this authority which ensures civil intercourse, disseminates a widespread sense of public responsibility, and fosters affection for one's own people. Where these arts and affections are lacking, or to the extent to which they are lost, a malaise spreads through civic life, and freedom becomes insecure—as happened throughout Western Europe, including England, during the 1930's.

Various writers, both in Britain and America, have accordingly acknowledged in recent years that traditions—specifically the traditional practices of freedom—can alone secure the continued existence of free institutions. These writers attempt to reconcile progress with its original enemy, tradition, by affirming that the process of continuous social improvement forms a part of the traditions of a free society (as against that of a feudal or ritualistic society) and that any progress which proceeds step-wise must rely on the existing society as its matrix, and thereby testify to its own respect for tradition.

We shall better appreciate this appeal to tradition as the ultimate ground on which all explicit formulations of liberty must rest by recalling how the same appeal was made 165 years ago by Edmund Burke in the face of a rising Jacobinism.

The Jacobins had got hold of two English political theories in a French version. The first originating with Hobbes, claimed the absolute sovereignty of a secular society in pursuit of its own interest and, in consequence, also the absolute power of the sovereign to enforce what is necessary in the social interest. The second theory, going back to Locke, sought to establish freedom by demanding that governments should derive their powers from the consent of the governed. The two were amalgamated by Rousseau into the doctrine of the General Will, which may force men to be free.

The Jacobins used this theory to justify the comprehensive destruction of the historic framework of France and the establishment in its place of a rule of perfect virtue and happiness. Such a comprehensive transformation leaves no justification to any opposition, for it abolishes all standards by which it could be criticised. The revolutionary authority thus eliminates the logical possibility of ever being judged wrong: and any opposition to it must appear, therefore, as always totally evil.

Burke's appeal to tradition involved a qualification both of Locke's theory and of Hobbes'. When he described society as 'a partnership in all science, a partnership in all art, a partnership in every virtue and in all perfection' and declared that 'as the ends of such a partnership cannot be obtained in many generations, it becomes a partnership not only between those who are living, but between those who are living, those who are dead, and those who are to be born', he restricted the freedom of the subjects to exercise their consent, as well as the sovereign's right to exercise his power. Thus he also restrained the political theory of freedom from ever carrying its own conclusions to the point where it might destroy the framework of a civic tradition on which this theory is predicated.

The Legacy of Jacobinism

Burke's teaching, which appealed from the spoken to the unspoken rules of freedom, remained henceforth the silent presupposition of British liberalism. It was not explicitly incorporated in its theory as formulated by Mill, and it could not be, for the prevailing liberal movement of the time was Benthamite in its emphasis on legal and social reform, and denounced tradition as the chief obstacle to progress. But reliance on civic tradition was retained implicitly in the presuppositions of a natural social harmony and of a common good—presuppositions on which the liberal theory of the 19th century rested.

In the light of Burke's teaching, the outbreak of Jacobinism was due to the literal pursuit of sound political principles within a community not equipped with the traditional practice and wisdom through which these principles must be interpreted. The Rights of Man were a good summary of the legal maxims defining the ancient liberties enjoyed by Englishmen and as such could be effectively incorporated into the Constitution of the United States whose people shared the practice of these liberties. To Frenchmen it was merely a speculative doctrine, the attempted realisation of which inevitably led to disaster: as they tried to work from a recipe without the know-how, the stuff blew up into their faces.

But Burkeian admonitions were inevitably condemned to remain fruitless. For it is of the essence of a tradition to remain unformulated, and traditions can therefore be transmitted only by the personal apprenticeship of succeeding generations to the example of their elders. The doctrine of Burke could only prophesy the doom of communities not already blessed with a tradition of civic freedom: they must choose between continued stagnation or the risk of being disrupted and destroyed by speculative excesses.

The disasters of the 20th century were essentially the fulfillment of this doom to which Burke's teaching so casually assigned the non-English-speaking peoples. The heritage of Jacobinism continued to alienate European intellectuals from the existing social order and to fix their aspirations on a comprehensive reconstruction of society to be achieved by a violent upheaval. Yet before these disasters set in, liberalism had gained great achievements in Europe, well beyond the limits allowed by the prognosis implied in Burke's teaching. The soil of Europe was not so unprepared for the implantation of freedom as it might have seemed at the time of the outbreak of Jacobinism For, though most continental countries lacked a complete liberal tradition, many ancient strains of freedom were woven into the fabric of their culture. The religious freedom of Jews and Mohammedans was secure in the 13th century over important Mediterranean regions of Europe. Intellectual emancipation from priestly authority prevailed throughout most of Italy during the Renaissance, and intellectual freedom was renewed under Enlightened Absolutism. Frederick II of Prussia established a large measure of religious tolerance. Though the legal guarantees of freedom were incomplete under his rule, the majesty of the law was acknowledged by Frederick as superior to that of the King. And, already, the new spirit of nationalism was fostering everywhere that sense of civic conviviality which makes popular self-government possible.

Deriving guidance from these traditional strains, liberalism spread gradually into Europe after the French Revolution. The process became steady and rapid after the defeats of Austria by Prussia and Italy in 1866–67. The period from 1867 to 1914, in which free institutions arose throughout the Continent, also saw the gradual assuagement of the revolutionary spirit, at least in Western and Central Europe. The spectre which—according to Marx's Manifesto—haunted the Chancelleries of Europe in 1848 had dissolved by the beginning of the 20th century, Marxism itself having been domesticated by the German Social Democratic party.

Thus, for a time, the prophecy flowing from Burke's teaching was mercifully mocked by the victory of civility all over Western and Central Europe. But this prophecy came true further East, in Russia, with shattering effects on all the previous achievements of liberalism. Here in Russia, there had arisen an excess of theoretical aspirations over practical wisdom, even more extravagant than in 18th century France. The years in which this explosive mixture was formed were those of the seventh decade of the 19th century, which Trotsky has called the 'little 18th century' of Russia. This decade produced the nihilist movement with its almost insane hatred of existing institutions, amounting to a total repudiation of all human ties. Nihilism called for merciless violence to destroy society and achieve power on its ruins, and thus produced the conspiratorial conception of political action on which the Communist movement was to be based. In this conspiratorial milieu, the theories of Marx spread rapidly, for they endowed the prevailing apocalyptic vision with an aura of scientific necessity.

The totalitarianism of Lenin was more comprehensive than that of Jacobinism, to the same extent to which nihilist scepticism goes beyond mere anti-religious rationalism. A dictatorship of 'Virtue' and 'Reason' retains idealistic standards which a strict materialism ignores, and the scope of a materialistic ideology is correspondingly much wider and more detailed. Its imposition necessarily involves a more complete suppression of liberty.

Russian totalitarianism spread in the wake of liberal ideas in Asia and Eastern Europe, carried mainly by discontented and zealous intellectuals, Konrad Heiden's 'armed bohemians', inexperienced in peaceful political life. Its example gained followers also throughout Europe, in sufficient numbers to disrupt civic concord and to imperil freedom in countries like Germany, Austria, Italy, and Hungary, which had already successfully passed through the danger zone of liberal transformation. Freedom was eventually destroyed in those regions by a Fascist counter-revolution which had armed itself with the nihilism of its Communist opponents.

The Second World War ravaged large parts of Europe and left dominion over them divided between Stalin and his Western allies. But during the time which has since elapsed, a new stage of political development seems to have emerged in these areas. The peoples of countries which had previously been internally divided by frenzied factions have shown a new capacity for attending harmoniously to the conduct of their public affairs. Germany, Austria, Finland, Belgium, which were scenes of latent or open civil war during the 1930's, represent today examples of civic reconciliation which offer prospects for the lasting establishment of free institutions. In France, also, political warfare is much less violent than it was in the 1930's, and the tension seems to be ebbing year by year. Even in countries which do not strikingly show this process of recivilisation, the intensity with which violent political illusions are held has undoubtedly decreased. The shattering floods raised by the Russian Revolution seem to be receding in Europe even while they are still mounting higher in Asia. Of the eight European satellites which came under the dominion of Soviet Russia after the Second World War, one of the most important, Yugoslavia, has since deserted her, and has achieved a measure of internal reconciliation. In at least four others, East Germany, Poland, Czechoslovakia, and Hungary, Communism is as universally rejected as in neighbouring Finland, West Germany, and Austria.

A Rebirth of Liberalism?

However, the souring of old illusions does not necessarily produce a fresh appetite for reality. There is still an inordinate amount of political hysteria about. Much of it is the hysteria of anti-capitalists who nurse their unchanging resentment of existing society, even though they no longer can see any radical alternative to this society. But in part it also stems from excited anti-socialists who still keep confusing public life by their hypochondriac fears. With their gaze fixed on the lands stricken by Communism, they detect incipient symptoms everywhere of 'creeping socialism': an obsession quite widespread in America. Too many people are still glaring at each other through the angry masks of obsolete ideologies.

Moreover, our discarded costumes have become the raging fashion among hundreds of millions of Asiatics and Africans, deluded by our past examples and precepts. The theorie of Marxist Socialism, about to be forgotten in the countries of their origin, are fast becoming the centrepiece of Asiatic and African folklore. The violent sentiments of the illiterate native masses—universal hatred of the white man, Moslem fanaticism in the Arab countries, orgiastic frenzy in Africa—are all harnessed without difficulty by a Westernised native intelligentsia to their own sophisticated conspiratorial projects.

Even though Western opinion may be on its way to recover its balance, can it appease the turmoil which its earlier teachings have caused among its Eastern and African followers? Perhaps not, unless the Soviet Union adds its influence to our own in this direction—as it might conceivably do. The loss of Yugoslavia to the Soviet Empire may have educational effects on the successors of Stalin similar to those which the loss of the United States to the British Empire had on the successors of Lord North and George III. Assume, for example, that Tito finds he has profited, in term of internal stability, by his lenience towards Djilas and Dedjier. May not the Russians then plump for Nagy against Rákosi in Hungary?* If so, they could hardly fail to try this method of stabilisation by relaxation also internally in Russia, and in its relation to other affiliated states.

These speculations may seem fantastic; but then who would have believed in 1948 that six years later Tito would be forming a military alliance with Greece and Turkey, even while amicably negotiating a trade agreement with Soviet Russia? The next six years may offer chances for even more profound transformations. In any case, the kind of speculations I have outlined do illustrate in my view the kind of world policies to which an energetic revival of liberalism throughout the West might open the way.

We are spending far too much time beating our breasts and sympathetically trying to see the follies of Russians, Asiatics, and Africans from *their* point of view (which in any case is but the point of view we held and transmitted to them thirty years ago). If we looked at these

---

* Imre Nagy did replace Rákosi but in October 1956 the Russians invaded Hungary to depose him and two years later he was hanged.

happenings instead from our point of view, on which we now stand, we would be more likely to discover right ways of taking action; and besides, this might also give us a chance of recovering the intellectual leadership of the world which the exportation of a doctrinaire liberalism has foolishly lost us.

Part III

The Theory and Practice
of Science

Introduction to Part III

The articles grouped in Part III present together a comprehensive version of Polanyi's philosophy of science. The main features are: his rejection of Objectivist and Positivist accounts of it as a precise, impersonal, body of knowledge, acquired by following strict and explicit rules, which is based solely on observed data and does not refer beyond them to any supposed reality; and, in contrast, his own proof, by appeal to the actual history, procedures and results of scientific research, that it is necessarily imprecise and personally upheld and accredited; that its rules and methods can only be partially formulated and always have to be applied, modified and supplemented by the personal judgment of the scientist; and that its whole purpose and value lies in its bearing on reality. These points are articulated in the first four articles, the fourth appropriately summing up Polanyi's work in this field, while the fifth and sixth expound Polanyi's defence, against Reductionism, of the distinctiveness of biology and his account of how living beings, as comprehensive entities, transcend the physical elements and forces of which they are composed, and thus also the conceptions and methods of physics and chemistry.

15

Science: Observation and Belief

A part of the general Objectivist and Positivist account of knowledge is that it is impersonal, a knowledge without a knower, a knowledge to which the knower makes no contribution, or, if he does, he thereby vitiates it with 'subjectivism'. Polanyi took his arguments against such conceptions to the very sciences which Objectivists and Positivists claimed to exemplify them. All knowledge, he showed, rests upon personal acts of integration, judgment and commitment, and these are directed to the truth *and* validity *of what we know. But Objectivists and Positivists try to eliminate the notion of truth. This article is included because it contains some arguments and examples for the fiduciary basis of natural science which are not found in Polanyi's books.*

I

People who believe in science do not usually regard this as a personal act of faith. They consider themselves as submitting to evidence which by its nature compels their assent and which has the power to compel a similar measure of assent from any rational human being. For modern science was founded on a critical struggle against authority. Critical thought broke the fetters of Aristotelian and of Biblical authority. Descartes led the way by his programme of universal doubt: *de omnibus dubitandum*. The Royal Society was founded with the motto: *nullius in verba*. We accept no authority. Bacon had claimed that science was to be based on purely empirical methods, and *hypotheses no fingo*, No speculations! echoed Newton. Science has been through the centuries the scourge of all creeds which embodied an act of faith and was supposed—and is

[44]. Reprinted from *Humanitas* (Manchester), I, Feb. 1947, pp.10–15.

commonly still supposed—to be built, in contrast to these creeds, on a foundation of hard facts. It is thought that in science facts alone count.

Yet it is quite easy to see that this is not true, as David Hume had found jut already some 200 years ago. The argument can be stated without any verbal ambiguities in simple mathematical terms. Suppose the evidence on which a scientific proposition is to be based consists of a number of measurements made at various observed times or in coincidence with some other measurable parameters. Let us in other words have pairs of two measured variables V_1 and V_2. Can we decide from a series of points V_1 blotted against V_2 whether there is a function $V_1 = f(V_2)$ and if so, what it is? Clearly we can do nothing of the kind. Any set of pairs of V_1 and V_2 variables is compatible with an infinite number of functional relations between which there is nothing to choose from the point of view of the underlying data. To choose any of the infinite possible functions and give it the distinction of a scientific proposition is so far without any justification. The measured data are insufficient for the construction of a definite function $V_1 = f(V_2)$ in exactly the same sense as two elements of a triangle are insufficient to determine a definite triangle.

This conclusion is not altered but only obscured by introducing the element of scientific prediction. For one thing, prediction is not a regular attribute of scientific propositions. Kepler's laws and the Darwinian theory predicted nothing. At any rate, successful prediction does not fundamentally change the status of a scientific proposition It only adds a number of observations, the predicted observations, to our series of measurements and cannot change the fact that any series of measurements is incapable of defining a function between the measured variables.

Since some readers may be reluctant to accept this, I shall illustrate it a little further. Suppose a player of roulette observes the numbers or colours that have turned up in a hundred consecutive throws. He may plot them in a graph and derive a function in the light of which he will make a prediction. He may try it out and win. He may try again and win. And win a third time. Would that prove this generalisation? No, it would, in our view, only prove that some roulette players are very lucky—i.e., we would consider these predictions to be mere coincidences.

A few years ago I saw in *Nature* a table of figures proving with great accuracy that the time of gestation, measured in days, of a number of different rodents is a multiple of the number π. An exact relationship of this kind makes no impression on the modern scientist and no amount of further confirmatory evidence would convince him that there is any relation between the period of gestation of rodents and multiples of the number π. Anyone who has friends among astrologers can have from them instances of strikingly fulfilled predictions which would be hard to rival in science. Yet scientists refuse even to consider the merits of astrological predictions. In science itself I could tell you of the most amazing predictions gone true, like the discovery of heavy hydrogen, which turned out to be based on premises which later were found to be quite erroneous. There is no definite and rational criterion by which the accidental fulfillment of a prediction can be discriminated from its true confirmation.

Scientists and philosophers who are convinced that science can be based exclusively on data of experience, have tried to avoid the weight of such critical analysis of science by reducing the claims of science to a more moderate level. They point out that scientific propositions do not claim to be true, but only to be likely. That they do not predict anything with certainty, but only with probability. That they are provisional and make no claim to finality.

All this is entirely beside the point. If anyone claims that, given two angles of a triangle, he can construct the triangle, his claim is equally nonsensical, whether he claims to give a true construction or merely a probable construction, or the construction of a merely probable triangle. The selection of one element out of an infinite set of elements all of which satisfy the conditions set by the problems, remains equally unjustifiable whatever positive quality we attach to our selection. Its value is exactly nought. In fact, scientists would object just as much to serial rules in games of chance or astrological predictions, or to relations between time of gestation of rodents and the number π, whether these are claimed with certainty, or only with probability or else merely provisionally. They would be regarded as no less nonsensical for that.

Nor does another attempt to lessen the burden of responsibility on scientists' shoulders prove more successful. Science, it is said, does not claim to discover the truth but only to give a description or summary of observational data. But why then object to astrology or to the description of periods of pregnancy in multiples of the number π? Obviously, because these are not held to be true or rational descriptions; which brings the problem back exactly to where it was before. For it is no easier to find a justification for picking out one description of the observational data as true or as rational than it is to pick out any other relationship whatever its claims may be.

Again, the attempt has been made to lessen the difficulty of justifying the claims of science by suggesting that the statements of science do not claim to be true except in the sense of being simple. But this of course is pure nonsense. Scientists do not reject astrology, magic or the cosmogony of the Bible because these are not simple enough. That has nothing to do with it; unless indeed the word 'simple' is tortured into meaning 'rational', and finally made to coincide with 'true'.

II

So whichever way we turn we cannot avoid being faced with the fact that the validity of scientific statements is not compellingly inherent in the evidence to which they refer. Those who believe in science must, therefore, accept that they are placing on the evidence of their senses an interpretation for which they must themselves take a considerable amount of responsibility. In accepting science as a whole and in subscribing to any particular statement of science, they are relying to a certain extent on a personal conviction of their own.

Some of these personal convictions we derive from our own upbringing. The commonly accepted causal interpretation of nature on which all scientific thought is based we absorb automatically when growing up in a modern environment. It is in sharp contrast to the magical outlook of primitive cultures in which all events that have any bearing on the interests of man are exempted from ordinary causation and assumed to be due to magic influence, whether beneficent or malign. This magical outlook is apparently more readily acceptable to man than the causal view of events. It prevails in the child's approach to its surroundings, who is inclined to think that everything that happens to it is the result of a purposive action of some obscure agency. The magic outlook underlies also our works of fiction in which everything that happens to a character in the course of the story must have some justification in the sense of the story; otherwise it is not a work of art but a meaningless chronicle. Not fiction, but simply an untrue and irrelevant statement. People who normally use the magical outlook are of the same average grade of intelligence as their naturalistically instructed fellow men. But to them the scientific way of thinking is inaccessible over a large area, namely wherever human interests are involved.

The rejection *in limine* of the evidence of astrology is a definite consequence of a break with the magical outlook. But there are more specific beliefs than that involved in the acceptance of science. Take for example our rejection of the evidence connecting the period of gestation of rodents with the multiples of the number π. This represents a comparatively recent point of view in science. To a scientist like Kepler there would have been nothing repugnant in the relationship suggested here. He had himself derived the existence of the then known seven planets and the relative size of their orbits from a supposed connection with the existence of seven perfect solids and the relative size of spheres inscribed in them and enveloping them, the edges of the solids being taken to be constant. The science of his generation was still largely pursuing the Pythagorean supposition of the world being governed by the number rules and geometrical relationships. The fundamental discovery of Pythagoras of acoustic harmonies connected with simple ratios of the length of chord emitting the tone, had impressed this supposition for centuries on the speculative mind. The discovery of Copernicus was still largely based on it.

It would take me too long to trace here in detail the successive stages through which the premisses of science have passed from Kepler's day to our own. The main period from Galileo to Young, Fresnel and Faraday was dominated by the idea of a mechanical universe consisting of matter in motion. This was modified by the field theories of Faraday and Maxwell but not radically changed so long as the postulate of a material ether was upheld. Until the end of the 19th century, scientists believed implicitly in the mechanical explanation of all phenomena. In the last 50 years these premisses of science were abandoned but not without having caused considerable delay in the progress of discoveries which were inaccessible from such premisses. A good deal of evidence for the existence of the electron had been available for a long time before it overcame the resistance offered by the assumptions of Galileo that all properties of matter had to be explained by mass in motion. An entirely new assumption was imported into science from Mach's philosophy by Einstein in his discovery of relativity. Mach had set out to eliminate all tautologies from scientific statements: Einstein assumed that by modifying our conceptions of space and time on the lines of such a programme it should be possible to draw up a system which would eliminate some existing anomalies and possibly lead to new verifiable conclusions. This is the 'epistemological' method which is profoundly ingrained today in our conception of the universe. We may illustrate this by the following event. In 1928 a reputable American physicist called Milner repeated for the first time after a generation, Michelson's experiment on which the theory of relativity was originally based. Equipped with the most modern instruments he thought he had a good right to check up on these rather hoary observations of a great master. His results controverted those of Michelson and he announced this to a representative gathering of physicists. But not one of them thought for one moment of abandoning relativity. Instead—as Sir Charles Darwin described it—they sent Milner home to get his results right.

Twenty years after the discovery of relativity there came a further fundamental modification of our outlook on nature by the acceptance of a purely statistical interpretation of atomic interactions. Einstein who was then 45 years old rejected this view on the grounds of common sense. He continued to believe, and still believes, alone among physicists, so far as I know, that atomic processes are fundamentally causal. He does not believe that any process can be fundamentally indeterminate. His old friends have reproached him that he was sticking to the same kind of prejudice by which the opponents of relativity had obstructed its path in earlier years. But in spite of that and of much persuasion on the part of Niels Bohr, Einstein holds fast to his dissenting view of nature. Maybe he is right.

III

We can see even from this brief sketch how the beliefs of scientists regarding the essence of nature are held by them on their own responsibility, underlying their methods of discovery and determining their readiness to accept a certain type of evidence or to reject it as the case may be.

The whole activity of scientists is based on a set of surmises of different grades. Some held as implicit, quite unconscious beliefs, others as more or less definite assumptions, others again entertained as personal hunches. They are embodied in the general aims of all sciences and in their general methods. They are to be found taking on special shapes in each separate branch.

Little or nothing of these beliefs of science is codified. They are not taught as such in textbooks, it is impossible to formulate them in explicit terms. They are impalpable, like the rules of an art They are, in fact, rules of an art. They are transmitted personally from master to pupil by the imitation of the practice of discovery and of the practice of verification. This is why science has such a strong local tradition in certain countries. It is extremely difficult to transplant science to new countries lacking that tradition.

There is no essential difference in this connection between science as it emerges in the process of discovery and science as established in textbooks. At all stages of consolidation science must ultimately rely on a set of beliefs derived mainly from the scientific tradition. That is why science cannot be taught properly unless its teaching is informed by the personal experience of discovery. Such a spirit alone can restore to science that fundamental uncertainty and plasticity, that sense of in exhaustible new possibilities, which are proper to science at all stages of achievement.

Moreover, we have to realise that apart from beliefs held in common with other people—whether other scientists or members of the general public—there is an element of personal judgment in every scientific affirmation. Personal creative judgment is at the source of all discovery. And again it is indispensable at each stage of research, not the least at the end when a claim is to be made in public. In the case of many great discoveries, such as the Copernican system, or Darwinism, Mendelism, the bacterial theory, relativity, quantum mechanics, etc., the evidence at first does not induce general approval among scientists. The discoverer has to put his claim forward supported by his own conviction alone. But in any case, there is always a conceivable doubt of any particular statement in science, and it is the last resort for the scientist's conscience to decide whether the doubt is reasonable or not.

Science, we find, cannot be based on a radical empiricism but is on the contrary invalidated from the empiricist point of view by an analysis of its observational foundations. The validation of science is based, in fact, apart from sense experience, on the holding of certain beliefs which are: (1) partly instilled in us by general tradition and held implicitly by all modern men; (2) partly accepted by scientists as an element of the scientific tradition; and (3) partly nurtured as individual hunches; or else (4) affirmed as the dictates of our personal consciences. In other words, science is based on experience selected and interpreted in the light of certain traditional, intuitive and conscientious beliefs.

IV

Science cannot go on relying much longer on an empiricism which does not in fact justify its claim to validity. Powerful forces are already taking advantage of this weakness. It leaves science defenseless against a radical denial of its objectivity. It opens the door to its Marxist interpretation which would reduce science to an ideology. It invites the intervention of the State to direct the pursuit of science in the visible interests of society. (I have discussed this situation at some length on other occasions).

Science, free science, can survive in future only by recognising and consciously affirming its true basis: its groundwork of scientific beliefs. Scientists must henceforth profess their adherence to these beliefs by an explicit declaration of faith. But why should we believe in anything? In anything that we could also disbelieve? Why should we follow a tradition that is the example of people who have died long ago and who knew less about our problems than we do? Why should we share the beliefs which scientists hold today, which they are quite likely to change again before long? Why should we allow ourselves to beguiled by our own hunches in research or in accepting or rejecting some modern theory? Why should we wrestle with our scientific conscience and try to satisfy its demands?

Why indeed? I do not propose to attempt a full answer to this question. But one or two suggestions my be made here. A path to a conscious acceptance of belief may be found in the fact that we must believe in something. There is no way short of death or idiocy to keep all our judgments in suspense. All we can do is to drive out all positive and explicit forms of beliefs until we are left to hold only instinctive and unconscious beliefs. *There is no reason why involuntary beliefs should be better than beliefs which we deliberately profess.* To assume this was the fundamental error of rationalism since Descartes. This critical age of ours has seen outbreaks of fanaticism rarely paralleled in the history of professed creeds. Our most critical and advanced minds have often succumbed to propaganda and shown a measure of gullibility which was not common among intellectual leaders of less hard-boiled centuries. Any thinking person must believe in something uncritically, for he must believe in the premisses of his own thinking. Cogito ergo credo—I think, therefore I believe. Let us accept this fact and believe with open eyes. We have then a chance to hold our beliefs in mature consideration of alternative beliefs, and not merely to succumb to some uncontrolled residue of belief.

For that end we may also seek contact with other essentials of our civilisation which require to be upheld by a positive belief. Science has close relations with other realms of truth. The new scientific approach to nature which arose in the 16th century was the fruit—and a late fruit— of the same movement which liberated art, literature, scholarship and religious conscience. The new demands for an open-minded and fair examination of evidence was paralleled in many other fields of life. It soon entered into public life by the new doctrine of tolerance—that great contribution of England, Holland and America to modern civilisation. The scientific mode of thought caused also a revolution in law. Within a few decades of the foundation of the Royal Society the law of evidence was radically reformed and placed on a scientific basis.

All these developments hang together and are commonly rooted in the great traditions of our civilisation: in the tradition of intellectual integrity descended from the Greeks, of legal reason inherited from Rome and of brotherhood inspired by Christianity. These traditions embody transcendent beliefs which for centuries could safely be taken for granted. They cannot be so taken any more today. Our whole civilisation, including science, now needs reformation by a positive profession of the beliefs which form its foundation.

16

Science and Reality

When he came to defend the freedom of scientific research against Marxist proposals for incorporating it within a central plan, Polanyi found that contemporary accounts of science virtually ceded the Marxist case in advance by denying that it had any claim to truth and to revealing reality and by saying that it was merely an 'economical' or 'simple' way of recording and mathematically manipulating observational data. Yet, because he also insisted that scientific methods, like everything else in human life, cannot be reduced to an explicit and precise casuistry or algorithm, but depend essentially upon the trained judgment and connoisseurship of the scientist which he has acquired by apprenticeship to an acknowledged master, he was denounced, as by Popper and his disciples, as a 'subjectivist'. This article is included because it is his fullest treatment of the way that science does bear upon reality and of the necessity of recognising that intention.

The purpose of this essay is to reintroduce a conception which, having served for two millennia as a guide to the understanding of nature, has been repudiated by the modern interpretation of science. I am speaking of the conception of reality. Rarely will you find it taught today, that the purpose of science is to discover the hidden reality underlying the facts of nature. The modern ideal of science is to establish a precise mathematical relationship between the data without acknowledging that if such relationships are of interest to science, it is because they tell us that we have hit upon a feature of reality. My purpose is to bring back the idea of reality and place it at the centre of a theory of scientific enquiry.

[126]. Reprinted, with permission from Oxford University Press, from *The British Journal for the Philosophy of Science*, XVIII, 1967, pp. 177–96.

The resurrected idea of reality will, admittedly, look different from its departed ancestor. Instead of being the clear ad firm ground underlying all appearances, it will turn out to be known only vaguely, with an unlimited range of unspecifiable expectations attached to it.

It is common knowledge that Copernicus overthrew the ancient view that the sun and the planets go round the Earth and that he established instead a system in which it is the sun that is the centre around which all planets are circling, while the Earth itself goes round the sun as one of the planets. But we do not see it recognised that in the way Copernicus interpreted this discovery, he and his followers established the metaphysical grounds of modern science. We cannot find this recognised, since these grounds of science are predominantly contested today.

The great conflict between the Copernicans and their opponents, culminating in the prosecution of Galileo by the Roman hierarchy, is well remembered. It should be clear also that the conflict was entirely about the question, whether the heliocentric system was real. Copernicus and his followers claimed that their system was a real image of the sun with the planets circling around it; their opponents affirmed that it was no more than a novel computing device.

For thirty years Copernicus hesitated to publish his theory, largely because he did not dare to oppose the teachings of Aristotle by claiming that the heliocentric system he had set up was real. Two years before the publication of his book is 1543, the Protestant cleric Osiander responded to preliminary publications of the Copernican system by a letter pressing Copernicus to acknowledge that science can only produce hypotheses representing the phenomena without claiming to be true. Later, Osiander succeeded in introducing an Address to the Reader into the published book of Copernicus denying once more the reality of the Copernican system. The issue was still the same, more than half a century later, in Kepler's defence of Tycho Brahe against his critic Ursus, and the same again when Galileo confronted Cardinal Bellarmine and afterwards Pope Urban VIII.

The conflict was settled, at least for secular opinion, when the Copernican system was confirmed by Newton. Copernicus and his followers were recognised then to have been right; and for the two following centuries their steadfastness in defending science was unquestioningly honoured among modern educated people.

I myself was still brought up on these sentiments; but by that time some eminent writers were already throwing cold water on them. The positivist critique of science, initiated by Ernst Mach[1], and vigorously supported by Henri Poincaré[2], declared that the claim which Copernicus, Kepler and Galileo so bitterly defended was illusory. This radical positivism taught that science consisted merely in establishing functional relationships between the data observed by our senses and that any claim that went beyond this was undemonstrable. A reality underlying mathematical relations between observed facts was a metaphysical conception, without tangible content.

During the past half century these formulations of positivism have been first sharpened into logical positivism, which claimed to establish strict criteria for the meaning and validity of all empirical statements. But logical positivism, after reaching its highest prestige in the forties, presently declined for its aims proved unattainable. Its theories were softened down then by a series of qualifications, which amounted to abandoning any attempt at establishing a formal criterion of the meaning and validity of a scientific statement. The rise of analytic philosophy confirmed this abdication by abandoning the critique of science. Thus we are left today without any accepted theory of the nature and justification of natural science.

There has been sharp opposition to the positivist movement by individual authors, among them Planck[3] and Einstein,[4] as well as the great historian of science, Alexandre Koyré;[5] but these authors supplied no statement of the true metaphysical foundations of science. This is the situation in which I shall examine the Copernican's claim that the heliocentric system was a true account of reality. And I shall show that in their conception of reality we can find the actual grounds on which science has rested ever since Copernicus established modern science on these grounds.

In order to explain what made Copernicus feel that the new system he proposed was real, I shall give an outline of an important feature of the old system and show the way the new system dealt with this feature.

When you watch a planet night after night you see its position shifting through the firmament of fixed stars. Seen from a point in the northern hemisphere, it moves predominantly from west to east, but does not move steadily. It speeds up, slows down, retraces its path and continues eastward again. It passes through these loops at regular intervals. The Ptolemaic system explained these loopings by assuming that the planet—instead of simply moving round its orbit—is carried round this orbit, as it were, on the edge of a wheel. While the wheel moves round the planet's orbit,

FIGURE 1

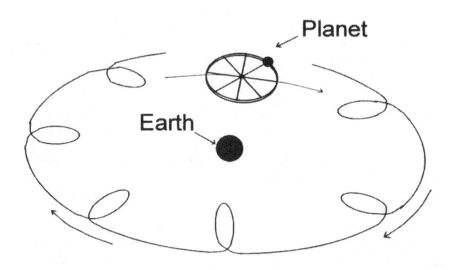

it keeps turning around its own axle and thus—when seen from the Earth—produces the loops in the planet's journey round its orbit. Such wheels are known as epicycles, and the particular type I have described, are the major epicycles. (Fig. 1.) The path along which the epicycles are carried round is known as the deferent.

The effect of epicyclic motion can be analysed more closely by assuming that the planet has for a moment discontinued its main eastward motion around its orbit. Viewed from the Earth at rest, the image of the plant among the fixed stars would oscillate then at the rate of its passage around the epicycle (Fig. 2.). Add then to the oscillation once more the orbital motion from west to east and you obtain the looping as observed from Earth. (Fig. 3.)

The fundamental idea of Copernicus was that instead of having the planets circling on epicyclical wheels, we can get the same effect by putting the Earth into a circular motion round the sun. You can see how this works if you imagine once more, a planet arrested for a moment in its orbital motion and then trace its image against the firmament of stars. The image oscillates in the same way as the planet was seen to oscillate in the Ptolemaic system. (Fig. 4.) And if we again add to this oscillation

FIGURE 2

PTOLEMY

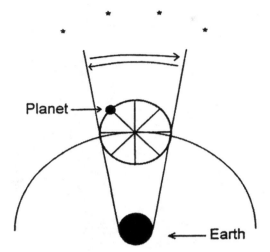

the eastward orbital motion of the planet, we see arising the observed looping. But the loops are now mere illusions, without any underlying epicyclical motion.

Let me add some further features of the Ptolemaic system which were known before Copernicus. *First,* all the wheels representing major epicycles were seen to go round at the same rate, and this common period of the epicycles was found to equal *one year.* Hence a planet like Mars, with an orbit of about two years, passes through one loop in rounding its orbit; while Jupiter, which completes its orbit in twelve years, passes through eleven loops, and Saturn, taking about thirty years to go round, makes twenty-nine loops on its way[6]. *Second,* it was observed and noted that the apparent size of the loops decreases with the increasing length of orbital periods from Mars, through Jupiter to Saturn.

To these two observations about the major epicycles, we may add as a *third* point a widespread speculative idea abut the size of the orbits around which the planets and the sun were thought to circle round the Earth. In order to understand, however roughly, the grounds for this idea, suppose for a moment that all these circling bodies go round their orbit at the same speed, so that the time each takes to get round its orbit would be

FIGURE 3

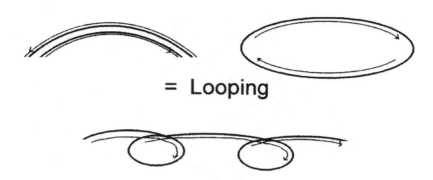

Oscillation + Circling

= Looping

proportional to the radius of its orbit. The orbit of Saturn should then be the largest, Jupiter's smaller and Mars's smaller still. More will be said later about the derivation of this sequence.

Turning now to the heliocentric theory of Copernicus, we find that the three main features of the Ptolemaic system fit in well with the new theory. Firstly, once epicycles are replaced by an illusory oscillation corresponding to the annual motion of the Earth around the sun, all these oscillations must occur at the same rate equalling one year. Secondly, we can see that, in the Copernican system, differences in the observed angles of oscillations imply that the planets are at different distances from the sun (Fig. 5). The observed decrease in the angles of oscillations in the sequence of Mars, Jupiter and Saturn yields then the conclusion that the orbital radii of these planets increase in this order, which accords with the ancient surmise, that the size of planetary orbits steadily increases as the orbital period gets longer.

I have so far based the transformation of the Ptolemaic system into Copernican terms on the three outer planets known to Copernicus, and must now introduce the two inner planets Venus and Mercury. When applied to the inner planets, the meaning of Fig. 1 is inverted. The period

FIGURE 4

COPERNICUS

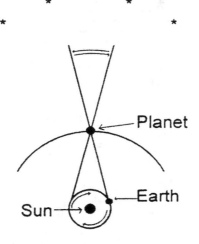

of the epicycle becomes the orbital period of the planet, and the period of the deferent becomes the period of the planet's oscillation, i.e. of its illusory motion due to the Earth's annual passage round the sun. For Venus and Mercury the amplitude of these oscillations is found to fall in line with that of the outer planets, and accordingly the calculated solar distance of Venus comes out smaller than that of Mars and the solar distance of Mercury smaller still than that of Venus. All three features of the Ptolemaic system are thus confirmed for the inner planets, when their deferents are taken as equivalent to the major epicycles of the outer planets.

Looking at this result with the eyes of a modern scientist, I would say that the most striking achievement of the new theory was that it explained the strange fact that the observed periods of loopings were all identical and equal to one terrestrial year. But these coincidences strike us as strange only because they are inexplicable in terms of mechanics. Copernicus had no idea that planetary motions were due to mechanical causes and hence his explanation of these coincidences, which is a triumph to our way of thinking, made no such impression on him. To us the very fact that the Copernican system eliminates the major epicycles by which Ptolemy explained the loopings of the planets, is a great achievement.

FIGURE 5

COPERNICUS

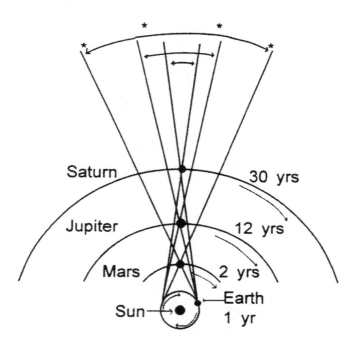

But Copernicus does not explicitly mention this, presumably because he used epicycles readily in other parts of his system, and so they were nothing strange to him.

To the scientist today the mere prediction of the relative orbital radii of the planets is a great achievement of the Copernican system. But Copernicus sees it mainly in relation to the sequence of planetary distances derived from a mistaken theory.

His theory of this sequence is stated in *De Revolutionibus*, book I, chapter 10, in two passages, one at the beginning the other later. I quote the second passage first for it is more explicit.

Quapropter prima ratione salve manente, nemo enim conventiorem allegabit, quam ut magnitudinem orbium multitudo temporis metiatur, ordo spaerum sequitur in hunc modum a summo capiens initium... (Capiens||capientes MS.) (*De Revolutionibus*, ed. Thoruni 1873, L. Prowe, E. de Losson, Boethke, Hagemann, p.28.)

This reads in translation:

> Therefore, if the first law is still safe—for no one will bring forward a better one than that the magnitude of the orbital circles should be measured by the magnitude of time—then the order of the planets will follow in this way...
> (C. G. Wallis, *Great Books of the Western World*, vol. 16, Chicago (1952)).

To say that the radii are 'measured by the magnitude of time' is to assert that the linear velocity of all planets is the same[7]. The words at the opening of the chapter appear to bear this out.

> Errantium vero seriem penes revolutionum suarum magnitudinem accipere voluisse priscos philosophos videmus, assumpta ratione, quod aequali celeritate delatorum, quae longius distant, tardius ferri videntur, ut apud Euclidem in Opticis demonstratur.

'aequali celeritate delatorum', i.e. 'objects moving with equal speed' could conceivably be construed as a hypothetical statement by Euclid but as it fits in with the subsequent description of the planets, this description appears to be its meaning.

Copernicus rejoices that the sequence of the planets computed by him conforms to the law derived from the equality of linear speeds. But, of course, the same sequence is obtained by Kepler's Third Law under which it is the squares of times that are proportional to the cube of the radii. The relation from which Copernicus derived the sequence of the planets was grossly erroneous. Could he have failed to notice the error? I think he knew his mistake.

In his *Commentariolus*, composed a number of years before *De Revolutionibus*, Copernicus presents the computation of the relative radii for the three outer planets as follows:

> Saturn's deferent revolves in 30 years, Jupiter's in 12 years, and that of Mars in 29 months; it is as though the size of the circles delayed the revolutions. For if the radius of the great circle is divided into 25 units, the radius of Mars' deferent will be 38 units, Jupiter's $130^1/_5$ and Saturn's $230^1/_6$. By 'radius of the deferent' I mean the distance from the centre of the deferent to the centre of the first epicycle.
> (*Three Copernican Treatises*, translated with introduction by E. Rose 2nd ed., Dover Publications, New York, p. 74. Note that the 'great circle' means the orbit of the Earth.)

The ratios of the figures $230^1/_6 : 130 : 38 : 25$ agree within about 2 per cent with Kepler's Third Law, but they greatly differ from the corresponding ratios of the orbital periods, which are $29.5 : 12 : 2 : 1$. Comparing the ratios for Saturn and Earth, that is the ratio $230^1/_6$: 25 with the ratio 29.5 : 1, the discrepancy between them amounts to about a *factor three,* and when we extend these ratios to include Mercury, the deviation from proportionality rises *nearly to a factor five.* I believe it was these deviations from proportionality that Copernicus had in mind when he wrote: 'It is as though the size of the circles delayed the revolutions'. This delay would, e.g. have to reduce the speed of Saturn to close on one-fifth of the value predicted by Copernicus in order to make its actual speed agree with the observed speed of Mercury. This could not have gone unnoticed by Copernicus.

Consultations with historians have failed to reveal a place in literature mentioning this error; it seems to have been overlooked. My point in bringing it up is to suggest that Copernicus disregarded this discrepancy, because his conception of physical magnitudes in the celestial domain was but vague and that this vagueness must have been worsened still further by his knowledge of this discrepancy. Seen against this background, his prediction of the radii could not have for him the solidity which it has for the modern scientist, for whom most other details of the Copernican system are, by contrast, mere fictions.

What remained then for Copernicus to convince him of the reality of his system? We can sum it up in one sentence. He had succeeded in explaining planetary loopings by a theory which, when introducing the actually observed periods and amplitudes of oscillations, predicts a plausible sequence of orbital radii. It was this achievement to which Copernicus fastened his hopes during thirty years of travail and on the grounds of which he and his followers claimed, against bitter opposition, that the heliocentric system was real.

In his preface addressed to Pope Paul III Copernicus writes that he has

at last discovered that, if the motions of the rest of the planets be brought into relation with the circulation of the Earth and be reckoned in proportion to the orbit of each planet, not only do their phenomena presently ensue, but the orders and magnitudes of all stars and spheres, nay the heavens themselves, become so bound together that nothing in any part thereof could be moved from its place without producing confusion of all the other parts and of the universe as a whole.

Everything is now bound together, he claims, and this is a sign that the system is real[8].

But why did this claim evoke such protest among his contemporaries, particularly the clergy? The objection was not raised primarily in de-

FIGURE 6
Three Views of Science

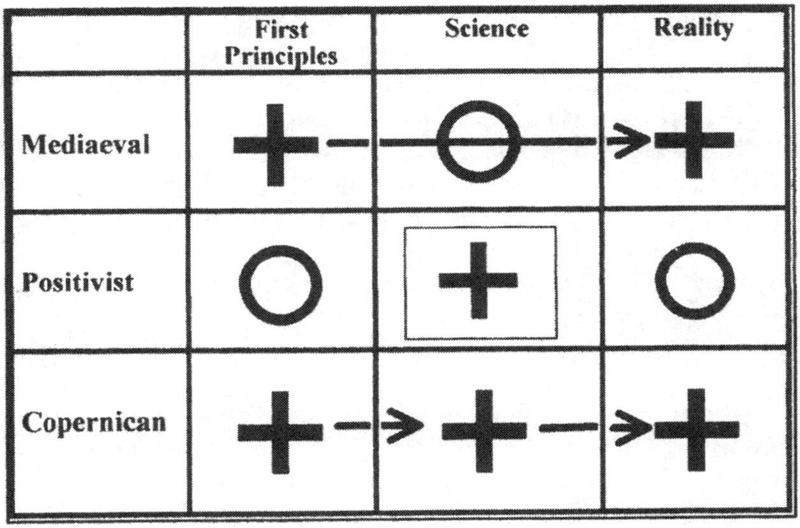

	First Principles	Science	Reality
Mediaeval	➕	⭕	➤➕
Positivist	⭕	➕	⭕
Copernican	➕➤	➕➤	➕

fence of the bible, but of medieval philosophy held by clerics and lay scholars alike, since the day of Aquinas 300 years before. The philosophic view which clerics from Osiander to Bellarmine and lay scholars like Melanchton defended, goes back to Aristotle. It assumed that all basic features of the universe can be derived from necessary first principles; for example, the perfection of the universe required that the course of all heavenly bodies be represented by steady circular motions. Such views excluded the possibility of discovering basic features of nature by the empirical observations of the astronomer; any theory established by representing astronomical observations could only be regarded as a mere computing device, and this applied as much to the Ptolemaic system as to that of Copernicus. Only philosophy was competent to arrive at an understanding of essential reality in nature.

Centuries later the positivists declared once more that science can say nothing about ultimate reality, but theirs was a very different reason, namely that they thought any such claim to be meaningless. Their purpose was not to preserve to philosophy the competence for metaphysical theories, but on the contrary, to purify science from making any such empty claims.

The meaning of these two different attacks on Copernicanism, the medieval and the positivist attacks, and the position of Copernicus himself, can be illustrated by a diagram as follows.

(1) In the medieval position first principles bear directly on reality, while excluding science from such bearing. (2) The positivist movement is shown isolating science on the one hand from any extra-scientific first principles and on the other hand from reality, since neither of these is recognised. Science, regarded merely as a convenient summary of given facts, is strictly self-contained. (3) Copernicanism is shown, thirdly, claiming to apply basic principles *through empirical science* for discovering reality.

Copernicus did not contest the competence of philosophy to arrive at necessary conclusions about the nature of things. When Osiander reminded him that his astronomy falls to explain the motions of the planets[10], he must have agreed that these motions could be understood only from first principles and not from his astronomy. His strict adherence to the steady circular motion of heavenly bodies, which made his system inordinately complicated and clumsy, showed him to be basically an Aristotelian. But he was irresistibly compelled by the appearance of his own system to claim that this particular feature of the celestial order, though derived essentially from experience, was true and real. Thus did he make for the first time the metaphysical claim that science can discover new knowledge about fundamental reality and thus did this claim eventually triumph in the Copernican revolution.

Such is the claim of science to know reality, that positivism disowned in our time; and it is this same metaphysical claim, now widely discredited, that I want to re-establish today.

Let me start by asking, what Copernicus meant by saying, that his system was real? What had he actually in mind when believing that the planets really circle the sun? We shall find a clue to this question if we first look at the more active form of this belief which Kepler and Galileo manifested when undertaking their enquiries. They testified to their belief that the Copernican system was real, by relying on it as a guide to discovery.

I shall show this for Kepler. His Third Law, discovered seventy-six years after the death of Copernicus, developed the feature of the helio-centric system which Copernicus had mentioned as its most striking harmony, namely the fact that all six planets recede steadily further from the sun in the sequence of their longer orbital periods. Kepler lent precision to this relationship by showing that the cube of solar distances is proportional to the square of the orbital periods. His other great discovery—ten years earlier—of his First and Second Laws, was in some sense a departure from Copernicus. It broke away from the doctrine of steady circular planetary motions and introduced instead an elliptic path and a law of variable velocities related to the ellipse. Yet this elliptic path, with the sun in one focus of it, was firmly tied to the helio-centric system. It could not have been discovered from Ptolemy's image of the planetary system.

I would not hesitate to say that these discoveries proved the reality of the Copernicus system, but this is only because I know that Newton discovered towards the end of the same century that these three laws of Kepler were expressions of the law of universal gravitation. At the time at which Kepler put his laws forward, mixed up with a number of other numerical rules that were to prove fallacious, the effect of his three laws was not widely convincing; Galileo himself was unimpressed by them. But for the moment I can set these questions aside, for I am only trying to understand what Kepler and Galileo themselves believed about the Copernican system, when they relied on their conviction that it was real and thus a proper guide to their enquiries.

At first glance it seems easy to see what happened in Kepler's and Galileo's minds. Relying on the reality of the Copernican system, they recognised the presence of problems, which by many years of labour they proved to have been fruitful. But this leaves open the question, how the Copernican system could indicate to them good problems that were not visible in the Ptolemaic system.

We meet here a general issue, which to my knowledge, has never been systematically examined. We must ask: What is a problem? Not the kind of problem set to students of mathematics, or to chemists in practical classes, but a scientific problem the solution of which is unknown, and on which the scientist may yet embark with a reasonable hope of discovering something that is new and that will prove also worth the labour and expense of the search.

I would answer that to have such a problem, a good problem, is to surmise the presence of something hidden, and yet possibly accessible, lying in a certain direction. Problems are evoked in the imagination by circumstances suspected to be clues to something hidden; and when the problem is solved, these clues are seen to form part of that which is discovered, or at least to be proper antecedents of it. Thus the clues to a problem anticipate aspects of a future discovery and guide the questing mind to make the discovery.

We may say then that Kepler's conviction that the Copernican system was real, was expressed by his belief that its image anticipated aspects something hidden and possibly accessible by an enquiry in a certain direction. And we may add that he *confirmed* these anticipations when, by following their guidance, he discovered his three laws.

Nor was this all. For in their turn, Kepler's discoveries raised new problems in Newton's mind, insofar as they anticipated aspects of the still hidden laws of gravitation, which Newton was to discover. Thus Newton was guided still further by a belief in the reality of the Copernican system.

The confidence which the followers of Copernicus placed in the reality of the Copernican system consisted, then, in surmising still hidden implications in it, as were suggested to them by certain features of the system. Their belief in the system's reality was an act of their imagination that spurred and guided them to discovery.

Let us take stock of the position we have reached so far. In the history of the Copernican Revolution we have found it possible to discriminate the explicit statements of a theory from its anticipatory powers. The celestial time-table set out by Copernicus was not markedly different from that of Ptolemy. Close on to a century following the death of Copernicus, all efforts to discriminate convincingly between the two systems on the grounds of their observable quantitative predictions had failed. While the discoveries of Kepler and Galileo based on the heliocentric system greatly increased its plausibility and eventually convinced most astronomers, the general effect, judged for example by the critical responses of Bacon or Milton, was far from conclusive. Yet all this time the theory of Copernicus was exercising heuristic powers absent in the system of Ptolemy. We are faced with the question then how one of two theoretical systems, having virtually the same explicit content, could vastly exceed the other in its anticipations.

In a way I have given the answer to this question in the anticipatory suggestions offered by the Copernican system to the followers of Copernicus. Its anticipatory powers lay in the new image by which

Copernicus recast the content of the Ptolemaic system. It is in the *appearance* of the new system that its immense superiority lay; it is this image that made the Copernican revolution.

I am drawing here a distinction which will prove decisive. I distinguish between the precise predictive content of a mathematical theory consisting in a functional relation of measured variables and a meaning of the theory which goes beyond this. While the functional relations remain the same, the surplus of meaning which goes beyond them may vary, as manifested in this case by the appearance of the theory.

The way this may come about can be illustrated from everyday life. Suppose we have a list of all the towns of England, each with its precise longitude and latitude, and the number of its inhabitants, and we now represent these data in a map, each town being marked by a circle corresponding to its size. The mapping of the list adds no new data to it, yet it conveys a far deeper understanding of these data. It reveals, for example, the way the population is distributed through the country and suggests questions about the reasons of physical geography and history which will account for this distribution. The map will guide the imagination to enter on fruitful enquiries to which the original list would leave us blind.

E. M. Forster has shown a similar difference between two kinds of characters in a novel. There are *flat* characters whose behaviour can be precisely predicted and *round* characters which develop creatively; the latter, says Forster, are more real and hence have the power convincingly to surprise us. By bearing on reality, scientific theories too have the power convincingly to surprise us.

But here I must enter a warning. The distinction between explicit content and informal heuristic powers is profound, but not absolute. No mathematical theory means anything except as understood by him who applies it, and such an act of understanding and applying is no explicit operation; it is necessarily informal. Indeed, great discoveries can be made by merely finding novel instances to which an accepted theory applies. For example, Van t'Hoff's demonstration that the mass action law of chemistry was an instance of the Second Law of thermodynamics was a fundamental discovery. When I speak of the explicit content of a theory, I refer to such applications of it which are fairly obvious, and I distinguish these from *a yet indeterminate meaning of a theory that may be revealed only much later, through a scientist's imagination.*

But was Copernicus himself, when expressing his belief in the reality of his system, in fact asserting that it had anticipatory powers, which the Ptolemaic system had not?

It is not clear how anticipatory powers can be known at all, apart from relying on them as clues to an enquiry. Copernicus obviously did not know that his system represented an aspect of Kepler's laws and of Newton's theory of general gravitation; indeed, being wedded to an explanation of the planetary system in terms of steady circular motions, he would have strictly rejected Kepler's laws and Newton's theory based on these laws. Yet his belief that his system was real, was basically akin to that of his great successors. For he saw the essence of his system in those features of it which were to serve as clues to the problems of Kepler and Newton. He saw in the increase of orbital periods with increasing solar distance the characteristic feature of a system in which the sun centrally controls the order of planets, and this is the feature on which Kepler and Newton were to build their discoveries.

But there is actually a more general kinship between the commitment of Copernicus to his belief that his system was real and that of his followers relying on it for their problems. What Copernicus believed of this system was what we all mean by saying that a thing is real and not a mere figment of the mind. What we mean is that the thing will not dissolve like a dream, but that, in some ways it will yet manifest its existence, inexhaustibly, in the future. For it is there, whether we believe it or not, independently of us, and hence never fully predictable in its consequences. The anticipatory powers which Kepler, Galileo and Newton revealed in the heliocentric system, were as many particulars of *the general anticipations that are intrinsic to any belief in reality.*

This defines reality and truth. If anything is believed to be capable of a largely indeterminate range of future manifestations, it is thus believed to be *real*. A statement about nature is believed to be true if it is believed to disclose an aspect of something real in nature. A true physical theory is believed to be no mere mathematical relation between observed data, but to represent an aspect of reality, which may yet manifest itself inexhaustibly in the future.

We can ask then why the general appearance of the heliocentric system made Copernicus and his followers believe that it was real—why its close coherence, its intellectual harmonies had such power to convince them of its reality. And to this we reply that the existence of a harmonious order is a denial of randomness, and order and randomness are mutually exclusive. Moreover, anything that is random is meaningless, while anything that is orderly is significant[11].

To recognise the principle at work here, think of the difference between a tune and a noise; or, more generally, between a message and a noise. Communication theory defines a noise, in contrast to any distinctive series of signals, as random sequence, and it says that, being random, noise conveys no information—means nothing. This implies an important difference in the identifiability of an ordered sequence, as compared with a noise. Any single message is represented ideally by only one configuration of signals, while for a noise the very opposite holds. No significance must be attached to any particular configuration of signals that are a noise; we must indiscriminately identify any one configuration of a noise with any other configuration of it.

This is true of any aggregate deemed random: we must assume that the chance events which compose it could have as well happened otherwise. And, by contrast, once we have recognised an aggregate of events as orderly and meaningful, we may not believe that they might as well have happened differently. Such an aggregate is an identifiable thing, possessing reality in the sense I have defined it; namely, that it may yet manifest itself inexhaustibly in the future. To distinguish meaningful patterns from random aggregates is therefore to exercise our power for recognising reality.

Our capacity for discerning meaningful aggregates, as distinct from chance aggregates, is an ultimate power of our personal judgment. It can be aided by explicit argument but never determined by it: our final decision will always remain tacit. Such a decision may be so obvious, that in it our tacit powers are used effortlessly and thus their use remains unnoticed; our eyes and ears continuously commit us to such effortless decisions. But other decisions of the same class may be hard and momentous. A jury may be presented with a pattern of circumstantial evidence pointing to the accused. It is always conceivable that this pattern may be due to chance; but how unlikely a chance should they admit to be possible? Or else, what degree of coincidence should be deemed quite unbelievable? The prisoner's life and the administration of justice will depend on the decision, and there is no rule by which it can be decided. This is precisely why it is left to the jury to decide it.

I have said that reality in nature is a thing that may yet manifest itself inexhaustibly, far beyond our present ken. Something must be added to this description, if the pursuit of natural science is to be justified. Consider that the Copernican revolution was but a continuation of a structuring that had its origins in antiquity. Copernicus deepened and beautifully clarified a coherence transmitted to him by Ptolemy. And this triumph pointed further beyond itself in the mind of Copernicus. In Kepler, passionately embracing the system of Copernicus, its image was to evoke anew the kind of creative hunger which Copernicus had satisfied by discovering it. And the presence of yet hidden truth worked its way further. To Newton, Kepler's three laws appeared to hang covertly together and he established this fact by his theory of gravitation, which derived all the laws jointly from the mechanics of Galileo. Nor was this the end, for a quarter of a millennium later, Einstein was to find unsatisfying the co-existence of the Newtonian system with the electromagnetic theory of light, and was to discover an even deeper coherence reconciling the two.

The continued pursuit of science is possible, because the structure of nature and man's capacity to grasp this structure, can be such as is exemplified by this sequence of discoveries covering two millennia. It does happen, that nature is capable of being comprehended in successive stages, each of which can be reached only by the highest powers of the human mind. Consequently, to discover a true coherence in nature is often not only to discern something which, by the mere fact of being real, necessarily points beyond itself, but to surmise that future discoveries may prove the reality of the thing to be far deeper than we can at present imagine.

It may seem strange that I insist on a belief in the reality of theoretical suppositions as the driving force to discovery. Such belief would seem a conservative assumption, rather than a source of innovation. The positivist view of science would indeed claim that the major discoveries of modern physics were based on a sceptical attitude towards the framework of hitherto accepted scientific theories. The discovery of relativity involved abandonment of the current conceptions of space and time, and quantum mechanics achieved its breakthrough by discarding Bohr's planetary system of electrons circling the nucleus. Einstein himself acknowledged that Mach's positivist philosophy had inspired his work and Heisenberg's quantum mechanics was deliberately framed to reduce atomic theory to a functional relation of observable quantities.

These revolutionary heresies may seem to contradict my thesis, but I think they fall in line with it, once I make clearer the opposite extreme of creative procedure, based on a firm belief in the reality of the current framework of scientific theory. We may recognise the prototype of such a feat in the discovery of America by Columbus. He triumphed by taking literally, and as a guide to action, that the earth was round, which his contemporaries held vaguely and as a mere matter of speculation. The egg of Columbus is the proverbial symbol for such breath-taking originality guided by a crudely concrete imagination. I remember having this feeling when first hearing of Einstein's theory of Brownian motion. The idea that the meandering oscillations of small floating particles seen by a botanist under the microscope, should reveal the impact of molecules hitting the articles in tune with the highly speculative equations of the kinetic theory of gases, impressed me as grossly incongruous. I experienced the same shock of a fantastic idea, when I heard Elsasser suggesting (in 1925) that certain anomalies observed in the scattering of electrons by solids may be due to the optical interference of their de Broglie waves. We had all heard of these waves since 1923, yet were astounded by the fact that they could be taken as literally as Elsasser did.[12.]

This should remind us that the first great move towards the discovery of quantum mechanics was de Broglie's idea of the wave nature of matter. This revolutionary idea and Schrodinger's development of it into wave mechanics, shows no trace of positivistic influences. Add to this, that Max Planck, the founder of quantum theory, actively opposed Mach's analysis of science and also dissented from Heisenberg's claim of basing physical theories on directly observable quantities[13]; and that Einstein himself, whose principle of relativity served as an inspiration to modern positivism, was sharply critical of Mach's analysis of science as a mere relation of observed facts[14]. It appears then, that the predominant principle that shapes modern physical theory was not the positivist programme, but the transition from a mechanical conception of reality to a mathematical conception of it, which sometimes coincided with the positivistic programme for the purification of science.

We can thus bring the revolution of the twentieth century in line with the Copernican revolution of the sixteenth and seventeenth centuries. Both revolutions consisted in a stepwise deepening of coherence with simultaneous extension of its range. The modern revolution differed from its precursor only in establishing mathematical harmonies in place of beautiful mechanical systems.

The mathematical image of reality is more abstract than the mechanical but its capacity to point beyond its immediate predicative content is similar to that of the mechanical image. I have said that the fact that the wave nature of particles postulated by de Broglie could be confirmed by diffraction experiments, came as a fantastic surprise to physicists. The discovery of the positron occurred just as unexpectedly in confirmation of a prediction contained unnoticed in Dirac's quantum theory of the electron (1928).

In my account of the Copernican revolution and of the modern revolution in physics, I have mentioned only in passing the contributions made by new experimental observations. But the examples I gave were typical of the way at this time experiments often followed their theoretical anticipation, the connection being sometimes not recognised at first. Usually, theoretical speculation and experimental probing enter jointly to the quest towards an ever broader and deeper coherence.

This brings up the question, how the actual process of discovery is performed. Much has been written about this with which I disagree, but for the moment I can put my own views only quite summarily. To see a good problem is to see something hidden and yet accessible. This is done by integrating some raw experiences into clues pointing to a possible gap in our knowledge. To undertake a problem is to commit oneself to the belief that you can fill in this gap and make thereby a new contact with reality. Such a commitment must be passionate; a problem which does not worry us, that does not excite us, is not a problem; it does not exist. Evidence is cast up only by a surmise filled with its own particular hope and fervently bent on fulfilling this hope. Without such passionate commitment no supporting evidence will emerge, nor failure to find such evidence be felt; no conclusions will be drawn and tested—no quest will take place.

Thus the anticipatory powers that we have seen at work in historical perspective, arouse and guide individual creativity. These powers are ever at work in the scientist's mind, because he believes that science offers an aspect of reality and may therefore manifest its truth ever again by new surprises.

In this essay I have tried to define the mental powers by which coherence is discovered in nature. But the coherence achieved by the Copernican Revolution filled with dismay those brought up on the medieval order of the universe. The Earth's central position which had been the symbol of man's destiny as the only thinking morally responsible being, was lost. Gone was the divine perfection of an immutable firmament encircling the place where fallen man was ever to strive for salvation beyond this place. 'It is all in pieces, all coherence gone', wrote John Donne as early as 1611.

The destruction was deepened by the revival of atomism. Dante had said of Democritus that he 'abandoned the world to chance'. And Dante was right. The assumption that all things are ultimately controlled by the same laws of atomic interaction, reduces all forms of existence to mere collocations of ultimate particles. Such is the kind of universe that we have inherited from the Copernican Revolution. In it no essentially higher things exist, nor can intangible things be real. To understand the world then consists in representing throughout all that is of greater significance in terms of less meaningful elements and if possible, in terms of meaningless matter. Accepting such a conception of truth and reality, man is confused by his own lucidity and blighted by his self-doubt.

The anti-metaphysical critique of science marks the stage at which a false conception of truth and reality attacks science itself, from which it had first originated. If we can overcome these false ideals of knowledge in science, this might set an example for our whole outlook and, backed by the very prestige of science, might help to overcome scientism everywhere.

Once the recognition of anticipatory powers in science establishes a conception of reality transcending tangible things, we might be able generally to acknowledge higher entities, intangible and yet real—as real as matter and yet meaningful. We shall recognise thus a cosmic hierarchy in which man has once more his own place[15].

Notes

1. Ernst Mach, *Die Mechanik in ihrer Entwicklung* (1883).
2. Henri Poincaré, *Science et Hypothese*, Paris (1902), pp. 140–1, and Henri Poincaré, *La Valeur de La Science*, Paris (1914), pp. 271–4. In the latter book Poincaré defends himself against being taken to reject Galileo's affirmation that the Copernican system was true. He identifies convenience with coherence and ascribes to coherence the value of a greater truth than that which Galileo had claimed.
3. See n.13 below.
4. Albert Einstein, Biographical Notes in *Albert Einstein Philosopher-Scientist*, ed. P.A. Schlipp, New York (1949), p.49, writes about Ostwald and Mach:

   'The antipathy of these scholars towards atomic theory can indubitably be traced back to their positivistic philosophical attitude. This is an interesting example of the fact that even scholars of audacious spirit and fine instinct can be obstructed in the interpretation of facts by philosophical prejudices. The prejudice—which has by no means died out in the meantime—consists in the faith that the facts by themselves can and should yield scientific knowledge without free conceptual construction'.

5. Alexandre Koyré, *Les Origines de la Science Moderne*, Diogene, October 1956, no. 16, attacks positivism for denying that science has knowledge of reality.

6. In reply to an enquiry, Professor S. Sambursky of the Hebrew University of Jerusalem wrote as follows: 'The Almagest in fact does mention the relevant figures for the epicyclic loops of the planets and their amplitudes (in Book IX, ch.3, and Book XII), but Ptolemy of course fails to interpret these data, and their numerical relations are mere coincidences for him'. The knowledge of this relationship is clearly taken for granted by Rheticus in the *Oratio Prima* (1540), but I could find no mention of it in *De Revolutionibus*.

7. F. Dobson and S. Brodetsky, *Nicolaus Copernicus, De Revolutionibus*, Preface and book 1, Roy. Astron. Soc. 1947, translate 'prima ratione salve manente' as 'given the above view' which seems better than 'if the first law is still safe'. They translate 'quam ut magnitudinem orbium multitudo temporis metiatur' as 'that the periodic times are proportional to the sizes of the orbits' which is perhaps too free, even though substantially right.

8. 'The motion of the Earth, therefore, suffices to explain why so many apparent inequalities in the heavens', wrote Copernicus in *Commentariolus*. That coherence is a token of reality, is expressed by Rheticus in is *Narratio Prima* (1540) by the words: 'So wise is our maker, that each of his works has not one use, but two or three or often more'.

9. Note, the term 'science' is used here in the modern sense as applying to astronomy.

10. In his Address to the Reader prefacing the *De Revolutionibus*, Osiander says of the celestial movements, that the astronomer '...cannot by any line of reasoning reach the true causes of these movements...'

11. I disregard here statistical laws, as they apply to another level of reality. (See my *Personal Knowledge*, p.390).

12. This paper was delivered as a lecture at Duke University, Durham, N.C., in February 1964. James Franck lived at that time in Durham and we met to discuss my talk. Franck began very quietly, almost in a whisper, saying: 'You know, I am one of those literals'. He clearly was very pleased. During his great career, spent among conceptual revolutionaries like Planck, Einstein, Bohr, Heisenberg, Schrodinger, Born, he must often doubted the quality of his own genius and he as glad to find its place acknowledged in my analysis. I think that among great discoveries the one most purely based on a literal acceptance of current ideas, was Laue's discovery of the diffraction of X rays; but Langmuir too triumphed by the powers of a literal imagination, and many of Rutherford's discoveries were based on daringly primitive conceptions.

13. Max Planck, *Scientific Autobiography and Other Papers*, Philosophical Library, New York (1949), p. 129, Tr. Fr. Gaynor. (Original title of this essay was 'Der Causalbegriff in der Physic' first published in 1948.) 'It is absolutely false, although it is often asserted, that the world picture of physics contains, or may contain, directly observable magnitudes only. On the contrary, directly observable magnitudes are not found at all in the world picture. It contains symbols only'. In this essay (p. 139) he also objects to the elimination of seemingly unverifiable statements: 'I must take exception to the view (a very popular one these days, and certainly a very plausible one on the face of it), that a problem in physics merits examination only if it is established in advance that a definite

answer to it can be obtained. If physicists had always been guided by this principle, the famous experiment of Michelson and Morley undertaken to measure the so-called absolute velocity of the earth, would never have taken place, and the theory of relativity might still be nonexistent'.

14. In his Autobiographical Notes 1. c, p. 53, Einstein writes about his redefinition of reality as follows: 'The type of critical reasoning which was required for the discovery of this central point was decisively furthered, in my case, especially by the reading of David Hume's and Ernst Mach's philosophical writings'. But Einstein did not confirm Mach's teaching that the Newtonian doctrine of absolute rest is meaningless; Einstein proved, on the contrary, that Newton's doctrine, far from being meaningless, was false.

15. The basic ideas of this paper were first stated in Chapter 1, 'Science and Reality' of my *Science, Faith and Society* (1946), and summarised in the introduction to the Phoenix Edition(1964) of that book. For the relation of Copernicus to Medieval thought I have benefited from Ernan McMullin 'Medieval and Modern Science: Continuity or Discontinuity', *International Philosophical Quarterly* (1965), 103. Mr Rom Harré (Oxford) showed me unpublished evidence of Melanchton's anti-realistic views on astronomy expressed in his violent attack on Averroës. Mr Harré, Professor Samuel Sambursky (Jerusalem) and Mr J. R. Ravetz (Leeds) all read my manuscript and suggested corrections from which I substantially benefited. Dr J. D. North (Oxford) helped me not only by commenting on the finished manuscript, but also before this, by discussions during my final formulation of my historical account of Copernicus. But I am, of course, responsible for all the content of this paper.

17

Creative Imagination

In the previous article Polanyi briefly mentioned the creative role in science of the questing imagination. This article pays particular attention to the role of the questing imagination in going beyond what is already known in order to sense and articulate new coherences, something denied by Positivist views of science. Polanyi explicates that role by applying his account of how we tacitly integrate subsidiary clues, often not known in themselves, into a focal awareness of a comprehensive whole.

The enterprise that I am undertaking in this article has been severely discouraged by contemporary philosophers. They do not deny that the imagination can produce new ideas which help the pursuit of science or that our personal hunches and intuitions are often to the point. But since our imagination can roam unhindered by argument and our intuitions cannot be accounted for, neither imagination nor intuition is deemed a rational way of making discoveries. They are excluded from the logic of scientific discovery, which can deal then only with the verification or refutation of ideas after they have turned up as possible contributions to science.

However, the distinction between the production and testing of scientific ideas is not really so sharp. No scientific discovery can be strictly verified, nor even proved to be probable. Yet, we bet our lives every day on the correctness of scientific generalisations, for example those underlying our medicine and technology. Admittedly, Sir Karl Popper has

[118]. Reprinted from *Chemical & Engineering News*, XLIV, April 1966, pp.85–93, with permission from the American Chemical Society, © 1966, American Chemical Society.

pointed out that, though not strictly verifiable, scientific generalisations can be strictly refuted. But the application of this principle cannot be strictly prescribed.

It is true that a single piece of contradictory evidence refutes a generalisation, but experience can present us only with apparent contradictions and there is no strict rule by which to tell whether any apparent contradiction is an actual contradiction. The falsification of a scientific statement can therefore no more be strictly established than can its verification. Verification and falsification are both formally indeterminate procedures.

There is in fact no sharp division between science in the making and science in the textbook. The vision which guided the scientist to success lived on in his discovery and is shared by those who recognise it. It is reflected in the confidence they place in the reality of that which has been discovered and in the way they sense the depth and fruitfulness of a discovery.

Any student of science will understand—must understand—what I mean by these words. But their teachers in philosophy are likely to raise their eyebrows at such a vague emotional description of scientific discovery. Yet, the great controversy over the Copernican system, which first established modern science, turned on just such vague emotional qualities attributed to the system by Copernicus and his followers, which proved in their view that the system was real.

Moreover, after Newton's confirmation of the Copernican system, Copernicus and his followers—Kepler and Galileo—were universally recognised to have been right. For two centuries their steadfastness in defending science against its adversaries was unquestioningly honoured. I myself was still brought up on these sentiments.

But at that time some eminent writers were already throwing cold water on them. Poincaré wrote that Galileo's insistence that the earth was really circling round the sun was pointless, since all that he could legitimately claim was that this view was the more convenient. The distinguished physicist, historian, and philosopher, Pierre Duhem, went further and concluded that it was the adversaries of Copernicus and his followers who had recognised the true meaning of science, which the Copernicans had misunderstood. Although this extreme form of modern positivism is no longer widely held today, I see no essential alternative to it emerging so far.

Let us look then once more at the facts. Copernicus discovered the solar system by signs which convinced him, but these signs convinced few others. For the Copernican system was far more complicated than that of Ptolemy: It was a veritable jungle of ad hoc assumptions. Moreover, the attribution of physical reality to the system met with serious mechanical objections and involved also staggering assumptions about the distance of the fixed stars. Yet Copernicus (*De Revolutionibus*, Preface and Book 1, Chapter 10) claimed that his system had unique harmonies which proved it to be real even though he could describe these harmonies only in a few vague emotional passages. He did not stop to consider how many assumptions he had to make in formulating his system, nor how many difficulties he ignored in doing so. Since his vision showed him an outline of reality, he ignored all its complications and unanswered questions.

Nor did Copernicus remain without followers in his own century. In spite of its vagueness and its extravagances, his vision was shared by other great scientists like Kepler and Galileo. Admittedly, their discoveries bore out the reality of the Copernican system, but they could make these discoveries only because they already believed in the reality of the system.

We can see here what is meant by attributing reality to a scientific discovery:

- It is to believe that it refers to no chance configuration of things, but to a persistent connection of certain features, a connection which, being real, will yet manifest itself in numberless ways, inexhaustibly.
- It is to believe that it is there, existing independently of us, and that hence its consequences can never be fully predicted.
- Our knowledge of reality has then an essentially indeterminate content: It deserves to be called a vision. The vast indeterminacy of the Copernican vision showed itself in the fact that discoveries made later in the light of this vision would have horrified its author. Copernicus would have rejected the elliptic planetary paths of Kepler and, likewise, the extension of terrestrial mechanics to the planets by Galileo and Newton. Kepler noted this by saying that Copernicus had never realised the riches which his theory contained.

Clues Often Not Sensed

This vision, the vision of a hidden reality, which guides a scientist in his quest, is a dynamic force. At the end of the quest the vision is becalmed in the contemplation of the reality revealed by a discovery; but the vision is renewed and becomes dynamic again in other scientists and guides them to new discoveries. I shall now try to show how both the dynamic and the static phases of a scientific vision are due to the strength of the imagination guided by intuition. We shall understand then both the grounds on which established scientific knowledge rests and the powers by which scientific discovery is achieved.

I have pursued this problem for many years by considering science as an extension of ordinary perception. When I look at my hand and move it about, it would keep changing its shape, its size, and its colour, but for my capacity for seeing the joint meaning of a host of rapidly changing clues, and seeing also that this joint meaning remains unchanged. I recognise a real object before me from my awareness of the clues which bear upon it.

Many of these clues cannot sensed in themselves at all. The contraction of my eye muscles, for example, I cannot experience in itself. Yet I am very much aware of the working of these muscles indirectly, in the way they make me see the object at the right distance and as having the right size.

Some clues to this we see from corner of our eyes. An object is very different when we see it through a blackened tube, which cuts out these marginal clues.

We can recognise here two kinds of awareness. We are obviously aware of the object we are looking at but are aware also—in a much less positive way—of a hundred different clues which we integrate to the sight of the object. When integrating these clues we are attending fully to the object while we are aware of the clues themselves without attending to them. We are aware of them only as pointing to the object we are looking at. I shall say that we have a subsidiary awareness of the clues in their bearing on the object to which we are focally attending.

While an object on which we are focusing our attention is always identifiable, the clues through which we are attending to the object may be often unspecifiable. We may well be uncertain of clues seen from the corner of our eyes and we cannot experience in themselves at all such subliminal clues as, for example, the effort at contracting our eye muscles.

But it is a mistake to identify subsidiary awareness with unconscious or preconscious awareness, or with the Jamesian fringe of awareness. What makes an awareness subsidiary is the function it fulfills; it can have any degree of consciousness so long as it functions as a clue to the object of our focal attention. To perceive something as a clue is sufficient by itself therefore to make its identification uncertain.

Science is Seeing Things in Nature

Let me return now to science. A science is a manner of perceiving things in nature, we might find the prototype of scientific discovery in the way we solve a difficult perceptual problem. Take for example the way we learn to find our way about while wearing inverting spectacles. When you put on spectacles that show things upside down, you feel completely lost and remain helpless for days on end. But if you persist in groping around for a week or more, you find your way again and eventually can even drive a car and climb rocks with the spectacles on. This fact, well known today, was in essence discovered by Stratton some 30 years ago. This experience is usually said to show that after a time the visual image switches round to the way we normally see it. But some more recent observations have shown that this interpretation is false.

It happened, for example, that a person perfectly trained to get around with upside down spectacles was shown a row of houses from a distance. He was then asked whether he saw the houses right way up or upside down. The question puzzled the subject and he replied, after a moment, that he had not thought about the matter before, but now that he is asked about it he finds that he sees the houses upside down. Such a reply shows that the visual image of the houses, has not turned back to normal; it has remained inverted but the inverted image no longer means to the subject that the houses themselves are upside down. The inverted image has been reconnected to other sensory clues—to touch and sound and weight. These all hang together with the image once more and hence, though the image remains inverted, we can again find our way by it safely.

A new way of seeing things rightly has been established. And since the meaning of the upside down image has changed, the term 'upside down' has lost its previous meaning. It is confusing now to enquire whether something is seen upside down or right way up. The new kind of right seeing can be talked about only in terms of a new vocabulary.

We see how the wearer of inverting spectacles reorganizes scrambled clues into a new coherence. He again sees objects then, instead of meaningless impressions. He again sees real things, which he can pick up and handle, which have weights pulling in the right direction and make sounds that come from the place at which he sees them. He has made sense out of chaos.

In science, I find the closest parallel to this perceptual achievement in the discovery of relativity. Einstein has told the story how from the age of 16 he was obsessed by the following kind of speculations. Experiments with falling bodies were known to give the same result on board a ship in motion as on solid ground. But what would happen to the light which a lamp would emit on board a moving ship? Supposing the ship moved fast enough, would it overtake the beams of its own light, as a bullet overtakes the sound of the exploding cartridge by crossing the sonic barrier?

Einstein thought that this overtaking was inconceivable. Persisting in this assumption, he eventually succeeded in renewing the conceptions of space and time in a way which would make it inconceivable for a ship to overtake, however slightly, its own light rays. After this, questions about a definite span of time or space became meaningless and confusing— much as questions of 'above' and 'below' became meaningless and confusing to a subject who had adapted his vision to inverting spectacles.

It is no accident that the most radical innovation in the history of science appears most similar to the way we acquire the capacity for seeing inverted images rightly. For only a comprehensive problem, like relativity, can require that we reorganise such basic conceptions as we do in learning to see rightly through inverting spectacles. Relativity alone involves conceptual innovations as strange and paradoxical as those we make in righting an inverted vision.

The experimental verifications of relativity have shown that the coherence discerned by Einstein was real. One of these confirmations has a curious history. Einstein had assumed that a light source would never overtake a beam sent out by it, a fact that had already been established before by Michelson and Morley.

In his autobiography Einstein says that he made this assumption intuitively from the start. But this account failed to convince his contemporaries, for intuition was not regarded as a legitimate ground for knowledge. Physics textbooks described, therefore, Einstein's theory as his answer to the experiments of Michelson.

When I tried to put the record right, by accepting Einstein's claim that he had intuitively recognised the facts already demonstrated by Michelson, I was attacked and ridiculed by Professor Grünbaum of Pittsburgh, who argued that Einstein must have known of Michelson's experiment, since he could not otherwise have based his work on the facts established by these experiments.

However, if science is a generalised form of perception, Einstein's story of his intuition is clear enough. He had started from the principle that it is impossible to observe absolute motion in mechanics. When he came across the question whether this principle holds also when light is emitted, he felt that it must still hold, though he could not quite tell why he assumed this. However, such unaccountable assumptions are common in the way we perceive things and such unaccountable assumptions affect also the way scientists see things.

Newton's assumption of absolute rest itself, which Einstein was to refute, owed its convincing power to the way we commonly see things. We see a car travelling long a road and never the road sliding away under the car; we see the road at absolute rest. We generally see things as we do, for this establishes coherence within the context of our experience.

Likewise, when Einstein extended his vision to the universe and included the case of a light source emitting a beam, he could make sense of what he then faced only by seeing it in a way that the beam was never overtaken, however slightly, by its source. This is what he meant by saying that he knew intuitively that such was in fact the case.

We understand, then, why the grounds on which Copernicus claimed that his system was real could be convincing to him, though not convincing to others. For we have seen that the intuitive powers that are at work in perception integrate clues which, in being subsidiarily known, are largely unspecifiable; and we have seen that the way Einstein shaped his novel conceptions of time and space was also based on dues which were largely unspecifiable. We may assume, therefore, that this was true also for Copernicus in shaping his vision of reality.

And we may say this generally: Science is based on clues that have bearing on reality:

- These clues are not fully specifiable.
- Nor is the process of integration which connects them fully definable.
- And the future manifestations of the reality indicated by this coherence are inexhaustible.

These three indeterminacies defeat any attempt at a strict theory of scientific validity and offer space for the powers of the imagination and intuition.

Intuition Senses Hidden Truth

This gives us a general idea of the way scientific knowledge is established at the end of an enquiry; it tells us how we judge that our result is coherent and real. But it does not show us where to start an enquiry; nor how we know, once we have started, which way to turn for a solution. At the beginning of a quest we can know only quite vaguely what we may hope to discover. We may ask, therefore, how we can ever start and go on with an enquiry without knowing what exactly we are looking for.

This question goes back to antiquity. Plato set it in the *Meno*. He said that if we know the solution of a problem, there is no problem—and if we don't know the solution, we do not know what we are looking for and cannot expect to find anything. He concluded that when we do solve problems, we do it by remembering past incarnations. This strange solution of the dilemma may have prevented it from being taken seriously. Yet the problem is ineluctable and can be answered only by recognising a kind of intuition, more dynamic than the one I have described so far.

I have spoken of our powers to perceive a coherence bearing on reality, with its yet hidden future manifestations. But there exists also a more intensely pointed knowledge of hidden coherence: the kind of foreknowledge we call a problem. And we know that the scientist produces problems, has hunches, and, elated by these anticipations, pursues the quest that should fulfil these anticipations. This quest is guided throughout by feelings of a deepening coherence and these feelings have a fair chance of proving right. We may recognise here the powers of dynamic intuition.

The mechanism of this power can be illuminated by an analogy. Physics speaks of potential energy that is released when a weight slides down a slope. Our search for deeper coherence is guided likewise by a potentiality. We feel the slope towards deeper insight as we feel the direction in which a heavy weight is pulled along a steep incline. It is this dynamic intuition that guides the pursuit of discovery.

This is how I would resolve the paradox of the *Meno*. We can pursue scientific discovery without knowing what we are looking for because the gradient of deepening coherence tells us where to start and which way to turn, and eventually brings us to the point where we may stop and claim a discovery.

But we must yet acknowledge further powers of intuition, without which inventors and scientists could neither rationally decide to choose a particular problem nor pursue any chosen problem successfully. Think of Stratton devising his clumsy inverting spectacles and then groping about guided by the inverted vision of a single narrowly restricted eye for days on end. Stratton must have been firmly convinced that he would learn to find his way about within reasonable time, and also that the result would be worth all the trouble of his strange enterprise—and Stratton proved right.

Or think of Einstein, when as a boy he came across the speculative dilemma of a light source pursuing its own ray. He did not brush the matter aside as a mere oddity, as anyone else would have done. His intuition told him that there must exist a principle, which would assure the impossibility of observing absolute motion in any circumstances. Through years of sometimes despairing enquiry, he kept up his conviction that the discovery he was seeking was within his ultimate reach and that it would prove worth the torment of its pursuit; and again Einstein proved right. Kepler, too, might have reasonably concluded after some five years of vain efforts, that he was wasting his time, but he persevered and proved right.

The power by which such long-range assessments are made is practised every day on a high level of responsibility in industrial research laboratories. The director of such a laboratory does not usually make inventions but is responsible for assessing the value of problems suggested to him, be it from outside or by members of his laboratory staff. For each such problem the director must jointly estimate the chances of its successful pursuit, the value of its possible solution, and also the costs of achieving it. He must compare this combination with the joint assessment of the same characteristics for rival problems. On these grounds he has to decide whether the pursuit of a problem should be undertaken or not, and if undertaken, what grade of priority should be given to it in the use of available resources.

The scientist is faced with similar decisions. An intuition which would merely point him out problems could not tell him which problem to choose. He must be able to estimate the gap separating him from discovery and he must also be able roughly to assess whether the importance of a possible discovery would warrant the investment of the powers and resources needed for its pursuit. Without this strategic intuition, he would waste his opportunities on wild goose chases and be soon out of a job.

The intuition I have recognised here is clearly quite different from the supreme immediate knowledge called intuition by Leibniz or Spinoza or

Husserl. It is a skill for guessing with a reasonable chance of guessing right; a skill guided by an innate sensibility to coherence, improved by schooling. The fact that this faculty often fails does not discredit it; a method for guessing 10% above average chance on roulette would be worth millions.

Discovery Works in Two Steps

But to know what to look for does not lend us the power to find it. That power lies in the imagination.

I call all thoughts of things that are not present, or not yet present—or perhaps never to be present—acts of the imagination. When I intend to lift my arm, this intention is an act of my imagination. In this case imagining is not visual but muscular. An athlete keyed up for a high jump is engaged in an intense act of muscular imagination. But even in the effortless lifting of an arm, we can recognise a conscious intention, an act of the imagination, distinct from its muscular execution. For we never decree this muscular performance in itself, since we have no direct control over it. This delicately co-ordinated feat of muscular contractions can be made to take place only spontaneously, as a sequel to our imaginative act.

This dual structure of deliberate movement was first described by William James 70 years ago. We see now that it corresponds to the two kinds of awareness that we have met in the act of perception. We may say that we have a focal awareness of lifting our arm, and that this focal act is implemented by the integration of subsidiary muscular particulars. The structure of the act corresponds to that of perception, where we are focally aware of our intended performance and aware of its particulars only subsidiarily, by attending to the performance which they jointly constitute.

A new life, a new intensity, enters into this two-levelled structure the moment our resolve meets with difficulties. The two levels fall apart then and the imagination sallies forward, seeking to close the gap between them. Take the example of learning to ride a bicycle. The imagination is fixed on this aim, but our present capabilities being insufficient, its execution falls behind. By straining every nerve to close this gap, we gradually learn to keep our balance on a bicycle.

This effort results in an amazingly sophisticated policy of which we know nothing. Our muscles are set so as to counteract at every moment our accidental imbalance, by turning the bicycle into a curve with a radius proportional to the square of our velocity, divided by the angle of our imbalance.

Millions of people are cycling all over the world by skillfully applying this formula which they could not remotely understand if they were told about it. This puzzling fact is explained by the two-levelled structure of intentional action. The use of the formula is invented on the subsidiary level in response to the efforts to close the gap between intention and performance; *and since the performance has been produced subsidiarily, it can remain focally unknown.*

There are many experiments showing how an imaginative intention can evoke covertly, inside our body, the means of its implementation. Spontaneous muscular twitches, imperceptible to the subject, have been singled out by an experimenter and rewarded by a brief pause in an unpleasant noise; and as soon as this was done, the frequency of the twitches—of which the subject knew nothing—multiplied about threefold. Moreover, when the subject's imagination was stimulated by showing him the electrical effect of his twitches on a galvanometer, the frequency of the twitches shot up to about six times their normal rate.

This is the mechanism to which I ascribe the evocation of helpful clues by the scientist's imagination in the pursuit of an enquiry. But we have to remember here that scientific problems are no definite tasks. The scientist knows his aim only in broad terms and must rely on his intuition of deepening coherence to guide him to discovery. He must keep his imagination fixed on these growing points and force his way to what lies hidden beyond them. We must see how this is done.

Take once more the example of the way we discover how to see rightly through inverting spectacles. We cannot aim specifically at reconnecting sight, touch, and hearing. Any attempt to overcome spatial inversion by telling ourselves that what we see above is really below may actually hinder our progress, since the meaning of the words we would use is inappropriate. We must go on groping our way by sight and touch, and learn to get about in this way. Only by keeping our imagination fixed on the global result we are seeking, can we induce the requisite sensory reintegration and the accompanying conceptual innovation.

No quest could have been more indeterminate in its aim than Einstein's enquiry that led to the discovery of relativity. Yet he has told that during all the years of his enquiry, 'there was a feeling of direction, of going straight toward something definite. Of course', he said, 'it is very hard to express that feeling in words; but it was definitely so, and clearly to be distinguished from later thoughts about the rational form of the solution'. We meet here the integration of still largely unspecifiable elements into a gradually narrowing context, the coherence of which has not yet become explicit.

The surmises made by Kepler during six years of toil before hitting on the elliptic path of Mars were often explicit. But Arthur Koestler has shown that Kepler's distinctive guiding idea, to which he owed his success, was the firm conviction that the path of the planet Mars was somehow determined by a kind of mechanical interaction with the sun. This vague vision—foreshadowing Newton's theory—had enough truth in it to make him exclude all epicycles and spend his imagination in search of a single formula, covering the whole planetary path both in its speed and in its shape. This is how Kepler hit upon his two laws of elliptic revolution.

Intuition Guides Imagination

We begin to see now how the scientist's vision is formed. Guided by our intuition, our imagination sallies forward and our intuition integrates then what the imagination has hit upon. But a fundamental complication comes into sight here. I have acknowledged that the final sanction of discovery lies in the sight of a coherence which intuition detects and accepts as real but history suggests that there no universal standards for assessing such coherence.

Copernicus criticised the Ptolemaic system for its incoherence in assuming other than steady circular planetary paths and fought for the recognition of the heliocentric system as real because of its superior consistency. But his follower, Kepler, abandoned the postulate of circular paths, as causing meaningless complications in the Copernican system, and boasted that by doing so he had cleansed an Augean stable. Kepler based his first two laws on his vision that geometrical coherence is the product of some mechanical interaction. But this conception of reality underwent another radical transformation when Galileo, Descartes, and Newton found ultimate reality in the smallest particles of matter obeying the mathematical laws of mechanics.

I have described at some length elsewhere some of the irreconcilable scientific controversies which have arisen when two sides base their arguments on different conceptions of reality. When this happens, neither side can accept the evidence brought up by the other and the schism leads to a violent mutual rejection of the opponent's whole position. The great controversies about hypnosis, about fermentation, and about the bacterial origin of diseases, and about spontaneous generation are cases in point.

It becomes necessary to ask, therefore, by what standards we can change the very standards of coherence on which our convictions rest. On what grounds can we change our grounds? We are faced with the existentialist dilemma of how values of our own choice can have authority over us who decreed them.

We must look once more then at the mechanism by which imagination and intuition carry out their joint task. We lift our arm and find that our imagination has issued a command which has evoked its implementation. But the moment feasibility is obstructed, a gap opens up between our faculties and the end at which we are aiming, and our imagination fixes on this gap and evokes attempts to reduce it. Such a quest can go on for years; it will be persistent, deliberate, and transitive; yet its whole purpose is directed on ourselves: *it attempts to make us produce ideas.* We say then that we are racking our brain or ransacking our brain; that we are cudgelling or cracking it, or beating our brain trying to get it to work.

And the action induced in us by this ransacking is felt as something that is happening to us. We say that we tumble to an idea; or that an idea crosses our mind; or that it comes into our head; or that it strikes us, or dawns on us, or just presents itself to us. We are actually surprised and exclaim 'Aha' when we suddenly produce an idea. Ideas may come to us unbidden, hours or even days after we have ceased to rack our brain.

Discovery is made, therefore, in two moves: one deliberate, the other spontaneous—the spontaneous move being evoked in ourselves by the action of our deliberate effort. The deliberate thrust is a focal act of the imagination, while the spontaneous response to it, which brings discovery, belongs to the same class as the spontaneous co-ordination of muscles responding to our intention to lift our arm, or the spontaneous co-ordination of visual clues in response to our looking at something. This spontaneous act of discovery deserves to be recognised pre-eminently as the creative intuition.

But where does this leave the creative imagination? It is there, it is not displaced by the intuition, but it is imbued with it. When recognising a problem and engaging in its pursuit, our imagination is guided by our intuition. And the imaginative effort can evoke its own implementation only because it follows intuitive intimations of its own feasibility.

Remember, as an analogy, that a lost memory can be brought back only if we have clues to it; we cannot even start racking our brain for a memory that is wholly forgotten. The imagination must attach itself to clues of feasibility supplied to it by the very intuition that it is stimulating; sallies of the imagination that have no such guidance are idle fancies.

The honours of creativity are due then in one part to the imagination, which imposes on the intuition a feasible task and, in the other part, to the intuition which rises to this tasks a reveals the discovery that the quest was due to bring forth. Intuition informs the imagination which, in turn, releases the powers of the intuition.

But where does the responsibility for changing our criteria of reality rest then? To find that place we must probe still deeper. When the quest has ended, imagination and intuition do not vanish from the scene. Our intuition recognises our final result to be valid and our imagination points to the inexhaustible future manifestations of it. We return to the quiescent state of mind from which the enquiry started, but return to it with a new vision of coherence and reality. Herein lies the final acceptance of this vision; any new standards of coherence implied in it *have become our own standards*, we are committed to them. But can this be true? In his treatise on *The Concept of Law* (Oxford, 1961), Prof. H. L. A. Hart observes rightly that, while it can be reasonable to decide that something will be illegal starting tomorrow morning, it is nonsense to decide that something that is immoral today will be morally right starting tomorrow. Morality, Hart says, is 'immune against deliberate change'; and the same holds clearly also for beauty and truth. Our allegiance to such standards implies that they are not of our making. The existentialist dilemma, then, still faces us unresolved.

But I shall deal with it now. The first step is to remember that scientific discoveries are made in search of reality—of a reality that is there, whether we know it or not. The search is of our own making, but reality is not. We send out our imagination deliberately to ransack promising avenues. But the promise of these paths is already there to guide us. We sense it by our spontaneous intuitive powers. We induce the work of the intuition, but do not control its operations. And since our intuition works on a subsidiary level, neither the clues which it uses nor the principles by which it integrates them are fully identifiable. It is difficult to tell what were the clues which convinced Copernicus that his system was real; we have seen that his vision was fraught with implications so far beyond his own ken that, had they been shown to him, he would have rejected them. The discovery of relativity is just as full of unreconciled thoughts. Einstein tells in his autobiography that it was the example of the two great fundamental impossibilities underlying thermodynamics that suggested to him the absolute impossibility of observing absolute motion. But today we can see no connection at all between thermodynamics and relativity. Einstein acknowledged his debt to Mach and it is generally thought, therefore, that he confirmed Mach's thesis that the Newtonian doctrine of absolute rest is meaningless; but what Einstein actually proved was, on the contrary, that Newton s doctrine, far from being meaningless, was false. Again, Einstein's redefinition of simultaneity originated modern operationalism; but he himself sharply opposed the way Mach would replace the conception of atoms by their directly observable manifestations.

The solution of our problem is approaching here. If it is so difficult to identify the principles entailed in a discovery, this shows that they are subsidiarily present in it. And the latency of the principles entailed in a discovery indicates how we can change our standards and still uphold their authority over us. It suggests that while we cannot decree our standards *explicitly*, in the abstract, we may change them *covertly* in practice. The deliberate aim of scientific enquiry is to solve a problem, but our intuition may respond to our efforts with a solution entailing new standards of coherence, new values. In the solution, we tacitly obey these new values and thus recognise their authority over ourselves, over us who tacitly conceived them. This is indeed how new values are introduced, whether in science, or the arts, or in human relations. They enter subsidiarily, embodied in creative action. Only after this can they be spelled out and professed in abstract terms and this makes them appear then to have been deliberately chosen, which is absurd. The actual grounds of a value, and its very meaning, will ever lie hidden in the commitment which originally bore witness to that value.

Quest Presupposes Reality

I must not speculate here about the kind of universe which may justify reliance on our truth-bearing intuitive powers. I shall only speak of their part in our endorsement of scientific truth. A scientist's originality lies in seeing a problem where others see none and finding a way to its pursuit where others lose their bearings. These acts of his mind are strictly personal, attributable to him and only to him. But they derive their power and receive their guidance from an aim that is impersonal. For the scientist's quest presupposes the existence of external reality. Research is conducted on these terms from the and then goes on groping for a hidden truth towards which our clues are pointing; and when discovery terminates the pursuit, its validity is sustained by a vision of reality pointing still further beyond it.

Having relied throughout his enquiry on the presence of something real hidden out there, the scientist will necessarily rely on that external presence also for claiming the validity of the result that satisfies his quest. And as he has accepted throughout the discipline which this external pole of his endeavour imposed upon him, he expects that others, similarly equipped, likewise recognize the authority that guided him. On the grounds of the self-command which bound him to the quest of reality, he must claim that his results are universally valid; such is the universal intent of a scientific discovery.

I speak not of universality, but of universal intent, for the scientist cannot know whether his claims will be accepted; they may be true and yet fail to carry conviction. He may have reason to expect that this is likely to happen. Nor can he regard a possible acceptance of his claims as a guarantee of their truth. To claim universality for a statement indicates that it ought to be accepted by all. The affirmation of scientific truth has an obligatory character which it shares with other valuations, declared universal by our own respect for them.

Both the anticipation of discovery and discovery itself may be a delusion. But it is futile to seek for explicit impersonal criteria of their validity. The content of any empirical statement is three times indeterminate. It relies on clues which are largely unspecifiable, integrates them by principles which are undefinable, and speaks of a reality which is inexhaustible. Attempts to eliminate these indeterminacies of science merely replace science by a meaningless fiction.

To accept science, in spite of its essential indeterminacies, is an act of our personal judgment. It is to share the kin of commitment on which scientists enter by undertaking an enquiry. You cannot formalise commitment, for you cannot express your commitment noncommittally; to attempt to do so is to perform the kind of analysis which destroys its subject matter.

We should be glad to recognize that science has come into existence by mental endowments akin to those in which all hopes of excellence are rooted, and that science rests ultimately on such intangible powers of our mind. This recognition will help to restore legitimacy to our convictions, which the specious ideals of strict exactitude and detachment have discredited.

These false ideals do no harm to physicists who only pay lip service to them, but they play havoc with other parts of science and with our whole culture, which try to live by them. They will be well lost for truer ideals of science, which will allow us once more to place first things first: the living above the inanimate, man above the animal, and man's duties above man.

List of Suggested Additional Reading

For Copernicus, see his work *De Revolutionibus*, its Preface and Book 1, Chapters 4 and 10; also Herbert Dingle, *The Scientific Adventure*, London (1952).

You find in almost all the pertinent literature the false statement that adaptation to inverting spectacles consists in the reversion of the visual image. The facts were first clearly stated by F. W. Snyder and N. H. Pronko, *Vision with Spatial Inversion*, Wichita, Kan. (1952). Much fuller evidence as well as the interpretation I gave in this article are to be found in Heinrich Kottenhoff, 'Was ist richtiges Sehen mit Umkehrbrillen und in welchem Sinne stellt sich das Sehen um?' *Psychologia Universalis,* Vol. 5, (1961).

About Einstein and relativity, see *Albert Einstein, Philosopher-Scientist*, ed. P. A. Schlipp, New York (1949), also Adolf Grünbaum, *Philosophical Problems of Space and Time*, New York (1963)*.

The training of covert muscular twitches was reported by R. F. Hefferline et al. in Science, Vol. 130, page 1338 (1959) and Science, Vol. 139, page 834 (1963). About Kepler, see Arthur Koestler, *The Sleepwalkers* (1959). Passionate scientific controversies are described in my *Personal Knowledge,* London and Chicago, 1958.

---

* See also item [105] in the Bibliography.

18

Genius in Science

This article fittingly summarises Polanyi's philosophy of science over the years since his first publication on the subject, 'The value of the inexact' in 1936 [5].

Inexactitude of Science and the Work of Genius

We accept the results of science, and we must accept them, without having any strict proof that they are true. Strictly speaking all natural sciences are inexact. They could all conceivably be false, but we accept them as true because we consider doubts that may be raised against them to be unreasonable. Juries base their findings on the distinction between reasonable doubts which they must accept, and unreasonable doubts which they must disregard. They are instructed to make this distinction and to do it without having any set rules to rely upon. For it is precisely because there are no rules for deciding certain factual questions of supreme importance that these questions are assigned to the jury to decide them by their personal judgment. The scientist combines the functions of judge and jury. Having applied to his findings a number of specifiable criteria, he must ultimately decide in the fight of his own personal judgment whether the remaining conceivable doubts should be set aside as unreasonable.

Once it is recognised that all scientific discoveries ultimately rest on the scientist's personal judgment, the path seems open for unifying the whole sequence of personal decisions, beginning with sighting a problem and then pursuing the problem throughout an enquiry, all the way to the discovery of a new fact of nature.

[141]. *Boston Studies in the Philosophy of Science*, Vol. XIV, 1972, pp.57–71.

We shall meet the main features of the principle that controls scientific enquiry from the dawn of a problem to the finding of its solution, by looking first at its highest actions in the work of genius.

Genius is known for two faculties which may seem incompatible. Genius is a gift of inspiration, poets back to Homer have asked their Muse for inspiration, and scientists back to Archimedes have acknowledged the coming of a bright idea as an event that suddenly visited them. But we have also ample evidence of an opposite kind; genius has been said to consist in taking infinite pains, and all kinds of creative pursuits are in fact extremely strenuous.

How can these two aspects of genius hang together? Is there any hard work, which will induce an inspiration to visit us? How can we possibly conjure up an inspiration without even knowing from what corner it may come to us? And since it is ourselves who shall eventually produce the inspiration, how can it come to us as a surprise?

Yet this is what our creative work actually does. It is precisely what scientific discovery does: We make a discovery and yet it comes as a surprise to us. The first task of a theory of creativity, and of scientific discovery in particular, must be to resolve this paradox.

The solution can be found on a biological level, if we identify inspiration with 'spontaneous integration' and look out for the effort that induces such integration. Suppose I move an arm to reach for an object: my intention sets in motion a complex integration of my muscles, an integration that carries out my purpose. My intention is about something that does not yet exist: in other words it is a project, a project conceived by my imagination. So it seems that it is the imagination that induces a muscular integration to implement a project that I form in my imagination.

Could we say that this integration is spontaneous? I think that in an important sense we can call it spontaneous, for we have no direct control over it. Suppose a physiologist were to demonstrate to us all the muscular operations by which we have carried out our action, we would be amazed at the wonderful mechanism that we had contrived in achieving our project. We would find that we had done something that profoundly surprises us.

This exemplifies a principle that controls all our deliberate bodily actions. Our imagination, thrusting towards a desired result induces in us an integration of parts over which we have no direct control. We do not *perform* this integration: we *cause it to happen*. The effort of our imagination evokes its own implementation.

And the way we evoke here a desired event by the action of our body offers in a nutshell a solution of the paradox of genius. It suggests that inspiration is evoked by the labours of the thrusting imagination and that it is this kind of imaginative labour that evokes the new ideas by which scientific discoveries are made.

These conclusions may seem too fast, but they will be confirmed and enlarged by passing on from voluntary action to visual perception. The constancy of objects seen is achieved by an integration of clues which takes place beyond our direct control. We see objects and their surroundings coherently by integrating two to three snapshots per second, which present to us overlapping images ranging over the area before us. The intelligent scanning of these consecutive snapshots shows that our imagination is at work guiding our integration. And we can add that in case of any difficulty in recognising what it is that we see, the imagination explores alternative possibilities by letting our eyes move round to look for such possibilities.

Different branches of science are based on different ways of seeing. When an object is composed of parts that function jointly, our vision integrates the sight of these parts to the appearance of a coherent functioning entity. This is how the engineer, who knows the way a machine works, sees the machine as a working whole. Such integration underlies all biology and psychology. The view of an organism, the sight of an intelligent animal, the image of a human person, are all based on such integrations. We may call these visual integrations spontaneous because their parts are not directly controlled and often cannot even be directly noticed. The process of scientific discovery consists generally of such integrations evoked by the work of the imagination.

Powers of Anticipation

The progress of discovery falls into three main periods. The first is the sighting of a problem and the decision to pursue it; the *second*, the quest for a solution and the drawing of a conclusion; the *third*, the holding of the conclusion to be an established fact.

I have spoken of the way our eyesight organises consecutive snapshots by scanning them in an intelligent way, and how, in case of difficulty, the imagination explores alternative possibilities to find out what it is that we are seeing. These efforts of our eyesight are based on the assumption that any curious things before us are likely to have some hidden significance. Scientists speculating about strange things in nature act on a similar assumption. They try to interpret the facts they know, and go on collecting more facts, in the hope that these will reveal a coherence that is of interest to science. Such is the act of seeing a problem and pursuing it.

But here we meet a strange fact. In accepting the task of pursuing a problem, the scientist assumes it to be a *good* problem, a problem that he can solve by his own gifts and equipment and that it is worth undertaking in comparison with other available possibilities. He must estimate this; and such estimates are guesses.

But such guesses have proved sufficiently good to secure the progress of scientific enquiry with a reasonable degree of efficiency. It is rare to come across years of futile efforts wasted, or else to find that major opportunities were patently missed. Indeed, the opportunities for discovery are so effectively exploited that the same discovery is often made simultaneously by two or three different scientists. There is no doubt therefore of the scientist's capacity to assess in outline the course of an enquiry that will lead to a result which, at the time he makes his assessment, is essentially indeterminate.

How can we explain this capacity? I have said that scientific discovery is in essence an extension of perception. Remember how the different images of an object presented to our eyes from various distances, at different angles and in changing light, are all seen jointly as one single object, and that it is in terms of this coherence that our eyes perceive real things. This bears deeply on science. Copernicus laid the foundations of modern science by claiming his discovery of the heliocentric system in these very terms. He showed that his system included a parallelism between the solar distances of the planets and their orbital periods, and on this coherence he based his insistence that his system was no mere computing device, but a real fact.

But such claims to know reality are questioned by our antimetaphysical age. Can we define what it means to claim that an object is real? I think we can.

To say that an object is real is to anticipate that it will manifest its existence indefinitely hereafter. This is what Copernicus meant by insisting that his system was real. Copernicus anticipated the coming of future manifestations of his system, and these were in fact discovered by later astronomers who had accepted his claim that his system was real. *We can conclude then that, in nature, the coherence of an aggregate shows that it is real and that the knowledge of this reality foretells the coming of yet unknown future manifestations of such reality.* This concept of reality will now be extended to include all the phases of a scientific enquiry. It will explain the way discovery is anticipated, from the sighting of a problem to its final solution.

But let me stop first to recall the antecedents which led to this theory. I began my work on the nature of science twenty-five years ago guided by the idea that we make scientific discoveries in the same way we strain our eyesight to perceive an obscure object; and that in this effort we are guided by anticipating to some extent the direction which will prove most fruitful. 'A potential discovery', I wrote, 'may be thought to attract the mind which will reveal it—inflaming the scientist with creative desire and imparting to him intimations that guide him from clue to clue and from surmise to surmise'.[1]

For years I have written about this kind of anticipation.[2] At one stage I was joined in this idea by George Polya,[3] whose observations of mathematical discovery I had relied on from the start of my enquiry. And more recently I met with a brilliant description of anticipation in the posthumous work of C.F.A. Pantin, who writes that: '(Intuition) does not only suddenly present solutions to our conscious mind, it also includes the uncanny power that somehow we know that a particular set of phenomena or a particular set of notions are highly significant: and we are aware of that long before we can say what that signification is'.[4]

But only now can I see an explanation for such anticipations. I see that the anticipations offered to us by good problems should be understood in the same way as the anticipations aroused by all true facts of nature. Thus, when a coherent set of clues presents us with the sense of a hidden reality in nature, we are visited by an anticipation similar to that which we feel in seeing any object already recognised to be real. The expectations attached to a good problem differ only in their dynamic intensity from the expectations that will be attached to any facts eventually to be discovered in the end, once the problem has been solved. Of course, the sense of reality implied in adopting a problem, is pointing more clearly in a particular direction. And also the results anticipated in this kind of reality are expected to appear more soon than are the prospects implied in affirming the reality of an established fact; but I regard this difference as a mere matter of degree.

The whole of science, as it is known to us, has come into existence by virtue of good problems that have led to the discovery of their solution. The fact that scientists can espy good problems is therefore a faculty as essential to science, as is the capacity to solve problems and to prove such solutions to be right. In other words, the capacity rightly to choose a line of thought the end of which is vastly indeterminate, is as much part of the scientific method as the power of assuring the exactitude of the conclusions eventually arrived at. And both faculties consist in recognising real coherence in nature and sensing its indeterminate implications for the future.

This conclusion fulfills in substance my hopes of finding the same principles of personal judgment at work at all stages of a scientific enquiry, from the sighting of a problem to the discovery of its solution. Problems are discovered by a roaming speculative imagination, and once a problem is adopted, the imagination is thrust in the direction of the problem's expectations. This evokes new ideas of coherence which, if true, reduce the indeterminacy of the enquiry. The speculative or experimental examination of these ideas directs yet new thrusts of the imagination that evoke yet further surmises; and so the pursuit is narrowed down ever further, until eventually an idea turns up which can claim to solve the problem.

This rough sketch must suffice for the moment to outline the sequence of 'infinite pains' that finally evoke a surprise claiming to be the solution of the problem.

Rationality to the Rescue?

But scientific opinion has been reluctant to accept the fact that the scientist is guided essentially by a vague sense of still unrevealed facts. Hence textbooks of physics have taught for decades that Einstein discovered relativity as an explanation of Michelson's observation that the earth's rotation causes no flow in the surrounding ether, and so, when I pointed out about twelve years ago that this was a pure invention,[5] the only response I evoked was from Professor Adolf Grünbaum of Pittsburgh[6] who said that my description of Einstein's way to discovery was like Schiller's story that his poetic inspiration came to him by smelling rotten apples. Fortunately, a study recently published by Professor Gerald Holton has shown at last in great detail, that I had been right.[7]

I have mentioned this story to illustrate the temper of our age which prefers a tangible explanation to one relying on more personal powers of the mind, even though the plain facts do show these less tangible forces at work. The theory of scientific discovery—most influential today—expresses this preference by dividing the process of discovery sharply into the choice of a hypothesis and the testing of the chosen hypothesis. The first part (the choice of a hypothesis) is deemed to be inexplicable by any rational procedure, while the second (the testing of the chosen hypothesis) is recognised as a strict procedure forming the scientist's essential task.

This theory of scientific discovery would save the strictness of science by declaring that scientific discoveries are merely tentative hypotheses which can be strictly tested by confronting their implications with experience. And that if any of the implications of a hypothesis conflicts with experience, the hypothesis must be instantly abandoned; that indeed, even if the hypothesis is accepted on the grounds of having been confirmed in its predictions, it will ever remain on trial ready to be abandoned if any experience turns up that contradicts one of its claims. We are told that unless a hypothesis produces testable conclusions it should be disregarded as lacking any substantial significance.[8]

Let me test this theory. There may be cases where a scientific discovery was made and only claimed as such after some additional implications of it had been tested; but there is plenty of evidence to show that this is not necessary and, indeed, is often impracticable. On November 11, 1572 Tycho Brahe observed a new star in Cassiopeia, and this discovery refuted the Aristotelian doctrine of an unchangeable empyrean. This happened before the days of the telescope, and indeed the same observation was made also in China. The discovery was complete without producing testable implications, exactly as the eruption of Vesuvius on August 24, A.D. 79 was established as a fact, without any tests of its vast implications. Or take Kepler's discovery that for the six then known planets the square of the orbital period was proportional to the cube of the solar distance. The figures underlying this discovery had been known for eighty years or more; I happened to test the relative solar distances of the planets made available by the work of Copernicus and found that they agree with Kepler's Third Law within two per cent. All that Kepler did was to recognise this relationship, which is his Third Law. Yet Kepler hailed his discovery as the crowning of his search for celestial harmony, even though no testable implications of it were known at the time and indeed for a long time after his death.

Admittedly, many discoveries were not made at one stroke. But of these too, many fail to exemplify the orthodox 'hypothetico-deductive model'. On March 13,1781. William Herschel observed a slowly moving nebulous disk which he first took to be a comet, but, after a few weeks of watching its motion, recognised as a new planet, to be named Uranus. Later on, Leverrier and Adams, basing themselves on the irregularities of Uranus, derived the existence of one more planet, and the prediction of its position promptly led to its discovery. It was named Neptune. Thus the existence of Uranus and Neptune were claimed the moment they were observed and this observation completed their discovery, without regard to particular testable implications.

Turning to physics, we can take Max von Laue's discovery of the diffraction of X-rays in 1912 as a parallel case to this. A conversation with P. P. Ewald aroused in Laue the idea that X-rays would show optical diffraction when passing through a crystal. His attempt to find experimental help to test his idea met with opposition from the director of the laboratory, but when his request finally prevailed, the result confirmed his expectation, and he announced his discovery, which was accepted on this evidence.

Further, we sometimes find examples of beautiful discoveries neither based on any new observation nor predicting anything which would confirm or refute them—e.g., in theoretical work in physics and physical chemistry. Van't Hoff's derivation of the chemical mass action law from the Second Law of Thermodynamics was a fundamental discovery based only on known facts and predicting nothing. In a period extending close on half a century, no one has been able to find a test for the statistical interpretation of quantum mechanics that we owe to Max Born. Its radically new conception of physical laws as predicting only the probability and not the actual course of events controlled by the law is generally accepted today, though it was originally grounded on no new facts and has never offered factual implications that could test it.

Such unempirical theories can be of supreme importance in all the experimental sciences, including biology. Darwinism is an example of it, and indeed in two senses. First, for seventy years Darwinism was accepted by science, even though its evolutionary mechanism could not be understood in terms of known facts, and second, up to this day no such empirical implications of it are known which, if experimentally tested, could disprove the theory.

The second point is widely recognised, so I shall only demonstrate the first. During the first forty years following on the publication of the *Origin of Species* in 1859, it became increasingly clear that the kind of variations known at that time were not sufficiently hereditary to form the basis of a selective process producing evolutionary transformation.[9] Yet the authority of scientific opinion continued to support the theory of evolution by natural selection and spread its deep influence on the world view of humanity. After the re-discovery of Mendelian mutations in 1900 the opposite difficulty arose. These variations were hereditary, but they were much too massive for producing a process of gradual adaptation. Yet the acceptance of Darwinism as our world view, supported by science, remained unshaken, while the new contradictions remained unexplained for another three decades. This difficulty may have been overcome since 1930 through the rise of Neo-Darwinism, and if this new theory holds, the previous disregard of the fact that the theory of natural selection conflicted with the known laws of nature, may turn out to have been justified.[10]

To sum up, we have seen examples to show that important scientific discoveries can be made at a glance and established without any subsequent tests; and that there have been great theoretical discoveries which had no testable experimental content at all. We have seen also that a theory interpreting in a novel way a vast range of experience was accepted by science, and then firmly held for many years by science, though its assumptions contradicted the laws of nature as known at the time, and also that it continues to be held by science, as other important theories are, though it has never been testable by predictions that could be empirically refuted.

Personal Judgment in Science

My own theory of scientific knowledge is, and has been from my the start twenty-five years ago, that science is an extension of perception. It is a kind of integration of parts to wholes, as *Gestalt* psychology has described, but in contrast to *Gestalt*, which is a mere equilibration of certain pieces to form a coherent shape, it is the outcome of deliberate integration revealing a hitherto hidden real entity. There are no strict rules for discovering things that hang together in nature, nor even for telling whether we should accept or reject an apparent coherence as a fact.[11] There is always a residue of personal judgment in deciding whether to accept or reject any particular piece of evidence, be it as a proof of a true regularity or, on the contrary, as a refutation of apparent rules. This is how I saw and accepted the fact that, strictly speaking, all empirical science is inexact. And as I came to realise that all such integration is largely based, like perception itself, on tacit elements of which we have only a vague knowledge, I concluded that science too was grounded on an act of personal judgment.

To show this, I became for many years a scandal-monger, collecting cases where the most generally accepted rules of scientific procedure had been flaunted and flaunted to the advantage of science. My first such case showed that even though a new idea conflicts from the start with experience, it may be generally accepted by science. The periodic system of elements shows that the sequence of rising atomic weights produces a striking pattern of the elements in respect of their chemical character. But two pairs of elements fit into the pattern only the wrong way round, that is, the direction of decreasing weights. Yet at no time has this caused the system to be called in question, let alone to be abandoned.

Another example: The idea that light is composed of particles was proposed by Einstein—and upheld, still unexplained, for twenty years—in spite of its being in sharp conflict with the well-established wave nature of light. Commenting on the later history of these cases, (which were among my first scandals) I concluded that any exception to a rule may involve not its refutation but the indication of its deeper meaning.

And I went on to declaring that the process of explaining away observed deviations from accepted teachings of science is in fact indispensable to the daily routine of research. In my laboratory—I said—I find the laws of nature formally contradicted every day, but I explain these events away by the assumption of experimental error. I know that this may cause me one day to explain away a fundamentally new phenomenon and to miss a great discovery; such things have happened in the history of science. Yet I shall continue to explain away my odd results, for if every anomaly observed in a laboratory were taken at its face value, research would degenerate into a wild-goose chase after fundamental novelties.

But these products of my early scandal-mongering were surpassed by a statement of Einstein which recently came to my notice.[12] Werner

Heisenberg has told the story how, in the course of shaping his quantum theory, he told Einstein that he proposed to go back from Bohr's theory to quantities that could be really observed. To which Einstein replied that the truth lay the other way round. He said, 'whether you can observe a thing or not depends on the theory which you use. It is the theory which decides what can be observed'. Max Planck has also rejected Heisenberg's claim to deal with observables, on the grounds that science is a theory bearing on observations, and never including observations.[13]

The position of observations in the face of prevailing theories is of course precarious. Take once more the famous experiment of Michelson and Morley demonstrating the absence of the ether drift corresponding to the rotation of the earth. Far from rejoicing at this great discovery, which was eventually to form the main experimental support for Einstein's relativity, Michelson called his result a failure. Professor Holton has told in the paper that I quoted before, how both Kelvin and Rayleigh spoke of Michelson's result as 'a real disappointment' and Sir Oliver Lodge even said that this experiment might have to be explained away. Thus the ether theory, which was firmly supported by the current interpretation of physics, caused the experiment to be distrusted. But when some thirty-five years later the same experiment was repeated, with improved instruments by D. C. Miller, and this time did show the presence of an ether drift, this result was rejected in its turn. By this time relativity had overthrown the ether theory. And of course, this time, the theory was rightly preferred to the experiment.[14]

I have no space here to tell in detail the story that I picked up at the very beginning of my scandal-mongering[15], how the way scientists of the first rank came out with experiments showing a transformation of elements, because they were encouraged by the radio-active transmutations discovered by Rutherford. There was one epidemic of such publications from 1907 to 1913 that was evoked by Rutherford's discovery (in 1903) that radioactivity involves a transformation of elements; and a second epidemic spread from 1922 to 1928, in response to Rutherford's discovery (in 1919) of an artificial transformation of elements. The observations published during these epidemics would otherwise of course have been cast aside as mere 'dirt effect'.[16]

Let me add a counter example, where plausibility justly triumphed over observation. I have in mind Eddington's derivation from his theory of the universe, developed in the mid-nineteen twenties, that the reciprocal of the fine-structure constant usually denoted by $h\,c/2pe^2$ is equal to the integer 137. The theory was widely rejected and this was facilitated by the fact that the experimental value for Eddington's figure was at the time 137.307 with a probable error of ±0.048. However, by the passing of twenty years, new experiments gave a value of 137.009, which brilliantly confirmed Eddington's theory. But this agreement was rejected as fortuitous by the overwhelming majority of scientists; and they were right.[17]

To sum up: Science is the result of an integration, similar to that of common perception. It establishes hitherto unknown coherences in nature. Our recognition of these coherences is largely based, like perception is, on clues of which we are often not focally aware and which are indeed often unidentifiable. Current conceptions of science about the nature of things always affect our recognition of coherence in nature. From the sighting of a problem to the ultimate decision of rejecting still conceivable doubts, factors of plausibility are ever in our minds. This is what is meant by saying that, strictly speaking, all natural science is an expression of personal judgment.

The machinery of genius, which I have described before, is at work all the way from the start to the finish of an enquiry. And once we have recognised this mechanism we can see that we are ourselves the ultimate masters of its workings. Exactitude is recognised then to be always a matter of degree and ceases to be a surpassing ideal. The supremacy of the exact sciences is rejected and psychology, sociology, and the humanities are thus set free from the vain and misleading efforts of emulating mathematical rules.

I started on this way many years ago in a short paper entitled 'The Value of the Inexact'.[18] I pointed out that if we insisted on exactitude of procedure, we would have no chemistry, or at least none to speak of. For chemistry relies for its guidance on judgments of 'stability', 'affinity', 'tendency' as descriptions of chemical processes and also on the skilful application of rules of thumb as guides for acting on such judgments. But the value of the inexact goes much further. It alone makes possible the science of biology. For the structure of living things can be recognised only if we allow our vision to integrate the sight of its parts to the view of a coherently functioning entity, an entity which vanishes if analysed in terms of physics and chemistry.

Hence I have defined scientific value as the joint produce of three virtues, namely (1) accuracy, (2) range of theory, and (3) interest of subject matter.[19] This triad of values distributes our appreciation evenly over the whole range of sciences. We have then greater exactitude and elegance being balanced by a lesser intrinsic interest of subject matter— or else the other way round. For example, most subjects of modern physics are interesting only to the scientists, while the horizon of biology ranges over our experience of animals and plants, and of our own lives as human beings; so the glory of mathematical precision and elegance in which physics far surpasses biology, is balanced in biology by the much greater interest of its subject matter.

Once science is appraised by a threefold grading, all scholarship is elevated to the same pride: as a pride free of pangs about not being a 'real science'. The foolish hierarchy of Auguste Comte is smashed and flattened out.

I am not making excuses for the inexactitude of science and for our personal actions that ultimately decide what to accept to be the truth in science. I do not see our intervention as a regrettable necessity, nor regard its result as a second-rate knowledge. It appears second-rate only in the light of a fallacy which systematically corrupts our conception of knowledge and distorts thereby wide regions of our culture.

Notes

1. Michael Polanyi, *Science, Faith and Society*, published in 1946 by Oxford University Press; Phoenix Edition, 1964, p. 33.
2. Michael Polanyi, 'Problem-solving', *Brit. Journ. Philos. Science* **8** (1957), 89–103.
3. George Polya, *Mathematical Discovery*, John Wiley & Sons, New York, London, Sydney, 1965, Vol. II, p. 63.
4. C. F. A. Pantin, *The Relation between the Sciences* (ed. by A. M. Pantin and W. H. Thorpe), Cambridge Univ. Press, 1968, pp. 121–122.

   We may look also at other creative work. Kant has described in *The Critique of Pure Reason* the part of anticipation in the pursuit of philosophic problems. He wrote: 'It is unfortunate that not until we have unsystematically collected observations for a long time to serve as building materials, following the guidance of an idea which lies concealed in our minds, and indeed only after we have spent much time in the technical disposition of these materials, do we first become capable of viewing the idea in a clearer light and of outlining it architectonically as one whole according to the intentions of reason'.

   H. W. Janson (*History of Art*, New York 1962, p. 11) describes anticipation in making a painting: 'It is a strange and risky business in which the maker never quite knows what he is making until he has actually made it, or to put it another way, it is a game of find-and-seek in which the seeker is not sure what he is looking for, until he has found it'.

Northrop Frye (*T. S. Eliot*, 1963, p. 28) speaks of Eliot's account of anticipation: 'The poet has no idea of what he wants to say until he has found the words of his poem...[He] may not know what is coming up, but whatever it is, his whole being is bent on realising it'.

Anticipations of this kind resolve the problem of Meno in which Plato questions the possibility of pursuing an enquiry in our inevitable ignorance of what we are looking for.

5. Michael Polanyi, *Personal Knowledge*, Routledge and Chicago, 1958, pp. 9–13.

6. Adolf Grünbaum, *Philosophical Problems of Space and Time*, New York 1963, pp.385–386.

7. Gerald Holton, 'Einstein, Michelson and the "Crucial Experiment"', *Isis* **60** (1969), 133–197.

8. Clearly, the position to which I am referring is that Sir Karl Popper stated in *Logik der Forschung* (1934), translated into English as *The Logic of Scientific Discovery* (1946). It is this statement that has been most widely influential and though it was modified in some parts in Popper's *Conjectures and Refutations* (1963), the changes do not substantially affect the principles of 'refutationalism' which I shall test here.

9. D. Darlington, *Darwin's Place in History*, Basil Blackwell, Oxford, 1960, p. 40.

Professor Darlington described in Chapter 8 entitled 'The Retreat from Natural Selection' how in the successive editions of Darwin's *Origin of Species* natural selection is gradually abandoned and evolution 'shored up with Lamackian inheritance'.

10. The present situation was described as follows by Julian Huxley, *Evolution the Modern Synthesis*, Allen and Unwin, London, 1942, p. 116 and repeated in the same words in its revised edition in 1963.

'It must be admitted that the direct and complete proof of the utilisation of mutations in evolution under natural conditions has not yet been given...Thus it is inevitable that for the present we must rely mainly on the convergence of a number of separate lines of evidence each partial and indirect or incomplete, but severally cumulative and demonstrative'.

J. Maynard Smith in an article entitled 'The Status of Neo-Darwinism', pp. 82–89 in *Towards a Theoretical Biology* (ed. by C. H. Waddington), Aldine Publishing Co., Chicago, 1969, has listed some evidence as proving that Neo-Darwinism is not 'tautological'. But he merely shows, as Huxley does, that the evidence so far supports the theory.

11. The view that discovery is an informal process was anticipated by William Whewell in his brilliant critique of the mechanistic scheme of induction effectively propounded at that time by John Stuart Mill. The way intuition suddenly follows on a time of strenuous searching has been described by Poincaré in his famous account of an experience of his own. These examples have supported me in my enterprise.

12. W. Heisenberg, 'Theory, Criticism and a Philosophy', 71 in *From a Life of Physics,* special supplement of the *Bulletin of the International Atomic Energy Agency*, Vienna, pp.36–37. This publication is not dated.

13. Max Planck in *Positivismus und Reale Aussenwelt*, Akademische Verlagsgesellschaft, Leipzig, 1931, p.21, says, '...there exists absolutely no physical magnitude which can be measured in itself' (my translation).

14. For details of this event see my *Personal Knowledge*, pp.12–13.

15. *Op. cit., Science, Faith and Society*, pp.91–92.
16. For details see my *Science, Faith and Society*, 1946, Appendix 2.
17. For further details see *Personal Knowledge*, 1958, pp. 43,151,158,160.
18. Michael Polanyi, *Philosophy of Science* 3 (1936), 233.
19. See *Science, Faith and Society*, 1946, Chapter II, Section II.

19

Life Transcending Physics and Chemistry

Two consequences of Polanyi's rejection of Objectivist and Positivist accounts of science and knowledge generally are his rejection also of the reductionism that accompanies them and his re-instatement of a hierarchical conception of the universe and of the comprehensive entities within it, structured by the tacit integration which we reperform or reconstitute in our apprehension of them. These themes were mentioned in 'Science and reality' and 'The creative imagination'. This article deals with attempts to reduce biology to physics and chemistry, and life to the objects studied by them. It provides a fuller statement of the points made in the first part of 'Life's irreducible structure' [131]. It is preceded by Polanyi's own summary.

Form and function in an object may not be explicable in terms of the laws that govern the properties of its atomic constituents. Both animate and inanimate systems can illustrate this proposal.

DNA (deoxyribonucleic acid) may determine the boundary (the morphology) of a biological system. But the form and function of the resulting biological system cannot be explained by the laws governing its parts. An example of this principle may be found in administrative hierarchies. Here, a higher authority governs lower levels while relying on the autonomous workings of these lower levels.

A similar irreducibility may be found in machines. Their design, shape, and operation are comprehensive features not due to physical and chemical forces. A description of a machine in physical or chemical terms would result in a topography of atoms and molecules unique to the subject. It could not identify the machine as belonging to a class of machines based on certain operational principles.

Biological systems, like machines, have, therefore, functions and forms inexplicable by chemical and physical laws. The argument that the DNA molecule determines genetic processes in living systems does not indicate reducibility. A DNA molecule essentially transmits information to a developing cell. Similarly, a

[125]. Reprinted from *Chemical & Engineering News*, August 21st, 1967, pp.54–66, with permission from the American Chemical Society, © 1967 American Chemical Society.

book transmits information. But the transmission of the information cannot be represented in terms of chemical and physical principles. In other words, the operation of the book is not reducible to chemical terms. Since DNA operates by transmission of (genetic) information, its function cannot be described by chemical laws either.

The life process is essentially the development of a fertilised cell, as the result of information imparted by DNA. Transmission of this information is non-chemical and non-physical, and is the controlling factor in the life process. The description of a living system therefore transcends the chemical and physical laws which govern its atomic constituents.

The discovery by Watson and Crick of the genetic function of DNA (deoxyribonucleic acid), combined with the evidence these scientists provided for the self-duplication of DNA, is widely held to prove that living beings can be interpreted, at least in principle, by the laws of physics and chemistry. Barry Commoner has queried this view by citing evidence to show that the self-duplication of DNA is not proven (*Science and Survival*). But the latter point, though important, is not in fact decisive. For even if we granted the self-duplication of DNA, this would not show that living beings can be represented in terms of physics and chemistry. It would, for example, not offer a possible physical-chemical explanation of human consciousness.

Moreover, Commoner disregards the fact that, viewed by his own criteria for the reducibility of biological processes, his challenge of the self-duplication of DNA presents no difficulty to the reduction of genetics to physics and chemistry. For Commoner shares the view held by most biologists, that so far as life can be represented as a mechanism, it is explained by the laws of inanimate nature, and there is nothing in the observations he cited that could not be ascribed to some yet undiscovered mechanical operations.

For my part, I differ from Commoner and from most biologists, by holding that no mechanism—be it a machine or a machine-like feature of an organism—call be represented in terms of physics and chemistry. This principle precludes the possibility of biology ever becoming a molecular science and thus leads to Commoner's conclusion on grounds very different from his. But my principle has so far been accepted by few biologists and has been sharply rejected by Francis Crick, who is convinced that all life can be ultimately accounted for by the laws of inanimate nature (*Of Molecules and Men*). Thus my conclusions conflict both with Crick's view, as with the grounds on which Barry Commoner takes an opposite view. If I am right, both these positions must be radically revised.

My account of the situation will seem to oscillate in several directions, and I shall set out, therefore, its stages in order.

I shall show that:

- Commoner's criteria of irreducibility to physics and chemistry are incomplete; they are necessary but not sufficient conditions of it.
- Machines are irreducible to physics and chemistry.
- By virtue of the principle of boundary control, mechanistic structures of living beings appear to be likewise irreducible.
- The structure of DNA, which according to Watson and Crick controls heredity, is not explicable by physics and chemistry.
- Assuming that morphological differentiation reflects the information content of DNA, we can prove that the morphology of living beings forms a boundary condition which, as such, is not explicable by physics and chemistry (the suggestion arrived at in the third item).

Let me proceed on these lines now.

Commoner's Incompatible Views

Commoner holds two views (A and B) that are incompatible. His view A, shared by a number of scientists who acknowledge the existence of irreducibility, is that when the joint presence of parts shows features which cannot be observed in the isolated parts, these features are not explicable by the laws governing the separate parts. Hence, when the parts are governed by the laws of physics and chemistry, their joint entity is considered to be irreducible to physics and chemistry.

His view B, long since predominant among all scientists, is that the explanation of living functions in terms of a mechanical model amounts to explaining them in terms of physics and chemistry. These two views are incompatible, for machines—or living functions operating mechanically—are entities the characteristic features of which are absent in their separate parts. I hold both view A and B to be erroneous. I shall be first concerned with A—Commoner's criteria of irreducibility.

Criteria of Irreducibility

Let me show that the presence of joint properties not observed in the isolated parts does not prove irreducibility to terms of the laws controlling the parts. Take the fact that the sun is a sphere. Its separate parts are not spheres; nor does the law of gravitation speak of spheres. But the mutual gravitational interaction causes the parts of the sun to form a sphere. The same law causes the planets to move on elliptic paths around the sun.

Physics is rich in examples of comprehensive features of a system that cannot he observed in the isolated parts of the system. Crystals are marvelously ordered aggregates. Their particles are arranged in the pattern of one out of 230 space groups, which are not observed in the separate atomic parts. But these patterns can be derived from the interaction of their component parts. Snell's Law says that a beam of light passing through a medium of variable refractive powers will take the path along which it reaches its end-point in the shortest time, and this comprehensive feature is derived from the laws that determine the curvature of the path at any single point in space.

These comprehensive features, which cannot be observed in any single particle or any pair of particles nor, for the case of Snell's law, at any point of a beam, are all computable by the mathematical integration of the laws observed in the isolated components. And this is true also for the theory of superconductivity, which Commoner quotes as an example for the emergence of irreducible principles. It is but an integrated form of laws applying to parts or pairs of parts.

Clearly, holistic systems which can be computed from the laws of physics do not point to the existence of irreducible biological principles. They have often suggested on the contrary that all organised functions of living things might well be explicable in terms of physics and chemistry. Whenever the complex order of morphogenesis evoked the thought that there was manifested here a principle not present in inanimate nature, the answer came that this order of life might well be derived from physical laws, as the order of crystals is derived from them. Wolfgang Koehler has likewise used the harmonious distribution of the electric current in a system of parallel conductors as an example for suggesting that we should explain gestalt-like perception and its corresponding neural processes, by a physical equilibration of their parts.

Machines are Irreducible

But while we have met so far no irreducible holistic systems in inanimate nature, we find such systems among inanimate artifacts, like machines.[1] Machines seem obviously irreducible, since they have comprehensive features that are not due to a spontaneous integration of physical and chemical forces. They do not come into being by physical-chemical equilibration, but are shaped by man. They are shaped and designed for a specific purpose, which they achieve by the interaction of their characteristic parts working in accordance with distinctive operational principles. But I must argue this conclusion in detail, if I want it to carry conviction.

Try to describe a machine in physical-chemical terms. A complete physical-chemical topography of my watch—even though the topography included the changes caused by the movements in the watch—would not tell us what this object is. On the other hand, if we know watches, we would recognise an object as a watch by a description of it which says that it tells the time of the day, by hands sweeping round a face, marked by the hours of the day. We know watches and can describe one only in terms like 'telling the time', 'hands', 'face', 'marked', which are all incapable of being expressed by the variables of physics, length, mass, and time. The impossibility is of a logical kind, similar to that by which a poorer deductive system cannot define the terms of a richer one. For example, propositional calculus cannot define arithmetics.

But we can still sharpen this argument. A physical-chemical topography of my watch might make it possible, at least in principle, to identify this particular watch as an object. But it would fail to identify it as a watch, for it is incapable of defining a class of watches, as needed for assigning the watch to that class. To realise more clearly what I mean, suppose you had invented the watch and made one, and you applied for a patent specifying the watch you made, by its precise physical-chemical topography. Your patent would protect only the manufacture of an exact replica of your model. Your competitor could circumvent your patent by merely displacing one single atom of the patented topography. Only the principles underlying the operations of the watch in telling the time could specify your invention of the watch effectively, and these cannot be expressed in terms of physical-chemical variables. (This is the refutation of Commoner's view B.)

Now, from machines let us pass on to books and other means of communication. Nothing is said about the content of a book by its physical-chemical topography. All objects conveying information are irreducible to the terms of physics and chemistry.

Up to a point, we can transfer what has been said of machines to machine-like aspects of living beings. Take some examples from the higher animals—their organs of circulation, breathing, digestion, secretion, and thermal regulation. Think of their anatomy and of the way they operate in performing their functions. None of these conceptions can be defined in terms of physics and chemistry. In his treatise, *The Structure of Science*, Ernest Nagel has attempted to eliminate the purposive character of physiological functions by describing these as mere events that happen to be beneficent to the organism, without purposively serving this benefit. But the fact still remains that a process can be regarded as a biological function only if it does benefit the organism. This remains its essence, as much as it is the essence of a machine to serve a purpose acknowledged by its designer. We can see this from the fact that the concept of functional disorders interfering with normal achievements applies equally both to living and inanimate mechanisms.

Moreover, despite his reductionist claims, Nagel admits irreducibility of vital functions by using their biological names for talking about them. He must do so, for the mere shape of a living being defeats any physical-chemical definition and this is true throughout the anatomical features of life. And again, even supposing we did produce a mathematical expression for the shape of one living specimen, including all its anatomy at one particular moment, the formula would not cover its changes due to growth and decline and it would of course fail even more widely to cover the variety of specimens belonging to one species and to cover at the same time the innumerable future additions due to accrue to a species in the course of time.

Living Systems Seem Irreducible, Too

But might this barrier to physical-chemical reduction not prove to be temporary? Before Newton, the geometrical shapes of the sun and of the planetary paths appeared to be ultimate facts, not reducible to any laws governing their ultimate particles. Might machines and machine-like aspects of living things not be shown one day to result from the working of physical or chemical laws?

We can exclude this for machines. Our incapacity to define machines and their functions in terms of physics and chemistry is due to a manifest impossibility, for machines are shaped by man and can never be produced by the spontaneous equilibration of their material. But morphological structures are not shaped by man; could they not grow to maturity by the working of purely physical-chemical laws?

To answer this question, we must first deal with a more general problem. Let us go back and ask how it is possible for machines to be controlled by two independent sets of principles. For the material of the machine is subject to the laws of physics and chemistry, while the shape and the consequent working of the machine are controlled by its structural and operational principles. The solution is found by remembering that no given material system can be wholly determined by the laws of physics and chemistry.

The laws of physics are given in terms of differential equations which determine a definite system only within a set of fixed conditions. The spherical shape of the sun, the elliptic paths of the planet, the trajectory of a beam of light covered in a minimum of time—each of these arrangements arises under the dual control of a differential equation working within the bounds of a particular set of conditions. Laplace thought we would know all that can be known in the world, if we knew the course of its atoms. But for this he required a complete map of atomic positions and velocities to start with. Physics is dumb without the gift of boundary conditions, forming its frame; and this frame is not determined by the laws of physics.

The laws of chemistry have similar limitations. We can demonstrate chemical change by pouring a solution of reagents into a container and setting the concentration and temperature as required. Generally, to have a definite chemical process, we must frame it by boundary conditions not by the laws of chemistry.

We speak of such boundaries as 'fixed conditions' rather than 'controlling principles', for their intervention, though indispensable, is not highly significant. This is different for a machine. The boundary conditions of the physical-chemical changes taking place in a machine are the structural and operational principles of the machine. We say therefore that the laws of inanimate nature operate in a machine *under the control of operational principles that constitute* (or determine) *its boundaries*. Such a system is clearly under dual control.

The relationship between the two controls—the devices of engineering and the laws of natural science—is not symmetrical. The machine is a machine by having been built and being then controlled according to principles of engineering. The laws of physics and chemistry are indifferent to these principles; they would go on working in the fragments of the machine if it were smashed. But they serve the machine while it lasts; machines rely for their operations always on the laws of physics and chemistry.

Returning now to living beings, we may start by observing that to speak of life as something to be explained by the laws of physics and chemistry is strictly speaking absurd, for physical and chemical processes do not determine by themselves any finite system. We must ask what the boundary conditions are within which physics and chemistry do explain biotic phenomena. The answer is found in the fact that biochemistry and biophysics are always concerned with processes *that have a bearing on an existing organism.* These sciences seek to determine the chemical and physical principles on which the organism relies for its operations. Any chemical or physical study of living things that is irrelevant to the working of the organism is no part of biology, just as the chemical or physical studies of a machine must bear on the way the machine works, if it is to serve engineering.

It is this basic principle of biology that the physiologist, J. S. Haldane, insisted upon throughout his philosophical writings.

I have written elsewhere at some length about higher principles that govern the working of lower laws on which they rely for operating a system. Administrative hierarchies are common examples of a higher authority governing lower levels, while relying on the autonomous workings of these lower levels. Hierarchies formed by successive levels of the organism have been described similarly. My own theory expands the structure of hierarchic levels to the relation between biological principles and the laws of physics and chemistry. Biological principles are seen then to control the boundary conditions within which the forces of physics and chemistry carry on the business of life. This dual action of a system is said to work by *the principle of boundary control.*

But is it not conceivable that an organism developing from a fertilised cell might shape the boundary conditions of the developed organism, without itself being subject to such boundaries? One may reply that a machine that manufactures machines for a factory produces them within its own boundaries, as set to the machine by its operational principles. The embryo producing the biological boundaries of maturity works likewise within its own embryonic boundaries. Indeed, *no biological pro-*

cess ever takes place in an unstructured medium; at least not in the world today. But I must yet show that this is necessarily so.

Boundary Conditions for DNA

The next step takes us back all the way to the claims made currently for DNA as an explanation of life in terms of chemistry. I shall assume here the currently prevailing view that DNA determines altogether the outcome of embryonic growth, including the whole design of the final organism. Does this not face us with the fact that a pure chemical compound controls supreme biological functions? Where is then the boundary condition which controls this chemical effect?

One might be tempted to reply that a DNA molecule produces nothing by itself, its genetic programme being initiated within the richly structured framework of a fertilised cell, and that subsequently DNA controls morphogenesis within a steadily developing framework. But this is not to the point. For it is DNA itself that introduces within its chemical structure a pattern that acts as a controlling framework to the ensuing generative process. This is what is meant by saying that DNA controls the genetic development of an organism by transmitting to its cells a quantity of information that induces in them an equivalent amount of organic differentiation. Where, then, is the boundary condition?

Remember then our earlier conclusion that a book, or any other object bearing a pattern that communicates information, is essentially irreducible to physics and chemistry. It would follow that we must refuse to regard the pattern by which DNA spreads information as part of its chemical properties. Its functional pattern must be recognised as a boundary condition located within the DNA molecule. This is what I shall try to demonstrate. The boundary conditions forming a machine have two interrelated aspects: They consist in a distinctive structure sustaining a purposive operation. The various functions of a living organism are similarly sustained by its structure known as its morphology. A written or printed text functions by its structure alone, without generating motion; it acts passively by being read. A plan or an animal, recognisable by its shape, its pattern, and its colouring may be said to transmit information likewise passively, by being seen. The boundary condition generating this function consists in the case of such a plant or animal in its typical appearance, its morphology. If DNA is regarded as bearing a pattern that forms part of an organism and as transmitting information through this pattern, then such a pattern is to be classed likewise as a morphological feature of the organism, and hence be irreducible to terms of physics and chemistry.

By the same token, any chemical compound bearing a complex structure and transmitting thereby substantial information to its neighbourhood must be irreducible to physics and chemistry in respect of this particular feature. Let me show this.

All chemical compounds consist of atoms linked in an orderly manner by the energy of chemical bonds. But the links of a compound forming a code are peculiar. A code is a linear series of items which are composed, in the case of a chemical code, of groups of atoms forming a chemical substituent. In the case of DNA, each item of the series consists of one out of four alternative substituents. In an ideally functioning chemical code—to which I shall limit myself—each alternative substituent forming a possible item of the series must have the same mathematical chance of appearing at any point of the series. Any difference of alternative chances would reduce the amount of information transmitted, and if there were a chemical law which determined that the constituents can be aligned only in one particular arrangement, this arrangement could transmit no information. Thus in an ideal code, all alternative sequences being equally probable, no sequence is unaffected by chemical laws, and is an arithmetical or metrical design, not explicable in chemical terms.

The conception of a purely metrical structure in a chemical compound is exemplified by the configuration of two optical antipodes which have the same statistical probability. A chemical synthesis of any particular compound of this kind tends to produce both antipodes in equal quantities. They can then be separated, and Pasteur separated them, by letting them crystallise and picking out the pure forms by their differently shaped crystals. But this discrimination is not due to chemical forces. A chemical discrimination of the two antipodes can be brought about by using optically active reagents or solvents, but this leaves open the problem as to the origin of these optically active partners. To prepare chemically a compound that is one out of millions of equally probable DNA alternatives would produce, along with it, about equal amounts of each of these millions of alternatives. Moreover, the task of separating the desired compound from the others would present many times over the kind of problem presented by the chemical separation of optical antipodes.

One could build a chain of substituents arranged according to any desired pattern by adding each consecutive link of the series separately. But the resulting pattern would not be the product of chemical forces, and if it functioned as a code transmitting information, this would be the information which we had imparted to the pattern by the sequence of operations that built it up. Such a code might be made to transmit the words of a national anthem, or to serve as a message for military secrets, neither of which could be regarded as the product of chemical forces.

Another way of reaching the same conclusions is by considering the theory advanced by a number of neuro-physiologists, that the nervous system registers the memory of a habit acquired by an organism in the structure of its RNA molecules. This is called the fixation of experience by RNA in the manner of a tape recording, and this analogy illustrates what I am saying here. The information imparted to a molecule of this type is received and held by it in a way similar to that in which a tape recorder would do this. The pattern of its traces is the pattern of the impacts in which the message was embodied. The pattern can no more be derived from the laws of physics and chemistry when engraved in an RNA molecule than it can be when inscribed on a tape or, for that matter, on the surface of a rock.

Morphology is the Framework

We can now lend greater precision and force to the conclusion that morphological features are the boundary conditions of physical-chemical laws in living things and thus are not accountable by these laws, on which they rely for their functions. The functional structure of machines, products of man's designing and shaping, manifestly represent boundary conditions imposed on the laws of in animate nature to press them into the service of a technical purpose. We have before us now the corresponding process that shapes the morphological development of the germ cell. What happens here, according to the theory of Watson and Crick, is that DNA transmits to the developing body of cells a quantity of information in an equivalent amount of organic differentiation. And thus it follows that the shape and structure of living beings has the structure of an information.

When this structure reappears in an organism, it is a configuration of particles that typifies a living being and serves its functions; at the same time, this configuration is a member of a large group of equally probable (and mostly meaningless) configurations. Such a highly improbable arrangement of particles is not shaped by the forces of physics or chemistry. It constitutes a boundary condition, which as such transcends the laws of physics and chemistry.

This brings the vital shaping of offspring by DNA into consonance with the shaping of a machine by the engineer. The manufacturing of a machine also represents a distinctive distribution of matter not due to the working of physical-chemical forces and it, too, forms the characteristic boundary conditions of the system in question. We can see now more clearly why such shaping of boundaries may be said to go beyond a mere 'fixing of boundaries' and establishes a 'controlling principle'. It achieves control of the boundaries by imprinting a significant pattern on the boundaries of the system. Or, to use information language, we may say that it puts the system under the control of a non-physical-chemical principle by *a profoundly informative intervention.*

We can see then also why a selection of the crystals of one optical isomer from a mixture of the crystals including both antipodes is a non-chemical procedure. It is that because it produces a significant distribution of matter not determined by the laws of chemistry. And we can note that the same holds obviously for the construction of a polymer chain by joining a preselected sequence of substituents.

I have accepted here the view of Watson and Crick that the information content of an organism equals the information conveyed by its DNA. But I doubt that we have as yet a quantitative measure of the information—or negentropy, as Schrodinger has called it—of a living thing. The currently discussed question, whether the information content of the developed organism does not exceed that of its DNA, seems therefore not ripe for evaluation in the light of the principles I have put forward here.

Finally, a word on the way the boundary conditions controlling physical-chemical processes in an organism may have come into existence from inanimate beginnings. The question is whether or not the logical range of random mutations includes the formation of novel principles not definable in terms of physics and chemistry. It seems very unlikely that it does include it. This is the ground on which emergence has been defined in my recent writings, including my book *The Tacit Dimension.*

But the problem of evolution lies beyond my subject here. When I say that life transcends physics and chemistry, I mean that biology cannot explain life in our age by the current workings of physical and chemical laws.

In Retrospect

The moment one succeeds in proving that machines cannot be explained in terms of physics, this appears so obvious that one wonders whether something so trivial could have ever been overlooked, and if it has been, what use there can be in forcing it to our attention now.

It may seem unbelievable, but it is yet a fact, that for 300 years writers who contested the possibility of explaining life by physics and chemistry by affirming that living things are *not,* or not wholly, machine-like, instead of pointing out that the mere existence of machine-like functions in living beings proves that life cannot be explained in terms of physics and chemistry. In the late 17th century, we find the Neo-Platonist Cudworth, and likewise the naturalist John Ray, opposing the view that life can be explained in terms of matter in motion, by affirming that living beings are *not* machines. And 200 years later, Driesch and his supporters fought for the recognition that life transcends physics and chemistry, by arguing that the powers of regeneration in the sea urchin embryo (discovered by Driesch) were not explicable by a machine-like structure. Up to this day one speaks of the mechanistic conception of life both to designate an explanation of life in terms of physics and chemistry, and an explanation of living functions as machineries—though the latter excludes the former. The term 'mechanistic' is in fact so well established for referring to these two mutually exclusive conceptions, that I am at a loss to find two different words that will distinguish between them.

- No physical-chemical topography will tell us that we have a machine before us and what its functions are.
- Such a topography can completely identify one particular specimen of a machine, but can tell us nothing about a class of machines.
- And if we are asked how the same solid system can be subject to control by two independent principles, the answer is: The boundary conditions of the system are free of control by physics and can be controlled therefore by non-physical, purely technical, principles.

Turn next to living things. Of the points that apply to machines the first point fails to apply to living beings. For it is not obviously clear that living things are not formed by mere physical-chemical equilibration. And at this point, strangely enough, the discovery of DNA, which is so widely thought to prove that life is mere chemistry, provides the missing link for proving the contrary. The theory of Crick and Watson, that four alternative substituents lining a DNA chain convey an amount of information approximating that of the total number of such possible configurations, amounts to saying that the particular alignment present in a DNA molecule is not determined by chemical forces. And the additional theory, that the information of a DNA molecule is embodied in the morphology of the corresponding offspring, assures us of the fact that this morphology is not the product of a chemical equilibration but is designed by other than chemical forces. This is the step my present paper adds to my arguments.

This story of long gradual progress toward proving my point shows, in my view, that such proof is not easily established. Add to this the widespread, erroneous argument which those who share my basic views have put forward—as exemplified by my critique of Commoner's argument. It may appear then less surprising that these views have not gained ground so far, and that the confusion of the past centuries continues to prevail. The effort of dispelling confusion may also appear worthwhile then.

Note

1. In my *Personal Knowledge*, pages 390–92, I have pointed out that the entire system of conceptions based on randomness (such as the ideas of chance, the theory of gas pressure and temperature, and all thermodynamics) is unspecifiable in terms of atomic physics, and that hence we must recognise randomness as a comprehensive principle above mechanics, quantal- or macro- dimensional. I know of no other pair of inanimate principles, both valid (not complementary) where one of them (the 'higher' one) excludes application of the other, the other, even while its operations are based on the latter. We may also note that boundaries of inanimate systems established by the history of the universe, are found widely in geological, geographic and astronomic domains and that their information content per unit of matter is very much less than that of a living thing.

Suggestions for Additional Reading

1. Commoner, Barry, *Science and Survival*, Viking Press, New York, 1966, Chapter 3, "Greater than the Sum of its Parts", and writings of the author quoted by him.
2. Crick, Francis, *Of Molecules and Men*, University of Washington Press, Seattle, 1966.

3. Polanyi, Michael, *The Tacit Dimension*, Doubleday, New York, 1966; Routledge and Kegan Paul, Ltd., London, 1967, pp. 87–91.

Previous publications of the author containing much of the present argument include: *Personal Knowledge: Towards a Post-Critical Philosophy*, Routledge and Kegan Paul Ltd., London, and University of Chicago Press, Chicago (1958), pp. 328–35; *The Study of Man*, Routledge and Kegan Paul, Ltd. London, and University of Chicago Press, Chicago (1959), pp. 47–52; *The Scientist Speculates*, ed. L. J. Good, G. P. Putnam's Sons, N.Y., and Wm. Heinemann, Ltd., London (1962), pp. 71–78; *Science as a Cultural Force*, ed. Henry Woolf, Johns Hopkins Press, Baltimore (1964), pp. 54–76; *Rev. Mod. Phys.*, 34, 601 (1962); *Encounter*, London, 24, No. 5 (1965); *Brain*, London, 88, Part IV, 799 (1966); *Philosophy*, London, 40, 369 (1966).

20

Do Life Processes Transcend
Physics and Chemistry?

This short paper, introducing a discussion of the previous article, re-fines the formulation given there.

Ladies and gentlemen, I shall talk for quite a while about a subject which might seem far-fetched, namely, machines. But you will see shortly that this leads up to our main question.

Let me introduce the subject by suggesting that if all men were exterminated, which is not so difficult to imagine today as it used to be, the laws of inanimate nature would not be affected, but the production of machines would stop. Not until men rose again could machines be formed once more. Some animals can produce tools, but only men can construct machines. Machines are human artifacts consisting of inanimate material.

Now, the Oxford dictionary which one usually invokes at this point, describes a machine as an apparatus for applying mechanical power, consisting of a number of interrelated parts, each with a definite function. It might be, for example, a machine for sewing or painting. Let us assume that the power is built into the machine and disregard the fact that we have to supply it with power from time to time. We can then say that the manufacture of machines consists in cutting suitably shaped parts and fitting them together, so that their joint mechanical action will serve a human purpose. The structure and working of machines are thus shaped by men, even while their material and the forces that operate in them obey the laws of inanimate nature.

[130]. Reprinted, with permission from Basil Blackwell Inc., from *Zygon*, III, Dec. 1968, pp.44–7.

In constructing a machine and supplying it with power, we harness as it were the laws of nature at work in its material and in its driving force and make them serve our purpose. But this harness is not unbreakable. The structure of the machine and its working can break down. Nothing is more well-known. But this will not affect in the least the forces of inanimate nature on which the operation of the machine relies. It merely releases these forces from the restrictions the machine imposed on them before it broke down. So the machine as a whole works under the control of two distinct principles. The higher principle is that of the machine's design. This higher principle harnesses the lower one, which consists in the physicochemical processes on which the machine relies for its working.

We commonly form such a two levelled structure, as I shall call it, in conducting an experiment. But there's a difference between constructing a machine and rigging up an experiment. The experimenter imposes restrictions on nature in order to observe its behaviour under these restrictions, while the construction of a machine restricts nature in order to harness its working. We may borrow a term from physics and describe both these useful restrictions of nature as the imposing of boundary conditions on the laws of physics and chemistry.

Let me enlarge on this. I have exemplified two types of boundaries. In the machine we are interested in the effects of the boundary conditions, while in the experimental setting we are interested in the natural processes controlled by the boundaries. Both types of interest are common. When a saucepan bounds a soup that we are cooking, we are interested in the soup, not in the saucepan; likewise, when we observe a reaction in a test tube, we are studying the reaction, and not the test tube. The reverse is true, for example, for a game of chess: The strategy of the player imposes boundaries on the several moves which follow the laws of chess, but our interest lies in the boundaries, that is, in the strategy, not in the several moves. Similarly, when a sculptor shapes a stone, or a painter composes a painting, our interest lies in the boundaries imposed on the material, not in the material itself. I would distinguish these two types of boundaries by saying that the first represents the test-tube type of boundary, while the second represents the machine type. We'll see that this is useful.

All communications have machine types of boundaries, and these boundaries form a whole hierarchy of consecutive levels. A vocabulary sets boundary conditions to the utterance of the voice, a grammar harnesses words to form sentences, and the sentences are shaped into a text which conveys a communication. These are the consecutive levels. At each level we are interested in the boundaries imposed rather than in the principles harnessed. Communications will prove of particular interest to our main problem, to which I'll now return.

From machines, we pass to living beings. We arrive there by remembering that animals move about mechanically and that they have internal organs which perform functions as the parts of a machine do, functions which sustain the life of the organism in the way that machines serves the interests of their uses. For centuries past, the workings of life have been likened to the workings of machines, and physiologists have been seeking to interpret the organism as a complex network of mechanisms. Any single part of the organism is puzzling to physiology and meaningless to pathology until the way it benefits the organism is discovered. We may add that any description of such a system in terms of its physicochemical topography would be quite meaningless but for the fact that the description covertly recalls the system's physiological interpretation. Similarly, the topography of a machine is meaningless until we guess how it works and for what purpose.

In this light, the organism is shown to be, like a machine, a system under dual control. Its structure serves as a boundary condition, harnessing the physicochemical processes by which its organs perform their functions. Thus, morphogenesis, the process by which the structure of living beings develops, can be likened to the shaping of a machine which will act as a boundary for the laws of inanimate nature. As these laws serve the machine, so they also serve the developed organism.

Let me emphasise here the fact that the boundary condition is always extraneous to the process which it delimits. In Galileo's experiments of balls rolling down a slope, the angle of the slope was not derived from the laws of mechanics but was chosen by Galileo. This choice of slope was extraneous to the laws of mechanics, as the shape and manufacture of test tubes is extraneous to the laws of chemistry. The same holds for machine-like boundaries. Their structure cannot be derived from the forces which they harness. Nor can a vocabulary determine the content of a text. And so on. Therefore, if the structure of living things is a set of boundary conditions, this structure is extraneous to the laws of physics and chemistry governing the forces which the organism is harnessing. Under this supposition, the morphology of living things transcends the laws of physics and chemistry.

But before being satisfied with this argument, we should admit that the analogy between machines and functioning organs is weakened by the fact that the organs are not shaped artificially as the parts of a machine are. It is an advantage, therefore, to find that the morphogenetic process is explained in principle by the genetic transmission of information stored in a chemical compound, the famous DNA interpreted in this sense by Watson and Crick.

The informations [*sic*] stored in DNA, which control morphogenesis can be shown to be boundary conditions like those imposed on a material by shaping it into a machine. That's why I talked so much about machines. For, just as the information contained in a printed page is conveyed in a distinctive arrangement of letters which is not due to any physical interaction between the letters, so the information content of a DNA molecule inheres in an ordering of its constituents which is not due to any physical interaction between them. It is a boundary condition, and as such, it is extraneous to the chemical forces composing the molecule, just as if their pattern were artificial, as that of a machine is.

Its ordering has, in fact, a negentropy, which will give some additional precision to what I have just submitted to you. This negentropy is due to the fact that the chemical forces in the molecule permit any alternative isomeric sequence to be formed with an equal or virtually equal probability. This means that the sequence of substituents which bears the molecule's information is virtually extraneous to the molecule's chemical forces. In other words, the information-bearing function of a sequence of substituents is a boundary condition harnessing the molecule's chemical forces, and as such, it is extraneous to the laws of chemistry. Analogously, the arrangement of printed letters is extraneous to the chemistry of the paper and ink forming the printed page.

According to the theory of Watson and Crick, the negentropy—the negative entropy—content of DNA is transmitted to the offspring in the negentropy of its bodily structure. It follows then, by the same analysis that I have applied to the DNA molecule, to the machine, and to a number of other cases, that the distinctive improbability, or negentropy, of a living structure is extraneous to the laws of inanimate matter at work in the organism.

The structure of living things is a boundary condition which harnesses the physicochemical forces of the organism and as such, the structure of the organism transcends the laws of physics and chemistry. This is what

I meant by writing a short time ago a paper entitled 'Life Transcends Physics and Chemistry'. But that formulation is too loose, and I want to amend it in the sense I have just suggested. Thank you.

Part IV

Mind, Religion, and Art

Introduction to Part IV

The five articles in Part IV follow on from the last two articles in Part III wherein Polanyi outlined the structure of the tacit integration of comprehensive entities and of our tacit integration of our awareness of their subsidiary details into our focal knowledge of those entities themselves, and intimated that this structure entailed a multi-level universe in contrast to the uni-level world of Reductionism. We now turn to the human world, a series of yet higher levels. The following articles apply Polanyi's philosophy of personal knowing and tacit integration to the workings of the mind, its relation to the body and our knowledge of it, to the presence of faith in religion and all forms of knowing, to the inescapability of moral judgment in the study of human affairs, and to the structure of paintings and our awareness and appreciation of them.

21

The Hypothesis of Cybernetics (1951)

This article elaborates a part of Polanyi's argument against the reduction of minds to machines: viz. that machines cannot perform necessarily personal and unformalisable acts of judgment, belief and validation. Compare PK *pp.261–64.*

The publication of the following notes formulated some time ago on the question whether machines can be said to think may supplement the discussion of cybernetics conducted in this *Journal* by K. R. Popper (vol. I, pp. 194–195), J. O. Wisdom (vol. 2, p. I), D. M. MacKay (vol. 2, p. 120), F. M. R. Walshe (vol. 2, p. 161–163) and W. Mays (vol. 2, pp. 249–250).

Since the conception of the machine involves some complications which I consider to be not strictly relevant to the argument (and I want to be as brief as possible) I shall limit myself at first to the question whether the operations of a formalised deductive system might conceivably be considered equivalent to the operations of the mind. I believe that such a suggestion involves a logical fallacy.

The declared purpose of formalisation is (1) to designate undefined terms, (2) specify unproved asserted sentences (axioms), and (3) strictly to prescribe the handling of asserted sentences, which leads to the writing down of new asserted sentences (formal proof). There prevails throughout a desire to eliminate elements that are called 'psychological'. Thus, (1) undefined terms are chosen without aiming to signify commonly understood logical relations; (2) 'unproven asserted sentences' replace 'statements believed to be self-evident' and (3) the operations constituting 'formal proof' are intended to replace 'merely psychological' proofs.

---

[58]. Reprinted, with permission from Oxford University Press, from *The British Journal of Philosophy of Science*, II, Feb. 1951, pp.321–25.

I think it is logically fallacious to speak of a *complete* elimination of what have been called 'psychological' but might better be called 'unformalised' elements of deductive systems; for:

(1) No undefined term can be introduced unless its use is first explained by ordinary speech or demonstrated by examples. An undefined term is a sign indicating the proper use which is to be made of it. The acceptance of an undefined term implies, therefore, that we believe that we know its proper use though this is not to be formally described. This proper use is a skill of which we declare ourselves to be possessed.

(2) Similarly for 'unproved asserted sentences': the fact that they are asserted is irrelevant. Asserted by whom? 'Asserted' merely disguises the unavowed yet indispensable 'believed': namely believed by the writer and held by him to be deserving universal belief. 'Sentence' is a disguise for statement: a statement about something. For if there is nothing that can satisfy a sentence there is no use deriving any other sentences from it; and only sentences that are statements can be satisfied or not satisfied. A 'proof' cannot be recognised as such unless it is true that whatever satisfies the axioms from which it starts will satisfy the theorems arrived at. In accepting a statement as an axiom we express the belief that we know what does and what does not satisfy it, and that everything does. Thereby we imply the unformalised knowledge of an indefinite range of operations and of their expected result.

(3) The mere handling of symbols according to the rules of formal proof constitutes a proof only to the extent to which we accredit these operations in advance with the power of carrying conviction. But 'proof' (as I think Ryle would say) is a success-word. The success in this case lies in the capacity of the 'proof' to convince us (and to convince us also that others ought to share our conviction) that an implication has been demonstrated. No handling of symbols to which we refuse to award this success can be said to be a proof, no matter what pre-established rules it is said to conform to. And again the award of this success is a process which is not formalised.

Thus, I maintain that a formal system of symbols and operations functions as a deductive system only by virtue of unformalised supplements. We must know the meaning of undefined terms, understand what is stated in our axioms and believe it to be true, and acknowledge an implication in the handling of symbols by formal proof. These acts of knowing, understanding and acknowledging are not formalised: they may be jointly designated as the 'semantic operations' of the formalised system.

Formalisation can be extended to hitherto unformalised semantic operations, but only if the resulting formal system can in its turn rely on yet unformalised semantic operations. The elimination of 'psychological elements' by formalisation thus remains necessarily incomplete. The purpose of formalisation lies in the reduction of informal functions to what we believe to be more limited and obvious operations; but it must not aim at their elimination.

The semantic operations attached to a formal system are functions of the mind which understands and correctly operates the system. To believe that I understand and correctly operate a formal system implies that I know how to operate its unformalised functions. Since a formal system will always require supplementation by unformalised operations, it follows that none can ever function without a person who performs these operations. A formalised deductive system is an instrument which requires for its logical completion a mind using the instrument in a manner not fully determined by the instrument; while the mind of the person using the instrument requires no such logical completion. A person can carry out computations with the aid of a machine (or formal system) or without it, but a computing machine cannot be said to operate except within a tripartite system:

I   II   III
mind $\rightarrow$ machine $\rightarrow$ things to which the machine informally refers.

Herein lies the difference between mind and machine.

If in this system we replace 'machine' by a mind (mind (2)) we have,

I'   II'   III'
mind (1) $\rightarrow$ mind (2) $\rightarrow$ things to which mind (2) informally refers,

where the unformalised functions III' are those of mind (1), while the experimentally observed mind (2) functions as a formalised *instrument* of mind (1). This is the behaviourist model of mind (2) which attributes to the experimentally observed mind an entirely different character from that required for its experimental observation by mind (1). Such a disparity, arising merely from different temporary functions of minds, can be accepted only as representing two aspects of the mind. Both are significant and both incomplete, though in different ways. The experimentally observed aspect of the mind (mind (2)) is the brain surgeon's aspect of it. It does not include the unformalised functions of mind and lacks any element of responsible judgment, since only an observing mind ('mind (1)') can exercise such responsibility through its unformalised functions. The concept of the observed mind presupposes the observing mind but the reverse is not true. (Thus the behaviourist's intention of replacing the concept of mind by the concept of 'observed mind' necessarily defeats itself.) On the other hand, while mind (1) can function without ever practising experimental neurology, it cannot discover within itself the facts of neurology. Mind (1) *may* be supplemented by neurology; mind (2) must be supplemented by experience of consciousness and responsible judgment.

Only observing minds (minds (1)) can be supposed to communicate with each other. Inter-personal dealings like listening to or addressing a person exclude the observing of one person's mental operations by the other in the sense in which mind (1) experimentally observes mind (2).

A machine is an interpretation of an observed mind ('mind (2)') and not of an observing mind ('mind (1)'). You can see the difference for example in the process of reaching an inductive inference. Mind (1) can reach an inductive inference and a machine can be used by it as an instrument in the process, but the inference represents its own conviction. The experimental neurologist's model, mind (2), cannot be properly said to draw an inductive inference since it lacks the elements for representing the act of reaching a conviction.

22

The Body-Mind Relation

This article appropriately follows on from the previous one and the last two in Part III, because it is a restatement of Polanyi's treatment of the nature of the mind and its relation to the body in terms of their tacit integration such that we attend from someone's bodily expressions and actions and to his mind. I have included it because it contains some additional items, such as a clearer account of the functions of bodily processes of which the subject is not in any way aware and of why a neurologist studying them cannot dwell in them as he does in other aspects of the person whom he is studying.

When I point my finger at the wall and call out: 'Look at this!' all eyes turn to the wall, away from my finger. You are clearly attending to my pointing finger, but only in order to look at something else; namely, at the point to which my finger is directing your attention. We have here two different ways of being aware of things. One way is to look at a thing. This is the way you look at the wall. But how is one to describe the way you see my finger pointing at the wall? You are not looking at my finger, but away from it. I should say that you do not see it as a mere object to be examined as such, but as an object having a function: the function of directing your attention away from itself and at something else. But this is not to say that my pointing finger was trying to make you disregard itself. Far from it. It wanted to be seen, but to be seen only in order to be followed and not in older to be examined.

[132]. Reprinted, with the permission of Dr. W.R. Coulson, from *Man and the Science of Man*, ed. W.R. Coulson and C.R. Rodgers (Charles Merrill Pub. Co, 1968), pp.85–102.

I shall call my pointing finger a subsidiary thing or an instrumental thing that functions by pointing at an object which is at the focus of our attention. And I suggest that we have here two different kinds of awareness. We are subsidiarily aware of the pointing finger and focally aware of the object at which it points. We establish an integrated relationship between them by recognising the direction in which the finger directs us and by following this direction.

This relationship is not symmetrical. The finger points at the wall, but the wall does not point at the finger. The relationship that we have established has an intrinsic direction: it is directive. Thus, the finger has a meaning that the wall lacks. It can raise a problem: If you come across a pointing finger by itself, in a wood, it makes you wonder what it may be pointing at. This shows that it is for us to establish the coherence of the pointing finger with that to which it points. It is for us to comprehend the coherent system connecting a subsidiary element with the focal point on which the subsidiary element bears. And note that we perform this comprehending without a word. No syllogism is set up; no evidence is cited. The performance is tacit, and since its result is valid, we may call it an act of tacit inference.

Another case of this kind will reinforce this analysis and develop it further. Think of a pair of stereoscopic photographs, viewed in the proper way, one eye looking at one, the other eye at the other. The objects shown in the two pictures appear in their joint image as distributed in depth, and tangible. This is what we see at the focus of our eyes; but it involves also the sight of the two component pictures: cover these up and we see nothing at all. But we do not see these two pictures in themselves. In a way, we look through them, or from them, at their joint image. So I shall class our awareness of them as subsidiary and observe that the way we look at them integrates their sights into the spatially deepened image to which they contribute. Thanks to our integration, the two flat pictures effectively function as clues to a spatial image.

We may say that this image is their joint meaning,. and that this joint meaning lies in the focus of our attention. So far, the structure of this tacit integration is analogous to that of a finger pointing at an object. But something important is added here. The joint meaning of the subsidiaries is expressed in a new sensory quality. Sights in depth have come about by integrating sights that were comparatively flat.

This change of appearance is, in fact, a regular accompaniment of tacit integration. A pointing finger also looks a little different from the finger fixed in the same position by arthritis. This kind of difference is more noticeable in the closely analogous case of a word denoting an object. The word, when functioning in this way, appears transparent by contrast to its opaque appearance when we listen to it as a sequence of sounds. I shall come back to this case later.

Professor Hadley Cantril of Princeton has shown that when we introduce two fairly disparate pictures into the stereoscope, we see fanciful integrations of them. Such images are illusory. But we may limit ourselves to the case that the two pictures viewed are proper photographs, and that, hence, their stereoscoping image is a reasonably correct evaluation of their joint meaning. We can then regard stereoscopic viewing as a feat of tacit inference; that is, as a tacit counterpart to a process of explicit inference.

But let me stop to warn here against a misconception. It is a mistake (and I often find it done) to identify subsidiary awareness with subconscious or pre-conscious awareness, or with the fringe of consciousness described by William James. The relation of subsidiaries to that on which they bear is a logical relation similar to that which a premise has to the inference drawn from it, with the great difference that the inferences arrived at here are tacit. Subsidiary awareness can be fully conscious, as that of a pointing finger or a pair of pictures viewed in the stereoscope, though in other cases out consciousness of subsidiaries may be on a very low level and may be altogether subliminal. Such is the case, for example, when sensory clues inside our eyes and inner ear are integrated to a percept. Such variations in their level of consciousness in no way affects the functions of subsidiary elements contributing to an act of tacit knowing.

Jean Piaget has strikingly contrasted the act of acquiring knowledge by a sensory act like perception as compared with a process of explicit inference. He points out that explicit inference is *reversible* in the sense that we can go back to its premises and go forward again to its conclusions as often as we like, while this is not true for the sensory act. And since perception is always combined with action, and action with sensation, Piaget contrasts all sensory-motor acts with explicit inferences and calls them *irreversible*.

Actually, all acts of tacit integration are irreversible, and this can be understood from the structure of tacit knowing. We find, indeed, that tacit knowing can have two kinds of irreversibility. One consists in the fact that we may not be able to identify all the clues which we have integrated in establishing their joint meaning. The other kind of irreversibility goes beyond this. It is due to the fact that when we shift the focus of our attention from the meaningful result of tacit integration, and focus on the subsidiaries, their integration is wiped out. The subsidiary particulars cease to have a bearing on their prospective target and are reduced to an aggregate of meaningless objects. The first kind of irreversibility can be called contingent, by contrast to the second, that is logically necessary.

The joint viewing of two stereoscopic photographs offers a simple example both of contingent and logical irreversibility. Think of the differences in the two pictures, by virtue of which their joint viewing offers the sight of spatial depth: these differences are very small and are scattered all over the pictures. It is almost impossible to identify them; they are virtually unspecifiable. This is the first kind of irreversibility. But even if we could overcome this and identify the clues of stereoscopic vision, it would not be the same as retracing the steps of a mathematical proof. To reconsider a mathematical deduction is to deepen our understanding of the idea which it embodies. We can see now in the premises the whole panorama of their implications. By contrast, if we take out the stereo pictures from the viewer and look at them separately, they cease to tell us anything of what they jointly mean; we see nothing of what they would jointly present to our eyes. To go back to the antecedents of our tacit inference has not deepened our grasp of its result, but rather has made us lose sight of it.

I have already mentioned in passing the most widely known example of this disintegration of meaning, caused by the shifting of our focal attention to that which has this meaning. A spoken word loses its meaning if we repeat it a number of times while carefully attending to the movement of our lips and tongue and to the sound we are making. These actions are meaningful, so long as we attend to that on which they jointly bear; they lose their meaning when we shift our attention to the actions, themselves.

Admittedly, the disintegration of tacit knowledge by shifting our attention to its clues is not irreparable. The two stereo pictures can be viewed jointly once more; the word that has lost its meaning will regain it if we once more use it—once more subsidiarily be casting our mind forward to something we can say by it.

But it is important to note that this recovery never brings back the original meaning. It may improve on it. Motion studies, which tend to paralyse a skill, will improve it when followed by practice. The meticulous dismembering of a text which can kill appreciation of it, can also supply material for a much deeper understanding of it. In these cases, the detailing of particulars, which, by itself, would destroy meaning, serves as a guide to their subsequent integration, and thus establishes a more secure and more accurate meaning.

But the damage done by the specification of particulars may be irremediable. Meticulous detailing may obscure beyond recall a subject like history, literature, or philosophy. In his essay on the *Name and Nature of Poetry*, A. E. Housman has described the disastrous effect of spelling out in detail the allusions of Edgar Poe in his poem *The Haunted Palace*. My former colleague at Manchester, the distinguished French scholar Mansell Jones, has written that the humanities are discredited and rejected because of their unconscious abuse of erudition in the teaching of humane subjects. 'Research [he wrote] is at once the flower and the virus of Arts'.[1]

But it is not the unintentional damage done to our tacit knowledge, by reducing our capacity to reintegrate its subsidiaries after having brought them to the light of focal consciousness, that is the main issue here; it is a deliberate refusal to rely on the tacit mode of integration. The modern mind refuses to accept the necessity for tacit assumptions and wants to keep the grounds of its beliefs clearly in focus, as one does in an explicit deduction. Our whole culture is pervaded by the resolve to avoid unspecifiable commitments and to get down ruthlessly to the hard facts of this world, and to keep our eyes firmly fixed on them.

The purpose of this paper is to show that the relation between body and mind has the same logical structure as the relation between clues and the image to which the clues are pointing. I suggest that the body is a subsidiary thing which bears on the mind that is its meaning. The problem of the body-mind relation is that no examination of a person's neural processes (however meticulously carried out) can make the neuro-physiologist share the person's sensations and thoughts. I want to show that this deficiency is but an instance of the general fact that when we turn our attention on the subsidiaries which bear on their joint meaning, that meaning is wiped out. I have cited the obvious case that we lose the sight of a stereo image by looking at the two pictures separately; and I have mentioned also that a word, when used for designating something, appears transparent, and that it becomes opaque and meaningless when we attend to its physical details, such as the movements of our lips and tongue and the sound we are making. I would add now that we find something like this happening for any skilled performance. It loses its meaning and becomes paralysed if we attend to its several motions in themselves. The famous tightrope walker, Blondin, says in his memoirs that he would instantly lose his balance if he thought directly of keeping it; he must force himself to think only of the way he would eventually descend from the rope. Similarly, we lose a pattern from sight if we look at it too closely. When flying by airplane first started, the traces of ancient sites were revealed in fields over which generations of country folk had walked without noticing them. And once landed, the pilot could no longer see them either.

Furthermore, we recognise animals and plants by shapes, their structures, and functions. We know them as comprehensive entities by integrating their parts; and when we concentrate our attention on their several parts, and lose sight of the entity on which these bear, the parts lose their meaning.

In all these cases, we have two kinds of awareness meaningfully related in an act of tacit knowledge, and find that this knowledge is wiped out by directing our attention to the subsidiary particulars.

But we must yet take a further step in deepening our conception of tacit knowledge. We must realise that whenever we observe an external object, be it by sight or smell or touch, we know it by being subsidiarily aware of the impact the object makes on our body, as well as of the responses that our body makes to the object. All conscious transactions we have with the world involve our subsidiary use of our body.

We may indeed say that our body is the only collection of things which we know almost exclusively by relying on our awareness of them for attending to something else. Such is the exceptional position of our body in the universe; and this is what it means to live in our body.

Every deliberate act of consciousness, therefore, has not only an identifiable object as its focal point, but has also a set of subsidiary roots, inside our body. And this is where our body is related to our mind. As our sense organs—our nerves and brain, our muscles and memories—serve us to implement our conscious attention, our awareness of them enters subsidiarily into every meaningful entity which forms the focus of our attention.

And having thus identified the body-mind relation particular instance of the logical relation between he subsidiary and the focal, we can say conversely that all subsidiary elements function as our body does in bearing on conscious experiences. Anything bearing subsidiarily on the focus of our attention can be said then to function logically as part of our body.

Let us say that in such a relationship we attend from subsidiary particulars to their focus. Acts of consciousness are then not only conscious of something, but are also from certain things, that include our body. Remembering that Brentano has taught that all conscious attention has *intentionality*, we recognise now that it also invariably has a rootedness which enters into its content.

Let me restate my theory of the body-mind problem in these terms. When we examine a human body engaged in conscious action, we meet no traces of consciousness in its organs; and this can now be understood in the sense that subsidiary elements, like the bodily organs engaged in conscious action, lose their functional meaning and appearance when we cease to look from them at the focus on which they bear, and look instead at them, as they are in themselves.

This kind of process can also take place in the opposite direction; it can work constructively as well as destructively. We can be looking at something and then, recognising it to have a bearing on something else, we can pass from an at-awareness of it to a from-awareness of it. And again, we can go back on this, as I have just described, changing our from-awareness again into an at-awareness.

But this way of speaking is clumsy; we should have some simpler language for describing the way in which we establish tacit knowledge and the way in which we destroy it. For this, we shall assimilate all kinds of subsidiary awareness to the kind of awareness we normally have of our body when attending from it to an external event that impinges on it. We shall say then that when we become subsidiarily aware of something with a bearing on its meaning, we make it function as if it were part of our own body; in other words, we interiorise it and, in doing so, make ourselves *dwell in it*. The opposite action, of switching our attention to something of which we had hitherto been subsidiarily aware, can then be described as turning that thing into a mere external object, devoid of functional meaning; an action which can be said to *objectivise* the thing, or else to *externalise* it.

This formulation of tacit knowing is particularly suited for describing the way in which we know another person's mind. We know a chess

player's mind by dwelling in the stratagems of his games and know another man's pain by dwelling in his face distorted by suffering. And we
may conclude that the opposite process; namely, of insisting to look at
the parts of an observed behaviour, and thus regarding them as mere
objects, must make us lose sight of the mind in control of a person's
behaviour.

But what then should we think of the current school of psychology
which claims that it replaces the study of mental processes by observing
the several particulars of behaviour as objects, and then establishes experimentally the laws of their occurrence? We may doubt that the identification of the particulars is feasible, as these will include many
unspecifiable clues. But the feasibility of the programme will not only be
uncertain, but also logically impossible. To objectivise the parts of conscious behaviour must make us lose sight of the mind and dissolve the
very image of a coherent behaviour.

Admittedly, behaviourist studies do not reach this logical consequence
of their programme. This is due to the fact that we cannot wholly shift
our attention to the fragments of a conscious behaviour. When we quote
a subject's report on a mental experience instead of referring to this experience, it leaves our knowledge of that experience untouched; the report retains some meaning, by bearing on this experience. An experimenter
may speak of an electric shock as an objective fact, but he administers it
only because he knows and remembers its painful effect. Afterwards, he
may observe changes in the conductivity of the subject's skin which, in
themselves, would be meaningless, and register them because they actually signify to him the expectation of an electric shock by the subject.

Thus, a behaviourist analysis merely paraphrases mentalist descriptions in terms known to be symptoms of mental states, and the meaning
consists in these mentalist connotations. The practice of such paraphras-
ing might be harmless and sometimes even convenient, but a preference
for tangible terms of description will tend to be restrictive and misleading. The behaviourist analysis of learning, for example, has banned the
physiognomies of surprise, puzzlement, and concentrated attention by
which Köhler described the mental efforts of his chimpanzees. It avoids
the complex, delicately graded situations which evoke these mental states.
The study of learning was thus cut down to its crudest form known as
conditioning. And this oversimple paradigm of learning was then misde-
scribed by Pavlov when he identified *eating* with an *expectation to be*

fed, because both of these induce the secretion of saliva. Wherever we define mental processes by objectivist circumlocutions, we are apt to stumble into such absurdities.

The actual working of behaviourism therefore confirms my conclusion that strictly isolated pieces of behaviour are meaningless fragments, not identifiable as parts of behaviour. Behaviourist psychology depends on covertly alluding to the mental states which it sets out to eliminate.

Principles of Boundary Control

But is not the material substance of all higher entities governed throughout by the laws of inanimate matter? Does it not follow then that it must be possible to represent all their workings in terms of these laws? Yes, this would follow. If I claim that these higher entities are irreducible, I must show that they are governed in part by principles beyond the scope of physics and chemistry. I shall do so. I shall show first that a number of different principles can control a comprehensive entity at different levels. I have repeatedly presented this theory before in more particular terms; it will be developed here on general lines.

There exist principles that apply to a variety of circumstances. They can be laws of nature, like the laws of mechanics; or be principles of operation, like those of physiology, as for example those controlling muscular contraction and co-ordination; or they can be principles laid down for the use of artifacts, like the vocabulary of the English language or the rules of chess. Not all important principles have such wide scope; but I need not go into this, for it is enough to have established the fact that some principles of widely variable applicability do exist.

We can then go on to note that such a principle is necessarily compatible with any restriction we may choose to impose on the situations to which it is to apply; it leaves wide open the conditions under which it can be made to operate. Thus, these conditions lie beyond the control of our principle, and may be said to form its boundaries, or more precisely its *boundary conditions*. The term 'boundary conditions' (borrowed from physics) will be used here in this sense.

Next, we recognise that, in certain cases, the boundary conditions of a principle are, in fact, subject to control by other principles. These I will call higher principles. Thus, the boundary conditions of the laws of mechanics may be controlled by the operational principles which define a machine; the boundary conditions of muscular action may be controlled by a pattern of purposive behaviour like that of going for a walk; the boundary conditions of a vocabulary are usually controlled by the rules of grammar; and the conditions left open by the rules of chess are controlled by the stratagems of the players. And so we find that machines, purposive actions, grammatical sentences, and games of chess ar all entities subject to *dual control*.

Such is the stratified structure of comprehensive entities. They embody a combination of two principles: a higher and a lower. Smash up a machine, utter words at random, or make chess moves without a purpose, and the corresponding higher principles—that which constitutes the machine, that which makes words into sentences, and that which makes moves of chess into a game—will all vanish, and the comprehensive entity which they controlled will cease to exist.

But the lower principles—the boundary conditions of which the higher principles had control—remain in operation. The laws of mechanics, the vocabulary sanctioned by the dictionary, and the rules of chess will all continue to apply as before. Hence, no description of a comprehensive entity in the light of its lower principles can ever reveal the operation of its higher principles. *The higher principles which characterise a comprehensive entity cannot be defined in terms of the laws that apply to its parts in themselves.*

On the other hand, a machine does rely for its working on the laws of mechanics; a purposive motoric action, like going for a walk, relies on the operations of the muscular system which it directs; and so on. The operation of higher principles rely, quite generally, on the action of the laws governing lower levels.

Yet, since the laws of the lower level will go on operating whether the higher principles continue to be in working order or not, the action of the lower laws may well disrupt the working of the higher principles and destroy the comprehensive entity controlled by them. Such is the mechanism of a two-levelled comprehensive entity.

It presents us with an ontological counterpart of the *logical disintegration* caused by switching our attention from the centre of a comprehensive entity to its particulars. For to turn our attention from the actions of the higher principle, which defines the two-levelled entity, and direct it to the lower principle, controlling the isolated parts of the entity, is to lose sight of the higher principle and, indeed, of the whole entity con-

trolled by it. The logical structure of tacit knowing is seen to cover the
ontological structure of a combined pair of levels.

Application of These Principles to Mind and Body

We must ask now whether the functioning of living beings and of their
consciousness is, in fact, stratified. Is it subject to the joint control of
different principles working at consecutive levels?

We may answer that the laws of physics and chemistry do not ascribe
consciousness to any process controlled by them; the presence of consciousness proves, therefore, that other principles than those of inanimate matter participate in the conscious operations of living things.

And there are two other fundamental principles of biology which are
beyond the scope of physics and chemistry. The structure and functioning of an organism is determined, like that of a machine, by construc-
tional and operational principles which control boundary conditions left
open by physics and chemistry. We may call this a structural principle,
lying beyond the realm of physics and chemistry. I have explained this a
number of times elsewhere and will not argue it here again.

Other functions of the organism not covered by physics and chemistry
are exemplified by the working of the morphogenic field. Its principles
are expressed most clearly by C.H. Waddington's 'epigenetic landscapes'.
These show that the development of the embryo is controlled by the gradient of potential shapes, in the way the motion of a heavy body is controlled by the gradient of potential energy. We may call this principle an
organising field or speak of it as an *organismic principle*.[2]

Most biologists would declare that both the principles of structure
and of organising fields will be reduced one day to the laws of physics
and chemistry. But I am unable to discover the grounds (or even understand the meaning) of such assurances, and hence I will disregard them
and recognise these two principles as they are actually used by biology.

Living beings consist therefore, in a hierarchy of levels, each level
having its own structural and organismic principles. On the mental level,
explicit inferences may be taken to represent the operations of fixed mental
structures, while in tacit knowing, we meet the integrating powers of the
mind. In all our conscious thoughts, these two modes mutually rely on
each other; and it is plausible to assume that explicit mental operations
are based on fixed neural networks, while tacit integrations are grounded

mainly in organising fields. I shall assume that these two principles are interwoven in as their counterparts are in thought.

The purpose of this paper has been to explain the relation between body and mind as an instance of the relation between the subsidiary and the focal in tacit knowledge. The fact that any subsidiary element loses its meaning when we focus our attention on it, was used to explain the fact that when examining the body in conscious action, we meet no traces of consciousness in its organs. We are now ready to complete this project.

We have seen that we can know another person's mind by dwelling in his physiognomy and behaviour; we lose sight of his mind only when we focus our attention on these bodily workings and thus convert them into mere objects. But a neuro-physiologist, observing the events that take place in the eyes and brain of a seeing man, would invariably fail to see in these neural events what the man, himself, sees by them. We must ask why the neurologist cannot dwell in these bodily events, as he could in the subject's physiognomy or intelligent behaviour, in which he witnesses his mind.

We may notice that this kind of indwelling, for which we appear to be equipped by nature, enables us to read only *tacit* thoughts of another mind: thoughts and feelings of the kind that we may suitably ascribe to organismic processes in the nervous system. We can get to know the *explicit* thoughts of a person (which probably correspond to anatomically fixed functions of the nervous system) only from the person's verbal utterances. The meaning of such utterances is artificial; though ultimately derived from demonstrations pointing at tacit experiences, such utterances have no direct appeal on the native mind. The facility for indwelling can be seen to vary also in the case that prehistoric sites, unperceived from the ground, are discerned from the air. I suggest that our incapacity for experiencing the neural processes of another person in the manner he experiences them himself may be aligned with these gradual variations of indwelling.

We arrive, thus, at the following outline. Our capacity of conducting and experiencing the conscious operations of our body, including that of our nervous system, lies in the fact that we, ourselves, fully dwell in them. No one but ourselves can dwell in our body directly and know fully all its conscious operations; but our consciousness can also be experienced by others to the extent to which they can dwell in the external workings of our mind from outside. They can do this fairly effectively for many tacit workings of our mind by dwelling in our physiognomy and behaviour. Such powers of indwelling are fundamentally innate in us. By contrast, our explicit thoughts can be known to others only by dwelling in our pronouncements, the making and understanding of which is founded on artificial conventions.

Objectivisation, whether of another person's gestures or of his utterances, cancels out dwelling in them, destroys their meaning, and cuts off communication through them. The nervous system, as observed by the neuro-physiologist, is always objectivised and can convey its meaning to the observer only indirectly, by painting at a behaviour or at reports that we understand by indwelling.

The logic of tacit knowing and the ontological principles of stratified entities were derived here independently of each other, and we found that our tacit logic enables us to understand stratified entities. Tacit logic shows us: (1) that the higher principle of a stratified entity can be apprehended only by our dwelling in the boundary conditions of a lower principle on which the higher principle operates and (2) that such indwelling is logically incompatible with fixing our attention on the laws governing the lower level. Applied to mind and body, as to two strata in which the higher principles of the mind rely for their operations on the lower principles of physiology, we arrive at three conclusions.

1. No observations of physiology can make us apprehend the operations of the mind.

2. At the same time, the operations of the mind will never be found to interfere with the principles of physiology, or with the even lower principles of physics and chemistry on which they rely.

3. But as the operations of the mind rely on the services of lower bodily principles, the mind can be disturbed by adverse changes in the body, or be offered new opportunities by favourable changes of its bodily basis.

But I must yet show how the mind actually controls the body. For, from the point that we have reached so far, we cannot see how this is done. Let me recall how far we have gone in comparing our own relation to our own mind with the relation that another person has to our mind. We attend to what we have in mind from our awareness of our body; we do this by living in our body and by using it consciously. Others can see what we have in our mind only by watching our facial expression and our gestures; all their knowledge of our consciousness, however sophisticated it be, is derived, in the last resort, from this way of watching us. To sum up then: Others know our mind superficially from their superficial awareness of our body, and we know our own mind more fully from a much more intimate awareness of this body. So far, nothing has been said then, about the fact that we can use our own body actively and no one else can.

This fact can indeed be accounted for only by substantially enlarging our conception of the body-mind relation. The main point to account for is that while another person may watch what I am doing and guess from it what I am after, it would be absurd for me to watch what I am doing in order to guess what I am after. I *first* know what I am after and *then* do something about it. We shall have to expand our conception of tacit knowing and give it a dynamic form to explain how this sequence of intention and action arises. It will be explained by introducing the power of the imagination.

This goes back to William James. He explained the way we deliberately move our body as the work of our imagination. We start imagining the action that we are about to perform, and this forward thrust of our intention evokes the muscular contractions which will implement it.

I have said that to take a walk is to suitably control the boundary conditions of a normal physiological function. My project is at the focus of my attention, and this focal action relies on my subsidiary operation of the muscular contractions which implement it. I now have to supplement this mechanism by including the imaginative process by which we start setting our body in motion. I shall say that in a deliberate bodily action we thrust the focus of our attention ahead of the subsidiary muscular contractions which will bring the action about. Thus, we anticipate the action by the powers of our imagination, and this focal anticipation causes the subsidiary elements to emerge and implement what we imagined.

This is the way our mind takes control of the body and makes it serve our purpose; this is the dynamics of tacit knowing. This dynamism endows tacit knowing with creativity. It lends us the power of acquiring a skill, and, by the same token, enables us to invent a machine; indeed, to perform any possible creative action. I have shown elsewhere in some detail how the mechanism by which the mind sets the body in motion can be made to cover the whole range of creative originality.

At this point, there comes into sight a defect in our conception of consecutive levels of control. The way I described such stratified structure does not allow for the fact that in the embryonic development and in the growth of animals we see higher levels emerging by continuous changes, and that the same happens in phylogenetic evolution. The theory of consecutive levels must be somehow supplemented by a conception of the continuous transition of a lower level to a higher level. But the moment we see this problem, we are also presented with its solution. The development of an infant into a grown person illustrates a transition between successive levels. It shows that such a transition may take place gradually by a steady intensification of a higher principle from initial rudimentary traces, up to the stage where it fully takes control over the lower level from which it has emerged.

But here arises a further problem of great importance on which I can touch only briefly. The image of consecutive levels, unaccountable by the principles governing the levels below them, offers us a sharp definition of creativity. It defines creativity as the emergence of a new, irreducible higher principle. We can equally define in these terms both the action of intellectual originality and the creative processes by which new principles emerge in nature, whether this happens in the maturing infant or in the process of evolution. What the imagination achieves in the mind, the process of growth performs spontaneously in the child, and evolution performs likewise in the rise of higher forms of life.

This brings us back to Samuel Butler and Henri Bergson who thought of the evolution of species as a creative process akin to the acts of genius and not accountable by the laws of inanimate matter. I think that I have lent firm substance to this belief by defining more closely the process of creativity, by showing that evolution, like the rise of life itself, cannot be accounted for by the laws of inanimate nature. I believe to have shown also, that the logical relation between successive stages of evolution is the same as the logical relation between two stages of thought before and after a major invention or discovery. We find that creativity has a similar structure in both cases.

Admittedly, the imagination is a motive force of invention, which has no counterpart in the process of organic evolution. But I could reduce this disparity by showing, as I have done elsewhere,* that the imagination alone does not achieve inventions or discoveries, but merely evokes

---

* See 'Creative Imagination', no. 17 in this collection.

a spontaneous, integrative event which brings about the discovery. It appears that the effort of the imagination merely prepares the ground for a creative act which eventually takes place of its own ac cord. This is how Poincaré described discovery in mathematics many years ago, and it can be shown to happen mostly like this. Discovery or invention are, as it were, processes of spontaneous growth induced by the labours of the questing imagination. Originality is deliberate growth. The way my conclusions bear on Teilhard de Chardin's book *Le Phenomene Humain* is fairly clear. I agree with his vision of evolution as a continuous sequence of creative acts. I do not think that he has done much towards meeting the difficulties arising when we try to spell out this vision in terms of biological detail. I would think that a precise conception of creativity and the proof of its being equally present in human originality, individual ontogenesis, and phylogenetic evolution will remedy this deficiency up to a point. But I think that this involves an idea of the body-mind relation that is very different from the dualism accepted and elaborated by Teilhard de Chardin and all his predecessors. In my theory, the distinction between the inner and outer view of things applies to every kind of comprehensive entity. It applies in a series of stages: the outer view looks at a lower level of a comprehensive entity, while the inner view sees a higher level of it. More generally speaking, the difference lies between looking at and looking from some coherent subsidiary things.

The problem of the body-mind relation is thus resolved by being shown to represent but an instance of these two alternative ways of knowing the subsidiaries of a coherent entity.

The hierarchy of levels I am postulating cannot be represented in a Cartesian dualism. I believe that this hierarchy gives a truer picture of the phenomenon of man.

Notes

1. P. Mansell Jones, *Modern Humanities in the Technological Age with Reference to the study of French*. Manchester University Press; 1957.
2. Comp. e.g. C. H. Waddington, *The Strategy of Genes*. London, 1957; particularly the explanation of genetic assimilation on p. 167.

23

The Scientific Revolution

Although restating much that is familiar, this article, like 'Science and religion: separate dimensions or common ground?' [112], extends Polanyi's philosophy of personal knowledge and tacit integration somewhat further and aligns it with I-Thou and I-It relations, while introducing I-Me ones, and also with the specifically theological distinction between faith and reason which it generalises to cover all knowing.

Illness has given me a chance to reconsider once more the theme which I have been asked to write about. During my stay in hospital there fell into my hands—by the kindness of its author—a book which has revealed to me a new, and I think much better, understanding of the situation we are facing today in consequence of the modern scientific revolution. The author is Josef Pieper, Professor of Philosophical Anthropology at the University of Munster, and his book which so impressed me is entitled *Scholastik*[1]. Owing to this book, I can see now that the conflict between faith and reason evoked by natural science today is but a modern variant of a problem which has filled the thoughts of men in other forms ever since the dawn of philosophic speculation 2,500 years ago.

You will notice that by dating the beginning of philosophy in the sixth century B.C., I am localising this event in Greece and more particularly in Ionia and the Greek isles. I know this may be challenged and shall not argue it. Suffice it to say that, in my view, our anxiety about the relation between faith and reason here in Europe today is the legacy of a particular intellectual family. Modern science has recently been spreading this disturbance all over the planet, but it has formed no part of the heritage

[100b]. Reprinted from *Christians in a Technological Era*, ed. H. C. White (New York, The Seabury Press, 1964, pp.25–45).

of Chinese or Hindu thought. It has originated with, and has remained for two and a half millennia the preoccupation of, that part of humanity that has culturally centred mainly on Europe.

Greek, Medieval, and Modern Rationalism

But even accepting these limits, the simplification I now see appearing before me may seem excessively sweeping. I see extending behind us three consecutive periods of rationalism, the Greek, the medieval, and the modern. Greek rationalism rose from a bed of mythopoeic thought. We may define this for brevity as a predominantly personal interpretation of all things. Myths and ritual couch most thoughts of men in terms of I-Thou and leave nothing of importance to be spoken of in terms of I-It. Greek speculative thought tended to liberate the mind from this personal network, by establishing a broad area of objective thought. It extended I-It relations into a new philosophic interpretation of things. In this Greek rationalism, reason was used for eroding and replacing traditional beliefs, unquestioningly held or tacitly taken for granted.

The Christian message exploded into this scene as an outrage to rationalism. It restored the relation of I to Thou to the centre of everything. It proclaimed that a man put to death a few years before in a remote provincial capital was the Son of the Almighty God ruling the universe, and had atoned by his death for the sins of mankind. The Christian's duty was to believe in this event and be totally absorbed by its implications. Faith, faith that mocks reason, faith that scornfully declares itself to be mere foolishness in the face of Greek rationalism, is what St. Paul enjoins on his audiences.

The picture is familiar. But you may ask me where I see any trace here of a new Christian, medieval rationalism, striving to reconcile faith with reason. It emerged later as this message spread among an intelligentsia steeped in Greek philosophy. It was to be formulated by St. Augustine in terms that became statutory for a thousand years after. Reason was declared ancillary to faith, supporting it up to the point where revelation took over, after which in its turn faith opened up new paths to reason. What Professor Pieper has shown to me for the first time is that the entire movement of scholastic philosophy from Boethius to William of Ockham was but a variation on this theme.

Ockham brought scholasticism to a close by declaring that faith and reason were incompatible and should be kept strictly separate. Thus he ushered in the period of modern rationalism, established on this division, with the proviso that reason alone can establish true knowledge. Henceforth, as John Locke was soon to put it, faith was no longer accepted as a higher power that reveals knowledge lying beyond the range of observation and reason, but as a mere personal acceptance which falls short of rational demonstrability. The mutual position of the two Augustinian levels was inverted. In a way this step would have brought us back to Greek rationalism, and many of its authors did so regard it. They hoped that the new secular world view would appease religious strife and bring back the blessings of an antique dispassionate religious indifference. However, post-Christian rationalism soon entered on paths never trodden before by man, and we stand here today at the dismal end of this journey.

Toward a Restoration of the Lost Harmony between Faith and Science

But my purpose is not to denounce modern rationalism. The arts, the intellectual splendours, and moral attainments of the past three hundred years stand unrivalled in the history of mankind. The very failures and disasters that surround us may themselves bear testimony to this greatness. Only gigantic endeavour could precipitate us into such absurdities as the modern scientific outlook has made current today, and could set millions ablaze with a new bitterly sceptical fanaticism.

I shall take today these manifold and profoundly serious shortcomings of our present situation for granted, and shall bend all my effort to tracing a new line of thought along which, I believe, we may recover some of the ground rashly abandoned by the march of the modern scientific outlook. I believe indeed that this line of thought, if pursued systematically, may eventually restore the balance between belief and reason on lines essentially similar to those marked out by St. Augustine at the dawn of Christian rationalism.

I shall try to show you what I have in mind by speaking of the human person, and then expanding this into an analysis of discovery. Modern science and scientific philosophy cannot analyse the human person without reducing it to a machine. This flows from assuming that all mental processes are to be explained in terms of neurology, which in their turn must be represented as a chart of physical and chemical processes. The damage wrought by the modern scientific outlook is actually even more extensive: it tends towards replacing everywhere the personal I-Thou by an impersonal I-It.

Any attempt to restore a more sane and truthful view of the human person must go to the very roots of the conception of knowledge, and I shall start off in this direction by giving you an example to illustrate some of the essential features of knowledge which are disregarded by the modern conception of positive scientific knowledge.

The Two Forms of Knowledge

A few years ago a distinguished psychiatrist demonstrated to his students a patient who was having a mild fit of some kind. Later the class discussed the question whether this had been an epileptic or an hystero-epileptic seizure. The matter was finally decided by the psychiatrist: 'Gentlemen', he said, 'you have seen true epileptic seizure. I cannot tell you how to recognise it; you will learn this by more extensive experience'. This psychiatrist knew how to recognise this disease, but he was not at all certain how he did this. In other words, he recognised the disease by attending to its comprehensive appearance, and did so by relying on a multitude of clues which lie could not clearly specify. Thus his knowledge of the disease differed altogether from his knowledge of these clues or symptoms. He recognised the disease by attending to it, while he was not attending to the symptoms in themselves, but only as clues. We may say that he was knowing the clues only by relying on them for attending to the pathological physiognomy to which they contributed. So if he could not tell what these clues were, while he could tell what the disease was, this was due to the fact that while we can always identify a thing we are attending to, and indeed our very attending identifies it, we cannot always identify the particulars on which we rely in our attending on the thing.

This fact can be generalised widely. There are vast domains of knowledge—of which I shall speak in a moment—that exemplify in various manners that we are in general unable to tell what particulars we are aware of when attending to a whole which they constitute. So we can declare that there are two kinds of knowing which invariably enter jointly into any act of knowing a comprehensive entity. There is (1) a knowing by attending to something, as we attend to the entity in question, and (2) a knowing by relying on our awareness of certain things in the way we rely on our awareness of the many particulars of the entity in the act of attending to it.

We can go further. Evidently, any attempt to identify the particulars of an entity would involve a shift of attention from the entity to the particulars. We would have to relax the attention given to the whole for the sake of discovering its particulars which we had noticed until now only by being aware of them as parts of the whole. So that once we have succeeded in fully identifying these particulars, and are in fact attending to them now directly in themselves, we clearly shall not be relying any more on our awareness of them as particulars of a whole, and therefore will inevitably have lost sight of the whole altogether.

This fact is abundantly borne out by half a century of Gestalt psychology. We may put it as follows. It is not possible to be aware of a particular in terms of its contribution to a whole and at the same time to focus our attention on it in itself. Or again, since it is not possible to be aware of anything at the same time subsidiarily and focally, we necessarily tend to lose sight of an entity by attending focally to its particulars.

But we may add that this loss need not be definitive. We may successfully analyse the symptoms of a disease and concentrate our attention on its several particulars, and then return to our conception of its general appearance, by becoming once more subsidiarily aware of these particulars as constituent parts of the comprehensive picture of the disease. Indeed, such an oscillation of detailing and integrating is the royal road for deepening our understanding of any comprehensive entity.

Knowing and Comprehending

In saying this, I have pronounced a key word. I have spoken of understanding. Understanding—comprehension: this is the cognitive faculty cast aside by a positivistic theory of knowledge, which refuses to acknowledge the existence of comprehensive entities as distinct from their particulars, and this is the faculty which I recognise as the central act of knowing. For comprehension can never be absent from any process of knowing, as it is indeed the ultimate sanction of any such act. What is not understood cannot be said to be known.

Lest this analysis appear too abstract, let me rapidly run through various forms of knowing to which it strikingly applies. I have so far used as my leading example the process of medical diagnostics. We have a closely similar process in the identification of the species to which an animal or a plant belongs. An expert who can identify 800,000 species of insects must rely on a vast number of clues which he cannot identify in themselves. This is why zoology and botany cannot be learned from printed pages, any more than medicine can. This is why so many hours of practical teaching in the laboratory has to be given also in many other branches of the natural sciences. Wherever this happens, there some knowledge of the comprehensive aspect of things is being transmitted, a knowledge of those things which we must acquire by becoming aware of a multitude of clues that cannot be exhaustively identified.

We must learn to identify the physiognomy of such things by relying on clues which cannot be clearly identified in themselves. But we hardly ever do such diagnosing without examining the object in question, and this testing itself has to be learned together with the physiognomies of the tested objects. We must jointly learn to be skilful testers as well as expert knowers. Actually, these are only two different and inseparable processes of comprehension. Expert knowing relies on a comprehension of clues, as skilful examination relies on a combination of tricks for tracing these clues.

Skills and Tools

This reveals the structure of skills quite generally. A performance is called skilful precisely because we cannot clearly identify its component muscular acts. The craftsman's cunning consists in controlling these component acts jointly with a view to a comprehensive achievement. Such also is the sportsman's and musical performer's mastery. Neither can tell much, and mostly can tell very little, about the several muscular tricks he combines in accomplishing his art.

Skills usually require tools—instruments of some kind, and these are things patently akin to the particulars of a comprehensive entity. For they are tools or instruments by virtue of the very fact that we rely on them for accomplishing something to which we are attending by using the tool or instrument. In this case we can admittedly identify that on which we rely, though mostly we do not quite know how we actually use it. In any case, it still remains strikingly true that we cannot direct our attention to the thing on which we rely as our tool while relying on it for a skilful performance. You must keep your eye on the ball, and if you look at your racket instead, you inevitably lose the stroke. Any skilful performance is paralysed by attending focally to its tools.

The same is true of speech. Listen to the sound of your words, while forgetting their context and meaning, which is the comprehensive entity which it is their function to subserve, and you will be instantly struck dumb. This brings in the whole multitude of signs, symbols, and gestures by which human communications are achieved and by the practical use of which the intelligence of man is developed far beyond that of the animals. Here is another vital area of skilful doing and knowing, all over which we are met with comprehensive entities to which we attend, and can attend only, by relying subsidiarily on things and acts of our own, to which we do not attend, and must not attend in themselves, for the time being.

Perception

We may add lastly that, deep down, in the most primitive forms of knowing, in the act of sensory perception, we meet with the very paradigm of the structure which I have postulated for all kinds of knowledge at all levels. It was indeed sensory perception, and particularly the way we see things, that has supplied Gestalt psychologists with material for their fundamental discoveries which I am expanding here into a new theory of knowledge. They have shown that our seeing is an act of comprehension for which we rely in a most subtle manner on clues from all over the field of vision, as well as on clues inside our body, supplied by the muscles controlling the motion of the eyes and the posture of the body. All these clues become effective only if we keep concentrating our attention on the objects we are perceiving. Many of the clues cannot be known in themselves at all, others can be traced only by acute scientific analysis, but all of them can serve the purpose of seeing what is in front of us only if we make no attempt to look at them or to attend to them in any way in themselves. They must be left to abide in the role of unspecifiable particulars of the spectacle perceived by our eyes, if we are to see anything at all.

This concludes my list. We have now before us the art of diagnostics and of the testing of objects to be diagnosed, as taught in universities; we have the practice of skills in general and the skilful use of tools in particular which leads on to the use of words and other signs by which human intelligence is developed; and finally we have the act of perception, the most fundamental manifestation of intelligence, both in animals and men. In each of these cases we have recognised the typical elements of comprehension. I now want to show how this panorama of knowing suggests a new conception of knowledge, equally comprising both the I-It and the I-Thou, and establishing at the same time a new harmony between belief and reason.

Knowledge and Learning

Clearly, the new element I have introduced here into the conception of knowing is the knowing of things by relying on our awareness of them for attending to something else that comprehends them. Now, we have an obvious experience of certain things which we know almost exclusively by relying on them. Our body is a collection of such things; we hardly ever observe our own body as we observe an external object, but continuously rely on it as a tool for observing objects outside and for manipulating these for our own purposes. Hence we may identify the knowing of something by attending to something else, as the kind of knowledge we have of our own body by living in it. This kind of knowing is not an I-It relation, but rather a way of existing, a manner of being. We might call it an I-Myself or I-Me relation.

We are, of course, born to live in our body and to feel that we are relying on it for our existence, but the more skilful uses of our body have to be acquired by a process of learning. For example, the faculty of seeing things by using our eyes is not inborn; it has to be acquired by a process of learning.

We may say then that when we get to know something as a clue, as a particular or a whole, as a tool, as a word, or as an element contributing to perception, by learning to rely on it, we do so in the same way as we learn to rely on our body for exercising intellectual and practical control over objects of our surroundings. So any extension of the area of reliance by which we enrich our subsidiary knowledge of things is an extension of the kind of knowledge we usually have of our body; it is indeed an extension of our bodily existence to include things outside it. To acquire new subsidiary knowledge is to enlarge and modify our intellectual being by assimilating the things we learn to rely on. Alternatively, we may describe the process as an act of pouring ourselves into these things.

These ways of acquiring knowledge may sound strange, but then we are dealing with a kind of knowledge which, though familiar enough to us all, seems never to have been identified by students of the theory of knowledge. Evidently, all hitherto recognised processes for acquiring knowledge, whether based on experience or deduction, only apply to knowledge of things we are attending to, and not at all to what we know of things by relying on our awareness of them in the process of attending to something else. I shall continue, therefore, undeterred, my account of the way such knowledge is acquired and held, however curious this account may sound at first hearing.

Knowledge by Indwelling

When we rely on our awareness of some things for attending to something else, we may be said to have assimilated these things to our body. In other words, subsidiary knowledge is held by indwelling. Thus we comprehend the particulars of a whole in terms of the whole by dwelling in the particulars. We grasp the joint meaning of the particulars by dwelling in them.

My examples of comprehension will illustrate these conclusions. To diagnose a disease is to grasp the joint meaning of its symptoms, many of which we could not specify. These particulars we know subsidiarily by dwelling in them. Indwelling has a more obvious meaning when applied to a skilful testing of an object or any other feat of expert handling. Here we literally dwell in the innumerable muscular acts which contribute to our purpose, and this purpose is their joint meaning. Indwelling is most vivid in man's use of language. Human intelligence lives only by grasping the meaning and mastering the use of language. Little indeed of our mind lives in our natural body; our person comes into existence when our lips shape words and our eyes read print. The intellectual difference between a naked pygmy of Central Africa and a member of the French Academy is grounded in the cultural equipment by which Paris surpasses the African jungle. The French academician's superior personality is formed and manifested by his intelligent use of this superior equipment.

Foreknowing the Unknown

This brings us to the very threshold of our understanding of the way we know a human person. But let us consider first for a moment the way comprehension is achieved, as envisaged in the extended sense given to it by my examples. More often than not we comprehend things in a flash.

But it is more instructive to think of the way we struggle from a puzzled incomprehension of a state of affairs toward its real meaning. The success of such efforts demonstrates man's capacity for knowing the presence of a hidden reality accessible to his understanding. The active foreknowledge of an unknown reality is the true motive and guide of discovery in every field of mental endeavour. The explicit forms of reasoning, whether deductive or inductive, are impotent in themselves; they can operate only as intellectual tools of the creative power residing in man's capacity to anticipate a hidden meaning of things.

This confidence in the hidden coherence of a puzzling state of affairs is guided by an external aid when a student is taught how to identify a disease or a specific biological specimen. When the psychiatrist in the example I mentioned said to his students that they will learn to recognise in practice the characteristic appearance of an epileptic seizure, he meant that they would learn to do so by accepting his own diagnosis of such cases and trying to understand what he based it on. All practical teaching, teaching of comprehension in all the senses of the term, is based on authority. The student must be confident that his master understands what he is trying to teach him and that he, the student, will eventually succeed in his turn in understanding the meaning of the things which are being explained to him.

Plato has argued that the task of solving a problem is logically absurd and therefore impossible. For if we already know the solution, there is no occasion to search for it, while if we don't know it, we can do nothing to find it, for we don't know then what we are looking for. The task of solving a problem is indeed self-contradictory, unless we admit that we can possess true intimations of the unknown. This is what Plato's argument proves, namely, that every advance in understanding is moved and guided by our fundamental power of seeing the presence of some hidden comprehensive entity behind the as yet incomprehensible clues which we see pointing toward this yet unknown entity. Our confidence in these powers of our own may arise from the depth of our own inquiring mind, or it may be guided by our confidence in the judgment of our masters. Yet it is always the same dynamic power, and its dynamics are akin to the dynamics of faith. Tillich says that 'that which is meant by an act of faith cannot be approached in any other way than through an act of faith'. And the same holds here. There is no other way of approaching a hidden meaning than by entrusting ourselves to our intimations of its yet unseen presence. These intimations are the only path toward enlarging our intellectual mastery over our surroundings.

A Dynamic Conception of Knowledge

Tillich says that his dynamic conception of faith 'is the result of conceptual analysis, both of the objective and subjective side of faith'. This is precisely what I claim for my derivation of the dynamic conception of knowing. It is derived in the last resort from our realisation of the two kinds of knowledge which combine to the understanding of a comprehensive entity when we rely on our awareness of particulars for our knowledge of the entity to which we are attending. Our awareness of the particulars is the personal, our knowledge of the entity the objective, element of knowing.

The dynamic force by which we acquire understanding is only reduced and never lost when we hold knowledge acquired by its impulse. It sustains the conviction for dwelling in this knowledge and for developing our thoughts within its framework. Live knowledge is a perpetual source of new surmises, an inexhaustible mine of still hidden implications. The death of Max von Laue a short while ago should remind us that his discovery of the diffraction of X-rays by crystals was universally acclaimed as an amazing confirmation of Boyle's speculation on the structure of crystals, which itself was a development of ideas originating with Lucretius and Epicurus. And Dalton's theory was amazingly confirmed in its turn by the experiments of J. J. Thompson eighty years later. To hold knowledge is indeed always a commitment to indeterminate implications, for human knowledge is but an intimation of reality, and we can never quite tell what reality will do next. It is external to us, it is objective, and, by the same token, its future manifestations can never be completely under our intellectual control.

So all true knowledge is inherently hazardous, just as all true faith is a leap into the unknown. Knowing includes its own uncertainty as an integral part of it, just as, according to Tillich, all faith necessarily includes its own dubiety.

The traditional division between faith and reason, or faith and science (which Tillich reaffirms), reflects the assumption that reason and science proceed by explicit rules of logical deduction or inductive generalisation. But I have said that these operations are impotent by themselves, and I could add that they cannot even be strictly defined by themselves. To know is to understand, and explicit logical processes are effective only as tools of a dynamic commitment by which we expand our understanding and then hold on to it. Once this is recognised, the contrast between faith and reason dissolves, and a close similarity of structure emerges in its place.

Admittedly, religious conversion commits our whole person and changes our whole being in a way that an expansion of natural knowledge does not do. But once the dynamics of knowing are recognised as the dominant principle of knowledge, the difference appears only as one of degree. For—as we have seen—all extension of comprehension involves an expansion of ourselves into a new dwelling place, of which we assimilate the framework by relying on it as we do on our own body. Indeed, the whole intellectual being of man comes into existence in this very manner, by absorbing the language and the cultural heritage in which he is brought up. The amazing deployment of the infant mind is stirred on by a veritable blaze of confidence sensing the hidden meanings of speech and other adult behaviour and grasping these meanings. Moreover, the structure of the child's dynamic intellectual progress has its counterpart on the highest levels of creative achievement, and both these structures resemble closely that of the self-transformation entailed in a religious conversion.

From Objective Observation to Personal Knowledge

But a deeper division between reason and faith may be found in the urge toward objectivity which tends to break up the I-Thou axis of the religious world-view and establish everywhere I-It relations in its place. Has not the modern positivist outlook exercised its pressure even on the purely secular studies of the human mind, as well as of human affairs whether past or present, in favour of a mechanical conception of man which represents him as a bundle of appetites, or as a mechanical toy, or as a passive product of social circumstances?

It has, but this is due in my opinion to the obsessive limitation of knowledge to the outcome of explicit inferences. Persons can be identified only as comprehensive entities by relying on our awareness of numberless particulars, most of which we could never specify in themselves. This is the same process by which we diagnose an elusive illness or read a printed page. Just as we assimilate the symptoms of a disease by attending focally to the disease itself, and as we assimilate the printed text by attending to its meaning, so we assimilate the workings of another man's mind by attending to his mind. In this sense we may be said to know his mind by dwelling in its manifestations. Such is the structure of empathy (that I would prefer to call conviviality) which alone can establish a knowledge of other minds and indeed of any living being whatever.

Behaviourism tries to replace convivial knowledge by I-It observations of the particulars by which the mind of an individual manifests itself and tries to relate these particulars to each other by a process of explicit inference. But since most of the particulars in question cannot be observed in themselves at all and, in any case, their relation cannot be explicitly stated, the enterprise ends up by replacing its original subject by a grotesque simulacrum of it in which the mind itself is missing. The kind of knowledge which I am vindicating here, and which I call personal knowledge, casts aside these absurdities of the current scientific approach and reconciles the process of knowing with the act of addressing another person. In doing so it establishes a continuous ascent from our less personal knowing of inanimate matter to our convivial knowing of living beings, and beyond this to the knowing of our responsible fellow men. Such, I believe, is the true transition from the sciences to the humanities and also from our knowing the laws of nature to our knowing the person of God.

Scientific and Christian Conceptions of Man

But is the kind of person we may know in this manner not floating vaguely above its own bodily substance, outside of which it actually cannot exist at all? The answer to this question will reveal a surprising affinity between my conception of personhood and a central doctrine of Christianity.

I have said that the mind of a person is a comprehensive entity which is not specifiable in terms of its constituent particulars; but this is not to say that it can exist apart or outside of these particulars. The meaning of a printed page cannot be specified in terms of a chemical analysis of its ink and paper, but neither can this meaning be conveyed without the use of ink and paper. Though the laws of physics and chemistry apply to the particles of the body, they do not determine the manifestations of the mind; their function is to offer an opportunity for the mind to live and manifest itself. Our sense organs, our brain, the whole infinitely complex interplay of our organism offer to the mind the instruments for exercising its intelligence and judgment, and, at the same time, they restrict the scope of this enterprise, deflecting it by delusions, obstructing it by sickness, and terminating it by death.

The knowing of comprehensive entities establishes a series of ascending levels of existence, and the relationship I have just outlined obtains throughout between succeeding levels of this hierarchy. The existence of a higher principle is always rooted in the inferior levels governed by less comprehensive principles. Within this lower medium and by virtue of it, the higher principle operates freely, but not unconditionally, its range being restricted and its every action tainted by the lower principles on which it has to rely for exercising its own powers. As the rising levels of existence were created by successive stages of evolution, each new level achieved higher powers entrammelled by new possibilities of corruption. Our inanimate beginning was deathless, subject neither to failure nor suffering. From this have emerged levels of biotic existence subject to malformation and disease, and then, at higher stages, to illusion, to error, to neurotic affliction—finally to produce in man, in addition to all these liabilities, an ingrained propensity to do evil. Such is the necessary condition of a morally responsible being, grafted on a bestiality through which alone it can exercise its own powers.

Such is the inescapable predicament of man which theology has called his fallen nature. Our vision of redemption is the converse of this predicament. It is the vision of a man set free from this bondage. Such a man would be God incarnate; he would suffer and die as a man and by this very act prove himself divinely free from evil. This is the event, whether historic or mythical, which shattered the framework of Greek rationalism and has set for all times the hopes and obligations of man far beyond the horizon of here and now.

Natural and Supernatural Knowledge

I have mentioned divinity and the possibility of knowing God. These subjects lie outside my argument. But my conception of knowing opens the way to them. Knowing, as a dynamic force of comprehension, uncovers at each step a new hidden meaning. It reveals a universe of comprehensive entities which represent the meaning of their largely unspecifiable particulars. A universe constructed as an ascending hierarchy of meaning and excellence is very different from the picture of a chance collocation of atoms to which the examination of the universe by explicit modes of inference leads us. The vision of such a hierarchy inevitably sweeps on to envisage the meaning of the universe as a whole. Natural knowing expands continuously into supernatural knowing. The very act of scientific discovery offers a paradigm of this transition. It is a passionate pursuit of a hidden meaning, guided by an intensely personal foreknowledge of this hidden reality. The intrinsic hazards of such efforts are of its essence; discovery is defined as an advancement of knowledge that cannot be achieved by any application of explicit modes of inference, however diligent. Yet the discoverer must labour night and day. For though no labour can make a discovery, no discovery can be made without intense, absorbing, devoted labour. Here we have, in paradigm, the Pauline scheme of faith, works, and grace. The discoverer works in the belief that his labours will prepare his mind for receiving a truth from sources over which he has no control. I regard the Pauline scheme, therefore, as the only adequate conception of scientific discovery.

Such is, in bold outline, my programme for reconsidering the conception of knowledge and restoring thereby the harmony between faith and reason. Few of the clues which are guiding me today were available to the scholastics. The modes of reasoning which they relied on were inadequate; their knowledge of nature was poor and often spurious. Moreover, the faith they wanted to prove to be rational was cast into excessively rigid and detailed formulas, presenting intractable and sometimes even absurd problems to the reasoning mind. Even so, though their enterprise collapsed, it left great monuments behind it. I believe that we are today in an infinitely better position to renew their basic endeavour. The present need for it could not be more pressing. We should therefore spare no effort for advancing this enterprise.

Note

1. Published in English by Pantheon Books, Inc., New York [and Faber, London].

24

Polanyi's Logic—Answer

These notes, although short, provide a valuable and concise development of Polanyi's argument against the possibility of non-evaluative and morally neutral studies of man. (See 'The Message of the Hungarian Revolution' [121].) They are a reply to a comment on Polanyi's article, 'On the Modern Mind' [116]. Professor Gwynn Nettler of the University of Alberta stated that Polanyi's statements, 'To assume that you can explain an action without regarding it whether it is good or bad is to assume that moral motives play no part in it' and 'To extend this assumption to all social action is to deny the very existence of genuine moral motives in men', are untrue and non sequiturs.

Professor Nettler raises an extremely important question. After Rickert had first affirmed in 1902 that science could understand human affairs without making moral judgments, this view was spread widely by Max Weber. In fact, a whole academic culture has grown up in pursuit of this aim. It has been sometimes questioned whether it was possible to give 'value-free explanations' of all actions without denying the existence of moral motives, but these doubts have not prevailed. Professor Nettler has, therefore, the established opinion of sociology on his side, when contradicting my view that to explain all human actions without considering whether they are good or bad, is to deny that moral motives ever enter in our actions. What is simply obvious to me, is quite unacceptable to him and to most of his colleagues in sociology.

But how can one prove the obvious? Let me try it by suggesting two exercises in logic.

---

[119]. Reprinted, with the permission, of Mr. M. Lasky, from *Encounter*, XXVII, Sept. 1966, p.9.

First Exercise. Suppose we were told that a particular decision of judge can be explained scientifically, without considering what the law says in the matter. This would clearly mean that the state of the law has played no part in motivating the judge's decision.

It may then be suggested to us that science can explain the judge's decision, by observing that the judge believed his decision to conform with the law. (This is Rickert's and Max Weber's way of replacing *Werturteil* by *Wertbezogenheit*.) To this we would answer that it leaves the judge's decision unexplained, for we must yet explain the judge's belief that he was acting according to law. And if we are then told that the judge's belief that he had followed the law can be explained without considering what the law actually says, this means once more that the law had no part in motivating the judge's decision.

Second Exercise. President Johnson has introduced the Civil Rights Bill on the grounds that this was morally right. If a sociologist can explain this action without asking whether the Bill was in fact morally right, he implies that its moral rightness had no bearing on Johnson's action. If then (see the First Exercise) to avoid thus conclusion, the sociologist would limit himself to observing that the President acted as he did because he believed the Bill was morally right, this would leave Johnson's action unexplained. It would yet have to be explained why the President believed that the Bill was morally right. And if the sociologist claimed that he can explain this belief without judging whether the Bill was in fact right, this means once more that moral motives played no part in the President's action.

Conclusion. Therefore, if the sociologist claims that he can explain all human action without judging whether it is good or bad, he denies that moral motives play a part in human action. And this is what I said.

25

What is a Painting?

In this article Polanyi applies the structure of tacit integration to the understanding of paintings and art generally.

There is a strange painting covering the vault of the church of St. Ignazio in Rome. It is the work of the Jesuit Andrea Pozzo, done about the turn of the seventeenth century. The painting shows among a number of figures a set of columns which appear to continue the pilasters supporting the vault. But these subjects of the painting can be seen in their normal shape only if the viewer stands in the middle of the aisle. If he moves away from that point even by a few yards, the columns appear curved and lying down at an angle to the structure of the church. If you walk around the centre of the aisle, the painted columns keep moving round, always lying down away from your position.

In a paper published in 1963 M. H. Pirenne[1] offered an interesting explanation of these facts and in a book, now in print with the Cambridge University Press[†], he has extended this argument further. I think his ideas have important consequences of which I shall speak here.

At first sight the Pozzo phenomenon may seem to present no problem to speak of. We know that a perspective painting represents its subject from one central position; hence when viewed at an angle to this direction the painting must appear distorted. Pozzo himself gave this as the reason that his painting is distorted when seen at an angle to its perspectival axis. But this explanation settles Pozzo's case at the cost of raising a much wider problem. For it follows from it that all perspective paint-

[138]. Reprinted, with permission from Oxford University Press, from *The British Journal of Aesthetics*, 1970, pp. 225–36.

[†] *Optics, Painting and Photography*, Cambridge, CUP, 1970.

ings must be distorted to a similar degree when viewed at an angle to their perspectival axis. But this does not happen. One can walk past a painting, for example in a picture gallery, without its appearance being distorted as Pozzo's painting is. Yet the distortion should actually be much greater here than in the Pozzo case, since the deviations from the line of perspective caused by passing a picture must exceed by far those due to viewing the vault of a church from a spot a few yards away from the centre of the aisle.

This problem is of course well known in a general way. The fact that a perspective design continues to be seen virtually unchanged from directions at wide angles to its axis has been well noted. But its treatment seems to have been rather cursory, perhaps because no estimates were made of the amount of the distortion to be expected.

However that may be—and I shall return to it again—the Pozzo case confronts us with the full measure of this problem. It forces us to look for a powerful factor which protects ordinary paintings from being distorted; and this must be a factor that is absent in the Pozzo painting, leaving it therefore defenceless against distortion when viewed at an angle. This is where Pirenne comes in. He suggests that the factor which protects ordinary perspectival paintings from distortion by angular vision consists in our subsidiary awareness of the fact that paintings are normally based on a flat canvas. Our awareness of the canvas reduces, in Pirenne's view, the depth of a painting's perspectival design and thus protects the painting against the distorting effect of being viewed at an angle. According to this theory the Pozzo painting is subject to distortion because its perspective is not counteracted by an awareness of the ground on which it is painted.

But if this is so, we would expect the Pozzo painting to look different from ordinary paintings even when both are viewed correctly along the axis of their perspectives. They do in fact look different, and different in a way that Pirenne's theory predicts. The Pozzo picture is deceptive; its pilasters appear to be a continuation of the church's architecture: the picture is seen as fully three-dimensional. By contrast ordinary pictures are not deceptive and not fully three-dimensional. We do not mistake a still life of Cézanne for real fruits and vegetables placed in a recess of the exhibition's wall, nor do we see Manet's *Dejeuner sur l'herbe* as two undressed women sitting in the company of their fully dressed male companions on a grassy sward in the open air. Even a more strictly perspectival picture is not mistaken for the presence of its subject; though its perspective design is marked, it does not appear to be a hole in the wall behind it. According to Pirenne our subsidiary awareness of the plane of the canvas combines with the perspectival appearance of the picture and thus produces a normal painting's manner of showing objects not present on the spot. A painting's liability to be distorted by angular vision is thus linked to its deceptiveness, and a subsidiary awareness of the canvas is supposed both to protect a painting against such distortion to prevent it from being deceptive. Thus the Pozzo vault shows angular distortion plus deceptive power owing to our lack of awareness of its ground, while a normal painting, because of our awareness of its canvas, is protected against angular distortion and also deprived of deceptive power. This is Pirenne's theory.

But are we not relying here too heavily on the evidence of a single painting, the vault of Pozzo, with its peculiar hemi-cylindrical shape? Pirenne answers this by additional evidence from the case of anaglyphs. Anaglyphs combine two stereoscopic images with different colours which, when viewed through a corresponding pair of coloured glasses, present a fully three-dimensional image. When viewed from different angles such a deceptive image shows strong deformation—just as required by Pirenne's theory.

We have independent evidence also for another element of this theory. There is evidence that, seen from an angle, the perspective design of an ordinary painting is distorted if the distortion is not counteracted by the perception of the painting's flatness. We find that the photograph of a painting taken from an angle is heavily distorted, because the camera does not let us sense the presence of the canvas, which would counteract distortion.

But let me return now to the current explanations of the fact that the appearance of a painting is undisturbed by viewing it at an angle. Gombrich mentions the problem in *Art and Illusion* several times and classes it with other cases in which we see a painting in a particular way because it thus makes sense to us.[2] Such a tendency is said to be akin to the way we see an object constantly though it is presented to us at different distances and angles and in various illuminations. One can try to regard Pirenne's theory in this light as affirming that a painting's appearance remains constant when viewed at an angle provided its perception includes the subsidiary awareness of its canvas, whilst otherwise it is distorted when we view it sideways. We could thus link deceptiveness to angular distortability and lack of deceptiveness to angular stability. Pirenne's theory could thus be expressed in terms already current in a rather vague manner.

But at this juncture, just when all seems neatly settled, new problems arise owing to the modern rejection of the traditional conception of painting. Remember the kind of statements that inaugurated modern painting towards the end of the last century. Whistler described his own paintings as the arrangement of colours and tones on canvas.[3] In France Maurice Denis declared about the same time that a painting is 'essentially a plane surface covered with paint in a certain arrangement'. The twentieth century opened with a series of novel works in Italy and Switzerland, France, Germany and Russia, paintings that radically rejected any aim of resembling nature. Pirenne's theory affirming that we are invariably aware of the canvas might appear to side with the modern movement, which would identify all painting with brush-strokes on a canvas. But this is not so. Pirenne speaks of our *subsidiary* awareness of the canvas and in doing so makes reference to my writings, which sharply distinguish between our subsidiary awareness and our focal awareness of an object. This distinction—the distinction between a subsidiary and a focal awareness—changes the situation. I shall demonstrate this by recalling Sir Kenneth Clark's experiment made about twelve years ago when viewing *Las Meninas* by Velasquez. Owing to its rough structure the *Meninas* must be viewed from a distance. Clark wanted to observe how as one approaches it closer, one sees the painting dissolving into fragments. He hoped to see a gradual transition—but there was none. He wrote:[4]

> I would start from as far away as I could, when the illusion was complete, and come gradually nearer, until suddenly, what had been a hand, and a ribbon, and a piece of velvet dissolved into a fricassee of beautiful brushstrokes.

Now if we are asked two questions: (1) Which view showed a canvas plus brush-strokes and (2) Which view showed the painting? the answer would be that the view at close quarters showed a canvas plus brush-strokes and the view from a distance showed the painting. We can see only *one or the other* of these two sights, never the two at the same time. And this is indeed what Gombrich concludes from this kind of observations. He says that we see *either* a canvas and blobs *or* a painting *never the two at the same time*. But the situation changes if we admit two different ways of seeing an object. Gestalt psychology has long since observed that to look at the several parts of a whole can destroy our view of the whole. Let me recall a case of this kind which resembles the experiences of Kenneth Clark. When flying first started pilots discovered the traces of ancient sites over which people had walked for centuries without noticing them. Back on the ground the flyers themselves lost track of the ancient sites. It would be nonsense to say that when by moving to some distance away we come to see a collection of parts as one whole we no longer see these parts. What happens is that we now see the parts in a new way, namely as parts of a whole. To introduce my own terms, let me say that to look at the parts separately is to see them focally, while to see them together forming a whole is to be aware of them subsidiarily. And this is the structure that Pirenne ascribes to a normal representational painting. The perception of it is said to include a subsidiary awareness of the canvas. This subsidiary awareness distinguishes the normal painting both from a focal awareness of the canvas plus brush-strokes, in which the painting falls apart; and from a total unawareness of the canvas, which produces a deceptive painting like the Pozzo ceiling.

We can illustrate this in a diagram.

Focal awareness of:	Subsidiary awareness of:	No awareness of:	Focally seen results:
—	paint blobs	canvas	Illusion
—	canvas + paint blobs	—	Normal representational painting
canvas + paint	—	—	Meaningless fragments*

* Canvas + paint seen focally could be an abstract painting and a transition from representative painting to abstract painting might be formed by gradually expanding the part of flatness in the painting. Further remarks on this to follow.

(1) Starting from below, we have the parts of the painting as seen focally. When viewed closely the painting is dismembered into brush-strokes and canvas, into a meaningless aggregate of parts.

(2) Passing next to the top level, we find the structure of a deceptive painting like Pozo's vault. Such a painting is full of meaning, indeed overfull of it. It displays the meaning of the paint viewed subsidiarily, untrammelled by any awareness of the canvas or of any other base sup-

porting the paint. Hence arises its capacity to deceive, which may produce absurd results while it also suffers from being defenceless against distortion by a side view.

(3) Between these two levels—the lower one, deprived of meaning, and the upper one, overflowing with absurd and unstable meaning—we find the level of a normal painting. Here we have a subsidiary awareness of canvas and paint, combining the quality of these two.

We can now see what went wrong in the controversy about the nature of a painting. To say that a painting is 'essentially canvas plus brush-strokes' is wrong if you refer to a focal awareness of these two, but right if you refer to a subsidiary awareness of them. To say (with Gombrich) that one either sees canvas plus blobs or a painting, misses the fact that in a painting we do see canvas plus blobs but subsidiarily, not focally. Such a painting includes both the perspectival depth of its paint and the flatness of its canvas, these two contradictories being seen as one joint quality, and this is indeed the quality that distinguishes a normal painting. This quality is perspectival, but its perspective is restrained by a suffusion of flatness. And it is this quality of depth-cum-flatness that keeps a normal painting from being deceptive and secures it against distortion when it is viewed from the side.

These observations broadly answer the question: 'What is a painting?' But a closer look reveals an incongruity. We have seen that the fragments into which a painting is decomposed when seen at close quarters are united into a coherent image when the viewer recedes to a distance, and I have compared this with the way an ancient site is discovered by rising above it in an aeroplane. I said that Gestalt psychology accounts for this transformation when parts are united to form a whole. Rudolf Arnheim has developed this relation throughout his *Art and Visual Perception* (1954) by explaining the coherence of a painting in terms of Gestalt psychology.[5] But there is something peculiar—not mentioned by Arnheim—in the way Gestalt formation takes place when forming a painting. This union is not a fusion of *complementary parts* into a whole, but a fusion of *contradictory features*. The flatness of a canvas is combined with a perspectival depth, which is the very opposite of flatness.

Such integration of incompatibles is not unknown to psychology. Binocular vision is based on the fusion of incompatibles. This action works even more strikingly in the use of stereoscopic photography. Stereoscopic pictures are taken about four inches apart. At a glance they look much the same, but actually they differ at every point. When we view them jointly, by using one eye for each, they are fused into a single image, uniting their incompatible features into one strikingly novel sight. A deep three-dimensional appearance is produced here by fusing two conflicting flatnesses.

This fusion produces a radical extension of our eyesight, but the integration of canvas with perspectival design goes much further in its radical innovation. Binocular integration adds wonderfully to our powers of perceiving what is there, but the integration of incompatibles in a painting reveals to us something beyond all that exists in nature or human affairs: for what we see is a flat surface having a deep perspective in three dimensions. This quality of flat-depth, which is the hallmark of a normal painting, may be said to be transnatural.

It has been frequently noticed that the colours and tones available to the painter cannot equal the variety we meet in nature; but to possess a flat-depth goes far beyond nature. We are facing here no mere deficiency of a painting which reduces its capacity for imitation of nature, but its possession of a peculiar quality that is altogether lacking in nature. And thus we realise that the painter must aim from the very start at producing an image essentially different from natural appearance.

This capacity to fuse incompatible features of an artefact into radically novel qualities has been expanded by modern painting. I have mentioned before the view repeatedly expressed since the end of the last century that a painting is essentially a canvas with brush-strokes arranged on it. This view was mistaken, but it did express the urge of the time for always going to rock-bottom. In painting this was done by reducing simulation and increasing thereby the part played by flatness. Cubism and Epressionism, for example, went a long way towards flatness by reducing simulation and abstractionism achieved total flatness by foregoing all representation. My theory of the integration of incompatibles admits of all such variations, which have opened the way to modern art in all its various branches.

But before developing further these ideas of the transnatural, let me enlarge the basis of my argument by including other kinds of representational art. We shall see that evidence from poetry and drama will support my conception of painting. Take drama first. The actor on the stage resembles the painter in trying to simulate something, while the simulation is kept firmly short of deception. In playing Hamlet the actor must simulate killing Polonius and being killed by Laertes; but if any of these actions were to give the impression that someone had been actually killed on the stage, this would disrupt the play. The actor's simulation is kept from turning into a deception by an opposing force that is intrinsic to his art. Opposition to simulation, which in the case of a painting consists in its flatness, consists in the play in the apparatus of stagecraft. The playwright, the director, the designers and the actors producing a play jointly restrain the range of simulation. The painting's self-contradictory flat-depth has its counterpart here in equally paradoxical stage murders and other such stage scenes. Art appears to consist, for painting as for drama, in representing a subject within an artificial framework which contradicts its representational aspect, and I think we find the same structure in all representational arts.

This view of representational art was anticipated by I. A. Richards in respect to poetry.[6] In 1924 he wrote this of metre in poetry:

> Through its very appearance of artificiality metre produces in the highest degree the 'frame' effect, isolating the poetic experience from the accidents and irrelevancies of everyday experience.

But metre is only one artificiality of a poem among many others. Rhyme, expressive sounds and distinctive grammatical construction, strange connotation of words, and above all metaphor, are other fixtures of the poetic frame. They all function as subsidiaries, which together with such content of the poem as can be put into prose, form the meaning of the poem. Take Shakespeare's 28th Sonnet ('Shall I compare thee to a summer's day?'). This poem of supreme power says little more in prose than: 'You are beautiful, but you will fade and die except that you will be remembered in my immortal verse'. The power and beauty of the poem lies in a subsidiary framework embracing a simple idea.

We can then define representational art as art comprising images, actions or statements within an incompatible artificial framework. Paintings representing objects are thus placed firmly in the same class as plays representing action and poems making statements. They all are works of art which by the fusion of their contents with incompatible frames have a quality wholly detached both from nature and from man's personal affairs.

There seems then nothing tangible left that a work of art could tell us. And this is not far from the truth. The factual information content of art is slight, its main purpose being to evoke our participation in its utterance. And again it is for poetry that this action of the arts was first identified. I. A. Richards has contrasted the vagueness and incoherence of our own experiences with the severely circumscribed statements of a poem.[7] And Eliot spoke likewise of the ordering powers of poetry: 'the ordinary man's experience', he wrote, 'is chaotic, irregular, fragmentary. The latter falls in love, or reads Spinoza, and these two experiences have nothing to do with each other, or with the noise of the typewriter or the smell of cooking; in the mind of the poet these experiences are already forming new wholes'.[8] From our lives ever meandering, and from things we pass by, poems and plays and paintings call up vague memories and cast them into structures firmly woven and well organised. And as the artist draws on his own rambling experiences for subjects to be shaped by his art, so do we, his public, turn to his works in order that their aspect may make sense of our own vague experiences. By means of its artificial framework, that is sharply incompatible with its subject, a work of art takes us into an experience beyond the realm both of nature and of practical affairs, and our understanding and acceptance of art consists in letting it thus carry us into its own transnatural domain. Art does not inform us about its subject but makes us live in it as its maker first lived in it—sometimes many centuries before.

However, this kind of participation does not explain the passion, the breath-taking effect that a poem, a play or a painting can evoke. Some responses occurring in other domains may suggest an explanation. Closest would be the comparison with music, but this would lead us away from the representational arts to more abstract kinds of art which are off my subject. Let us take rather the triumph of scientific discovery. Announcing his discovery that the square of planetary orbital periods was proportional to the cube of the corresponding solar distances, Kepler wrote:

> So now, since eighteen months ago the dawn, three months ago the proper light of day, and indeed a very few days ago the most marvellous contemplation has shone forth—nothing holds me; I will indulge my sacred fury....

This passion resembles that evoked by a great work of art, but there is a difference: the emotions of discovery are not transmitted to the student; he learns of the proportionality of cubes and squares in the planetary system without being deeply moved by this fact. The difference seems due to the fact that the feelings evoked by a work of art even in the viewer as distinct from the creator are existential rather than intellectual. Kepler himself did undergo a triumphant transformation when his discovery changed the image of the universe, but this experience had to remain his own. Perhaps we might find a closer analogy to the way one is carried away by a work of art in popular emotions. Look how a patriotic citizen of a country—or even one who merely feels at home in it—can be deeply moved by the unfurling of the nation's flag. All the incoherent and unspecifiable experiences which make up a person's national memories are mobilised by the sight of a national flag unfurled to the salute of a large crowd. We see how a closely circumscribed structure, the simple pattern of the flag, can draw from a man's diffuse life-space an intensely concentrated emotion. Replace the flag by a work of representational art and you see the same mechanism at work. From diffuse experiences of life the clear utterances of art draw a passionate response. Art does this first in the mind of its maker and then in the mind of its public.

One might think that to convey a matter drawn from experience is to transmit a communication; but this is not so. Once an experience of ours is transfused into an incompatible artifact—be it a poem, a play or a painting—our experience is turned into a matter unprecedented in nature or the affairs of men. And when such transnatural matters are evoked in us by art this event tells us nothing that can be true or false; it does not convey a factual communication.

This does not mean that the effect of representational art lies altogether outside our relation to nature or to human affairs. Works of art may imply certain facts and these may appear convincing or misleading. Art may even deliberately express ideas and these may be true or false. But the truth of such ideas does not qualify their evocation as a true work of art any more than their possible falsity—though it may be objectionable—would disqualify their utterance as a work of art

All this may be fairly obvious in respect of poetry and drama, but not quite so obvious for painting. So let me make it clear once more that it does apply also to painting, even in all its traditional forms which aimed at simulation. The normal painting of all times belongs to the same class as poetry and drama, for it possesses an artificial frame that contradicts its subject and yet is so closely fused with this subject that the union of the two acquires a quality of its own, a quality unexampled in nature and the affairs of men. In this artificial estrangement of its subject lies the power of all painting to represent matters drawn from experience in terms that transcend all natural experience. And therein lies equally the power of *all* representational art.

A few words about the imagination. Our imagination is mostly known for roaming at random; but it is actually our principal guide to reality. Perception works within our imagination, and when there is a difficulty in making out what it is that we see we send out thrusts of our imagination to explore what that thing may be. And, of course, as it is capable of finding truth the imagination is capable also of error: it can produce illusions. Most of the time our imagination seems to work instantly, but its scanning may take a long time, and, again, as perception works by stages, so does illusion. There are grades of perception and grades of illusion: stages of perception lead to the recognition of objects that are really before us, while stages of illusion lead to the sight of things that are not there.

Since the representational arts tell us of things that are not there, such arts have been classed as illusions. And then the illusions attributed to such art were graded according to degrees of illusion. But this is a mistake. The arts do not exhibit things that *could be* really there and yet *are not* there; they exhibit things of a kind that cannot exist either in nature or in human affairs.

I have said that both perception and illusion are works of the imagination. The making of a painting or a play or a poem is also a work of the imagination, but in a very different way. We have met this difference before when comparing the integration of parts into a whole by which we recognize facts of nature, with the integration of incompatible elements, by which a novel thing unknown to nature is brought into existence. The assembling of pieces expected to belong naturally together produces either a perception or an illusion, while the integration of artistic elements designed to be incompatible produces transnatural things like paintings, plays and poetry. This is the work of artistic imagination.

Modern art has extended the integration of incompatibles to ever new kinds of art. The unlimited inventiveness of our technology is matched today by the inventiveness of our arts. We have learnt also to see the coherence and value of arts from primeval beginnings to the artistic experiments of today. Such is the work of our modern imagination.

Once these powers of the artificious imagination are fully realised the widespread classing of paintings as illusions becomes clearly misleading. A painting lacks a place on the scale of illusions in the same way as the square root of minus one lacks a place among real numbers. The square root of minus one is called an *imaginary* number and not an *illusory* number, because it does not pretend to be something that it is not. It follows that Dr. Johnson, who warned against succumbing to the illusion of a play, and Coleridge, who advocated a voluntary suspension of our disbelief in artistic illusion, were both mistaken. Since no such illusion exists, instructions for dealing with it are pointless.

Thus I agree with Professor Wollheim when he objects to the way Gombrich spoke of illusions in normal paintings. I would say that when Gombrich writes about illusion he should be understood as referring to the imitative element in a painting and not to a painting as a whole. Otherwise, the conceptual framework used by Professor Wollheim in his several papers[9] differs so widely from the conceptions introduced by Pirenne and developed by me, that I cannot tell whether Professor Wollheim has anticipated any other of the ideas I have put forward and to what extent I may be dissenting from his views. I agree of course also in substance with Mr. Osborne's rejection of a complete illusion as being the perfect impression of a work of art,[10] but I cannot accept his view that our contemplation of art should be based on a limited illusion, which he calls 'near illusion'[11].

The 'integration of incompatibles' is reminiscent of A. Koestler's 'bisociation'.[12] But I prefer to speak of integration, as this links my remarks to my own analysis of intellectual achievement back to 1946.[13]

I think that the part illusion plays in painting was first clarified by Pirenne in 1963, when he suggested that a painting's imitative content is reduced by a fusion with a subsidiary awareness of the canvas. To this theory I have now added the view that works of art are generally formed through integration of two incompatible elements, one of these being an attempted communication and the other an artistic structure that contradicts the communication. The harmonious compound formed by these two elements has qualities found neither in nature nor in human affairs, and hence it can communicate no information about real events. But it can draw on our unorganised memories and embody them in its own structure, evoking thereby deep emotions in ourselves. The passions that the artist has spent in creating his work thus generate their counterpart in us who follow him.

This is how artistic structures, being essentially detached from nature and human affairs, can grip us more firmly than our own memories can do.

Notes

1. M. H. Pirenne, 'Les lois de l'optique et la liberté de l'artiste', *Journal de Psychologie normale et pathologique*, 60, pp.151–66 (1963).

2. E. H. Gombrich, *Art and Illusion* (1962), pp.234,253.
3. Whistler described his portrait of his mother (1871) as *Arrangement in Grey and Black.* See R. Arnheim, *Art and Visual Perception* (1954). p.430.
4. Sir Kenneth Clark, 'Six Great Pictures', *The Sunday Times*, 2nd June 1957. This quotation was drawn to my attention by E. H. Gombrich on p. 5 of *Art and Illusion.*
5. Rudolf Arnheim, *Art and Visual Perception* (1954).
6. I. A. Richards, *Principles of Literary Criticism* (1924) p.145.
7. *Ibid.*, p.237.
8. Quoted by Philip Wheelright, *Metaphor and Reality* (1963) pp.82–83.
9. Richard Wollheim, 'Art and Illusion', *The British Journal of Aesthetics*, Vol. III, No. 1, January 1963. *On Drawing an Object* (1964). *Art and Its Objects* (1968).
10. H. Osborne, 'On Artistic Illusion', *The British Journal of Aesthetics*, Vol. 9, Nos. 2 and 3, 1969.
11. *Ibid.*, p. 221.
12. A. Koestler, *Insight and Outlook* (1949). p.36 *et seq. The Act of Creation* (1964), p. 35 and *passim.*
13. Michael Polanyi, *Science, Faith and Society* (1946).

Appendix I

An Annotated Bibliography of Michael Polanyi's Publications on Society, Economics, and Philosophy

Where the same item was published more than once, all subsequent versions, with notes about any differences, have been included with the first. This bibliography does not include the Hungarian versions of some of his articles which were given as radio talks and have since been published in *Polanyiana,* the journal of the (Hungarian) Michael Polanyi Liberal Philosophical Society.

Michael Polanyi's books are referred to by means of the usual abbreviations, and 'Schwarz' refers to the collection of Polanyi's papers, *Science, Thought and Reality,* ed. F. Schwarz (*Psychological Issues,* VIII 4, Monograph 32, New York, International Universities Press, 1970). *Tradition and Discovery* is the journal of the (American) Polanyi Society.

I have used the following bibliographies: R. Gelwick, in *Intellect and Hope* (ed. T. Langford and W. Poteat, Durham (NC), Duke U.P., 1968); R. Brownhill (cyclostyled, 1976); E.P. Wigner and R. Hodgkin, in *Biographical Memoirs of the Fellows of the Royal Society* (Vol. 23, Dec. 1977) which also contains a complete list of Polanyi's scientific papers.

I have personally checked every item, except No.s [40] and [122], of which I have not been able to obtain copies.

1. *A békeszerzőkhöz* (*To the peacemakers*), Budapest 1917, 15pp. Also in: *Huszadik Század* (*Twentieth Century*), 1917, No. 2, pp. 165–176; *Polanyiana* I 1, Autumn 1991, pp. 15–23.

2. 'Uj szkepticizmus' ('New scepticism'), *Szabadgondolat* (*Free Thought*), 1, Feb. 1919, pp. 53–6. Also in: *Polanyiana* I 1, Autumn 1991, pp. 24–S.

3. 'USSR Economics—fundamental data, system and spirit', *The Manchester School of Economic and Social Studies,* VI, Nov. 1935, pp. 67–89. Also as: *USSR Economics,* Manchester, Manchester U.P., 1936; 'Soviet Economy: Fact and Theory', in *The Contempt of Freedom* [12], pp. 61–95, with the additions of n.1 p. 60 and n.2, p. 73.

4. 'The struggle between truth and propaganda', review of *Soviet Communism: A New Civilisation* by S. and B. Webb, *The Manchester School of Economic and Social Studies,* VII, 1936, pp. 105–118. Also in: *The Contempt of Freedom* [12], pp. 96–116.

5. 'The value of the inexact', (letter) *Philosophy of Science,* 3, April 1936, pp. 233–34. Also in: *Tradition and Discovery,* XVIII 3, 1992, pp. 35–6.

6. 'Az Orosz forradalom tanulságai' ('The Russian Revolution'), *Századunk,* 1937, pp. 160–70. Also in: *Polanyiana,* I 1, Autumn 1991, pp. 27–37. (A shortened version of a talk on the Russian Revolution, 1917–30, to a joint meeting of the Manchester branches of the Historical and Geographical Associations, in their 1936/7 sessions. The original paper is in the Polanyi Collection of the Joseph Regenstein Library, University of Chicago, Box 25 Folder 12.)

7. 'Congrès du palais de la découverte', *Nature,* 140, Oct. 23rd, 1937, p. 710.

8. *An outline of the working of money*, Manchester, The Manchester Statistical Society, 1938. (A commentary to accompany the diagrammatic film, *Money:* see [13] and [14].

9. 'The settling down of capital and the trade cycle', *The Manchester School of Economic and Social Studies,* IX No. 2, Nov. 1938, pp. 153–169.

10. 'The rights and duties of science', a review of J. Bernal's *The Social Function of Science, The Manchester School of Economic and Social Studies,* X, Oct. 1939, pp. 175–193. Also in: *The Contempt of Freedom* [12], pp. 1–26; Occasional Pamphlet No. 2, Society for Freedom in Science, 1945, 18pp.

11. 'Science in the USSR', (a letter) *New Statesman,* XIX, Feb. 10th, 1940, p. 174.

12. *The Contempt of Freedom,* London, Watts, 1940 (Arno Press, New York, 1975). Contents: items [3], [4], [10] and 'Collectivist Planning', pp. 27–60 (a lecture given to the South Place Ethical Society, London, April 1940).

13. 'Economics on the screen', *Documentary Newsletter,* Aug. 1940, pp. 5–6.

14. 'Economics by motion symbols', *Review of Economic Studies,* VIII, Oct. 1940, pp. 1–19. (On the film, *Unemployment and Money,* an expanded version of *Money*.)

15. 'Cultural significance of science', (a letter) *Nature,* CXLVII, Jan. 25th, 1941, p. 19.

16. 'The growth of thought in society', *Economica,* VIII, Nov. 1941, 428–56. The section, 'Two kinds of order' (pp. 431–3), was included in 'Planning and spontaneous order' [50], pp. 238–40, and then in 'Economic and intellectual liberties' [53]. When both of these articles were reprinted in *LL,* 'Two kinds of order' was omitted from the former and retained in the later.

The section 'Corporate order' in 'Planning and spontaneous order', pp. 240–3, has the same ideas in the same order but not in the same words, as the corresponding section, pp. 43 1–5, of 'The growth of thought in society'.

Four continuous paragraphs from pp. 444–5 were included as n. 1, pp. 442–3 in 'Economic and intellectual liberties' and consequently as n.1, pp. 194–5, in Chap. 10 of *LL*.

The paragraphs, pp. 450–4, referring to J.G. Crowther's *The Social Relations of Science*, were added to 'The planning of science' [31] when that was reprinted as *LL* Chap. 5.

17. 'Revaluation of science', (a letter) *Manchester Guardian*, Nov. 7th, 1942, p. 6.

18. 'Jewish problems', *Political Quarterly*, XIV, Jan.–Mar. 1943, pp. 33–45.

19. 'Autonomy of science', *Memoirs and Proceedings of the Manchester Literary and Philosophical Society*, LXXXV, Feb. 1943, pp. 19–38. Also in: *Scientific Monthly*, Feb. 1945, pp. 141–150; *LL*, as Chap. 4 'Self-Government of Science'; Schwarz.

20. 'Research and planning', (a letter) *Nature*, CLII, Aug. 21st 1943, pp. 217–8.

21. 'The Hungarian opposition', (a letter) *New Statesman*, XXVI, Sept. 25th 1943, 216–7.

22. 'The English and the Continent', *Political Quarterly*, XIV, Oct.–Dec. 1943, pp. 372–81. Also as: 'England and the Continent', in *Fortune*, XXXIX, May 1944, pp. 155–7, 178, 182, 185.

23. 'Science—its reality and freedom', *The Nineteenth Century and After*, CXXXV, Feb. 1944, pp. 78–83.

24. 'The Socialist error', a review of Hayek's *Road to Serfdom*, *The Spectator*, Mar. 31st, 1944, p. 293.

25. 'Science and the decline of freedom', *The Listener*, June 1st, 1944, p. 599.

26. 'Reflections on John Dalton', *Manchester Guardian*, July 22nd, 1944, pp. 4 and 6. Also in: as 'John Dalton's theory', *L. Farkas Memorial Volume*, ed. A. Farkas and E.P .Wigner, Jerusalem, Research Council of Israel, 1952, pp. 13–15.

27. 'Patent reform', *Review of Economic Studies*, XI, Summer 1944, pp. 61–76.

28. 'Science and the modern crisis', *Memoirs and Proceedings of the Manchester Literary and Philosophical Society*, LXXXVI, No. 6, June 1945, pp. 107–16. Also in: Schwarz.

29. 'Reform of the patent law in Britain', (a letter) *Nature*, CLVI, July 14th 1945, p. 54.

30. *Full Employment and Free Trade*, Cambridge, CUP, 1945, 155 pages. Second edition, 159 pages, 1948. Includes [44/1] as Appendix IV.

31. 'The planning of science', *Political Quarterly,* XVI, Oct–Dec. 1945, pp. 316–26. Also as: Occasional Pamphlet No. 4, Society for Freedom in Science, 1946, 14 pages; *LL* Chap. 5, with additional paragraphs from 'The growth of thought in society' (see note to [16]).

32a. 'Value of pure science', *Time and Tide,* 26, No. 50, Dec. 1945, pp. 1054–5. An abridged version of a paper read at a conference on 'Scientific Research and Industrial Planning', Dec. 7–8th 1945, organised by the Division for the Social and International Relations of Science of the British Association for the Advancement of Science. Also in: *LL* as Chap. 1; Schwarz.

32b. 'The social message of pure science', *The Advancement of Science,* April 1946, pp. 288–90. The full version of 32a.

33. 'Soviets and capitalism: What is the difference?', *Time and Tide,* April 6th 1946, p. 317.

34. 'Social capitalism', *Time and Tide,* April 13, 1946, pp. 341–2.

35. 'Can science bring peace?', *The Listener*, XXXV 902, April 25th, 1946, pp. 531–2. Also in: *The Challenge of Our Time,* ed. G. Wundham-Goldie, London, Percival Marshall, 1948.

36. 'Rededication of science in Germany', *Nature,* CLVIII, July 13th, 1946, p. 66.

37. 'Why profits?', *The Plain View,* No. 8, July 1946, pp. 197–208. Also in: *Humanitas* (Manchester), I No. 2, Autumn 1946, pp. 4–13; As 'Profits and polycentricity', *LL* Chap. 9.

38. 'Policy of atomic science', *Time and Tide,* Aug. 10th, 1946, p. 749.

39. 'Science: academic and industrial', *Universities Quarterly,* Vol. 2 No. 1, Nov. 1947, pp. 71–76. (No connection with [102]).

40. 'Free trade through full employment', *University Liberal (Oxford Guardian)*, III, Dec. 1946, pp. 1–2.

41a. 'The foundations of freedom in science', *Bulletin of the Atomic Scientists,* Vol. 2 No's 11 & 12, Dec. 1st. 1946, pp. 6–7; (A speech given at the Bicentennial Celebration of Princeton University.) Also in: *Physical Science and Human Values,* ed. E.P. Wigner, Princeton U.P., 1947, pp. 24–32 (see also pp. 132–4). As 'The foundations of academic freedom', *Occasional Pamphlet No. 6,* Sept 1947, 16 pages, Society for Freedom in Science. As 'The foundations of academic freedom', *The Lancet,* May 3rd, 1947, pp. 583–6. *LL* as Chap. 3, with additions.

41b. 'The foundations of freedom in science', *The Nineteenth Century and After,* CXLVI, April 1947, pp. 163–7. The Lloyd Roberts Lecture, Manchester, Nov. 19th 1946. A shorter version of [41a].

42. *Science, Faith and Society,* London, O.U.P., 1946. Paperback ed. with new Preface, Chicago, Chicago U.P., 1964. Lect. I (minus II) as 'Science and reality', *Synthèse,* 5, 1946, pp. 137–50.

43. 'Old Tasks and New Hopes', *Time and Tide,* Jan. 4th 1947, pp. 5–6.

44. 'Science: Observation and belief', *Humanitas* (Manchester) I, Feb. 1947, pp. 10–5.

44/1. 'Countering inflation: Problems of a Labour Government', *Manchester Guardian,* March 3rd 1947. Also in: *Full Employment and Free Trade* [30], 2nd ed., as Appendix IV.

45(a). 'Organisation of Universities I', *Time and Tide,* July 19th 1947, p. 777.

45(b). 'Organisation of Universities II', *Time and Tide,* July 26th, 1947, pp. 802–3. (An address read at a conference on 'The place of the universities in the community', May 10th 1947, organised by the Division for the Social and International Relations of Science of the British Association for the Advancement of Science.)

45c. Both [45a] and [45b] also as, 'The place of universities in the community', *The Advancement of Science,* April 1948, pp. 13–5.

46. 'What kind of crisis?', *Time and Tide,* Oct 4th, 1947, pp. 1056–8.

47. 'The universities today', *The Adelphi,* 24 No. 2, Jan.–Mar. 1948, pp. 98–101.

48. 'Ought science to be planned? The case for Individualism', *The Listener,* XL 1025, Sept. 16th 1948, pp. 412–3. Also in: *LL* as Chap. 6, 'Planned science'.

49. 'Profits and private enterprise', in *Economic Problems in a Free Society,* London, Central Joint Advisory Committee on Tutorial Classes, 1948, pp. 50–62.

50. 'Planning and spontaneous order', *The Manchester School,* XVI, Sept. 1948, pp. 237–68. Includes the section 'Two kinds of order' from 'The growth of thought in society' [16]. Also in: *LL* as Chap. 8, 'The span of central direction', minus the section from [16].

51. 'The nature of scientific convictions', *The Nineteenth Century and After,* CXLVI, July 1949, pp. 14–28. Also in: *LL* as Chap. 2; Schwarz.

52. 'The authority of the free society', *The Nineteenth Century and After,* CXLVI, Dec. 1949, pp. 347–60. Also in: as, with some additions, re-arrangements and deletions (principally from the middle of p. 357 to the end), 'The logic of liberty: perils of inconsistency', *Measure,* I, Autumn 1950, pp. 348–62; *LL* as Chap. 7.

53. 'Economic and intellectual liberties', *Zeitschrift für Die Gesamte Staatswissenschaft,* CVI 3, 1950, pp. 411–47. Parts of [16] were included in pp. 412–4 ('Two kinds of order') and n.1 pp. 442–3. Also in: *LL* as Chap. 10.

54. 'Scientific beliefs', *Ethics,* LXI, Oct 1950, pp. 27–37. Also in: as, 'Der Glaube und die Wissenschaft', *Physicalische Blätter,* VI 8, 1950, pp. 337–349; Schwarz.

55. 'Die Freiheit der Wissenschaft', *Physicalische Blätter,* VII 2, 1951, pp. 49–55.

56. 'Autorität und Freiheit in der Wissenschaft', *Physicalische Blätter,* VII 3, 1951, pp. 97–102.

57. 'Contemporary scientific mythology', (a letter) *The Listener,* XLV, March 15th 1951, p. 432.

58. 'The hypothesis of cybernetics', *Brit. J. of Philosophy of Science,* II, Feb. 1951, pp. 312–5.

59. 'Totalitarianism', a review of *The Burden of Our Time* by H. Arendt, *Time and Tide,* Aug. 25th 1951, pp. 801–2.

60. *The Logic of Liberty,* London, Routledge, 1951.
Contents:

    1. 'Social message of pure science'—see [32]
    2. 'Scientific convictions'—see [51]
    3. 'Foundations of academic freedom'—see [41]
    4. 'Self-government of science'—see [19]
    5. 'Science and welfare'—see [31], and [16] for pp. 78-83.
    6. 'Planned science'—see [48]
    7. 'Perils of inconsistency'—see [52]
    8. 'Span of central direction'—see [50]
    9. 'Profits and polycentricity'—see [37]
    10. 'Manageability of social tasks'—see [53] and [16].

61. 'The stability of beliefs', *Brit. J. of Philosophy of Science,* III, Nov. 1952, pp. 217–32. The greater part was included in *PK* pp. 187–94.

62. 'Skills and connoirseurship', in *Atti del Congresse di metodologia,* Turin, Dec. 17–20, 1952. Also in: *PK* pp. 49–57.

63. 'Science and faith', *Question,* V, Winter 1952, pp. 16–36; with Discussion, pp. 37–45. (A talk given at the 8th Present Question Conference, Oxford, Aug. 1952.) Also in: as 'Science and conscience', *Religion in Life,* XXIII, Winter 1953–4, pp. 47–S8.

64. 'Social illusions', *Christian Newsletter,* April, 1953, pp. 77–82.

65. 'Protests and problems', *Bulletin of the Atomic Scientists,* IX, Nov. 1953, pp. 322, 340. (The welcoming speech at the Congress for Cultural Liberty, Hamburg, July, 1953. See also [68] and [72].)

66. 'Pure and applied science and their appropriate forms of organisation', *Occasional Pamphlet No. 14,* Society for Freedom in Science, 1953, 13 pages. Also in: *Science and Freedom,* London, Secker and Warburg, 1955, pp. 36–46 (see [72]); *Dialectica* Sept. 1956, pp. 231–41.

67. 'On the introduction of science into moral subjects', *Cambridge Journal,* VII, Jan. 1954, pp. 195–207. Also in: Schwarz.

68. 'A letter from the Chairman', *Science and Freedom* (A Bulletin of the Committee on Science and Freedom), 1, 1954. Also in No. 6, Aug. 1956. (See also [65] and [72].)

69. 'On Liberalism and liberty', *Encounter,* IV, Mar. 1955, pp. 29–34.

70. 'From Copernicus to Einstein', *Encounter,* V, Sept. 1955, pp. 54–63. Also in: *PK* as Chap. 1; Schwarz.

71. 'Words, conceptions and science', *The Twentieth Century,* CLVIII, Sept. 1955, pp. 256–67. Also in: *PK* Chap. 5, pp. 69, 78–80, 102–8, 110–3.

72. 'Preface', *Science and Freedom* (the Proceedings of the Hamburg Congress on Science and Freedom, July 1953, convened by the Congress for Cultural Freedom), London, Secker and Warburg, 1955, pp. 9–11 (see also [65], [66] and [68]).

73. 'This age of discovery', *The Twentieth Century,* CXLIX, Mar. 1956, pp. 227–34.

74. 'The magic of Marxism', *Bulletin of the Atomic Scientists,* XII, June 1956, pp. 211–5, 232. Also in: *Encounter* VII, Dec. 1956, pp. 5–17; as 'Die Magie des Marxismus', *Der Monat,* XI, 13, Dec. 1958, pp. 3–15; *PK,* pp. 226–48.

75. 'Passion and controversy in science', *The Lancet,* CCLCC, June 16th, 1956. Also in: *Bulletin of the Atomic Scientists,* XIII, April 1957, 114–9; *PK* pp. 134–60, with some additions and omissions.

76. 'Ethics and the scientist', *Bulletin of the Institute of Physics,* 7 No.7, July 1956, pp. 188–93. (A talk given at a symposium at Manchester, March 24th 1956: see pp. 193–200 for discussion.)

77. 'The next stage of history: An appeal for intellectual co-operation', special supplement to *Science and Freedom,* Nov. 1956, pp. 22–4.

78. 'Beauty, elegance and reality in science', in *Symposium on Science Observation and Interpretation,* ed. S. Körner, London, Butterworth, 1957, pp. 102–6. Also in: *PK* Chaps. 5 and 6, but with additional material, and not continuously nor with contents in the same order.

79. 'Scientific outlook: its sickness and its cure', *Science,* CXXV, Mar. 1957, pp. 480–504.

80. 'Problem solving', *Brit. J. for Philosophy of Science,* VIII, Aug. 1957, pp. 89–103. Also in: *PK* Chap. 5, pp. 120–131, with some omissions and rearrangement.

81. 'The foolishness of history, Nov. 1917–Nov. 1957', *Encounter* IX, Nov. 1957, pp. 33–7.

82. 'Oscar Jaszi and Hungarian Liberalism', *Science and Freedom* 1957, p. 7.

83. 'On biased coins and related problems', *Z. für Physikalische Chemie,* Neue Folge, Frankfurter Ausgabe, XV, April 1958, pp. 290–6.

84. 'The Committee on Science and Freedom and Apartheid', *Science and Freedom* 10, Feb. 1958, pp. 9–11. (Introduction to a meeting in London in Nov. 1957).

85. 'Tyranny and freedom: ancient and modern', (pamphlet?) *Quest,* Calcutta, 1958. Also in: *Quest* No. 20, Bombay, 1959, pp. 9–18.

86. 'Editorial' (on Freedom and Responsibility), *Science and Freedom,* No. 11, June 8th, 1958, pp. 5–8.

87. 'The impact of science', *Quest,* Bombay, No. 19, 1958, pp. 32–5. (The text of a talk given on the BBC.)

88. *Personal Knowledge,* London, Routledge, 1958.
   Includes:
   [61] in Chap. 9, pp. 286–94.
   [62] in Chap. 4, pp. 49–57
   [70] as Chap. 1.
   [71] in Chap. 5, pp. 69, 78–80, 102–8, 110–3.
   [72] in Chap. 7, pp. 226–48.
   [73] in Chap. 6, pp. 134–60.
   [78] in Chaps. 5 and 6, not continuously, nor with contents in the same order, and with much other material. The other items mentioned on PK p. x (i.e. [58], [66], [67], [80] and [83]), were not included verbatim.

89. 'A philosophy of perception': a review of *The Nature of Experience,* by Sir Russell Brain, *Brain,* 82, 1959, pp. 292–3.

90. 'Darwin and his evolution': a review of G. Himmelfarb, *Darwin and the Darwinian Revolution, New Leader,* Aug 31, 1959, p. 24.

91. 'The two cultures', *Encounter,* XIII, Sept. 1959, pp. 61–4. Also in: *KB* Chap. 3.

92. 'The organisation of science and the claim to academic freedom', *Science and Freedom,* 13, Nov. 1959, pp. 135–43. (Read at the Study Group, of the Congress for Cultural Freedom, on 'Freedom and Responsibility: The Role of the Scholar in Society', Tunis, April 1959).

93. *The Study of Man,* London, Routledge, 1959.

94. 'An epic theory of evolution', a review of *The Phenomenon of Man* by Teilhard de Chardin, *Saturday Review,* Jan 30th 1960, p. 21.

95. *Beyond Nihilism,* London, C.U.P., 1960 (The Eddington Lecture). Also in: *Encounter,* XIV, Mar. 1960, pp. 34–43; *History and Hope,* ed. K.A. Jelenski, New York, A Praeger, 1962, pp. 17–35 (see pp. 69–81 for discussion; see also [112]); *Crisis and Continuity in World Politics,* ed. G. Lanyi and W. McWilliams, Random House, 1966, pp. 214–27; *KB* Chap. 1.

96. 'Acceptance speech—Le Comte du Nouy Foundation', *Christian Scholar,* XLIII, Mar. 1960, pp. 57–8.

97. 'Morals—a product of evolution': review of *The Ethical Animal* by C.H. Waddington', *New Scientist,* Vol. 8 No. 214, Dec. 22nd, 1960, pp. 1666–7.

98. 'Towards a theory of conspicuous production', *Soviet Survey,* XXXIV, Oct–Dec 1960 pp. 90–9. Also in: as 'Theory of Conspicuous Production', *Colloque de Rheinfelden,* Calman Levy, Paris, 1960; *Quest* (Bombay), No. 41, April–June 1964, pp. 16–21 (a shorter version).

99. 'The study of man', *Quest,* Bombay, 29, Spring 1961, pp. 26–35. (The opening address at the Bombay Seminar on 'The Place of Science and the Humanities in Higher Education'.)

100a. 'Faith and reason', *J. of Religion,* Oct 1961, pp. 237–47. Also, as *The Scientific Revolution,* Chicago, University of Chicago Press, 1961; Also in, as 'Faith and reason', Schwarz.

100b. 'The scientific revolution', *The Student World,* LIV, No. 3, 1961, pp. 287–302. A version of [100a]. Also in: *Christians in a Technological Age,* ed. H.C. White, New York, Seabury Press, 1964, pp. 25–45.

101. 'Knowing and being', *Mind,* LXX, Oct. 1961, pp. 458–70. Also in: *KB* Chap. 9.

102. 'Science, academic and industrial', *J. of Institute of Metals,* LXXXIX, 1961, pp. 401–6.

103. 'Commentary on "The genesis of the special theory of relativity" by Prof Grünbaum', in *Current Issues in Philosophy of Science,* ed. H. Feigl and G. Maxwell, New York, Holt, Rinehart and Winston, 1961, pp. 53–5.

104. 'The unaccountable element in science', *Transactions of the Bose Research Institute,* Calcutta, Vol. 24, No. 4, Dec. 1961, pp. 175–84. Also in: *Philosophy,* XXXVII, Jan. 1962, 1–14; *Philosophy Today,* VI Autumn, 1962, 171–82; as 'Experience and perception of pattern', in *The Modelling of the Mind,* ed. K.M. Sayer and F.J. Crosson, Notre Dame Univ. Press, 1963, pp. 207–222; *KB* as Chap. 8.

105. 'History and hope', *Virginia Quarterly Review,* XXXVIII 2, Spring 1962, pp. 177–95.

106. 'The republic of science, its political and economic theory', *Minerva,* I, Oct. 1962, pp. 54–73. Also in: *Criteria for Scientific Development, Public Policy and National Goals,* ed. E. Shils, Cambridge (Mass), M.I.T. Press, 1968 (see also [124]); *KB* as Chap. 4.

107. 'Tacit knowing: its bearing on some problems of philosophy', *Reviews of Modern Physics,* XXXIV 4, Oct. 1962, pp. 601–12. Also in: *Philosophy Today,* VI, Winter 1962, pp. 239–62; *KB* Chap. 11.

108. 'Clues to an understanding of mind and body', ed. I. Good, *The Scientist Speculates,* London, Heinemann, 1962 pp. 375–80.

109. 'Commentary on "The uses of dogmatism in science" by Thomas Kuhn', ed. A.C. Crombie, *The Structure of Scientific Change,* London, Heinemann, 1962, pp. 375–80. (Kuhn's article is a much shortened version of the first third of *The Structure of Scientific Revolutions,* which had not then been published. His reply to Polanyi's comments is given on pp. 391–5.)

110. 'My time with X-rays and crystals', in *Fifty Years of X-Ray Diffraction,* ed. P. Ewald, Utrecht, A. Oosthock, 1962, pp. 629–36. Also in *KB,* as Chap. 7.

111. 'A postscript', in *History and Hope,* ed. H.A. Jelenski, New York, F. A. Praeger, 1963, pp. 185–96 (see [95]).

112. 'Science and religion: separate dimensions or common ground?', *Philosophy Today,* VII, Spring 1963, pp. 4–14.

113. 'The potential theory of adsorption: authority in science has its uses and dangers', *Science,* CXLI, Sept. 1963, pp. 1010–13. Also in: *KB* as Chap. 6.

114. 'Science and man's place in the universe', in *Science as a Cultural Force,* ed. H. Woolf, Baltimore, John Hopkins U.P., 1964 (and O.U.P. 1965), pp. 54–76. A part, pp. 56–62 (top), was included in *TD* pp. 8–14.

115. 'The feelings of machines', (a letter) *Encounter,* XXII, Jan. 1964, pp. 85–6.

116. 'On the modern mind', *Encounter,* XXIV, May 1965, pp. 12–20. Also in: as 'Wider der Skepsis des modernen Denkens', *Gehort Gelesen,* Jan. 1968; Schwarz.

117. 'The structure of consciousness', *Brain,* LXXXVIII Pt 4, 1965, pp. 799–810. Also in *KB* Chap. 13.

118. 'Creative imagination', *Chemical & Engineering News,* XLVIV, April 1966, pp. 85–93. Also in: *Tri-Quarterly,* Winter 1967, pp. 111–24; as 'Schopferische Einbildungskraft', in *Z. für philosophische Forschung,* 1968; *Toward a Unity of Knowledge,* ed. M. Grene, *Psychological Issues,* Vol. VI 2, Monograph 22, New York, International Universities Press, 1969, pp. 53–70, plus Discussion, pp. 71–91.

119. 'Polanyi's logic—answer', (a note to a letter about [116]) *Encounter,* XXVII, Sept. 1966, p. 92.

120. 'The logic of tacit inference', *Philosophy,* XLI, Oct. 1966, pp. 1–18. Also in: *KB,* as Chap. 10.

121. 'The message of the Hungarian revolution', *The American Scholar,* XXXV, Autumn 1966, pp. 661–76. Also in: *Christianity and Crisis,* XXVI, Oct. 1966, pp. 240–3; *Psychology Today,* I, May 1968, pp. 62–5 (see [129]); *The Anatomy of Knowledge,* ed. M. Grene, London, Routledge, 1969, pp. 315–28; *KB* as Chap. 2.

122. 'Autobiographical note', *Mid-century Authors,* 1966. [No further details traced].

123. *The Tacit Dimension,* London, Routledge, 1966. Includes part of [114].

124. 'The growth of science in society', *Minerva,* V, Summer 1967, pp. 533–45; Also in: *Man and the Science of Man,* ed. W. Coulson and C. Rogers, Charles Merrill Pub., 1967 (see also [132]); *Criteria for Scientific Development, Public Policy and National Goals,* ed. E. Shils, Cambridge (Mass), M.I.T. Press, 1968 (see [also 106]); *KB* as Chap. 5. Note: 'The growth of

science in society' was wrongly stated in *TD*, p. 104, to be in *Encounter,* 1966. But as 'The society of explorers' it was preprinted for *Encounter* 1967 (and was listed by Brownhill as so published) yet was never published in *Encounter.*

125. 'Life transcending physics and chemistry', *Chemical & Engineering News*, XLV, Aug. 1967, pp. 54–66.

126. 'Science and reality', *Brit. J. for the Philosophy of Science,* XVIII, 1967, pp. 177–96.

127. 'Sense-giving and sense-reading', *Philosophy,* XLII, Oct. 1967, pp. 310–25. Also in: *Philosophy Today,* 11, 1969; as 'Sinngebung und Sinndeutung', *Das Problem der Sprache,* ed. H-G. Gadamer, Munich, 1967; as 'Sinngebung und Sinndeutung', *Seminar: Die hermeneutik und die Wissenschaften,* ed. H-G. Gadamer and G. Boehm, Frankfurt, 1978; *Intellect and Hope,* ed. T. Langford and W. Poteat, Durham (N.C.), Duke U.P., 1968, pp. 402–31; *KB* as Chap. 12.

128. 'Logic and psychology', *American Psychologist,* XII, Jan. 1968, pp. 27–43.

129. 'Conversation with Michael Polanyi', *Psychology Today,* I, May 1968, pp. 20–5, 66–7 (see also [121]).

130. 'Do life processes transcend physics and chemistry?', *Zygon,* III, Dec. 1968, pp. 444–7.

131. 'Life's irreducible structure', *Science,* No. 160, 1968, pp. 1308–12. Also in: *KB* Chap. 14.

132. 'The body-mind relation', in *Man and the Science of Man,* W. Coulson and C. Rogers, Charles Merrill Pub. Co. 1968, pp. 85–102. Discussion, pp. 103–127; other discussion with Polanyi, pp. 133–201. (See also [124]).

133. 'On body and mind', *The New Scholasticism,* XLIII No. 2, Spring 1969, pp. 195–204.

134. *Knowing and Being,* ed. M. Grene, London, Routledge, 1969. Contents: Editor's Introduction and items [91], [95], [101], [104], [106], [107], [110], [113], [117], [120], [121], [124], [127], [131].

135. 'The determinants of social action', in *Roads to Freedom: Fetschrift for F.A. von Hayek,* ed. E. Stressler, London, Routledge, 1969, pp. 165–79.

136. 'Foreword' to M.H. Pirenne, *Optics, Painting and Photography,* Cambridge, CUP, 1970.

137. 'Transcendence and self-transcendence', *Soundings,* LIII No. 1, Spring 1970, pp. 88–94.

138. 'What is a painting?', *Brit. J. of Aesthetics,* 1970, pp. 225–36. Also in: *The American Scholar,* Vol. 39 No. 4, Autumn 1970, pp. 655–69.

139. 'Science and man', *Proc. Royal Soc. of Medicine,* LXIII, Sept. 1970, pp. 969–76.

140. 'Why did we destroy Europe?', *Studium Generale,* XXIII No. 20, Oct 1970, pp. 909–16. Also in: *Knowledge in Search of Understanding: The Frensham Papers,* ed. P. Weiss, Mt Kisco (N.Y.), Futura Pub. Co., 1975, pp. 1–8.

141. 'Genius in science', *Archives de L'Institut International des Sciences Théoretiques,* 34 No. 2, 1972, pp. 593–607. Also in: *Boston Studies in the Philosophy of Science,* Vol. XIV, 1972, pp. 57–71.

142. 'Discoveries of science', *Archives de L'Institut International des Sciences Théoretiques,* 19, 'Science, Philosophie, Foi', 1974, pp. 71–6.

143. *Meaning,* with H. Prosch, Chicago, University of Chicago Press, 1975. Chap. 9, 'Truth in myths', also published in *Cross Currents,* Vol. 25 No. 2, 1975, pp. 149–63.

Appendix II

Summaries of Papers Not Republished
Either above or in Polanyi's Books

[3]. 'USSR Economics', 1935.

Socialism is now definitely installed in the USSR and Communism has been relegated to an uncertain future. 'A picture, drawn correctly at the present time, may, therefore, possibly forecast the ultimate meaning of the Russian upheaval. A new marketing system, and open market for all consumers goods as the only channel of distribution, has made it easier to review the economic system' (p. 67). The failure of Communism, 1917–21, and the return to private capitalism in the New Economic Policy of 1921. In 1928 the first Five-Year Plan was begun and has been claimed to have been fulfilled in 1932. The second was launched in 1933.

I. The Social Body: statistics and Polanyi's estimates relating to food, housing, wages, health, education and industrial production.

II. The Economic System: No planned economy, only planned production, and even then little systematic planning, for plans are frequently changed and over-production of one commodity is taken as compensating for under-production of another. In 1931 Stalin introduced three market principles: wages to be fixed so as to ensure a sufficient supply of workers with the required qualifications; enterprises to be profitably conducted; and business managers to have personal responsibility. This economic system, 'Socialism', is in effect indistinguishable from capitalism except that ownership is not transferable by private contract, for the Government appoints the 'owners', the managers. The Central Planning Commission does not *plan,* but allocates capital for selected proposals put to it by local soviets.

III. The USSR aims to overtake and outstrip capitalist countries but is, and is likely to remain, poor and inefficient.

IV. There is a notable driving force in the USSR, the hope of personal success, of higher wages and privileges in the towns and especially in some industries, for educated workers. The economic consciousness of the workers is unified under a common symbol of State ownership. In a reversal of capitalism, the State is the fountain of all benefits and the populace is execrated for failures. 'Medieval craftsmanship, and later, pioneer business life, in which everyone was an owner or hoped to become one, have been two forms of economic consciousness to the workers. They have passed; State management by a bureaucracy linked to the working class is a new and valid expression of economic consciousness for the workers: once more it gives a meaning to their labours. One of the tragedies of mankind seems to be that the most vivid forms of social consciousness are invariably destructive. If this destruction is to be avoided the community must be made conscious of purpose in its daily life by some other means than a social revolution. A way has to be found of clearing the sight of the citizens otherwise than by the smashing of a mechanism which they fail to comprehend' (p. 88).

[5]. 'The value of the inexact', 1936.
Polanyi's first statement of the inevitable vagueness of scientific, and especially chemical, concepts, laws and methods.

[7]. 'Congrès du palais de la découverté', 1937
An account of Polanyi's observations of the effects of totalitarian régimes upon science and scientists.

[8]. 'An outline of the working of money', 1938
A description of the film, *Money,* and the commentary which accompanied it.

[9]. 'The settling down of capital and the trade cycle', 1938
A mathematical treatment of the cycle of reinvestment elaborating the treatment presented in the diagrammatic film, *Money.*

[11]. 'Science in the USSR', 1940
Polanyi accuses J.S. Haldane and other Marxists of hushing up the evils of the USSR, demands that they state what they know about the position of the Rights of Man there, and gives his own examples of the imposition of Marxist-Leninism upon science and scientists.

[13]. 'Economics on the screen', 1940
Documentaries about economic matters favour Collectivism by being able to show only the physical and technological aspects of manufacture, and not the commercial ones. Hence their use by Russian propaganda. The diagrammatic film, *Unemployment and Money* (completed April 1940), does show the commercial aspects and the circulation of money.

[14]. 'Economics by motion symbols', 1940
An account of the contents of the six reels of the film, *Unemployment and Money*: 'Money', 'From Pictures to Symbols', 'Inflation and Reflation—the simplest version', 'Investment Campaign', 'Depreciation and Reinvestment', and 'The Trade Cycle'.

[15]. 'Cultural significance of science', 1941
Polanyi criticises the leading article in *Nature* Dec. 28th 1940, which opposed the independent pursuit of scientific research.

[17]. 'Revaluation of science', 1942.
Polanyi opposes the demand that science should recognise its social responsibilities, although it has had little effect, because it is part of a wider movement to subordinate science to the state.

[20]. 'Research and planning', 1943
A reply to a criticism of [19] in the leading article of *Nature* Aug. 7th, 1943.

[21]. 'The Hungarian opposition', 1943
A defence of the union of Hungarian democrats in the 'People's Front' in reply to the leading article of *The New Statesman* Sept. 25th.

[22]. 'The English and the Continent', 1943
The principal difference between English and Continental politics is that in the former social progress is not connected with enlightenment and anti-communism but often produced by religious sentiment. The opposite conjunction has produced the two Continental anti-moralist theories: that politics is the destruction of one group (or race or nation) by another and the exceptional individual is exempt from moral laws. The 17th century in England produced religious tolerance and the Bill of Rights, as a religious doctrine: to protect all Protestant churches against the Government, Catholicism and Atheism, in contrast to the repeal of the Edict of Nantes. When news of English liberty was taken to countries dominated by a single religion, it generated anti-clerical and anti-religious movements, again in contrast to English movements of reform. Continental admiration, in the 19th century, of English practices and manners did not include its moral restraints. Except for Byron, there was no literary treatment in England of the unrestrained individual, which enjoyed a secular Protestantism of 'manners, virtue, freedom, power' (Wordsworth). That tradition, and national self-confidence, were weakened in the First World War. National will has revived after Dunkirk. 'National feeling seems to be the only sentiment today in which that responsible devotion to a community

can be rooted, that bond of mutual confidence assured, which are needed if reason and equity are to gain acceptance as the guides of human affairs. National traditions appears as the most ample and most reliable embodiments of the principles of morality—at least so far as the guidance of popular behaviour is concerned. Germany's national traditional of political immorality appears now as an exception; as an aberration; as a break-through of the modern doctrine of group immorality in a national guise. It is an evil to be extirpated; not a valid argument against the 19th century conception of nationhood—of the nation as a source of honour and as an integral element of international order' (pp. 380–1). 'People on the Continent who want to live as human beings must recognise the moral principles for which England stands and must revive the kindred elements of their own tradition. Nothing will grow from moral unbelief. The bolder our plans for the future, the deeper must they be rooted in the original ideas of our civilisation' (p. 381).

[23]. 'Science: its reality and freedom', 1944
Pure science is distinguished by its universality, systematic nature, and progressive extension and deepening of its systems. It regulates itself. Marxism and Fascism, as Social Absolutism, require the subjection of science to social control. Science has no definite programme, only its own development, advancing without forethought. Science as an integral part of our civilisation, and founded in common ideals.

[24]. 'The Socialist error', 1944
A favourable review of Hayek's book. 'Freedom and tolerance succumbed only after Europe's most generous sons withdrew their support from these ideas in favour of Socialism'.

[25]. 'Science and the decline of freedom', 1944
Freedom and tolerance have been lost, on the Continent, to totalitarianism because of the dominance of what is taken to be a scientific view of man, as an animal whose appetites are real and enduring but whose ideals are passing shadows, and because of the belief in the necessity of smashing the existing system and efficiently replacing it without being affected by moral scruples. These also apply to Nazism and Fascism. Continentals see Britain as backward in terms of class war and belief in morality and its power. We can reassert or ideals in a scientific age. For science itself is based on an act of faith—in accepting the main body of scientific tradition and its ideals which therefore testify to power of traditional ideals on which our civilisation rests. The new scientific outlook will recognise that it is only one form of truth, and so will help to recognise traditional faith in which freedom and tolerance rest.

[26]. 'Reflections on John Dalton', 1944
Dalton was not inhibited, in forming and maintaining his theory of atoms, by the modern proscription of questions about the nature of things, which also threatens to turn each study into an isolated specialism.

[27]. 'Patent reform', 1944
Patents encourage inventions but incur costs to the general public by restricting their applications. Instead the Government should pay patentees, for leasing their rights on demand, a fixed proportion of the value created by each invention during the previous year. Reform is also needed of the provisions of patent law with respect to Utility, Novelty and Invention.

[28]. 'The universities and the modern crisis', 1945
Totalitarianism in Russia and Fascism elsewhere arise from common sources: both have hard-headed materialist view of politics and contempt for ideals of 19th century liberal civilisation. The origins of the modern crisis go back to the emergence of the secular authority of the State which replaced feudalism. Hobbes, the father of modern materialism, based on it a theory of the State as absolute master with full and undivided power, and denied the claims of religion, morality and science against the State, as in modern totalitarianism. But that was bookish speculation, and religion and ideals of justice, morality and truth constrained power in fact. But in France, because of the decline of religious belief, demands arose for purely secular political reform. Rousseau modified Hobbes: the ruler is truly sovereign only if power emanates from people, and then it can do no wrong. Jacobinism was the practical application of Hobbes. But the ideals of justice, humanity and truth still restrained it by revolting against it. But, while these ideals spread throughout Europe, so also did the naturalistic doctrine of man. Marx burned with humanitarian ideals which he explicitly denied and made it possible for others to do likewise by identifying them with the material forces which he supposed to govern man and history. This led to modern fanatical ruthlessness and enabled Hobbes' supreme secular power to be established in a perfect form. Fascism based itself on patriotic feeling, narrower than the desire for universal justice in Marxism, but also transformed patriotism into a purely materialist force. The logic of Hobbes was suspended in Britain because of the dominance of religion and lack of belief in scientific materialism, though the influence of the latter has been increasing.

[29]. 'Reform of the patent law in Britain', 1945
A reply to a criticism of [27]

[33]. 'Soviets and capitalism', 1946

The Soviet government only pretends to practise planning. Instead it practises forecasting, and its central plan is a only compilation of the plans of individual enterprises. It is guided by a commercial network, which it despises, and it conceals its dependence upon it.

[34]. 'Social capitalism', 1946
Socialism and Capitalism have both adopted the errors of Bentham, Ricardo and Malthus: that men are ruled by self-interest, that the laws of supply and demand apply to all spheres of society, and that labour's share of wealth tends towards the minimum needed for subsistence. Both take the capitalist system to be a mere mechanism of interlocking appetites which cannot be reformed, and must either be accepted or set aside at the Millenium. But while Marx wrote about it, it was being reformed. As for unemployment, Russia has reduced it by inflation, not planning, and the same Keynesian policies should be applied here, though they have their dangers which could lead to the control of wages, prices and labour. The market is a mechanism but it need not overrule respect for humanity and social justice, and we must dispel the monstrous callousness of Marxism.

[35]. 'Can science bring peace?' 1946
Polanyi's youthful enthusiasm for H.G. Wells. But he no longer believes that science can solve the problems of the age, which are political and not technical. Atomic power creates a need for world control by the free co-operation of states. Free government rests upon mutual trust, and therefore trust is also needed among nations, and likewise a shared belief in mutual obligations and that people can be relied upon to observe them. A suggestion for a Declaration of the Duties of Men—to respect truth, keep promises and observe justice, equity and general decency. From these, rights follow—freedom to act according to conscience and to the support and protection of free institutions. The chief obstacle to this is the materialist philosophy which takes man to be only a bundle of appetites to which it reduces, and thereby debunks, moral ideals. We need a new enlightenment to reassert the spiritual life of man and to release great moral forces of our time which have been led astray by false and degrading theories. This will bring men back to Christianity. The foundations of freedom are akin to those of religion.

[36]. 'Rededication of science in Germany', 1946
A commemoration of Fritz Haber, who was discredited by the Nazis, and remarks on the current difficulties of German scientists.

[38]. 'Policy of atomic science', 1946

Pure science cannot be directed by any government. Any attempt to keep secret basic research would stultify science. Liberty is to be supported by force of arms, including atomic ones, but not at the expense of the principles of liberty and the freedom of science. To do so would cause a decline into servitude, obscurity and corruption. We must hope for the eventual conversion of the USSR to liberalism.

[39]. 'Science: academic and industrial', 1947
Mostly an account of an advanced course at Manchester for scientists in industry, which was intended to cultivate their love of science.

[40]. 'Free trade through full employment', 1946
[No details: I have been unable to trace any copy.]

[43]. 'Old tasks and new hopes', 1947
Woodrow Wilson's Liberalism and Lenin's revolutionary Marxism. The former was defeated between the wars but there are new hopes for it now and time to resume its task. Soviet Marxism is now less violent than it used to be, and it should be possible to establish international confidence with Russia.

[45]. 'Organisation of universities', 1947
Universities need to be independent, although funded by governments, and scientists free to choose their own lines of research, in order to safeguard and promote systematic research without which teaching stultifies stagnates

[46]. 'What kind of crisis?', 1947.
The current inflation, and the low level of unemployment, are both the result of monetary expansion. Control of the former means acceptance of more unemployment but politicians will not face this consequence for fear of popular resentment based on reckless expectations. 'Planning' is no answer for it is logically impossible. Throughout Europe the workers are using inflationary pressure in a revolt against all management, private and public. Freedom is under threat by this questioning of the agreed coherence of society. The bourgeoisie must willingly give up its unjustified privileges, reconcile the workers and reassert its leadership.

[47]. 'The universities today', 1948
The universities foster creative dissent, seeing for oneself and not relying on authority. This method of doubt has proved enormously fruitful in science and scholarship. But it has also resulted in universal doubt, nihilism and totalitarianism. Scepticism cannot discover anything new but can only re-

lease our powers of discovery, which stem from belief and presuppositions about the nature of things. The universities now need to profess faith, not just in hard facts and the evidence of the senses, but also in the truths of the mind, ideals, and allegiance to transcendent powers. They need to be conscious of these their true foundations.

[54]. 'Scientific beliefs', 1950.
Science is supposed to be positive and mathematically exact and demonstrable, and therefore quite different from religious and moral beliefs. But the schism between Western and Soviet genetics disproves this. Science in fact has a fiduciary basis in 'scientific beliefs'. For no series of measurements can prove any generalisation; conversely the fulfillment of a prediction cannot validate a scientific statement for it be the result of chance. Nor can scientific generalisations be always strictly disproved: e.g. the Copernican theory of cycles and epicycles and Dalton's law of simple chemical proportions. No scientist does or could discard an hypothesis immediately it conflicts with experience, nor is there any fixed rule for distinguishing anomalies from genuine refutations. Attempts to minimise the claims of science, as merely 'probable' or as the 'simplest' description of observations, are verbal smoke-screens behind which we hide the fact that we believe scientific statements to be true, out of fear of offending an empiricist and sceptical philosophy which discredits our transcendent faculties and obligations. We need openly to admit our beliefs and that we acquire them uncritically. The most general of them is the naturalistic view of the universe, which we acquire against our native inclination to a magical view. Modern education, and the necessarily acritical learning of our mother tongue, break down the latter and instil the former. We are fully committed to our beliefs and pass them on to the next generation. Science is not an external power but a set of obligations: to seek a truth which is unambiguous and universal, even though we recognise this as impossible and strictly meaningless. In science, as in everything else, we have to commit ourselves in our concrete circumstances and on grounds that seem deficient on reflection. Examples of more specific scientific presuppositions and changes in them. The Positivist view of science tries to construct a machine that would produce universal results, but universal validity cannot apply outside a situation of personal commitment, of submission to an ultimate obligation which can appear only in a fiduciary declaration. Science is a body of beliefs, reasonably adopted with a view to evidence, which necessarily rests upon ultimate commitments personally and acritically held. Consequently, we can acknowledge that other have different commitments, such as to dialectical materialism. Our objections to what Lysenko has done rest upon the affirmation of our own beliefs.

[55]. 'Die Freiheit der Wissenschaft', 1951
The common goal of scientific research is best achieved when each researcher is free to work at what he thinks best. Science is a self-co-ordinating task, resting upon common beliefs and rules which cannot be exactly specified and can be transmitted only implicitly in traditions and by learning by example, within a scientific community.

[56]. 'Autorität und Freiheit in der Wissenschaft', 1951
Scientific value includes significance for science as whole and genuine human interest as well as demonstrability. Scientific opinion must be trusted to select what is important, and be supplemented by the 'guild system' of scientific recruitment. How then can the genius of an Einstein or Pasteur be cherished? Firstly such people are never totally revolutionary, and secondly, all scientitists are trained in respect for the ideal of truth and will not presuppose that they already possess it. The newcomer is not challenging scientific opinion as such, only its contemporary form. Scientific opinion is not a matter of decision but grows. We can trust in the reality and effectiveness of this system only from within it. The conditions and consequences of intellectual freedom.

[57]. 'Contemporary scientific mythology', 1951
Toulmin was wrong to argue that problems about the interpretation and application of the Second Law of Thermodynamics can be settled by linguistic analysis.

[59]. 'Totalitarianism', 1951
Hannah Arendt's account, unlike others, does apply to more than one form of totalitarianism. But she is wrong in saying that it arose amid ruthless competition, for the latter did not prevail in the semi-feudal states of Russia, Hungary and China. She is more correct in saying that it was established by Bohemian groups who had never participated in civic life and who gained the support of the previously indifferent masses, newly liberated from feudalism or absolutism, by infecting them with their own bookish nihilism. The intelligentsia's destructive analyses of man and society converted the masses to régimes of violence, but had little effect in the older democracies where the restraints of Liberal tradition were more effective.

[63]. 'Science and faith', 1952
The weakening of religious belief began in the Renaissance before the rise of modern science, and turned the moral passions generated by Christianity into demands for unlimited progress in this world, with firstly constructive and then destructive consequences. Science, as the current model of knowledge

and sanction of all claims, has led to the neglect of men's moral responsibilities in a mistaken pursuit of intellectual honesty. Communism is a radical attempt to carry out in practice these tendencies of modern thought. The error of eliminating what can be doubted. Moral beliefs cannot be proved. 'We must resolutely teach ourselves once more openly to hold these beliefs as an act of faith'.

[64]. 'Social illusions', 1953
Two illusions which arose with modern political thought: Say's Law, that there never could be an over-supply of all goods and therefore no general depressions; and the Socialist, Nihilist and Marxist total rejection of existing society. Keynes showed that budgetary deficits can correct depressions, which obviously do occur, and so Socialist planning is not required to restore full employment, not that it did in Russia. Although there are still some errors current about employment and the supply of money, the above illusions and passions are now weaker though rising in Asia. Can we accept our limitations without falling into apathy?

[65]. 'Protests and problems', 1953
The struggle for the freedom of science and scholarship under Communist totalitarianism requires a reassertion of the value of knowledge for its own sake and for public respect for it. Otherwise democratic as well as Marxist governments will direct science towards welfare. Likewise, the freedom of science is the exercise of an authority within science and requires a political authority for its protection.

[66]. 'Pure and applied science and their appropriate forms of organisation', 1953
The Neo-Marxist theory of science. The differences among science, empirical technology, systematic technology and technically justified science. Two forms of order, corporate (co-ordinated from above) and spontaneous (spontaneously co-ordinated by the mutual adjustments of the members). The former applies to technological research in commercial firms and public services (but not by independent inventors), but not to scientific research, including systematic technology, which has to be guided spontaneously by its own unofficial government of leading experts.

[67]. 'On the introduction of science into moral subjects', 1954
[This is the first publication in which Polanyi presents his distinction between subsidiary and focal awareness.]
Hume's unfulfilled intention to introduce experimental methods into moral subjects. Behaviourist psychology, positivism in jurisprudence and anthro-

pology, as attempts to study man and society in a detached manner supposedly like that of natural science. Logical positivism rejects moral utterances as meaningless for similar reasons. But science itself cannot meet the ideal of detached objectivity. The errors of Laplace's ideal of universal knowledge. Personal participation is required to establish a correspondence between a scientific formula and the experience to which it applies, which is an unspecifiable art, transmissible only by apprenticeship. Exact science rests upon and has meaning only in relation to a pre-scientific personal knowledge. Skills and connoisseurship are valid and indispensable forms of knowledge. Two forms of awareness in skills: subsidiary and focal. We incorporate into ourselves the tools and interpretative frameworks on which we rely. Subsidiary awareness of parts and focal awareness of wholes. Personal participation involved in all sciences but to varying degrees according to the degree of unspecifiability. We employ and appraise our skilful performances and acts of recognition and understanding by standards we take to be universal. We apply standards of health in biology and intelligence in psychology. Understanding another involves entering his situation and judging his actions from his point of view as an intelligent and morally responsible person. That applies also to ourselves and the historical situation in which we are placed. Science requires us to study man and society, not as detached observers, but as members of a human society. Crystallography is a system of appraisal within exact science which like morality, jurisprudence and artistic criticism, says nothing true or false about experience. Human concerns—ethics, law, religion—cannot be regarded as 'unscientific' in a bad sense, for science itself makes similar valuations.

[68]. 'A letter from the Chairman', 1954
The themes and aims of the Hamburg Conference, July 1953, and preparation for the Congress on Science and Freedom.

[72]. 'Preface' to Science and Freedom, 1955
Reflections on the Hamburg Congress: the division, in opposition to totalitarianism, between those who continue the rationalism of the Enlightenment and those who think that totalitarianism has resulted from scepticism.

[73]. 'This age of discovery', 1956
The modern age, begun in 1917, has been one of discovery, by Socialism that a centrally planned economy is impossible, and, by Liberalism, of Keynes' cure for mass unemployment. The more sober mood of the present. We again know liberty and its value, and recent experience may protect us from future delusions and disasters.

[76]. 'Ethics and the scientist', 1956
Citing the examples of scientists who intervened in politics in relation to the possibility, the use and the further development of the atomic bomb, Polanyi argues that scientists, as scientists and not just as citizens, have a duty to intervene when they alone have specialist knowledge, about applied science, which they cannot make public. Likewise those who spoke up to defend universities and freedom of research. Marxist proposals for directing science specifically to general welfare have come to nothing. Pure science can be pursued only for its own sake, and is to be appreciated as such.

[77]. 'The next stage of history', 1956.
The task for the next stage of history is to restore the balance between our critical powers and moral demands. The struggles of writers in Communist countries to speak the truth. Not the vote but respect for law and dignity of independent thought make men free. Not differences of economic systems but the ambition totally to transform society, separates the Communist world from the West. Desire to co-operate with intellectuals in Communist countries, and to see them have same inner and institutional liberties as we enjoy.

[79]. 'Scientific outlook: its sickness and its cure', 1957
The compulsion exercised by the model of science as detached observation. Bentham, Marx and other examples of 'moral inversion'. Detached observation destroys meanings. Moral passions therefore seek a covert and supposedly neutral expression. The same inversion in 'scientific' anthropology and sociology. Biology and technology deal with achievements, beyond the explanations provided by physics and chemistry. Behaviourism fails to distinguish focal observation of the workings of a mind and convivial reading them as signs of its working, but inevitably practises the latter which it denies. Science itself is a human commitment.

[82]. 'Oscar Jászi and Hungarian Liberalism', 1957
A tribute, on his death, to the leading Hungarian Liberal of the 20th century.

[83]. 'On biased coins and related problems', 1958
The Summary given at the end reads: 'The repeated flipping of an unbiased coin would result in a sequence which corresponds to the a priori probability of ½ for each side of the coin. If the coin is biased there will be a deviation from this in the direction of the bias. Take now a model in which the flipping is done by the Brownian motion of the coins. The probable distribution for biased dice will then be seen to depend on the temperature. At $T=0$ the bias will predominate to 100%, while at high temperatures the bias will vanish. It

follows more generally that the probability of biased systems, (coin, die, etc.) is indeterminate; it depends on the *intensity* of the random impacts to which the system is subject'. Polanyi also points out that random impacts do not generally produce random results, for they invariably release ordering forces which will counter act the disordering effects of random impacts.

[84]. 'The Committee on Science and Freedom and apartheid', 1958
A statement of the aims and 'campaigns' of the Committee on Science and Freedom. Apartheid violates the freedom required by the duty of universities to transmit the intellectual heritage of modern man.

[85]. 'Tyranny and freedom: ancient and modern', 1958
The modern demand for self-determination and for reshaping society as the people, or those acting for them, think fit, has taken two forms: gradual and piece-meal reform, extending legal order and liberty, and revolutionary to-talitarianism, aiming at an immediate perfection of society and destroying legality. Both emerged in the French Revolution, the Civil Code and Jacobinism, respectively. Revolutionary dynamism embodies a materialist conception of man which denies the reality of moral motives and results in fanatical ruthlessness. A liberal, dynamic society requires shared a belief in truth and fairness, mutual trust, and the validity of those ideals. A static order is based on an authoritarian teaching of explicit doctrines, assures each his birthright of traditional duties and privileges, and upholds a belief in the power of truth and the moral responsibility of man. A liberal, dynamic society is based on beliefs in reason and justice, which are not self-evident as formerly thought, and offers wide scope for independent thought. A totalitarian society imposes its orthodoxy as scientific fact not faith, suppresses doctrinal faiths and liberal convictions, and denies the very existence of the spontaneous powers of the mind. Reformist dynamism works by persuasion and parliamentary institutions but toleration was spread on the Continent by enlightened absolutism. A free society requires dedication to intellectual and moral ideals. Electoral procedures can extend or abridge them. The contemporary disenchantment with revolutionary Socialism has often left a void. The rebellious Communists of Hungary and Poland returned to the idealistic form of the principles of the French Revolution and 1848. Elective self-government is the final and most difficult achievement if democracy, not its first step. A free society cannot be defined by rules if procedure for a popularly elected government could uphold Stalinism if everyone believed in it. We must acknowledge our own beliefs which would reject such a result. We can uphold a demand to establish a free society only on the ground that it flows from man's nature as the only morally responsible creature in the world.

[86]. 'Editorial', *Science and Freedom,* 1958
A comment upon a series of addresses on Freedom and Responsibility given in Paris in August 1956.

[87]. 'The impact of science', 1958
The hopes that were placed in science and their disappointment. The materialist interpretation of man, stemming from the misapplication of an ideal of exact science, at first resulted in humanitarian reforms. But it has also resulted in the inhuman fanaticism of modern nihilism, whose moral passions are not susceptible to argument.

[89]. 'A philosophy of perception', 1959
Brain suggests that sensory experiences, located in the brain, are experienced as symbols of external objects. But that also requires an active personal centre to make sense of them.

[90]. 'Darwin and his evolution', 1959
The author reveals incongruities in Darwin's thought and character. The triumph of Darwinism: the theories of evolution and of natural selection (as the only conceivable explanation on mechanical principles) reinforced one another.

[92]. 'The organisation of science and the claim to academic freedom', 1959
The value and proper organisation of scientific research, and the freedom required for it, in contrast to the value and organisation of technology.

[94]. 'An epic theory of evolution', 1960
Teilhard de Chardin is really a poet and his book has attracted great attention because of widespread dissatisfaction with the scientific denaturing of man. But his work is too vague and does not solve the important problems which it raises.

[96]. 'Acceptance speech: Le Comte du Noily Award' (1959)
The importance of interest in the whole of reality. Scientific rationalism has resulted in progress, but it is also obscurantist in its reductionism. The Le Comte du Noily Foundation is helping to form a nucleus of a reformed scientific outlook.

[97]. 'Morals a product of evolution', 1960
Polanyi appreciates Waddington's clarification of the philosophical issues but doubts if he has solved them. His revised view of evolution can serve as a

moral inspiration but he has only marginally modified the 'mechanical' account of evolution as the product of random mutations; and while he is right to say that health is both a value and a scientific fact, this does not mean that we can observe a fact as morally binding on ourselves: we can only bear witness to and uphold our own moral beliefs.

[99]. 'The study of man', 1961
The destructive consequences, for man's image of himself, of Objectivism and scientific naturalism; the need for personal involvement and judgment in science; knowledge as personal knowledge; tacit integration in knowing and action; knowledge as indwelling; personal knowing as setting standards for itself; appraisals in knowing plants, animals and our fellow men; understanding men as intelligent and morally responsible as legitimate extension of scientific knowledge; likewise acceptance of the situation in which we find ourselves.

[102]. 'Science, academic and industrial', 1961
A longer restatement of the case for the value and free pursuit of pure science, its self-organisation, and its connections with but differences from technology, technological sciences and technically justified sciences.

[103]. 'Commentary on "The genesis of the special theory of relativity" by Prof. Grünbaum', 1961
A reply to Grünbaum's comments on Polanyi's account, in *PK,* of Einstein's discovery of relativity.

[108]. 'Clues to an understanding of mind and body', 1962
The application of the ontology and epistemology of tacit integration to the relation between body and mind. Knowledge of our own and other minds by means of indwelling. The impossibility of explaining machines in merely chemical and physical terms, and of consciousness in mechanical terms.

[109]. 'Commentary on "The uses of dogmatism in science" by Thomas Kuhn', 1962
Polanyi endorses the main points of Kuhn's paper, refines them with his own examples, and states that it raises, but does not supply, the need for a radical revision of the theory of scientific knowledge.

[112]. 'Science and Religion: Separate dimensions or common ground?' 1963
Tillich is wrong to take religion and science as by-passing each other. Science is not detached observation. The theory of tacit integration and indwelling. Comprehensive entities and the emergence of new and higher levels of exist-

ence. The errors of reductionism. The hierarchy of comprehensive entitles and levels of existence. The transition from I-It to I-Thou relations. The emergence of man. The Pauline scheme of an obligation to strive for the impossible in the hope of achieving it by divine grace. This new view of science and the Christian view of man reinforce each other. The impossibility of Existentialist self-determination. Acceptance of our limitations and our tasks as a calling.

[114]. 'Science and man's place in the universe', 1964
The first third was included in TD as pp. 54–7. The remainder contains: Indwelling of one's own body, subsidiary details of objects known, and intellectual tools. Increasing depth of indwelling in knowledge of physical objects, living beings and minds. Denial of indwelling by the false ideal of scientific detachment. Hierarchy of levels of comprehensive entities. Application to evolution and emergence of higher from lower beings: a creative power inherent in the universe, and man's own creative powers.

[115]. 'The feelings of machines', 1964
The proposition that computers simulating personal responses have feelings, rests on the false assumption that the meanings of words can be defined in specifiable tests.

[116]. 'On the modern mind', 1965
Scepticism and the mechanistic world-view. The tacit integration of levels in machines and living beings. What is most tangible has the least meaning and reality. Knowing as tacit integration and indwelling. Indwelling another's mind. The moral nihilism of neutral sociology. The union of scepticism and moral perfectionism in moral inversion, individualist or totalitarian. The need to recognise the power of ideas and the reality of intangible things.

[122]. 'Autobiographical note', 1966
[No details. I have not been able to trace any copy.]

[128]. 'Logic and psychology', 1968
Science rests on nonstrict rules of inference which have hitherto been neglected. Scientific knowledge is indeterminable in its content, the coherences which it establishes and its data. Tacit integration and inference in all knowledge, including science. The tacit dimensions of knowledge of other minds, universal terms, principles of explanation and empirical generalisations. Tacit integration in perception, language, and scientific investigation. Logic is the rules for reaching valid conclusions from premises assumed to be true, and

not, as is currently assumed, for reaching strict conclusions from strict premises.

[129]. 'Conversation with Michael Polanyi', 1968
Polanyi restates his case against scientistic positivism and behaviourism, and his accounts of moral inversion, tacit integration, personal knowing and responsibility, language and evolution.

[133]. 'On body and mind', 1969
The impossibility of an exact specification of mental acts and behaviour; tacit integration and indwelling; the subsidiary role of neural processes.

[136]. 'Foreword' to M. Pirenne's *Optics, Painting and Photography*, 1970
The role of the tacit integration of incompatibles in the viewing of paintings. Subsidiary awareness of the flat canvas makes the seeing of a perspectival painting immune to distortion when viewed at varying angles.

[137]. 'Transcendence and self-transcendence', 1970
The ontology of tacit integration versus the mechanistic world-view.

[139]. 'Science and man', 1970
The mechanistic world-view; scientific liberalism and the destruction of moral principles and liberal ideals by the scientific outlook; moral inversion; a new theory of knowledge, tacit integration; indwelling versus impersonal detachment and strict objectivity.

[142]. 'Discoveries of science', 1974
The power of imagination in scientific discovery, metaphor, art and symbols, and the dangers of a mechanical analysis of man.

Index